漠阳传承

Moyang Inheritance

阳江市文化广电旅游体育局　阳江市文化馆　编著

华南理工大学出版社
SOUTH CHINA UNIVERSITY OF TECHNOLOGY PRESS
·广州·

图书在版编目（CIP）数据

漠阳传承：汉英对照 / 阳江市文化广电旅游体育局，阳江市文化馆编著. —广州：华南理工大学出版社，2023.10

ISBN 978-7-5623-7365-0

Ⅰ. ①漠… Ⅱ. ①阳… ②阳… Ⅲ. ①非物质文化遗产－介绍－阳江－汉、英 Ⅳ. ① G127.653

中国国家版本馆 CIP 数据核字（2023）第 082359 号

漠阳传承

阳江市文化广电旅游体育局　阳江市文化馆　编著

出 版 人：柯　宁

出版发行：华南理工大学出版社

（广州五山华南理工大学 17 号楼，邮编 510640）

http://hg.cb.scut.edu.cn　E-mail：scutc13@scut.edu.cn

营销部电话：020-87113487　87111048（传真）

策划编辑：吴翠微

责任编辑：吴翠微　陈　蓉

责任校对：梁樱雯

印 刷 者：佛山家联印刷有限公司

开　　本：889mm × 1194mm　1/16　印张：19　字数：776 千

版　　次：2023 年 10 月第 1 版　印次：2023 年 10 月第 1 次印刷

定　　价：268.00 元

编委会

前言 Foreward

Intangible cultural heritage is an important symbol of a country and nation's historical and cultural achievements. It is an important component of excellent traditional culture, and the root of a nation and the soul of a city. It is also an important source and rich nourishment for enhancing cultural confidence and value identification, and also a unique cultural symbol with local characteristics. Since the 18th National Congress of the Communist Party of China, President Xi Jinping has repeatedly talked about the protection and inheritance of intangible cultural heritage on different occasions. In December 2022, President Xi Jinping made important instructions on the protection of intangible cultural heritage, emphasizing the need to solidly protect it systematically to better meet the growing spiritual and cultural needs of the people and build cultural confidence and strength. It is necessary to promote the creative transformation and innovative development of outstanding Chinese traditional culture, continuously enhance the cohesion of the Chinese nation and the influence of Chinese culture, deepen civilizational exchange and mutual learning, tell stories well about outstanding Chinese traditional culture, and promote its better integration into the world.

In its thousand-year history and cultural accumulation, Yangjiang has integrated various cultures from Central Plains, Li-Liao area, and overseas to form a rich and diverse collection of local cultural characteristics, such as poetry and couplet culture, calligraphy and painting culture, kite culture, knife culture, lacquer art culture, Tanka culture, Moyang culture, and the Maritime Silk Road culture. These have given birth to a wealth of intangible cultural heritage that is unique to the region. Currently, Yangjiang has 1 national-level intangible cultural heritage project, 13 provincial-level projects, 150 municipal-level projects, 159 county-level projects, and 19 intangible cultural heritage workshops. There is 1 national-level intangible cultural heritage representative inheritor, 25 provincial-level representative inheritors, and 268 municipal-level representative

非物质文化遗产是一个国家和民族历史文化成就的重要标志，是优秀传统文化的重要组成部分，是民族之根、城市之魂，是增进文化自信和价值认同的重要来源和丰厚滋养，也是独具地方特色的文化符号。党的十八大以来，习近平总书记在不同场合多次谈到非物质文化遗产的保护与传承。2022年12月，习近平总书记对非物质文化遗产保护工作作出重要指示，强调要扎实做好非物质文化遗产的系统性保护，更好满足人民日益增长的精神文化需求，推进文化自信自强。要推动中华优秀传统文化创造性转化、创新性发展，不断增强中华民族凝聚力和中华文化影响力，深化文明交流互鉴，讲好中华优秀传统文化故事，推动中华文化更好走向世界。

阳江在千年的历史发展和文化积淀中，融汇了中原、俚僚及海外等多种文化，形成了悠久深厚、延绵相续、异彩纷呈的诗词楹联文化、书画文化、风筝文化、小刀文化、漆艺文化、疍家文化、漠阳文化、海丝文化等多种地方特色文化，孕育了丰富而独具地方特色的非物质文化遗产。阳江现有国家级非物质文化遗产项目1项，省级非物质文化遗产项目13项，市级非物质文化遗产项目150项，县级非物质文化遗产项目159项，非物质文化遗产工坊19个；非物质文化遗产国家级代表性传承人1人，省级代表性传承人25人，市级代表性传承人268人；省级非物质文化遗产研究基地1个，省级传承基地4个，省级生产性保护示范基地4个，市级传承基地26个。

阳江漆器髹饰、阳江风筝、小刀制作、剪刀锻造、豆豉酿制等技艺文化展现着漠阳文化的悠久绵长；疍家婚俗、端午节、高流河墟等民俗文化蕴含着极致的地方特色；阳江山歌、阳江咸水歌等传统音乐和海陵舞狮、阳春根雕等传统舞蹈、美术凸显了阳江人崇文厚德的一面；“施一针”针法、谢氏药摩法等传统医药和洪拳（梁方伍系）、潭塘（杨氏）武术等传统体育、游艺与杂技展现了阳江人对健体修身的追求……这些非物质文化遗产无一不闪耀着阳江人民的智慧，无一不展示着阳江深厚的文化底蕴与文化魅力。

实际上，独特的漠阳文化一直都吸引着各方专家学者的关注，并由此出版了不少的专业论文和著作，但真正完整地科普和介绍阳江市非物质文化遗产的书籍还是少之又少，更是遑论对外宣传的相关中英文书籍。阳江市委、市政府高度重视非物质文化遗产保护工作，在2022年12月出台了《关于进一步加强我市非物质文化遗产保护工作的实施意见》，明确工作任务和保护措施，以期进一步健全阳江市非物质文化遗产保护传承体系，推动阳江市非物质文化遗产创造性转换、创新性发展。为更好地保护和传承阳江市非物质文化遗产，深化漠阳文化对外交流展示，《漠阳

inheritors. In addition, there is 1 provincial-level intangible cultural heritage research base, 4 provincial-level inheritance bases, 4 provincial-level productive protection demonstration bases, and 26 municipal-level inheritance bases.

The culture of Moyang is reflected in the art of lacquerware decorating, kites, knife manufacturing, scissors forging, and fermented soybean brewing, which have been passed down for generations. Folk customs such as Tanka wedding customs, Dragon Boat Festival, and Gaoliu River Fair are steeped in unique local characteristics. Traditional music such as Yangjiang Hill Song and Yangjiang Salty-water Song, traditional dances such as Hailing Lion Dance, and traditional fine arts such as Yangchun Root Carving highlight the cultural integrity and moral conduct of Yangjiang people. Traditional medicine techniques like “Shi Yi Zhen” Acupuncture and Xie’s Medicated Massage Method, and traditional sports, amusement and acrobatics such as Hong Quan (Liang Fangwu Branch), Tantang (Yang’s) Martial Art reveal the pursuit of Yangjiang people to keep fit and cultivate themselves. All of these intangible cultural heritages shine with the wisdom of Yangjiang people and showcase Yangjiang’s profound cultural heritage and charm.

Actually, the unique Moyang culture has attracted the attention of experts and scholars from all over the world ever since a long time ago, and those people have published many professional papers and books as a result. However, there are still very few books that truly and completely introduce Yangjiang intangible cultural heritage and much fewer books in Chinese-English version for foreign publicity. The Yangjiang Municipal Party Committee and Municipal Government have attached great importance to the protection of intangible cultural heritage. In December 2022, they issued *Implementation Opinions on Further Strengthening the Protection of Intangible Cultural Heritage in Our City*, which clarifies the work tasks and protection measures, aiming to further improve the protection and inheritance system of intangible cultural heritage in the city, and promote creative transformation and innovative development of it. In order to protect and inherit Yangjiang intangible cultural heritage and promote the foreign exchange and publicity of Moyang culture better, the compilation of the book *Moyang Inheritance* is high on the agenda. Since August 2022, Yangjiang Municipal Bureau of Culture, Radio, Television, Tourism and Sport has conducted a comprehensive investigation, excavation, and sorting of the city's intangible cultural heritage resources. Relevant experts and staff members consulted literature, visited the places of origin, interviewed inheritors, and obtained rich information, completing the writing and editing work of this book.

This book consists of seven parts. With the aim of being illustrated and lively, from traditional music, traditional dance, traditional medicine, traditional sports, amusement and acrobatics, traditional fine arts, traditional craftsmanship, and folklore, it introduces 31 intangible cultural heritages of Yangjiang region. Adopting both Chinese and English, it showcases the profound historical heritage and cultural connotation of Yangjiang to the readers, which provides an important channel for further telling the stories of Yangjiang, spreading Lingnan culture, and providing a foundation for the development and inheritance of Yangjiang's culture. This book will lead the readers to unlock the time memory of Yangjiang and appreciate its unique charm accumulated over thousands of years.

We sincerely thank the relevant leaders of the Yangjiang Municipal Party Committee and Municipal Government for their guidance and support in the process of writing this book, and thank all intangible cultural heritage inheritors for trying their best to provide us with relevant information and effective suggestions.

Although we have exhausted our ability, there may inevitably be inadequacies and omissions in the book for the rush of time and our limited talent. Your comments and criticism are greatly welcomed so that this book can be continuously enriched and improved.

传承》一书的编纂工作便提上日程。2022年8月起，阳江市文化广电旅游体育系统对阳江市的非物质文化遗产资源进行了全面调查、挖掘和整理，有关专家和工作人员查阅文献、实地调查发源地、采访非遗传承人，获取了丰富的资料，完成了本书的撰写和编辑工作。

本书包含七部分，力求图文并茂、生动有趣，从传统音乐，传统舞蹈，传统医药，传统体育、游艺与杂技，传统美术，传统技艺和民俗七个方面，介绍31项阳江地区的非物质文化遗产。全书采用汉英对照的形式向读者展示阳江深厚的历史底蕴和文化内涵，为进一步讲好阳江故事、传播岭南文化，让阳江文化发展有源、传承有序提供了一个重要的渠道。本书将带领读者解锁阳江的时间记忆，体味阳江在千年积淀中的独特魅力。

衷心感谢在本书的编写过程中阳江市委、市政府相关领导的指导和支持，感谢各非遗文化传承人不遗余力地为我们提供相关资料依据，并提出有效的建议。

虽然我们力求完善，但由于时间仓促、能力有限，书中难免存在不妥及疏漏之处，恳请读者不吝赐教，以使本书得以不断充实和完善。

目录
Contents

Part 1

Traditional Music

第一部分

传统音乐

阳江山歌

广东省第四批省级非物质文化遗产名录

保护单位　阳西县文化馆

Yangjiang Hill Song

The Fourth Batch of Provincial Intangible Cultural Heritage List of Guangdong Province

Protection Unit　Yangxi County Cultural Center

阳江山歌在阳江家喻户晓，流传于讲阳江话的地区。在日常生活中，民间迎亲嫁娶、老人生日、小孩满月、乔迁新居以及葬礼等红白之事，或者传统佳节、劳动之余、男女求爱之时，阳江群众都会用唱山歌的形式来表达他们的思想感情。因此，阳江从县到镇、从镇到村，田间地头，都有群众在唱山歌。阳江群众唱山歌已成为一种习俗。

2012年，阳江山歌被列入广东省第四批省级非物质文化遗产名录。

历史渊源

阳江在我国古代是少数民族聚居地。南北朝以前，阳江居住着少数民族俚、獠、瑶。南北朝宋元嘉九年（432），立宋康郡（在现阳江市阳西一带）。宋康郡是南粤巾帼英雄、岭南圣母冼夫人主要活动的地方，曾一度是冼夫人和冼夫人儿媳妇的食邑。冼夫人和其夫君构成的冼冯集团势力，在阳江的统治达百年之久。他们促进了阳江经济的兴旺发达，同时促进了阳江地方文化的发展。北史《冯融传》中如

Yangjiang Hill Song is well-known and popular in Yangjiang, spreading in the Yangjiang dialect speaking areas.In daily life, and during weddings, the elderly's birthday, babies's first month birthday, housewarming, funerals, traditional festivals, laboring, courtship between man and woman, Yangjiang people sing hill songs to express their thoughts and feelings. Therefore, people sing hill songs in the county, town, village, even in fields. It has become a custom for them to sing hill songs.

In 2012, Yangjiang Hill Song was selected into the fourth batch of provincial intangible cultural heritage list of Guangdong Province.

Historical Origin

Yangjiang was once inhabited by ethnic minorities in ancient China. Before the Southern and Northern Dynasties lived people of the Li, Liao, and Yao ethnic minorities. In the ninth year of the Yuanjia period in the Southern and Northern Dynasties (432), Songkang County was established (in the current area of Yangxi, Yangjiang City). Songkang County was where Madam Xian, the heroine of Southern Guangdong and the saintly mother of Lingnan, mainly lived, and was appanage granted to Madam Xian and her daughter-in-law. The Xian-Feng Family Group, formed by Madam Xian and her husband, had governed Yangjiang for more than hundred years. Owing to their fame, their rule boosted the economic growth of Yangjiang and the development of local culture. *Feng Rong Biography* of the Northern Dynasty history depicts the scene of Yangjiang at that time, "The intellectuals and scholars sing songs and write poetry, so the barbarism and uncivilization of this place dissipate. The string and reading sound are heard in the gathering place abundant in bananas and lychees." *Guangdong New Records* says a hill song praising Madam Xian was popular in the Gaoliang area (Songkang once belonged to the west of Gaoliang County). The song says, "The name of the leader of Gaoliang was Xian Ying, and she aged 18 was not married ..." *New Tang Book* records that in the seventh year of the Zhenguan period (633), Emperor Taizong of Tang held a feast for his ministers in Weiyang Palace, and ordered the Turkic Khan Jieli to dance as well as the chief of Nanman Feng Zhidai to sing poems. Feng Zhidai, the great-grandson of Madam Xian, was ordered to sing local hill songs by singing lyrics. We can see Yangjiang was already very popular for singing hill songs at that time. Yangjiang popular hill songs were also recorded in the Song Dynasty. According to the genealogy of Chongkou Village, Zhilong Town, Yangxi County, their ancestors moved to Yangjiang from Zhejiang in the Southern Song Dynasty. When they came, they took a boat with the Zhang family to enter the Zhilong River through the Yangbianhai and then saw the fertile fields on both sides of the river, so they agreed to settle there. The two families divided labor. The Chen family was responsible for building the embankment and opening the culvert gate. The Zhang family was accountable for ditching to draw water from the mountains. However, when the embankment was built, there was no water, and the reclaimed fields could not be cultivated. The two families were forced to move to other places to make a living. The nearby farmers sneered at them with hill songs, "Chen built the embankment as well as Zhang ditch up, and there was no water coming, making them pitiful ..."

In the Ming and Qing Dynasties, it was quite common for Yangjiang people to sing hill songs. Zhang Yuanxun, the general

此描绘当时阳江的情景："士相以为诗歌，蛮中化之，蕉荔之圩，弦诵日闻。"《广东新语》记载，高凉地区（宋康曾一度被划归为高凉郡西境地）流行歌颂冼夫人的山歌，歌曰："高凉首领名冼英，十八女子未完婜……"《新唐书》记载，唐贞观七年（633），唐太宗在未央宫大宴群臣，命突厥颉利可汗起舞、南蛮酋长冯智戴咏诗。冯智戴是冼夫人的曾孙，命他咏诗就是让他唱地方山歌。由此可见，当时阳江已经很流行唱山歌。阳江流行唱山歌在宋代也有记载。阳西县织箦镇冲口村族谱记载，其祖先在南宋时从浙江迁至阳江，来时与一张姓朋友两家坐船经洋边海进入织箦河，见河两岸平畴沃野，相约就此定居。两家人作了分工，陈家负责塞堤围开涵闸，张家负责开沟引山水。结果堤围塞好，水却没引来，开垦的田地无法耕种，两家被迫迁往他处谋生，附近的农民用山歌挖苦他们："陈筑堤围张挖沟，挪水无来眼勾勾……"

明清两代，阳江人唱山歌已相当普遍。明抗倭将领张元勋两度在阳江沿海地区抗击倭寇，取得了胜利，保住了一方平

阳江山歌传承人走进校园讲述阳江山歌的故事
The inheritor tells stories about Yangjiang Hill Song in the school

安，当地百姓用山歌赞颂他，流行下来的有《十哨歌》《赞张帅》等。清乾隆《阳江县志》载：“……六月村落，各建小棚，延巫女歌舞其上，名曰跳禾楼，用以祈年……”跳禾楼即是山歌表演的一种形式。又清道光《阳江县志》载：“……俗传跳禾楼即效刘三妈故事……”刘三妈即当时传说中的刘三姐，以唱山歌出名，现阳江仍流传着很多刘三姐唱山歌的故事，阳西县境内龙高山上有传说中的刘三姐唱歌台。

以上说明，阳江山歌源远流长，底蕴深厚，在民间传唱相当普遍，并同其他民族民歌一样，有其独特的文化蕴涵和历史研究价值，值得人们去发掘。中华人民共和国成立后，地方党委和政府十分重视阳江山歌文化的发展，有关文化部门组建了民歌社，开辟民歌榜，有组织地开展民歌创作竞赛和评论活动，曾创下群众一夜创作万首山歌的创作活动纪录。尤其是阳江建市以来，市委、市政府把发展传统文化作为一项重要工作，加强领导，精心组织，对山歌发展作出规划，推行各种措施，使阳江山歌这一古老的传统民间文化艺术形式焕发出新的活力，愈发根深叶茂，历久弥新。

against the Japan in the Ming Dynasty, fought against the Japanese pirates in the coastal areas of Yangjiang twice, won and kept the district safe. The local people praised him with hill songs, some of which spread widely, like *Ten Whistles Song*, *Praise General Zhang*, etc.. *Yangjiang County Annals* of Qianlong period in the Qing Dynasty records, "... In villages in the sixth lunar month, small sheds are built to invite witches to sing and dance. The custom is called Tiao Helou (meaning a custom that people dance in front of the cottage made of straw) , in order to pray for a harvest..." Tiao Helou is a form of hill song perfomance. *Yangjiang County Annals* of Daoguang period in the Qing Dynasty records, "... It is said that Tiao Helou follows the example of Liu Sanma's stories..." Liu Sanma was Liu Sanjie in the legend at that time, famous for singing hill songs. There are still many stories of Liu Sanjie singing hill songs in Yangjiang now. There is a legendary singing stage of Liu Sanjie on Longgao Mountain in Yangxi County.

All of the above illustrate Yangjiang Hill Song, with a long history and profound connotation, is quite popular among the folk. Like other ethnic hill songs, it has unique cultural implications and historical importance.Thus, these hill songs are worth exploring. After the founding of the People's Republic of China, the local party committee and government attached great importance to the development of Yangjiang Hill Song culture. The relevant cultural departments established folk song clubs, set folk song lists, and organized folk song composition competitions and commentary activities. There were composition records of people creating 10,000 hill songs overnight. Especially since the establishment of Yangjiang City, the municipal party committee and the municipal government have regarded the development of traditional culture as an essential task, strengthening leadership, making organizations carefully, planning the development of hill songs, and implementing various measures. Yangjiang Hill Song, as an ancient traditional folk culture and art form, has radiated new vitality, becoming more deeply rooted and enduring.

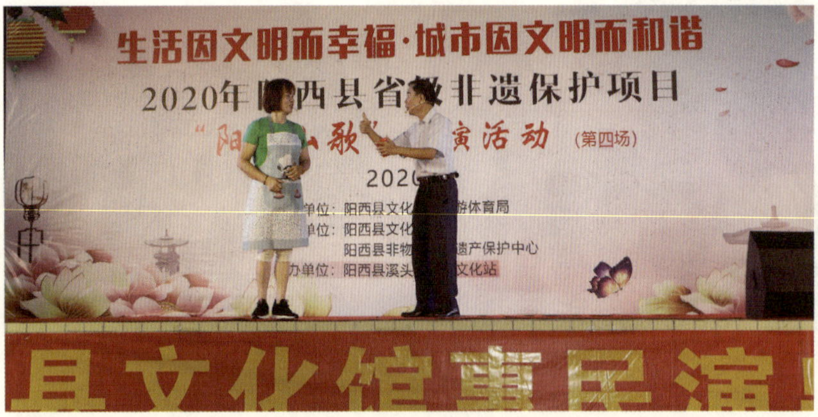

2020年阳西县文化馆举办“阳江山歌”惠民演出
"Yangjiang Hill Song" performance was held to benefit the public by Yangxi County Cultural Center in 2020

Basic Content

Up to now, Yangjiang Hill Song has had a variety of content genres. From the number of words, most of them are seven-character sentences, but according to the needs of the performance, there are also five-, six-, eight-, nine-, and ten-character ones. According to the intonation, there are Huajian tunes, wooden fish tunes, commanding cow tunes, reciting poem tunes, guessing horse tunes, murmur tunes, etc.. According to the form, there are long songs, short songs, and long-short songs. According to the content, there are children's songs, life songs, ritual songs, love songs, etc.. People sing hill songs to express their thoughts and feelings in their daily life. For example, in the labor-related song *Boating Song*, "It's hard to make a living by boating. Those people have sense of belonging when alive but are forgotten after death. There are many lives buried under the mud. The tombs are so lonely that people rarely remember to go for a worship. Young people are confident and don't worry about growing old. But they don't know time makes people get older and older. Time is making young make-up women disappear. They were wearing white hair, sighed in vain, and shed tears a lot." Another example is a song about life called *Crying for Marriage in Hall Song*, "The bride sits in front of the dresser. Two bright lights illuminate the hall of the house. She puts her feet on a rice sieve with thousands of mind's eyes as well as by the bucket which makes the moonlight brighter." Another example is the ritual song *Ten-month Pregnancy Song*, "Pregnancy in the first month is like dew. Blood is hazy in the second month. There is a shadow in the third month..." These hill songs are widely drawn from the daily life of people. The content of the lyrics is closely related to the life and production as well as thoughts and feelings of the masses. The words in the hill songs are plain, and the content is substantial.

Yangjiang hill songs, mainly love songs, are the most popular, the most distinctive, the most widely circulated, the most loved and imitated by the masses, and the most resonant and echoing. In production and life practice, young men and women like to use love songs to express their emotions, relieve worries, make fun of each other, and express their love affairs. Among the thousands of existing Yangjiang hill songs, love songs account for over half, and many love songs are narrative. For example, in *Free Girl*, "Blowing wind and golden scenery enter autumn, and every family plays music sentimentally in the Qiqiao Festival. I'm the only one left full of sadness and resentment. And I can't bear to look at Altair. The Cowherd and the Weaver Girl are separated by the Milky Way. The double stars are as clear as ever. There is still a chance to have a date in heaven. People in the human world have separated for too long. What can I do but hate when we separate in two places. Nobody knows I miss you so much that my heart is broken. It's hard

基本内容

发展至今，阳江山歌具有多种多样的内容体裁。从字数来划分，大都是一句七字，但根据演出内容的需要，也有五、六、八、九、十字不等；从唱调来分，有花笺调、木鱼调、使牛调、吟诗调、猜马调、喃呒调等；从形式来分，有长歌、短歌、长短歌；从内容上分，有儿歌、生活歌、仪式歌、情歌等。在日常生活中，群众都会用唱山歌的形式来表达他们的思想感情。如劳动类山歌《撑船歌》："撑船度日苦伶仃，生时有主死无明。香埋肉葬知多少，荒冢何人去踏清。青春思老气还高，岁月催人知得无。恨杀几多红粉女，白头空叹泪滔滔。"又如生活类山歌《哭嫁坐厅歌》："明镜妆台姐坐定，两盏明灯照屋厅。脚踏米筛千只眼，脚踏斗边月更明。"再如仪式类山歌《十月怀胎歌》："正月怀胎如露水，二月怀胎血朦朦，三月怀胎成有影……"这些内容各异的山歌，广泛取材于群众日常生活，歌词内容与群众的生产生活贴近，与群众的思想感情息息相关，语言质朴，内容充实。

阳江山歌以情歌最多，最有特色，流传最广，最受群众喜爱和效仿，也最能引起人们共鸣和附和。男女青年在生产和生活实践中，喜欢用情歌来抒发情思、排愁解忧、互相取乐、表达恋情。在现存的几千首阳江山歌中，情歌占了一大半，且很多情歌都具有故事性。如《自由女》："荡荡金风景入秋，家家乞巧乐绸缪。独我满胸愁以恨，伤情不忍看牵牛。牛郎织女隔银河，双星如切又如初。天上佳期还有会，人间心愿久分离。分疏两地恨何如，心中想烂有谁知。始末一言言不尽，执支笔写绝情书……"又如《新自由女》："回忆白沙母校时，那时奋力读书诗，可叹光阴如兔走，瞬息之间又转移，转移同学各回乡，仕工农业任所长，境遇不同人各别，果场悲苦更凄凉，凄凉团聚更无能，兄离兰妹苦伤神，二载同窗为密友，割爱与娇怎舍分……”这两首新旧对比的长诗，略带口语化，通俗易懂，雅俗共赏，特别顺口和押韵，它们利用周围的环境和事物来比兴，深刻引出所需表达的内容和思想感情。

除了上述的故事性叙事长诗情歌外，还有一种男女即兴对答的情歌也很有特色，如《笑磨谷》：

妻唱：两个合埋做一堆，中间助碌野来推。
双脚跨开腰出力，呼声推去呀声回。
夫唱：妻供唱时夫供随，呼声推去呀声回。
无奈与妻同改磨，周身磨得汗涔涔。

又如《袁大舵求婚》：

男唱：谭屋外公改坐呀？还无喊我做郎家？
我系姓袁人屋仔，无赌无吹使乜查！
女唱：果位乞儿讲乜呀？无赌无吹使乜查？
我系谭家人小姐，丝绸怎补烂衫那？
男唱：小姐原是果句差，丝绸怎补烂衫那？
七姐下凡配董永，何况凡人配怎差！

to explain the beginning and end completely. I hold a pen to write a letter of love...” Another example is *New Free Girl*, “I recalled the time in my old school in Baisha that I had tried my best to read books and poetry. It was so sorrowful that time ran away like a running rabbit. Time passed in an instant. The classmates went back to their hometowns. They worked on what they were good at, such as politics, agriculture, and industry. Opportunities differed from people to live. The misery destiny was more lonely. The desolate reunion was more incompetent. The elder brother left, and the orchid sister was sad, harming her spirits. Two-year classmates made close friends. How could we separate from love...” These two long poems that contrast the old and the new are slightly conversational, easy to understand, appreciated by both the elegant and the popular, and incredibly smooth and rhyming. It uses the surrounding environment and things to profoundly elicit the content of the desired expression, thoughts and feelings.

In addition to those long narrative poems mentioned above, there is also a kind of love songs with impromptu answers between men and women, such as *Milling Rice with a Smile*:

The wife: Our joint efforts rotate the wheel. They are pushed by using something in the middle.

The two feet straddle and the waist contributes. Push away with the sound “Hu” and take it back with the sound “Ya”.

The husband: When the wife sings, the husband follows. Push away with the sound “Hu” and take it back with the sound “Ya”.

I had no choice but to change the mill with my wife, and the whole body was worn to sweat.

Another example is *Yuan Datuo’s Proposal.*

Man: Grandpa Tan, you sit here? Why haven’t you called me son-in-law yet?

My surname is Yuan. You don’t need to check my information for no gambling and no drugs!

Woman: What are you talking about, poor man? Is there no need to check your information for no gambling and no drugs? I am the daughter of the Tan family. How can I use my silk clothes to mend rotten clothes?

Man: Miss, you are wrong. How can a girl wearing silk clothes mend rotten shirts?

The Seventh Fairy went down to the earth to marry Dong Yong. It’s not bad for a mortal girl to marry me!

The love songs mentioned above are understandable in language, and they are sung in the local dialect, full of local flavor. The vivid lyrics stimulate the listeners' interest and arouse emotional resonance, so for thousands of years, these love songs have prevailed and been sung widely among young men and women.

There are many expression forms of Yangjiang Hill Song activities. The primary forms include "Refuting Song", "Tiao Helou", "Playing Tangmei", "Dancing with Flower Branches", and "Fighting in the Ring".

"Refuting Song" means antiphonal singing. Generally, each person sings four sentences. After a singer sings the last sentence, the other singer must sing immediately. Otherwise, they will be coaxed off the stage by the audience. "Tiao Helou", used to pray for the harvest, is an entertainment activity held after the farmers finish farming in order to celebrate the agricultural harvest and hope for the next crop. It is mostly held on the night of the sixth or tenth lunar month. "Da Tangmei" is used for weddings and takes place in the hall of the groom's home. "Dancing with Flower Branches" is used when women pray for pregnancy, which has been lost.

"Fighting in the Ring" is developed based on "Refuting Song" and "Tiao Helou", adding modern performance forms. During the Spring Festival of 1987, the Yangjiang County Cultural Bureau held "The First Yangjiang County Hill Song Ring" in Zhongshan Park and the People's Square of the county. At that time, the lively scene of thousands of people was reported by provincial and municipal newspapers, radios, and televisions. Since then, the hill song ring has been carried out once or twice a year until now and has been active in Yangjiang urban and rural areas as a form of popular cultural activity.

Main Features

One of the characteristics of Yangjiang hill songs is that they are sung in slang and the Yangjiang dialect, a unique language. Its causes of formation are very complex. It not only maintains a large number of ancient language characteristics, but also is influenced by the surrounding local dialects. And it contains many dialect slang words. Therefore, Yangjiang hill songs are different from other hill songs in the use of words, rhymes, and level and oblique tones, full of their specificity. Due to the penetration of a large number of dialect slang in hill songs, Yangjiang hill songs have strong local language characteristics, some of which can only be sung but cannot be expressed in words.

上述情歌语言通俗，以当地方言土语入歌，富有乡土气息，歌词形象生动，能激发听歌人的兴趣，引起情感共鸣，以致千百年来，这些情歌盛行不衰，在青年男女中广泛传唱。

阳江山歌活动有多种表现形式，主要有“驳歌仔”“跳禾楼”“打堂枚”“跳花枝”和“打擂台”等。

“驳歌仔”即对歌。一般每人唱四句，前者唱完最后一句，对唱者必须立即接上，否则便会被听众哄下台。“跳禾楼”用于“祈年”，是农家农事完成了以后举行的娱乐活动，以庆祝农业丰收并寄托下一季丰收的希望，多在农历六月或十月夜晚举行。“打堂枚”用于婚礼上，活动地点在新郎家中厅堂。“跳花枝”是妇人祈子用，已失传。

“打擂台”是在“驳歌仔”和“跳禾楼”的基础上，引进现代表演形式发展而成。1987年春节，阳江县文化局在县城中山公园和人民广场举办“阳江县首届山歌擂台”，当时那万人空巷的热闹情景被省市报刊、电台、电视台报道。此后，每年一次至两次的山歌擂台一直开展到现在，并作为大众文化活动形式活跃于阳江城乡。

主要特征

阳江山歌特点之一是以俚语入歌、用阳江话说唱。阳江话是一种独特语言，成因十分复杂，它既保持着大量的古代语特征，又受周围地方方言的影响，夹杂着大量的方言俚语，因而，阳江山歌在用词、押韵、平仄音运用上都与别的民歌不同，有其特异性。由于大量方言俚语渗透在山歌中，阳江山歌具有浓厚的地方语言特色，一些歌句只能唱，没法用文字表述。

阳江山歌特点之二是对歌，歌手在相互对歌时，起唱者唱完四句后，答歌者在还歌时必须在答歌的第二句重复起歌者最后一句，唱完四句后，起歌者再还对方的歌，也要在答歌的第二句重复起歌者最后一句，如此连续，直到一方认输为止。比如：

The second characteristic of Yangjiang hill songs is that when the antiphonal singers sing against each other, after a singer has sung four sentences, the respondent must repeat the former's last sentence in the second sentence of the answering song. After singing four sentences, the former should return to the respondent's song and repeat the respondent's last sentence in the second sentence of the answering song. Singers keep singing like this until one of them is beaten. For example:

男唱：谭小姐你在家吗？还无喊我做夫呀！
　　我系单身独屋仔，无赌无吹使乜查。
女唱：乞儿仔你讲乜呀？无赌无吹使乜查？
　　我系千金人小姐，丝绸怎补烂衫那？

Man: Miss Tan, are you at home? You haven't called me husband yet!
I am a single man. There is no need to check my information for no gambling and no drugs.
Woman: What are you thinking about, little beggar? Is there no need to check your information for no gambling and no drugs?
I am a daughter of a wealthy family. How can I use my silk clothes to mend rotten clothes?

阳江山歌对歌时，基本是一韵到底，但逢歌手棋逢对手、难分难解、所唱的韵重复太多时，一方歌手会自动转韵，对方歌手还歌时跟着韵续下去，如此循环往复，连续不断。

阳江山歌的特点之三是可唱可说。边唱边说的形式多来自一些出名的歌手表演。歌手向观众表演时，有点类似北方的弹词，每唱一段，再解说一遍，演唱时声情并茂，解说时惟妙惟肖。说唱阳江山歌是知名歌手的拿手好戏，多为即兴表演，与观众互动，深受观众欢迎和喜爱。

阳江山歌的特点之四是以七字一句为多，四句为一段落。其写法，一般与竹枝词写法相同，但加入方言土语，通俗易懂，且注重平仄，押地方声韵，朗朗上口，能诵能唱。比较通行的写法有：

（1）比兴，山歌第一句对后面的歌词没有大的意义，只起衬托的作用，如：

Yangjiang hill songs are basically sung in one rhyme to the end. However, when the singer meets the rival, it isn't easy to win, and the rhyme sung is repeated too much, one of the singers will automatically change the rhyme, and the other singer will follow the rhyme when returning to the song continuously.

The third characteristic of Yangjiang Hill Song is that it can be sung or said. This form mostly appears in the performances of some famous singers. When the singer performs to the audience, he/she sings each paragraph and then explains it, which is similar to the northern lyrics strumming. When singing, the singer's voice is full of emotion. When presenting, the singer's words are vivid and abundant. Famous singers are good at this kind of performance and mostly play impromptu performances. They interact with the audience and are well-welcomed and loved by the audience.

The fourth characteristic of Yangjiang hill songs is that a sentence is mainly made up of seven characters, and a paragraph is made up of four sentences. The writing method of Yangjiang hill songs is generally the same as that of Zhuzhi poem. These songs add dialect language, which helps to be understood easily, lay emphasis on level and oblique tones with local rhyme, and can be catchy, recited and sung. The typical writing methods are as follows.

（1）Bixing: The first sentence of the hill songs has no great significance with lyrics behind it, and only plays a foil role. For example：

Restoring vegetables and watering flowers needs the round pump. Someone wants to find a wife but has no money.

He sleeps in bed thinking again. He wipes his beard until another year.

（2）Dingzhen: The last two words of the last sentence in the four seven-character sentences are the beginning of the first sentence in the subsequent four sentences. It keeps continuing. For example:

There was a blaze around the bank of Lugou Bridge. Cruel Japanese are mad and determined to destroy China. Everyone kills the enemies unswervingly with a sense of patriotism.

Whether people come from east, west, north and south, people are very determined to kill the enemies. There is no distinction between young, old, men, or women. To save the dying country is to save ourselves.

（3）Repetition: The second sentence of the respondent's repeats the fourth sentence of the former singer. Sing and respond in this way. It is inextricably connected. For example:

On the trip to Sanya, I run into a girl who peeled off hemp by chance. I greeted this girl to ask the direction. I forgot how to go and got lost.

I asked whose house you planned to go. You forgot how to go and got lost. The left road was through the highroad, and the right road to Changsha.

（4）Antithesis: If you write eight-sentence songs with seven characters, the third and the fourth, the fifth and the sixth are two groups of antithesis sentences, which are the same as the seven characters hill songs but are not so strict. Some can also make the first and the second, the seventh and the eighth into antithesis sentences, or they can be non-antithesis ones. For example, as the same as the seven characters hill songs :

One asks: It is drizzling today and the rain splashes my shoes. I have waited all morning for the boat to cross the river but no boat at all. Who can take me across the river? I have no money, but can give the golden hairpin on my head.

One answers: Who is so talkative and tactful? You say that you have no money, but can give the golden hairpin on head. It's so easy to take you across the river, which can be served as Xiuzhai（meaning offering monks vegetarian and worship the Bodhisattva）.

（5）Inlay: This kind of words such as numbers, directions, five elements, solar terms, and colors are embedded at the song's beginning, middle, end with a total of four- or eight-sentences with seven characters to enhance the content color and aggravate the language appeal. The following is the example that numbers are embedded in the sentence.

瓮菜打花泵泵圆，想揼老婆未有钱。

睡落床中凛（想）过数，抹抹须仔又一年。

（2）顶真，即七言四句的末一句的末两个字，就是下四句第一句的开头，一直如此接连下去，如：

卢沟桥畔起烽烟，残忍倭奴发赛癫。立心定要亡中国，大家杀敌爱心坚。

心坚你话系谁人，南北东西地不分。无分老幼同男女，救亡系救自家身。

（3）重复，即答歌者的第二句重复起唱者第四句。如此一唱一和，连接无间，如：

行程路上到三丫，有缘偶遇妹刨麻。借请贤娇问句路，果时忘记路行差。

问爷你，去谁家，果时忘记路行差。左边那条通大路，右边条路去长沙。

（4）对偶，如写七言八句民歌，第三与第四句、第五与第六句则是两组对偶句，似与七律相同，但没那么严格，有的也可将第一与第二句、第七与第八句成对偶句，也可全不对偶。与七律相同的如：

唱：水仔湄湄湄湿鞋，论朝等渡渡无埋。使个渡官撑我过，有钱头上扯金钗。

答：使个姐人嘴咁乖，有钱头上扯金钗。撑你过河容乜易，救人过水当修斋。

（5）镶嵌，即在七言四句或八句的句首、句中、句末镶嵌数字、方位、五行、节气、颜色等类词，以加浓内容色彩，加重语言感染力。句中嵌数字的如：

一生投着恶家婆，百样使奴受苦多。
千古少逢姑贡恶，万望良人替揣摩。

有的专用相同的一个数目镶嵌在句首的，如：

一把汗珠一把禾，一箩新谷一箩歌。
一双巨手山川改，一亩千斤未算多。

（6）借喻，用生动而形象的东西作比喻，使之如见其人、如闻其声，感人肺腑，如：

共妹插秧隔块田，魂魄过都妹那边。
怎得变成金纽扣，时时扣在妹胸前。

（7）双件，即在四句或八句中，运用一些类物词语，以及典故、同音或反义词，以加深内容的含义及情趣。运用五金词语的如：

皎洁银蟾映绣帷，怅郎铁马去辽西。
羞窥玉兔情难吐，只恨金龟婿未归。

此外，还经常运用双关、寄意、连字、猜谜等手法。

重要价值

·历史价值

阳江山歌历史悠久，早在4000年以前的新石器时代，人类始祖就在阳江海边一带活动。广东省考古队在这里发现了三处新石器时代遗址。春秋战国时，阳江为百越地，所形成的古代文化中，最主要的就是阳江山歌。阳江山歌内容丰富多彩，涉及面广，传播及影响范围广泛，参与群众较多，是一个历史产物。在千百年历史发展过程中，它表达了阳江人民的思想感情和对幸福、平安、健康的热烈追求，是阳江人民的智慧结晶，也是阳江历史文化的具体表现，对研究阳江各时代的历史、各时期社会情况、生产力发展情况以及文化娱乐生活状况等方面提供了宝贵的研究资料。

In my life, I have thrown myself to meet my malicious mother-in-law. I have been slaved and suffered a lot in a hundred ways. Through the ages, It's rare to meet a malicious mother-in-law. I sincerely hope my beloved can figure it out for me.

Some use the same number embedded at the beginning of the sentence. For example:

Take a handful of millet with a handful of sweat. Take a basket of new rice with a basket of songs. A pair of giant hands have changed mountains and rivers. An *mu* producing a thousand kilos of things is not so much.

(6) Metonymy: Use vivid things as metaphors so that it is like seeing someone, and hearing someone, which touches one deeply in the heart. For example:

When I transplant seedlings, I meet a girl across the field. The soul passes over the girl's side. How can I become a golden button? Then I can always be buttoned on her chest.

(7) Shuangjian. In a song with four or eight sentences, use some physical words, allusions, homonyms, or antonyms, to deepen the meaning and emotion of the content. For example, using hardware words:

The bright silver moon lights the embroidered curtain. Be sad about the man riding the strong horse and going to the western part of Liao. Too shy to meet Yutu and express my love feelings. Only hate that the precious husband has not returned.

In addition, puns, expressing meanings, linking words, guessing, and other techniques are often used.

Great Value

· Historical value

Yangjiang Hill Song has a long history. As early as the Neolithic Age 4,000 years ago, the ancestors of human beings were active in the seaside area of Yangjiang. The archaeological team of Guangdong found three Neolithic sites here. In the Spring and Autumn Period and the Warring States Period, Yangjiang was where hundreds of Yue people lived, creating the ancient culture. The most critical ancient culture formed was Yangjiang Hill Song. Yangjiang Hill Song has rich content, involves a wide range of aspects, and has a wide range of dissemination and influence with many participants. It's a historical product. In the process of thousands of years of historical development, these songs express the intelligence and emotional feelings of the Yangjiang people and their great desire for happiness, peace, and healthy. It is the crystallization of the Yangjiang people's wisdom and the specific manifestation of Yangjiang's history and

2020年阳西县安全生产系列活动中的阳江山歌表演
Yangjiang Hill Song performance in Series Activities for Safety Production of Yangxi County in 2020

culture. It provides valuable research materials for studying the history of Yangjiang in various eras, social conditions in multiple periods, development of productive forces, cultural life, and entertainment conditions.

· Cultural value

Yangjiang, located on the coast of the South China Sea, enjoys fertile land and abundant resources. At the earliest, Han and Li people lived together, and the production methods were highly backward. After the Southern Song Dynasty, many people of the Central Plains migrated to settle here. These people brought advanced production technology and culture, inspiring the masses' enthusiasm for labor and promoting the development of the masses' culture. The masses sang hill songs while working. Some people sang and got responded with reverberation from hills and valleys. The woodcutters going up the mountain, the workers in the row, and the farmers working in the fields all sang with each other and expressed their emotions, which became a way for the working people to express their thoughts and feelings. It has been passed down from generation to generation and has become a familiar atmosphere, forming a kind of hill song culture about self-creation and mutual communication.

· Entertainment value

In ancient times, the Yangjiang people sang hill songs to relieve the hardships of labor and express their thoughts and feelings. With the development of society, singing hill songs is gradually given new content, combining culture, art, entertainment, food, social interaction, and business. Large-scale hill song cultural activities such as hill song competitions and hill song talent shows appear, greatly enriching the masses' material and spiritual life.

· Aesthetic value

The hill song, as a folk culture, pursues beauty from language, music, rhyme, and form in various themes and content. It sings catchy. It sounds relish and humorous, giving people a kind of artistic enjoyment.

·文化价值

阳江地处南海之滨，土地肥沃，物产丰富。最先，这里俚汉杂居，生产方式极为落后。南宋以后，大批中原人迁徙至此定居。中原人带来了先进的生产技术和文化，激发了群众的劳动热情，促进了群众文化的开发，群众边劳动边唱山歌。有人歌起，山鸣谷应。不管是上山的樵夫，还是放排的工人，抑或田间耕耘的农民，都互相唱和，抒发情感。山歌成为劳动人民表达思想感情的一种方式，代代相传，蔚然成风，形成一种自我创作、互相交流的山歌文化。

·娱乐价值

古时阳江人唱山歌是为了减轻劳动的辛苦，表达自己的思想感情。随着社会的发展，阳江山歌渐渐被赋予了新的内容，它集文化、艺术、娱乐、饮食、社交、商业于一体，山歌擂台赛、山歌表演赛等大型山歌文化活动也应运而生，极大地丰富了群众的物质、精神生活。

·审美价值

山歌作为一种民俗文化，它所表现的各种题材和内容，都追求一种语言美、音乐美、节奏美和形式美，它唱起来朗朗上口，听起来津津有味，并富有幽默感，给人以美的享受。

主要传承人

谭闰瑜，男，生于1952年5月，其曾祖父辈就有人唱山歌。谭闰瑜生长在山歌世家，受父辈影响，自幼学唱山歌，几十年来一直坚持阳江山歌的创作和演唱，遇传统佳节、迎亲娶嫁、老人生日、小孩满月、乔迁新居以及葬礼哭丧等，都被人请去唱山歌，每年演出均在80场次以上。曾获市级山歌擂台比赛第一名5次、第二名3次，县级山歌擂台赛第一名12次；录制山歌音带20余盒。其代表作有山歌小剧《卖猪》《骗婚记》等。谭闰瑜现为广东省第四批省级非物质文化遗产项目代表性传承人。

谢计平，男，生于1961年8月，从小深受祖辈的影响，对阳江山歌非常热爱，八九岁时就会跟着大人学唱，从而产生浓厚的兴趣。从1983年开始，谢计平积极参加市、县、镇、村级的山歌演唱晚会和比赛，近十几年来多次参加市、县级的山歌擂台赛，取得了优异的成绩，获得了大量奖项。他创作山歌、白榄、花笺、山歌小品、对口词等280多首；同时积极主动培养唱山歌人才，把阳江山歌发展好、传承好。现为阳江市第四批非物质文化遗产项目代表性传承人。

Main Inheritors

谭闰瑜
Tan Runyu

Tan Runyu, male, was born in May 1952. The generation of his great-grandfather sang hill songs. He grew up in a hill song family. Influenced by his parents' generation, he learned to sing hill songs in childhood. He has insisted on creating and singing the Yangjiang Hill Song for several decades. In traditional festivals, weddings, the elderly's birthdays, babies' first month birthdays, housewarmings, and funerals, he has been invited to sing hill songs. He plays the performances more than 80 times a year. He has won the first place in the municipal hill song competitions five times, the second place three times, and the first place in the county hill song competitions 12 times. He has recorded more than 20 hill song tapes. His representative works include hill song performances, *Selling Pigs*, *The Story of Fraud Marriage*, etc.. Tan Runyu is now listed as the representative inheritor of the fourth batch of local intangible cultural heritage projects of Guangdong Province.

Xie Jiping, male, was born in August 1961. He was profoundly influenced by his ancestors since he was a child, loving Yangjiang Hill Song very much. At the age of eight or nine, he learned to sing from adults, resulting in a strong interest. Since 1983, he has actively participated in hill song-singing evening parties and competitions of municipal-, county-, town-, and village-level. In the last more than ten years, he has participated in municipal- and county-level hill song competitions many times, achieved excellent results, and won many awards. He has created more than 280 hill songs, white olives, Huajian, hill song sketches, and dialectical words. At the same time, he has actively cultivated talents for singing hill songs

谢计平
Xie Jiping

陈妹
Chen Mei

and has developed and inherited Yangjiang Hill Song well. Now he is the representative inheritor of the fourth batch of intangible cultural heritage projects of Yangjiang City.

Chen Mei, female, was born in a peasant family in Yangxi County, Yangjiang City, in May 1960, and is the third generation of inheritors of the Yangjiang Hill Song. When she was young, she followed her father to learn Yangjiang Hill Song through oral teaching in daily life. At the age of fifteen, she started to study singing formally. She has created more than 30 songs in more than 40 working years. She has participated in more than 200 Yangjiang Hill Song series activities and performances. She is good at creating and performing Yangjiang Hill Song sketches and antiphon. In the process of creation, she has integrated local cultural characteristics and living habits. Among them, the song *High Contribution of the Party to Alleviating Poverty and Difficulties* won the second class prize of the competition, "Practicing the Original Mission and Winning Victory in Poverty Alleviation—2020 Yangxi County Provincial Intangible Cultural Heritage Project 'Yangjiang Hill Song' ". In the process of inheritance, she pays attention to the development of new forces, actively cultivates enthusiasts and imparts oral skills of Yangjiang Hill Song. She won the honor of "The Most Beautiful Intangible Cultural Heritage Person of the Intangible Cultural Heritage Project 'Yangjiang Hill Song' " in 2017. Now she is the representative inheritor of the fifth batch of intangible cultural heritage projects of Yangjiang City.

陈妹，女，1960年5月出生在阳江市阳西县一个农民家庭，是阳江山歌第三代传承人。陈妹年幼时跟随父亲在日常生活中口耳相传学习阳江山歌，15岁时开始学艺。从艺40余年间，共创作阳江山歌作品30余件，参加阳江山歌系列活动和演出200余场。她擅长创作与表演阳江山歌小品和山歌对唱，在创作的过程中融入了当地文化特色和生活习惯。她创作并演唱的曲目《扶贫解困党功高》荣获"践行初心使命·决胜脱贫攻坚——2020年阳西县省级非遗项目'阳江山歌'大赛"二等奖。在传承过程中，陈妹注重新生力军的发展，积极培养阳江山歌爱好者并传授阳江山歌口头技艺，2017年荣获"非物质文化遗产'阳江山歌'项目最美非遗人"称号。现为阳江市第五批非物质文化遗产项目代表性传承人。

阳江咸水歌

广东省第五批省级非物质文化遗产名录

保护单位 阳东区文化馆

Yangjiang Salty-water Song

The Fifth Batch of Provincial Intangible Cultural Heritage List of Guangdong Province

Protection Unit Yangdong District Cultural Center

阳江咸水歌主要流传于当地渔民群体中，尤以阳东区东平镇，海陵岛闸坡镇，阳西县沙扒镇、溪头镇、上洋镇等最为集中、活跃。咸水歌起源于疍民，一直以来，疍民作为一个弱势族群，社会地位低下，生存环境险恶，劳动强度大，人与人之间交流机会少，生活单调艰难，长夜寂寞枯燥。为了排遣苦闷、抒发情思、调剂生活，疍民有感而发地吟唱出咸水歌，后来咸水歌逐渐被人们认可、传唱，演变为疍家人一种重要的精神生活载体。

2013年，阳江咸水歌被列入广东省第五批省级非物质文化遗产名录。

历史渊源

阳江南临浩瀚无垠的南海，在这里世代生活着以海为生的打渔人，他们作为一个特殊的群体，有着一个特殊的称呼——疍民。海洋是世世代代疍家人赖以生存的物质环境，“疍”原作“蜑”，古书作“蜑”，今通作“疍”。疍民是水上居民的统称，也称“渔民”。渔民又分为三种，一种是咸水渔民，另一种是半咸淡水

Yangjiang Salty-water Song has been mainly spread among local fishermen, especially in Dongping Town of Yangdong District; Zhapo Town of Hailing Island; Shapa Town, Xitou Town, and Shangyang Town of Yangxi County. The salty-water songs originate from the Tankas. As a minority group, they had low-level social status, dangerous living environment, high labor intensity, few opportunities to communicate with each other in a monotonous and challenging life, and were lonely and boring in the long nights, so they sang songs with emotion to relieve depression, express feelings and adjust to life. Gradually, salty-water songs were recognized and sung by people and evolved into a vital carrier of spiritual life for the Tankas.

In 2013, Yangjiang Salty-water Song was selected into the fifth batch of provincial intangible cultural heritage list of Guangdong Province.

Historical Origin

Yangjiang faces the vast South China Sea in the south, where fishermen have lived by the sea for generations. As a particular group, they have a unique name — Tankas. The sea is the material environment in which the clan of Tankas has lived for generations. The original word for “Dan” is “Tan”（a different word in Chinese）in ancient times. The Tankas are the general name of afloat residents, also known as “fishermen”. There are three kinds of fishermen: salty-water fishermen; semi-saline freshwater fishermen, and inland river fishermen. Salty-water fishermen are deep-water fishermen who work in the open sea mainly by trawling and lighting. Semi-saline freshwater fishermen belong to shallow-water fishermen. They work in

疍家渔民在捕鱼作业
Tanka fishermen go fishing

疍家渔民在劳作
Tanka fishermen are laboring

shallow water and offshore, and can go out early and return late. Their operation methods mainly include digging large fishnets, catching shrimp, and putting nets. Inland river fishermen belong to freshwater fishermen. They work in the regional inland rivers with a relatively small risk of labor environment. The fish and shrimp they caught are called river fish and shrimp.

Yangjiang Salty-water Song is an original ecological music culture in Yangjiang, also known as the "fishermen's song", which refers to the song sung by fishermen who engaged in fishing. However, there is a subtle difference from the fishermen's song. The fishermen's song refers to all the songs sung by fishermen engaged in water operations (including inland rivers) . In contrast, salty-water songs, by definition, are named because of the salty taste of seawater. Distinctly, it refers solely to the songs sung by the boat-dwelling people who make their living by going to sea to fish.

According to the *Guangdong New Language · Poetry · Cantonese Songs* by Qu Dajun in the early Qing Dynasty, "Tankas also like to sing. Two boats will meet each other in the sunset in the wedding. When the male wins during the antiphonal singing, he can pick up the female's clothes to cross the boat." It also recorded, "People in both eastern and western Guangdong enjoy singing, especially the chieftains in western Guangdong." *Yangjiang County Annals* (edition of the second year of Daoguang in the Qing Dynasty （1822）) also recorded, "People like to drink when getting married, and women and men drink by the waterside. The groom's and bride's family will go boating together at sunset and have fun singing songs, which can be as many as dozens of boats." These historical materials record the long history of the salty-water songs, proving that it has been popular in coastal areas since the late Ming and early Qing Dynasties.

As a minority group in a special environmental condition, the

渔民，还有一种是内河渔民。咸水渔民属于深水渔民，出远海作业，他们的作业方式以拖网、灯光作业为主。半咸淡水渔民属于浅水渔民，在浅海、近海作业，能早出晚归，他们的作业方式以打大围罟、捕虾和下网为主。内河渔民属于全淡水渔民，在区域内河作业，劳动环境的危险性相对小一些，所捕捞的鱼虾称为河鱼河虾。

阳江咸水歌是阳江本土的一种原生态音乐文化，也被称为“渔歌”，即打渔人唱的歌，但却又有区别于渔歌。“渔歌”泛指一切从事水上作业的渔民（包括内河）所唱的歌，而咸水歌顾名思义，是由海水的咸味而得名，从真正意义上来说，它是专指以出海打渔为生的疍民唱出的歌。

据清初屈大均撰写的《广东新语·诗语·粤歌》中记载：“疍人亦喜唱歌，婚夕两舟相合，男歌胜则牵女衣过舟也。”又载：“东西两粤皆尚歌，而西粤土司中尤盛。”清道光二年（1822）《阳江县志》也有记载：“婚娶率以酒相馈遗，妇子饮于洲岸，是夕两姓联舟，多至数十艇，更唱迭和以为乐。”这些史料都记录了咸水歌悠久的历史，证明了明末清初咸水歌就已在沿海地区流行。

疍民作为一个处于特殊环境中的弱势

疍家渔民在捕鱼作业时唱咸水歌
Tanka fishermen are singing salty-water songs when fishing

族群，他们也需要表达自己的情感，而叹唱咸水歌就成为他们表达情感的一种方式。这种方式不仅起到表达情感的作用，更发挥了音乐的独特功能，使语言在与旋律的互为衬托下，把生活升华为艺术。而正是这种艺术魅力，使咸水歌为疍家男女老少所接受和喜爱，使叹唱咸水歌成为他们生活的组成部分，并慢慢演变成他们一种重要的精神生活载体，成为疍民的一个特有的文化符号。现在的咸水歌还完整地保留了传统的唱法，如句首的"哎呀哩""细妹呀""哥兄呀"等呼语，以及句中、句尾"嗨""哩""呀""咧""啰哩""呀哩""那个""呢个""啰喂"等衬词的运用。

在阳东县的东平镇，阳西县沙扒镇、溪头镇，以及海陵岛的闸坡镇等地，渔民们为了调剂生活，以唱咸水歌增进相互间的沟通、交流和友情。在日常生活中，特别是在一些民俗活动中，如红白喜事、传统节日等，都一定要唱叹咸水歌，以表达他们的欢乐和悲伤的情感。直至20世纪60年代初，咸水歌也是渔民们的主流娱乐方式，盛行之处热闹非凡。但在"文革"期间，咸水歌被视为"四旧"曾一度被禁唱，遭受了毁灭性的打击，而被禁唱后的

Tankas must also express their feelings. Thus, singing the salty-water song has become a way for them to express their feelings. This way not only plays a role in expressing emotion but also sublimates life into art because of music's unique function, which makes language and rhythm set off each other. This artistic charm makes the salty-water song accepted and loved by men and women, the old and the young, and makes singing the salty-water song an integral part of their life. It slowly becomes an essential carrier of spiritual life for the Tanka family and a unique cultural symbol of the Tanka people. The current salty-water song also ultimately retains the traditional singing method, such as the vocative expression of "Ah Ya Li", "Sister Ya" and "Brother Ya" at the beginning of the sentence, as well as the use of lining words such as "Hai", "Li", "Ya", "Lie", "Luo Li", "Ya Li", "Na Ge", "Ne Ge" and "Luo Wei" at the end of the sentence.

In Dongping Town of Yangdong County, Shapa Town and Xitou Town of Yangxi County, and Zhapo Town of Hailing Island, to adjust their lives, fishermen sing salty-water songs as a means to enhance their communication and strengthen friendships. In daily life, especially in some folk activities such as weddings, funerals, and traditional festivals, fishermen must sing salty-water songs to express their joy and sadness. Until the early 1960s, salty-water songs were also the mainstream entertainment for fishermen, and the prevailing place is bustling. However, during the "Cultural Revolution", salty-water songs were regarded as the "four olds" that were once banned and suffered a devastating blow. After being banned, salty-water songs gradually lost vitality and were slowly forgotten, causing a historical fault. After bringing order out of chaos in the country, the salty-water song was reborn from the ruins and entered people's lives again.

With the development of history and the progress of times, Yangjiang Salty-water Song has shown its strong vitality. Singers of the salty-water songs also focus on innovation based on adhering to the original ecology. They gradually add instrumental music (mainly including erhu, dulcimer, flute, etc.) and percussion music (mainly including a crisp gong, waist drum based on twisting, small cymbals, small porcelain plate, bamboo board, etc.) to accompany Yangjiang Salty-water Song in the singing process. With clothes and props, they pay more attention to the performance, making salty-water songs easy to understand and more audible and visible, so salty-water songs are welcomed by the audience. In recent years, many Yangjiang Salty-water Song works have also been created, such as Salty-water Song performances *Towing the Flow with Girls Until Daylight*, *Weaving a Boat with Sincerity*, *Resisting Wind and Chopping Waves Without Getting Lost*; large-scale salty-water song dance performance *South China Sea Fish Dance*; Salty-water song drama *Love on the Raft, Sending Lover Off Ten Times*; and six-act large-scale mythical fishing opera *Strange Encounters on the South China Sea*. They have flourished the creation of the salty-water song, enriched the cultural life of fishermen, and played a positive role in promoting the construction of spiritual civilization and building a harmonious society.

Yangjiang Salty-water Song went through its earliest generation, the widespread singing, the prohibition of singing during the "Cultural

咸水歌在退出大众生活后也渐渐失去了生命力，慢慢地被人遗忘，造成了历史的断层。至拨乱反正后，重生的咸水歌再次走进了人们的生活。

随着历史的发展与时代的进步，阳江咸水歌显示了其顽强的生命力。咸水歌歌手们在坚持原生态的基础上注重创新，在阳江咸水歌的演唱过程中逐渐加入器乐（主要有二胡、扬琴、笛子等）、打击乐（主要有酥锣、文鼓、京镲、小瓷碟、竹板等）伴奏，再配以服装、道具，更加注重表演性，使咸水歌既通俗易懂，更具可听性、可看性，广受观众的欢迎。近年来，还创作了一批阳江咸水歌作品，如咸水歌表演《拖流共妹到天光》《织好心网哥开船》《抗风劈浪不迷航》，大型咸水歌舞表演《南海鱼舞》，咸水歌小剧《渔排情缘》《十送情郎》，以及六幕大型神话渔歌剧《南海奇缘》等，繁荣了咸水歌的创作，活跃、丰富了广大渔民的文化生活，为推进精神文明建设、构建和谐社会

渔民举行热闹的咸水歌渔歌会
Fishermen are holding a salty-water song concert

起到了积极的作用。

阳江咸水歌在经历最早的产生到普遍的传唱，又经历“文革”的禁唱，再到改革开放后的兴盛，到如今却面临濒危，主要表现为渔民生活方式的改变、历史断层的影响、多元化文化娱乐方式的冲击、咸水歌歌手高龄体弱现象普遍、年轻一代对咸水歌的认知程度低等。为保护和传承阳江咸水歌，阳江市各级政府累计投入资金上千万元，社会筹资近百万元，用于建设公共文化设施、组织项目参演参赛、利用媒体宣传传播、协助专家采风与调研，支持、鼓励、资助传承人和咸水歌歌手进行各种传承活动等，对阳江咸水歌的传承和发展起到积极和有效的推动作用。

基本内容

阳江咸水歌的歌词格式近似竹枝词，一般为七言四句，常采用比兴、对偶、镶嵌、借喻、双关、谐音、排比、重复、夸张等修辞手法。按歌曲内容分类，可分为儿歌、生产歌、生活歌、时政歌、情歌、叙事歌等几大类；按歌种分类，有“叹调”“哥兄调”“众人调”“先姐调”“媒娘调”“堂枚调”“哭嫁调”“哭妈调”“万寿歌”“索罟调”“小船调”“花笺调”“嗳仔歌”等十几种，其中以“众人调”“叹调”“哥兄调” “堂枚调”等几种最为常用；按调式分类，有五声徵调式和五声羽调式；按乐句结构分类，有以四句为一乐段的复乐段体，还有由上句和下句组成的单乐段体；按演唱形式分类，有合唱、独唱、对唱等。

Revolution", and the prosperity after the reform and opening-up. But it is in danger now, which is mainly manifested in these aspects: changes in the lifestyle of fishermen, the impact of historical faults, the impact of diversified cultural entertainment methods, the prevalence of aging infirmity of the salty-water song singers, and the low level of awareness of the younger generation of the salty-water song. To protect and inherit Yangjiang Salty-water Song, Yangjiang governments at all levels have invested about ten million yuan, and nearly one million yuan has been raised from society. The funds are used to build public cultural facilities; organize projects in performances and competitions; use media to propagate and disseminate; assist experts in collecting and researching; support, encourage and fund inheritors and salty-water song singers to carry out various inheritance activities; which play a positive and influential role in promoting the inheritance and development of Yangjiang Salty-water Song.

Basic Content

The lyrics of Yangjiang Salty-water Song are similar to those of Zhuzhi poem and generally have seven characters in a sentence and four sentences in a paragraph. It often uses rhetorical devices such as Bixing, antithesis, inlay, metonymy, puns, homophonic, parallelism, repetition, exaggeration, etc.. According to content of songs, it can be classified into children's songs, production songs, life songs, current political songs, love songs, narrative songs, etc.. According to the category of songs, there are more than ten kinds of songs, including "sigh tune", "brother tune", "people tune", "sister tune", "matchmaker tune", "Tangmei tune", "wailing marriage tune", "crying for mother tune", "longevity song", "Soko tune", "boat tune", "Huajian tune", "Aizai song", among which "people tune", "sigh tune", "brother tune", "Tangmei tune" are the most commonly sung. According to the mode classification, there are five-tone Zhi Mode and five-tone Yu Mode. According to the sentence structure classification, there are multiple paragraph styles with four sentences as a paragraph, single paragraph styles composed of the upper sentence and lower sentence. According to the singing form, there are chorus, solo, and duet, etc..

Main Features

Yangjiang Salty-water Song is a form of oral folk music widely sung by the Tankas along the Yangjiang coast. It's also one of the most primitive expressions of local fishermen's culture which are integrated into the blood of the Tankas. In daily life, fishermen express their feelings with songs, use songs to replace language communication, and tell the pain and joy in their hearts. It is an essential carrier of spiritual life of the Tankas, which has become a unique cultural symbol of them.

Yangjiang Salty-water Song has the following characteristics from the analysis of the lyrics:

(1) The format is rigorous. Generally, there are seven words in a sentence and four sentences in a paragraph as the basic unit. The format may also have seven words and two sentences; the number of words can be increased or decreased if necessary.

(2) The characteristics of spoken language are apparent. The Yangjiang dialect is unique in the world. So Yangjiang Salty-water Song is different from other salty-water songs in the use of words, rhyme, and level and oblique tones.

(3) It's sung in a dialect. Yangjiang dialect is mainly used for singing, and a few fishermen also sing in Hakka dialect and Haihua (Minnan dialect).

(4) It has strong improvisation. Singers sing for people when they see people and sing for things when they see things. They revive memories at the sight of places and sing songs in no time. They show their emotions on songs and express that with songs.

(5) Use the vocative expression and lining words according to the specific format. For example, the sigh tune usually adds a vocative expression before the four sentences as an introduction, the brother tune adds a vocative expression in the middle of the four sentences, and the Tangmei tune generally adds a lining word at the end of the odd sentence.

From the melody analysis, its main features are as follows:

(1) Yangjiang Salty-water Song is rich in lyricism. Its melody is fresh, beautiful ,natural, euphemistic, bleak, and easy to sing aloud with smooth singing and sighing. It has the characteristics of chanting.

(2) On the basis of basic rhythm, it has the characteristics of free rhythm.

(3) The basic characteristics of the mode are mainly Yu Mode and Zhi Mode, and the melody style is based on the frame forming with main notes and the altered notes such as Yu-Jue and Zhi-Shang.

主要特征

阳江咸水歌是阳江沿海疍家广为传唱的一种口头民间音乐表现形式，也是当地最原始的渔家文化表现形式之一，并已深深融入疍民的血液中。在日常生活中，渔民们以歌传情，用歌声代替语言沟通，用歌声诉说心中的苦与乐，它是疍家人重要的精神生活载体，且成为疍民的一个特有文化符号。

阳江咸水歌从歌词分析，具有如下特征：

（1）格式较严谨。其一般为七言四句，即以七字一句、四句一段为基本单位，也有七言二句格式，需要时也可增减字数。

（2）口语化特征明显。阳江话是一种世界上独一无二的方言，所以阳江咸水歌在用词、押韵、平仄运用上都与别的咸水歌不同，有其特异性。

（3）使用方言演唱。以阳江话演唱为主，也有少数渔民用客家话和海话（闽南话）演唱。

（4）即兴性强。歌者见人唱人，见物唱物，即景生情，随口而出，情动于中，故形于声。

（5）按特定格式运用呼语和衬词。如叹调一般是在四个乐句之前加一个呼语作引子，而哥兄调是在四句的中间加入一个呼语，堂枚调则一般在奇数句句尾加衬词。

从曲调旋律分析，其主要特征如下：

（1）阳江咸水歌善于抒情，其曲调清新，旋律优美，韵律天然，唱叹流畅，易于上口，委婉凄凉，具有咏叹特质。

（2）在基本节奏的基础上，又具有不拘一格、较自由的节奏特征。

（3）调式的基本特征是以羽调式和徵调式为主，构成以羽角和徵商为框架的调式色彩。

（4）曲式结构基本上是四句为一乐段的复乐段体，也有由上句和下句组成的单乐段体。

（5）旋律一般是以第一、二乐句为基本形态作旋律发展，音域跳度较小，且服从于语言声调的高低，随字求腔、因字落腔。

(4) The music structure is basically a polyphonic style with four sentences as a paragraph, and also a single style composed of upper sentence and lower sentence.

(5) The melody is generally based on the first and second sentence as the basic form for melody development. The vocal range is narrow, and it is submit to the pitch of language tune. Notably,the tune varies from the word.

重要价值

阳江咸水歌是疍民在劳动、生活中自创自唱、自娱自乐的一种民间音乐艺术形式，经祖祖辈辈口口相传下来。这种艺术形式源于生活、贴近生活，有着深厚、广泛的群众基础，富有阳江沿海地方特色，是广大渔民喜闻乐见的民间艺术形式之一。其重要价值表现在以下几方面。

· 历史价值

阳江咸水歌真实地记载了阳江沿海渔民各个历史时期的政治、经济、文化等各个方面的具体信息，如疍民的社会地位、核心价值观、宗教信仰、潮流崇尚、衣食住行状况等，具有人类学、历史学、民俗学、社会学等学科研究的价值，为追溯我国水上居民特别是阳江沿海疍民的形成以及千百年来其生活的演变和特有的民俗风情，了解当时社会生活及生产力发展状况以及文化娱乐状态提供了真实而宝贵的研究史料。

Great Value

Yangjiang Salty-water Song is an art form of folk music created and sung by the Tankas in their work and life and enjoyed by themselves. It has been passed down from generation to generation orally. This art form originates from life, and it is close to life. It has a deep and extensive mass base. It is rich in the local characteristics of the Yangjiang coastal area, and is one of the folk art that most fishermen like to see. Its essential value is shown in the following.

· Historical value

Yangjiang Salty-water Song truly records the specific information of the politics, economy, culture and other aspects of the fishermen along the Yangjiang coast in various historical periods, such as the social status, core values, religious beliefs, trend and worship, food, clothing, housing and transportation of the Tankas, etc.. It has the value of disciplinary research such as anthropology, history, folklore and sociology. It provides real and valuable research historical materials to trace the origin of the formation of domestic water residents, especially the coastal Tanka people of Yangjiang, and the evolution of their lives and unique folk customs over thousands of years, and to understand the social life, productive forces and the state of culture and entertainment at that time.

渔民在休闲娱乐之时闲谈歌唱
Fishermen chat and sing at leisure

· Humanistic value

The birth of Yangjiang Salty-water Song shows the cultural creativity of the Tankas along the Yangjiang coast, highlights the distinctive cultural characteristics of the Tankas, and produces the common language of the Tankas. As an essential link of cultural exchange, it carries the spirit and emotion of the Tankas, provides a continuous sense of cultural identity, and is passed down from generation to generation. It is constantly recreated during the interaction with nature and history, greatly enriching the spiritual and cultural life of the fishermen on the sea and promoting social harmony. Because of the spiritual nourishment of the salty-water song to the Tankas, a unique aesthetic orientation has been formed. They take "simplicity", "softness", "low" and "implicity" as the beauty. They have been at the bottom of society for a long time, creating the Tankas's conservative, introverted, patient, implicit, and cautious characters. With the sea life that has been struggling with the wind and waves for a long time, they has also shaped the other side of the dynamic, brave, plain, and tenacious characters. In addition, the salty-water song also has the educational and propaganda functions of "teaching with entertainment". Much common sense of production and life accumulated by the ancestors of the Tankas over a long period, as well as their experience with ideas in dealing with people, can be passed down from generation to generation through the continuous singing of the salty-water song.

· Social value

Since ancient times, the Tankas, as a minority group in a special environment, have been living on the water for generations, taking boats as their homes, the sea as their livelihood, and fishing as their life. "Going to the sea is dangerous, going ashore with lowering their

· 人文价值

阳江咸水歌的产生，展现了阳江沿海疍民的文化创造力，彰显了鲜明的疍家文化特色，形成了疍家人共同的语言。作为一种文化交流的重要纽带，它承载了疍民的精神与情感，提供了持续的文化认同感，并世代相传，在与自然和历史的互动中，被不断地再创造，极大地丰富了海上渔民精神文化生活，促进了社会和谐。咸水歌对疍民的精神滋养，形成了疍民独特的审美取向。他们以"朴"为美、以"柔"为美、以"低"为美、以"含蓄"为美，长期处于社会最底层的磨砺，亦造就了疍民保守内向、忍耐含蓄、谨言慎行的性格；而长年与风浪搏斗的海上生活，又塑造出疍民勤劳勇敢、朴实无华、坚韧不拔的性格特征的一面。此外，咸水歌还兼备了"寓教于乐"的教化作用和宣传功能，疍民先辈们长期学习积累到的许多生产生活常识，以及他们为人处世的经验和思想，通过咸水歌的不断传唱得以代代相传。

· 社会价值

自古以来，疍民作为一个在特殊环境中的弱势族群，他们世代袭居水上，以船

渔民出海捕鱼

Fishermen go fishing when going out to the sea.

为家、以海为生、以渔为命，“出海三分命，上岸低头行，生无立足所，死无葬身地”，就是过去疍民生活的真实写照。在漫长的封建社会里，疍民无论是在政治上还是在经济上都备受欺凌、歧视和压迫，他们没有部落，没有田地，没有固定的房产。岸上的原住居民“规定”疍民不准上岸居住，上岸不准穿鞋，不准读书识字，不准与岸上人家通婚，科举的名册中也从来没有疍民的名字，疍民在世人眼里就是被欺凌者的代名词。这种社会地位低下、生存环境险恶、劳动强度大、人与人之间交流机会少、生活单调艰难、长夜寂寞难耐、长期与风浪搏斗的以海洋捕鱼为生的生活环境，是咸水歌产生的社会背景。咸水歌中涵盖的所有内容，都是疍民以他们的道德规范、价值观为标尺，从他们特有的角度表达社会给予他们的感受以及他们对社会的看法和评价，所以咸水歌对疍民的思想意识、道德规范、核心价值观的形成和他们的特有的民俗风情有着举足轻重的社会研究价值。

· 艺术价值

阳江咸水歌从产生到不断传承、发展的过程中，形成了摇曳柔和、舒缓温婉的独特艺术风格。在文学方面，一个文化程度低下的群体却创造了格式严谨、平仄押韵、朴实无华、深入浅出、通俗易懂的歌词；在音乐方面，形成了调式特征明显、曲式结构清晰、节奏自由舒缓、具有咏叹特质的旋律。它既是民间民族音乐艺术的瑰宝，也是现代音乐创作的珍贵原始素材。

heads, living without a foothold and dying without a burial place” is the accurate portrayal of the life of the Tankas in the past. The Tankas were bullied, discriminated, and oppressed in the long feudal society politically and economically. They had no tribe, no land, and no fixed property. The aboriginal residents on the shore “stipulated” that the Tankas were not allowed to live on the land, wear shoes, learn knowledge, and intermarry with the people on the land. The name of the Tankas has never been included in the register of the imperial examination. The Tankas are synonymous with victims in a sense. Low social status, dangerous living environment, high labor intensity, few opportunities for communication between people, monotonous and difficult life, lonely and hard nights, and long-term struggling with the wind and waves are the social background of the birth of the salty-water song. All the contents covered in the salty-water song are based on their moral norms and values. With their unique perspective, they express their feelings about society and their views and evaluations of the world. Therefore, the salty-water song has a significant social research value on the formation of the ideology, moral norms and core values, and unique folk customs of the Tankas.

· Artistic value

Yangjiang Salty-water Song has formed a unique artistic style of soft, swaying, and gentle in its generation, inheritance, and development. In terms of literature, a group with a low level of education has created lyrics which are rigorous in format, rhyming with level and oblique tones, simple and plain, approachable and easy to understand. In terms of music, it has formed a melody with prominent characteristics, clear structure of music, free and slow rhythm, and aria characteristics. It is not only the treasure of folk music art but also the precious original material of modern music creation.

阳江咸水歌在舞台上有丰富的表演形式
Yangjiang Salty-water Song is abundant in performance forms on stage

Main Inheritors

Chen Changqing (1939–2018), male, was born at the seaside. At age 7, he followed his father and uncle to fish at sea. Under their influence, he began to fall in love with singing salty-water songs. In his youth, he learned to sing salty-water songs under the guidance of the famous lamplight seine worker Xian Zhenghui. Later,he got trained under the instruction of Zhang Guanting, a fisherman who sang salty-water songs best at that time, and Lin Guanyi, the leading role of Dongping amateur opera troupe. He mastered the various modes and singing methods of salty-water songs and followed Feng Yingchuang, Gao Weiwen, Yang Changfa, and other masters to learn song creation. He became the inheritor of salty-water songs with the capability of singing and writing. For decades, he has studied salty-water songs in-depth, sang salty-water songs everywhere, created salty-water songs wholeheartedly, and made every effort to inherit salty-water songs. He has become the leader of Dongping Salty-water Song and has a high reputation in Dongping. Over the years, he participated in national-, provincial-, municipal-, county-, and town-level rehearsals, performances and competitions and achieved good results. Salty-water song singers from other fishing ports often invited him to participate in the salty-water song exchange, get-togethers, contests, and other activities. He became a famous singer during important activities or festivals. And he was invited to sing salty-water songs everywhere. He also recorded salty-water song CDs to meet the needs of most salty-

陈昌庆
Chen Changqing

主要传承人

陈昌庆（1939—2018），男，出生于海边，7岁时跟随父亲、叔叔出海捕鱼，在他们的熏陶下开始学唱咸水歌。青年时期拜著名灯光围网作业大工冼正辉为师，并在当时最会唱咸水歌的渔民张贯庭、东平业余曲艺团正花林观益的指导下学唱咸水歌，熟练掌握了咸水歌的多种调式和唱法，后跟冯英创、高伟文、杨昌发等老师学习歌曲创作，成为能唱能写的咸水歌传人。他几十年如一日，深入研究咸水歌，四处演唱咸水歌，潜心创作咸水歌，竭力传承咸水歌，成为东平咸水歌的领头人，在东平有相当高的知名度。历年来参加过国家、省、市、县、镇的各级调演、汇演和比赛，并获得好成绩；经常被其他渔港咸水歌手邀请去参加咸水歌交流、联欢、比赛等活动，在重要活动或节庆期间更是抢手的歌手，被邀请到各处去演唱咸水歌；他还录制了咸水歌CD，以满足广大咸水歌爱好者的需求；央视“乡土”栏目和省、市、县的新闻媒体如电视台、电台、报纸等都有过专访和录制专题节目对他进行介绍和宣传。陈昌庆还与许多到当地采风调研的作家、音乐家和歌唱家等共同研讨阳江咸水歌，对阳江咸水歌进行更深入的挖掘、传承，并在保持原生态的基础上创新和发展。陈昌庆为广东省第四批省级非物质文化遗产项目代表性传承人。

杨爱，女，1955年10月出生，1967年开始跟母亲学唱阳江咸水歌，艺成后一直从事节日喜庆等渔家风俗活动及阳江咸水歌的演唱、比赛、宣传、传教、交流等传承活动，曾荣获“阳江渔歌传人”称号。杨爱使用阳江话演唱咸水歌，其曲调清新、韵律天然、唱叹流畅，节奏自由舒缓、委婉抒情。她演唱持续时间长，能连唱几小时。她的演唱风格主要表现在三个方面：一是声线较好，音色圆润，声音响亮，吐字清晰；二是反应敏捷，出口成歌，见人唱人、见物唱物；三是擅长叹调咸水歌，唱法保留了原始正宗韵味。现为广东省第六批省级非物质文化遗产项目代表性传承人。

water song lovers. CCTV's "Local Scene" column, and provincial, municipal and county news media, such as television stations, radio stations and newspapers, have had special interviews and recorded special programs for introduction and publicity. He also discussed Yangjiang Salty-water Song with many writers, musicians, singers and other experts and scholars who went to the local to collect and research, and carried out more in-depth exploration and inheritance of the Yangjiang Salty-water Song and innovation and development based on maintaining the original ecology. He is the representative inheritor of the fourth batch of provincial intangible cultural heritage projects of Guangdong Province.

杨爱
Yang Ai

Yang Ai, female, was born in October 1955. She began to sing Yangjiang Salty-water Song with her mother in 1967. After her skills being matured, she has been engaged in fishing folk activities in festivals and inheritance activities such as singing, competition, publicity, preaching, and exchange of Yangjiang Salty-water Song. She has won the title of "Inheritor of Yangjiang Fishery Song". Yang Ai uses the Yangjiang dialect to sing salty-water songs. And the melody is fresh, rhythm is natural, singing and sighing are fluent, and the tempo is free and slow, euphemistic and lyric. She can sing for a long time and even for several hours. Her singing style is advantageous in three aspects: First, her singing voice is good, the tone is mellow, the sound is superior, and the pronunciation clear. Second, she can respond quickly and sing songs instantly when she sees people or things. Third, she is good at singing salty-water songs with aria, and her singing method retains the original and authentic charm. Now she is the representative inheritor of the sixth batch of provincial intangible cultural heritage projects of Guangdong Province.

Li Xiaoying, female, was born at the seaside in September 1960. She learned to sing the Yangjiang Salty-water Song from her mother when she was young, inherited the traditional salty-water song's singing, and mastered all kinds of singing methods of the salty-water song. She is not only good at singing but also at acting. She does well in the brother tune of the salty-water song. Her voice is loud and clear, her tune is mellow and cadenced, her emotion is rich, her personality is distinctive, her singing and sighing are smooth, and her improvisation is intense. She is good at expressing her feeling with a singing drawl, her rhyme is loud and melodic, and her singing method is more primitive and authentic. She is now the representative inheritor of the third batch of intangible cultural heritage projects of Yangjiang City.

李小英，女，1960年9月出生在海边，从小跟母亲学唱阳江咸水歌，传承传统的咸水歌，并熟练掌握咸水歌的各种唱法，能唱能演。擅长哥兄调咸水歌，歌声响亮清脆，音饰圆润、抑扬顿挫，感情丰富，个性鲜明，唱、叹流畅，即兴性强，善于用拖腔抒发情感，歌韵嘹亮悠扬，唱法比较原始正宗。现为阳江市第三批非物质文化遗产项目代表性传承人。

李小英
Li Xiaoying

Zhang Changzhou, female, born in September 1947 in Dongping Town, Yangdong District, is the second generation inheritor of Yangjiang Salty-water Song. She started to learn the salty-water song from her aunt Zhang Hei in 1955 and has mastered the mode and singing method of the salty-water song. Zhang Changzhou, fascinated by the salty-water song for more than 60 years, attaches great importance to the inheritance and development of the salty-water song. To inherit the salty-water song, she had two apprentices, Lin Ruijuan and Zhang Meizai, and taught skills through singing and telling the customs and allusions of the salty-water song. And she trains the apprentices through singing and participating in activities in social practice. She is now the representative inheritor of the fifth batch of intangible cultural heritage projects of Yangjiang City.

张长州，女，出生于1947年9月，阳东区东平镇人，是阳江咸水歌第二代传承人。自1955年起，拜大姑张黑为咸水歌老师，熟悉掌握了咸水歌的调式、唱法。钟情咸水歌60多年的张长州，重视咸水歌的传承与发展，为把咸水歌传承下去，收有林瑞娟、张妹仔两位徒弟，通过教唱、讲述咸水歌习俗和典故传授技艺，并在社会实践中带徒演唱和参加活动培养弟子。现为阳江市第五批非物质文化遗产项目代表性传承人。

张长州
Zhang Changzhou

杨国珍，女，出生于1947年4月，阳东区东平镇人，是阳江咸水歌第三代传承人。杨国珍祖辈世代都是渔民，深受祖辈的影响，对叹咸水歌有种由衷的喜爱。杨国珍重视和支持咸水歌的传承发展，因此对有兴趣学唱咸水歌的妇女耐心教唱。跟杨国珍学唱咸水歌的东平妇女也较多——有冼益改等十多位渔民。通过杨国珍一句句教唱和讲授咸水歌传统习俗，并在实践活动中学习积累，徒弟们都能掌握咸水歌演唱技能，其中冼益改、黄丽珍、林广姐、杨计姐4位徒弟已成为渔歌队出色的成员，经常从事节日喜庆等渔家风俗活动及阳江咸水歌的演唱、宣传、传教等。现为阳江市第五批非物质文化遗产项目代表性传承人。

Yang Guozhen, female, born in April 1947 in Dongping Town, Yangdong District, is the third generation inheritor of the Yangjiang Salty-water Song. Yang Guozhen's ancestors have been fishermen for generations, and she was deeply influenced by her ancestors. She heartfully likes singing the salty-water song. Yang Guozhen highlights and supports the inheritance and development of the salty-water song, so she patiently teaches women who interested in learning the salty-water song. And many Dongping women have learned the salty-water song from Yang Guozhen. She took more than ten fisherwomen, such as Xian Yigai, as apprentices. And then, she taught them to sing sentence by sentence and taught the traditional customs of the salty-water song. Through learning and accumulation in practical activities, the apprentices can master the singing skills of the salty-water song. And four apprentices, Xian Yigai, Huang Lizhen, Lin Guangjie, and Yang Jijie, have become outstanding members of the fishing song team and often engage in fishing folk activities in festivals, as well as the singing, publicity, and preaching of Yangjiang Salty-water Song. She is now the representative inheritor of the fifth batch of intangible cultural heritage projects of Yangjiang City.

杨国珍
Yang Guozhen

冼益改，女，出生于1958年1月，阳东区东平镇人，是阳江咸水歌第四代传承人。为了阳江咸水歌的传承和发展，冼益改也像长辈一样把咸水歌传授给下一代，收有林掌体、林瑞娟2名徒弟，在日常生活和工作空闲时间中，聚集徒弟传授技艺，教唱咸水歌，讲述咸水歌有关习俗和典故。现为阳江市第五批非物质文化遗产项目代表性传承人。

Xian Yigai, female, born in January 1958 in Dongping Town, Yangdong District, is the fourth generation inheritor of Yangjiang Salty-water Song. To inherit and develop the Yangjiang Salty-water Song, Xian Yigai, like her elders, also taught the songs to the next generation. So she took Lin Zhangti and Lin Ruijuan as her apprentices. In her daily life and spare time, she gathered her apprentices to teach skills of singing the salty-water song and narrate the customs and allusions of the salty-water songs. She is now the representative inheritor of the fifth batch of intangible cultural heritage projects of Yangjiang City.

冼益改
Xian Yigai

阳江客家山歌

保护单位　阳东区非物质文化遗产保护中心

Yangjiang Hakka Hill Song

Protection Unit　Yangdong District Intangible Cultural Heritage Protection Center

Yangjiang Hakka Hill Song is an oral cultural expression widely sung by the Hakka people. It is a regional culture spread in the mountainous area around Xinzhou Town and Dongping Town in Yangdong District, with the taste of life in the mountains. Because the Hakka people were immersed in a unique language—the Yangjiang dialect, the tune of Yangjiang Hakka Hill Song is different from that of Meizhou, Huizhou, and other places. Moreover, for historical reasons, the Hakkas who stayed in the local area did not admit that they were Hakkas and seldom had cultural exchanges with outsiders. So Yangjiang Hakka Hill Song is only sung in the mountainous area around Xinzhou and Dongping. Yangjiang Hakka Hill Song is closely related to the origin of the Hakka. The Hakka people who had experienced the wars moved around and settled here. They shared the same hobby of singing with the local Yangdong people. In the long time, the local working people chant and sing songs to themselves or in an antiphonal style, forming a traditional custom. It is a folk art activity with a deep mass foundation and regional characteristics.

Historical Origin

The historical origin of Yangjiang Hakka Hill Song needs to be explored from the issue of the Hakka origin. The Hakkas are Han people who moved south from the Central Plains. Due to the invasion of the frontier tribes, the Hakka ancestors moved from the Central Plains to the south. Later, the Hakkas moved southward and scattered across the country, forming a situation where the Hakkas scattered in many areas. After many twists and turns of migration, the Hakka

阳江客家山歌是由客家人广为传唱的口头文化表现形式，是一种山区文化，流传于阳东区新洲镇和东平镇一带山区，具有山野生活味道。由于独特的阳江话环境，阳江客家山歌调子跟梅州、惠州等地的山歌有所不同。而且由于历史原因，留在当地的客家人不承认自己是客家人，少有跟外地交流，使这一传统风俗只流传于新洲和东平一带山区。阳江客家山歌与客家源流紧密相连，经历战乱的客家人几经辗转，定居此地，他们与当地的阳东人同样爱唱民歌，在时间的长河中，当地劳动群众自吟自唱，对歌斗歌，形成了传统风俗，是一种有着深厚群众基础又颇具地方特色的民间文艺活动。

历史渊源

对阳江客家山歌的历史渊源的考究，需从客家源流问题上探讨。客家是从中原南迁的汉人，由于受到边疆部族的侵扰，客家先民从中原辗转迁到南方，继而再往南、往各地分散迁徙，形成客家人散布于许多地区的局面。经过多次的辗转迁徙，客家人始得在各地安身立命，世代繁殖，终至今日成为中华民族一支重要的、特殊的民系。

阳江客家人是在清代后期的第五次迁徙中从鹤山、高明等地迁入的，集中在新洲、东平一带山区居住。阳江客家山歌之所以能传唱至今，其主要原因是历史上（清代）南迁的客家人在阳东选择山区而居，继承和发展客家山歌，同时影响当地文化，使阳东当地人也会唱客家山歌。

《阳江县志》载：清咸丰四年（1854）鹤山、高明客家人与土著发生械斗。客家人向新会、开平、阳江迁徙，清同治四年（1865）进入阳江东境（即现在的阳东县）田畔、那龙、那笃、乌石、河仔、东平等地。总兵陈佐光在那笃（新洲旧圩）镇压客家人，并诬禾叉坳客家村人通匪（客家），横加杀戮。越数月，又在那龙围杀客家人。清政府在咸丰四年至同治四年的10余年间在阳江对客家人进行杀戮驱赶。客籍人戴梓贵原为红巾军花翎副将，起义失败后从广西回到阳江，指挥客家军与官军抗争，无奈兵力不足，胜少败多，客家人被迫迁向韶关、广西等地，少部分散居于新洲山区上六、中六、下六、那六及东平一带。而在此之前早就居住在阳东县新洲镇北股村委会的禾叉坳客家人，在遭受了这一劫难后，仍留下了一座客家围屋。客家人也在阳东县留存了为数不多但很是珍贵的客家山歌。

基本内容

俗话说唱山歌，就说明“山歌是唱出来的”，唱，就明显地说明其有独特的音乐特点，应该是以其优美的情趣、动人的旋律、和谐的节奏充分表现出歌的主题内容，使人们听来感受到音乐美。

如《八才子花笺》中的“对花自叹”

people began settling down in various places and breeding for generations, finally becoming an essential and unique branch of the Chinese nation today.

In the fifth migration of the late Qing Dynasty, Yangjiang Hakka people moved from Heshan, Gaoming, and other places to live in the mountainous area around Xinzhou and Dongping. The main reason why Yangjiang Hakka Hill Song was transmitted orally from generation to generation is that the Hakka people in history who moved southward chose to live in the mountainous area of Yangdong. They inherited and developed original Hakka Hill Song, which influenced local culture, so local Yangdong people could sing this kind of songs.

According to *Yangjiang County Annals*, in the fourth year of Xianfeng of the Qing Dynasty (1854), Heshan and Gaoming Hakkas fought with the locals. The Hakkas migrated to Xinhui, Kaiping, and Yangjiang and entered Tianpan, Nalong, Nadu, Wushi, Hezai, Dongping, and other places in the east of Yangjiang (now Yangdong County) in the fourth year of Tongzhi of the Qing Dynasty (1856). Chief soldier Chen Zuoguang cracked down the Hakka people in Nadu (the old market of Xinzhou), framed the Hakka people in Hechaao Village for joining the bandits and killed them. A few more months passed, the Hakka people in Nalong were killed. From the fourth year of Xianfeng to the fourth year of Tongzhi, the Qing government killed and drove away the Hakka people in Yangjiang for more than ten years. Dai Zigui, a Hakka, was a deputy general of the Red Turban Army. After the uprising failed, he returned to Yangjiang from Guangxi to command the Hakka army to fight against the official army. However, due to the lack of military strength, the Hakkas were forced to move to Shaoguan, Guangxi, and other places. Still, a small number of them were scattered in the areas of Shangliu, Zhongliu, Xialiu, Naliu, and Dongping of the Xinzhou mountainous area. The Hakka people in Hechaao, who had lived in the village of Beigu, Xinzhou Town, Yangdong County before that, kept a Hakka circular house after the disaster. The Hakka people have left a few precious Hakka hill songs in Yangdong County.

Basic Content

As the saying goes, singing hill songs means “hill songs are made to sing”. Singing hill songs clearly implies that they have unique musical characteristics. The songs' theme should be fully expressed with its exquisite taste, moving melody, and harmonious rhythm so that people can feel the beauty of music.

For example, in *Eight Talented People's Envelopes*, the chapter of "Sighing at Flowers" says: "How beautiful oleaceae it is/I once brought one from moon palace /The lady in the moon named Chang'e did show no pity on the lonely man/ There is no way from the window to the ladder of the cloud which full of foggy /Ask where the Arcadia is/ Fluently/I hope that heavy door would be opened easily/Lovers can meet each other early." There are six words, three words, seven words, and even eleven words in a sentence, and their tones and rhythm are very clear.

Even crying songs, such as *Pregnancy of Ten Months*, it says: "Ten months pregnancy is known / When the baby is born/The mother feels in pain/She sits uncomfortably and sleeps in worry." Its tone is "ze ze ping ping (ze) ze ping/ping ping ze ze ze ping ping / (ping) ping ze ze ping ping ze/ze ze ping ping ze ze ping" , which meets the requirements of rhythm and colloquial.

Another example, the first part of *Meeting People on the Road is Difficult* meets the requirements of tone, while the second part is not as good as the previous one. This means that some Hakka hill songs still have their own characteristics despite their shortcomings in this respect.

In terms of the content and nature of Hakka hill songs, there are following three types: First, they are sung only for self-complacence or self-catharsis, and they may not be sung with a target audience. Sometimes they can be hummed by one person to unwind and escape from boredom. Second, they are sung as a method of courting and flirting between young men and women, which is the main part of Hakka Hill Song. Third, it belongs to a kind of bantering ballad, that is, one of the men and women sings a hill song to the other in a bantering manner. If the other responds, he or she will taunt the other with the hill song tone. If there is no response, it can be seen that the other person is honest, and can be deceived or can't sing hill songs, so the singer can be indulgent.

Main Features

Yangjiang Hakka Hill Song is rich in local characteristics and national artistic styles.The song has a wealth of content in emotional ous expression, life and entertainment, and social communication. As a feature of local art, Yangjiang Hakka Hill Song has the following main features:

(1) Yangjiang Hakka Hill Song is widely spread and sung by the Hakka people as oral cultural expressions, and becomes a mountainous culture. Yangjiang Hakka hill songs are all sung in Hakka dialect, which contain Hakka's local language characteristics

节："花貌好，是木樨/广寒曾带一枝归/嫦娥未肯怜孤客/书窗无路到云梯/借问桃源边处系/休阻滞/但愿重门唔锁闭/愁人及早到红闺。"其间有六字一句、三字一句、七字一句，甚至还有十一字一句的，其平仄、韵律节奏都是很清晰的。

哭歌，如《十月怀胎》："十月怀胎天地知/当来降世出生时/肚中削痛娘辛苦/坐不安时睡不安。"其平仄是"仄仄平平（仄）仄平/平平仄仄仄平平/（平）平仄仄平平仄/仄仄平平仄仄平"，既合律句要求，又口语化。

如《路上逢人万里难》第一首就很合乎平仄要求，第二首就不如前首。也就说明有的客家山歌在这方面虽存在不足，仍不失其特色。

就客家山歌的内容和性质来说，大致可分为下列三种：一是属于自我陶醉或自我发泄的，唱时未必有对象，有时可以单独一人随口哼几句来调剂枯燥的心情。二是属于男女间调情的山歌，这是客家山歌主要的部分。三是属于戏谑性的歌谣，即男女之一方以戏谑性的态度向对方唱一首山歌，对方如有反应则互相以山歌调闹讥讽对方，如无反应，可知她（他）是一个老实可欺或不会唱山歌的人，那就更可放任起来了。

主要特征

阳江客家山歌富有地方特色和民族艺术风格，在感情宣泄、生活娱乐、社会交际等方面都有极为丰富的内容。作为具有地方艺术特色的阳江客家山歌，其主要特征如下：

（1）阳江客家山歌是由客家人广为传唱的口头文化表现形式，是一种山区文化。阳江客家山歌全用客家话传唱，它富有客家人的地方语言特色，成为民歌中的独立一支。它源于生产生活并同生活紧密相连，集感情、娱乐、生活于一体，歌中流露出山区山野生活味道。客家人由于所处环境的关系，终日作业于田野山岭之间，保留着古代中原人的风气，在选用歌词、节奏、声调等方面都具有大量的即兴创作成分。客家山歌曲调清新、韵律天然、简单易懂、委婉抒情，具有浓厚的乡土气息和地方特色。

（2）客家山歌是中国民歌中最为浓情、最为放达，也最为卓越的歌种。它继承了《诗经》中的传统风格，受到唐诗律绝和竹枝词的重大影响，同时又吸取了南方各地民歌的优秀成分，广泛流传，久唱不衰。

（3）客家情歌内容十分丰富，遍及爱情生活的每个阶段、各个方面、各个角落，而歌中反映出来的感情、性格又是多种多样的，或纯真相爱，或贪财爱貌，或生死不渝，或移情别恋，或大胆泼辣，或委婉含蓄，或大方袒露，或温柔羞涩，真可谓千姿百态。

（4）客家山歌有多种唱腔，题材广泛、曲调丰富、旋律优美，几乎所有曲调中都有颤音、滑音、倚音等装饰音，因而旋律回环曲折、委婉动听。

（5）客家山歌富有感情浓烈、想象丰富，形象鲜明、意境清新，抒情叙事、感物即事，自然流畅等艺术特色。客家山歌要把无形无影的思想情感化为具体可见、生动感人的艺术形象，常常运用各种形象生动的表现手法，主要有双关、借喻、重复、反语、直叙、对比、排比、对偶、顶真、夸张、拆字等。

①双关，如《侹针督紧笑吟吟》。

②借喻，如《八月十五请你落来趟一时》，以月亮借代情人，约定时间地点，让情人别在外面转悠，急切地盼望心上人快快到来。

③重复，如《借钱纳利娶妹来》的

and form an independent branch of hill songs. Originating from life and production and closely connected with life, it integrates emotion, entertainment, and life. The song reveals the flavor of mountain life. Due to their environment, the Hakka people work in fields and mountains all day long, keeping the atmosphere of ancient people in the Central Plains. There is a lot of improvisation in the selection of lyrics, rhythm, tone, and other aspects. The song's melody is fresh, and the rhythm is natural. It's easy to be understood, euphemistic, and lyrical with a strong local flavor and characteristics.

(2) The Hakka hill song is one of China's most affectionate, broad-minded and outstanding hill songs. It inherits the traditional style in the *Book of Songs* and is greatly influenced by the rhythm of Tang poetry and Zhuzhi poem. At the same time, it also absorbs the excellent elements of hill songs from the south, and has been widely spread and sung for a long time.

(3) Hakka love songs are very rich in content, covering every stage, every aspect, and every corner of love life, and the feelings and characters reflected in the songs are diverse. Those songs show pure love, love for money and beauty, love beyond life and death, or love passed to another. The characters in those songs include bold and intense, discreet and implicit, generous and honest, or gentle and shy, which can be described as a variety of forms.

(4) The Hakka hill song has a variety of tunes with a wide range of themes, rich tunes, and beautiful melodies. Almost all tunes have vibrato, glide, appoggiatura, and other decorative tones, making the melody roundabout, tortuous, and euphemistic.

(5) The Hakka hill song is rich in emotion and imagination with vivid image and fresh artistic conception, which has lyrical narration, sense of things, natural style and other artistic characteristics. To transform invisible thoughts and feelings into concrete, vivid, and moving artistic images, Hakka hill songs often use various vivid expressions, including pun, metonymy, repetition, irony, direct narrative, contrast, parallelism, antithesis, Dingzhen, exaggeration, and deconstruction of words, etc..

①Pun, such as *Smiling While Stabbed by the Needle*.

②Metonymy, such as *Please Come Here on the 15th Day of the 8th Lunar Month*. In this song, it uses the moon to represent the lover, appoints the time and place, lets the lover not wander outside, and eagerly yearns for the sweetheart coming soon.

③Repetition, such as "This person who is not tall but not short is talented and the talent who is not tall and not short is perfect" in *Borrowing Money and Paying Interest for Marrying the Bride*.

④Irony, such as the love song *Elder Man Holds Young Lady's Hands, and She Nods*. In this song, the man clearly knows that there is nothing valuable in his house, but he still brags about himself to the young lady.

Great Value

· Historical value

Yangjiang Hakka Hill Song has been sung in Yangdong for over 100 years. Its emergence, development and gradually being in danger have their historical background and reasons. The Hakka ancestors had gone through several times of significant migration and gradually moved southward, and finally settled in Yangdong mountainous area, which is combined with various historical events, which has a specific reference value for the study of the Hakka origin.

· Cultural and artistic value

Yangjiang Hakka Hill Song is a mountainous culture with a wild flavor. Its artistic expression has unique characteristics compared with other hill songs. It is a freestyle, and improvisation in singing. It inherits the style of the *Book of Songs* and has rich cultural and artistic research value.

· Social value

(1) Yangjiang Hakka Hill Song has important reference value for studying Hakka's social production development and folk customs in this region.

(2) Yangjiang Hakka Hill Song is used in social life to communicate with people, express feelings, enhance friendship, promote unity, and coordinate relations and life. It is both a cultural and a social activity that can enrich social and cultural activities and promote social harmony.

(3) Yangjiang Hakka Hill Song is of great value to studying the Hakka's social culture and national customs.

"不高不矮好人材，不高不矮人材好"。

④反语，如情歌《阿哥捏手妹点头》中歌唱的，分明家中没什么值钱的东西，却向妹子夸口。

重要价值

· 历史价值

阳江客家山歌在阳东传唱百余年，其产生发展及日渐濒危都有其历史背景和历史原因。客家祖先历经多次大迁徙，渐渐地向南迁移，最后定居阳东山区。阳江客家山歌中结合种种历史事件变故，这对客家源流研究具有一定的参考价值。

· 文化艺术价值

阳江客家山歌是一种山地文化，有一定山野味，其艺术表现与一般民歌相比有独特的特色。它是自由体，即兴创作演唱，上承《诗经》遗风，具有丰富的文化艺术研究价值。

· 社会价值

（1）阳江客家山歌对于研究本区域客家人的社会生产发展以及民俗风情等具有重要的参考价值。

（2）在社会生活中，阳江客家山歌用于人与人之间沟通，表达感情，增进友谊，促进团结，协调关系和生活。它既是一种文化活动又是一种社交活动，能丰富社会文化活动，促进社会和谐。

（3）阳江客家山歌对研究客家人社会文化和民族风情有重要的价值。

主要传承人

刘昭光，男，出生于1952年7月，阳东区东平镇人，从小喜欢唱客家山歌，通过观看老一辈人演唱客家山歌，渐渐积累，自学掌握客家山歌歌调韵律。在农闲时同客家山歌爱好者对唱问答，交流心得；在实践中不断提高演唱技巧和能力，成为当地有名的客家山歌歌手。他歌声苍劲有力、吐字清晰、即兴性强，并掌握客家山歌的各种唱法。现为阳江市第三批非物质文化遗产项目代表性传承人。

刘昭光
Liu Zhaoguang

黄东缓，男，出生于1935年6月，阳东区新洲镇人，1948年起跟邻居黄仪信学唱客家山歌，练习歌本，通过自学掌握客家山歌歌调韵律。黄东缓在生活劳作时用客家山歌抒发感情、解除郁闷，几十年来，同周围村客家山歌爱好者共同交流演唱技巧和心得，不断提高演唱水平，成为新洲镇有名的客家山歌手。其技艺特色是能用客家话唱山歌，歌声洪亮、吐字清晰、即兴性强。现为阳江市第三批非物质文化遗产项目代表性传承人。

Main Inheritors

Liu Zhaoguang, male, was born in July 1952 and is a native of Dongping Town, Yangdong District. He has liked to sing Hakka Hill Song since childhood. Through watching the older generation sing Hakka hill songs, he gradually accumulates and learns to master the rhythm of Hakka hill songs. In the leisure season, he sang Hakka hill songs with Hakka hill song lovers, exchanges ideas, and constantly improved singing skills and abilities, which made him a famous local Hakka singer. His technical features are vigorous singing, precise articulation, and intense improvisation. He is mastering various singing techniques of Hakka hill songs. He is now the representative inheritor of the third batch of intangible cultural heritage projects in Yangjiang City.

Huang Donghuan, male, was born in June 1935 and is a native of Xinzhou Town, Yangdong District. He started to learn to sing Hakka hill songs with his neighbor Huang Yixin in 1948. He practiced the songbook, and mastered the rhythm of Hakka hill songs through self-study. Also, he sang Hakka hill songs to express feelings and relieve depression during daily work. For decades, he has shared singing skills and experiences with Hakka hill song lovers in surrounding villages, constantly improving singing level and has become a famous Hakka singer in Xinzhou Town. His technical features are the ability to sing hill songs in the Hakka dialect with a loud voice, clear articulation, and intense improvisation. He is now the representative inheritor of the third batch of intangible cultural heritage projects in Yangjiang City.

黄东缓
Huang Donghuan

Part 2

Traditional Dance

第二部分

传统舞蹈

海陵狮舞

保护单位 阳江市海陵岛经济开发试验区国珍武术培训基地

Hailing Lion Dance

Protection Unit Guozhen Martial Arts Training Base, Hailing Island Economic Development Pilot Zone, Yangjiang

海陵狮舞是流传于海陵岛区域的一项传统舞蹈，它通过仿生狮子头形象与鼓声节奏进行舞蹈，一般在传统节日，特别是在春节以及民间一些重大喜庆之日演出。海陵狮舞曾经在海陵岛19个行政村134个自然村都有分布，因寓意吉祥而受到海陵岛人民的喜爱。

历史渊源

海陵岛历史文化底蕴浓厚。受地理环境影响，岛上居民依靠农业、捕鱼业为生，并大多崇尚用武术强身健体。在科学不发达、信息落后的日子里，渔民在出海时，面对自然灾害等不可抗力因素，往往寄望神灵“指引和庇佑”，出海前拜神祈求平安也逐渐成为渔民必不可少的一项仪式。特殊的地理环境和人文文化造就了海陵人民对“好彩头”的渴望，催生了寓意吉利、喜庆的狮舞。

据老一辈狮舞师傅回忆，马桂良、董北养是海陵狮舞最早一批舞狮人。董北养，海陵岛北汀村人，约90岁，是海陵岛知名舞狮人，师承马桂良。

Hailing Lion Dance is a traditional dance spread in the Hailing Island area. Its performers danced with a biomimetic lion head accompanied by drums. It is usually held in traditional festivals, especially the Spring Festival and some major festivals of folk. Hailing Lion Dance has been distributed in 19 administrative villages and 134 natural villages of Hailing Island. The people of Hailing Island favor it because of its auspicious meaning.

海陵狮舞表演
Hailing Lion Dance performance

Historical Origin

Hailing Island has a long history and rich culture heritage. Influenced by the geographical environment, inhabitants on the island rely on agriculture and fishing to make a living. Thus, most advocate martial arts to keep fit. At the days when science was not developed and information was backward, fishermen going to sea faced with natural disasters and other force majeure factors. So they looked to the gods for guidance and blessing. Praying to the gods for safety before going to sea has gradually become an integral part of the fishermen's tradition. The unique geographical environment and humanities culture have made the people desire for good luck in Hailing, giving birth to the auspicious and joyous lion dance.

According to the memories of the older generation of lion dance masters, Ma Guiliang and Dong Beiyang were the earliest lion dancers in Hailing. Dong Beiyang from Beiting Village, Hailing Island, about 90 years old, is a well-known lion dancer on Hailing Island under the guidance of Ma Guiliang.

According to Dong Beiyang's dictation, Ma Guiliang, a native of Rudong, Yangxi, was born about 130 years ago and already passed away. He was 40 years older than Dong Beiyang. When Dong Beiyang was 15 years old, Ma Guiliang had been teaching lion dance for many years in Beiting Village, and Dong Beiyang started to learn the lion dance from Ma Guiliang. Dong Beiyang recalled that when he was young, the people in all villages and communities on Hailing Island had the habit of advocating and practicing martial arts, and performing lion and dragon dances. As a kind of traditional dance on Hailing Island, lion dances were ubiquitous at every major festival or celebration. However, at that time, most of the Hailing lion dances were small-scale and self-organized activities of small groups, lacking professional skills training and specialized props.

After Chen Xiangsheng and Li Youguo devoted themselves to it, the lion dance team gradually changed into a greater and more formal troupe. Chen Xiangsheng and Li Youguo learned the lion dance from the same master, Chen Jiu who converted to Buddhism. His master Shi Xuefeng was the auspice and eminent monk of Yangjiang Shijue Temple, and also good at Shaolin Hong Quan. At that time, Hailing District had two towns, Hailing Town and Zhapo Town. In June 1965, Chen Xiangsheng founded "Nan'an Village Youth Martial Arts Class" in Nan'an Village, Hailing Town. In October 1988, "Hailing Yinsheng Martial Arts Club" was officially established, which was later renamed "Nan'an Lion Art Troupe". Chen Xiangsheng's junior fellow apprentice Li Youguo founded "Zhapo Shaolin Martial Art Center" (later renamed "Guozhen Martial Arts Training Base") in July 1986 in Zhapo Town. The two venues were independent and complementary, and they also taught martial arts and lion dances together in each other's places. After nearly ten years of development, Nan'an Lion Art Troupe has developed into a giant lion art troupe with more than 30 members, more than ten lion tools, drums, gongs, martial art knives and guns, etc.. Since 2001, skills,

两只狮子抢灯笼，寓意吉利、喜庆

Two lions are grabbing lanterns, which means auspicious and joyous

据董北养口述，马桂良为阳西儒洞人，生于约130年前，已故，比董北养大40岁。董北养15岁正式向马桂良拜师学艺时，马桂良已在海陵岛北汀村开办醒狮队传授狮艺多年。董北养回顾年幼时，海陵当时岛内大小村庄、社区群众都有尚武、习武、舞狮龙的习惯。作为海陵岛一项传统舞蹈项目，每逢重大喜庆节日或者庆典节目，都有海陵狮舞。但当时海陵狮舞大部分都为一些小范围、民间自发组织的小型团体活动，缺乏专业的技艺训练以及专门的道具。

狮舞逐渐规范、壮大，在陈祥升和李有国投身于海陵狮舞项目后正式成立为团体。陈祥升与李有国为师兄弟关系，师承陈九。陈九皈依佛门，其师傅为阳江石觉寺主持、高僧释雪峰，善少林洪拳功夫。当时海陵区设有海陵镇、闸坡镇两个镇。1965年6月，陈祥升在海陵镇南安村创办“南安村青年武术班”，1988年10月正式成立“海陵银声武术馆”，后更名为“南安狮艺团”。陈祥升的师弟李有国于1986年7月在闸坡镇创办“闸坡少林武术馆”（后更名为“国珍武术培训基地”）。两个场馆独立又相辅相成，两人也互相在对方的场所共同执教武术和狮舞。南安狮艺

传承人指导徒弟训练狮舞
The inheritor instructed the apprentices to train the lion dance

专门的狮舞团队
Specialized lion dance team

团经过近十年的发展，成为一个拥有30余名队员、10多副狮具，鼓、锣、武术刀枪等器械齐备的大型狮艺团，2001年，逐步加入走梅花桩和钢丝绳，以及采七米高青的训练和表演。与此同时，闸坡少林武术馆也开始发展起来，主要吸收闸坡镇的狮舞人才，共同为海陵狮舞队伍扩张储备人才。2007年，“海陵南安舞狮”以“南安狮艺团”作为项目保护单位，陈祥升、李有国作为项目传承人，成功申报成为海陵区区级非物质文化遗产。

陈祥升经常与李有国交流狮舞技艺，两人30余年来为海陵狮舞的发展和传承、人才培养作出了重大贡献。后因陈祥升年事已高，指导传授狮舞技艺的工作主要由李有国负责，海陵狮舞的发展、传承重点也逐渐转移到闸坡镇。

基本内容

海陵狮舞特色明显，集舞蹈、武术、鼓点音乐为一体，注重基本功训练以及敲鼓师傅的技艺表现水平，鼓法伴奏多样灵活，并具有独特的仪式。狮舞表演时通常以“三响鼓”为信号起势，鼓点逐渐激昂急进，狮舞表演也随鼓点逐渐奋进起势；

such as lion dance on the quincuncial staggered stakes or wire line and plucking the greens of 7-meter-high, have gradually been trained and performed. At the same time, Zhapo Shaolin Martial Art Center also began to develop, mainly absorbing the lion dance talents from Zhapo Town and jointly expanding the talent reserve for the lion dance team of Hailing. In 2007, “Nan'an Lion Dance” took “Nan'an Lion Art Troupe” as the project protection unit, and Chen Xiangsheng and Li Youguo as the project inheritors, and successfully applied for the intangible cultural heritage of Hailing District.

Chen Xiangsheng often exchanges ideas of skills with Li Youguo, and they have contributed significantly to the development, inheritance, and cultivation of talents of Hailing Lion Dance for more than 30 years. Later, due to Chen Xiangsheng's oldness, it is Li Youguo who is mainly responsible for guiding and teaching the lion dance skills. The development of the Hailing Lion Dance gradually shifted the focus of inheritance to Zhapo Town.

Basic Content

With distinct features, Hailing Lion Dance integrates dance, martial arts, and drum music. It focuses on basic skills training and the performance of the drum master. The methods of drum accompaniment are diverse and flexible, and have unique rituals. The performance of the lion dance usually starts with the signal of “three drums”. The drums are vigorous gradually, and the lion dance performance gradually rises with the drums. The other method, the “Xingqing drum”, is a soft rhythm used to change the atmosphere in the middle of the performance, and accompanied by the drum, the lion dance performance also slows down. Other methods, such as the “seven-star drum”, are primarily used in the performance of quincuncial staggered stakes in the lion dance.

Main Features

(1) Hailing Lion Dance has very high requirements for the skill of the lion dancers. The lion dancers mainly control the power and show various forms of the lion through their movements.

(2) Hailing Lion Dance has unique rituals. The lion dance means good luck and happiness. Influenced by the geographical environment, the traditions derived from Hailing Lion Dance are closely related to the marine culture.

The apprentices of Hailing Lion Dance must go to the Mazu Temple to worship when finishing their apprenticeship, which means "consecration". The local temple will also give red envelopes to express the blessing of the lion dance team of Hailing. When the lion dance team of Hailing goes out for performances and activities, they will pay their respects to Huaguang the Great first to express their concern for the founder and pray for a smooth and successful trip, and wish all the staff safe and to have vital energy and spirit.

During the Spring Festival, the lion dance is usually performed in people's homes to bring good luck to the people. It is commonly known as the "lions worship the house". In addition, there is a custom of "dancing lions worship the sea" in Zhapo fishing port every Little New Year. The lion dance team first worships on the shore to pray for protection and then follows the fishing boat. During the voyage, the lion dances on the boat to ward off evils, guard the fishermen's safety and good weather, and express the fishermen's wishes for a good harvest.

"The Fishing Festival" is a major characteristic in Yangjiang, which is also celebrated with a lion dance. It is called the "lions worship the sea" ceremony to pray for a good harvest after fishing and send blessings to the fishermen.

舞狮人正在舞动狮子
The lion dancers are controlling the lions

另一鼓法“行青鼓”则为柔势节奏，多为表演中途转换气氛所用，狮舞表演也随之放缓舞动节奏；其余鼓法如“七星鼓”，则多为狮舞表演梅花桩时所用。

主要特征

（1）海陵狮舞对舞狮人的技艺水平有非常高的要求，主要通过舞狮人对力量的把控，舞动狮子以表现出狮子的各种形态。

（2）海陵狮舞拥有独特的仪式礼。狮舞寓意吉祥喜庆，受地理环境影响，海陵狮舞所衍生出的仪式礼与海洋文化息息相关。

海陵狮舞的培训弟子在出师时，必须前往妈祖庙参拜，意为“开光”，当地庙宇也会给“利是”，表达对海陵狮舞队伍的祝福。海陵狮舞队伍在外出表演、活动时，都要先参拜华光大帝，表示对祖师的尊敬以及祈祷此行顺利、圆满以及人员平安、弟子龙马精神。

春节期间，狮舞通常都会入到百姓家，寓意为百姓送福气，俗称“狮子拜屋”。此外，每逢小年之际，闸坡渔港都有“醒狮拜海”的习俗，狮舞队伍先在岸上拜祭四方祈求庇佑，随后跟随渔船航行。航行过程中狮子全程要在船上表演狮舞，寓意辟邪，庇佑渔民平安、风调雨顺，并表达海边渔民对渔业丰收的祈愿。

“开渔节”为阳江一大特色节日，同样有狮舞助兴，称为“狮子祭海”仪式，祈求开渔后渔民能够丰收，并为渔民送上祝福。

参加“南海（阳江）开渔节”祭海仪式的狮舞队

The lion dance team in the “South China Sea (Yangjiang) Fishing Festival” ceremony

（3）狮舞套路与武术相融合。海陵狮舞的主要套路招式有“勇攀高峰”“悬崖寻宝”“桥底探宝”“舞地龙”等，都是结合一些武术动作所呈现的套路，非常具有观赏价值。

(3) Hailing Lion Dance is an integration of lion dance routines and martial arts. The main performances of Hailing Lion Dance include “climbing the peak”, “hunting treasure on the cliff”, “exploring treasure at the bottom of the bridge”, “performing the earth dragon dance”, etc., all of which are presented by combining some martial arts movements and have great ornamental value.

重要价值

·历史价值

海陵狮舞是流传于海陵岛区域的一种传统舞蹈，通常用于庆典、各大喜庆节日助兴，并作为一种传统的庆典仪式流传至今，展现了海陵人民对“好彩头”的热衷和喜爱，并见证了海陵传统庆典文化的发展和延续。

·艺术观赏价值

海陵狮舞是融武术、舞蹈、鼓点音乐等为一体的文化活动，舞狮人通过仿生狮子形象、动态表现和鼓声伴奏的轻重缓急去体现狮子形态，具有很强的观赏性、艺术性。狮舞道具、服装多为订做并配套，狮头样式为南狮，配色多为红、黄等醒目喜庆的颜色，样式美观、生龙活虎并彰显精神气。

Great Value

· Historical value

Hailing Lion Dance is a traditional dance spreading on Hailing Island. It is usually performed to contribute to celebrations and festivals. As a conventional celebration ceremony, it has been passed down to the present day, showing the enthusiasm and love of the people of Hailing for “Hao Caitou” (good luck) and witnessing the development and continuation of the traditional celebration culture of Hailing.

· Artistic ornamental value

Hailing Lion Dance is a cultural activity integrating martial arts, dance, and drum music. The lion dancers embody the lion shape through the bionic lion image, dynamic performance, and the order of drum accompaniment, which is highly ornamental and artistic. The props and costumes of the lion dance are customized and matched. The lion is with the southern lion head style, with red, yellow, and other eye-catching and festive colors, which is beautiful and vibrant and highlights the spirit.

· Social value

As an intangible cultural heritage project in Hailing District, Hailing Lion Dance shows the characteristics and highlights the charm of the intangible cultural heritage of Hailing. At the same time, Hailing Lion Dance is loved by the masses, widely praised and has a high reputation.

· Educational value

As a traditional celebration ceremony with a long history, Hailing Lion Dance is still famous among the public, which has a specific significance for enhancing the masses' attention to the traditional ceremony. Meanwhile, the lion dance emphasizes cooperation and is a group activity, which has of educational importance for promoting collaboration.

· 社会价值

海陵狮舞作为海陵区一项非遗项目，展现了海陵非遗文化的特色特点，彰显了海陵非遗文化魅力。同时海陵狮舞被群众喜爱，受到广泛欢迎，也拥有较高的知名度。

· 教育价值

海陵狮舞作为一项历史悠久的传统庆典仪式延续至今，仍然深受大众喜爱，对提升群众对传统仪式的重视程度有着一定的意义，同时狮舞讲究协作，为群体性活动，对宣传合作精神有着教育意义。

配色众多的狮子
The lions with different colors

主要传承人

李有国，男，1967年出生，海陵舞狮第三代传承人。从艺近50年，4代传承，谱系清晰。李有国8岁开始跟师傅学习舞狮武术，现为中国武术协会会员、中国龙狮运动项目裁判员、国家二级武术裁判员、国家二级武术指导员、广东省健身社会体育指导员、广东省武术协会会员、海陵区南派舞狮非物质文化遗产传承人，具有“海陵工匠”之称。在非物质文化遗产项目宣传中作出了重大贡献。2011年10月2日，获得阳江市首届民间民俗艺术花会武术表演专场“鹬蚌相争”项目一等奖；继而在海陵创建“闸坡少林武术馆”，为海陵区文化体育事业培养了大批人才。现为阳江市第五批非物质文化遗产项目代表性传承人。

因海陵狮舞为群体性传统舞蹈，故需多人合作完成。李有国创建的武术培训基地现有狮舞队伍一支，人数30余人，为海陵狮舞的主要传承群体。

Main Inheritor

Li Youguo, male, born in 1967, is the third-generation inheritor of Hailing Lion Dance. He has been practicing arts for nearly 50 years, inherited by four generations with an evident pedigree. Li Youguo began to learn the lion dance from his master at the age of 8 and is now a member of the Chinese Martial Arts Association, a referee of Chinese dragon and lion sports, a national second-class referee of martial arts, a national second-class instructor of martial arts, an instructor of Guangdong Province Fitness Social Sports, a member of Guangdong Martial Arts Association, an inheritor of the intangible cultural heritage of Southern Style Lion Dance in Hailing District. He is known as “Hailing craftsman”. He has significantly contributed to the publicity of intangible cultural heritage projects. On October 2, 2011, he won first prize in the “ ‘A Snipe and a Clam Locked in Combat’, the Martial Arts Performance of the First Folk Art Exhibition Competition” in Yangjiang. Then he set up Zhapo Shaolin Martial Art Center in Hailing, training a large number of talents for Hailing’s culture and sports. Now he is the representative inheritor of the fifth batch of intangible cultural heritage projects in Yangjiang City.

Because Hailing Lion Dance is a traditional group dance, several people must cooperate to complete it. The martial arts training base founded by Li Youguo now has a lion dance team with more than 30 members, which is the leading inheriting group of Hailing Lion Dance.

李有国（左一）
Li Youguo (the first on the left)

Part 3

Traditional Medicine

第三部分

传统医药

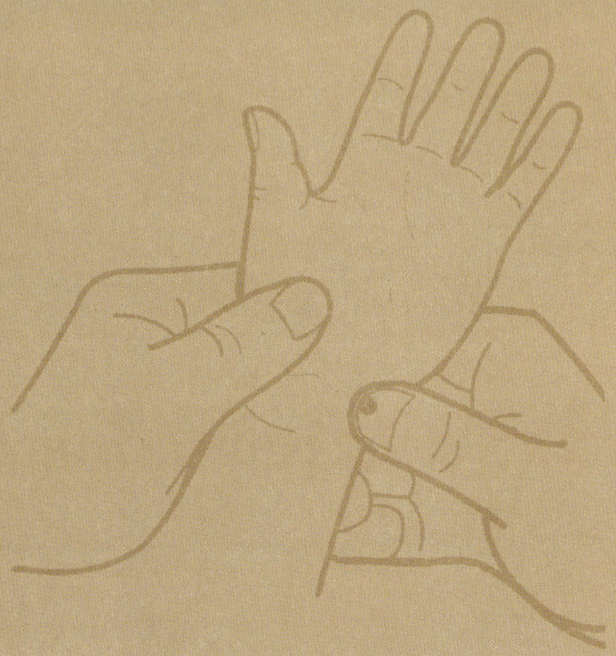

“施一针”针法

广东省第七批省级非物质文化遗产名录

保护单位 阳江海陵施粤响中医诊所

“Shi Yi Zhen” Acupuncture

The Seventh Batch of Provincial Intangible Cultural Heritage List of Guangdong Province

Protection Unit Shi Yuexiang Traditional Chinese Medicine Clinic in Hailing, Yangjiang

“施一针”针法（运动系统疼痛针灸治疗法，也可简称为“运动针法”），是治疗运动系统疼痛疾病的一种方法。它运用传统的针灸治疗方式，以经络学说、运动学原理为理论基础，把中医针灸和运动结合在一起，治疗运动系统功能受限的一系列疾病，如落枕、颈椎病、腰椎病、肩关节周围炎、肘劳、足跟病、腕关节疼痛、踝关节疼痛、髋关节疼痛、肌肉拉伤、风湿疼痛、痛风、运动伤痛及劳损等。

此针法主要分布区域以阳江市海陵区施粤响中医诊所为核心，在阳江市内的江城区、海陵区、阳东区、高新区、阳西县、阳春市等有一定的影响力，并逐步往珠三角区域扩展。2018年，“施一针”针法被列入广东省第七批省级非物质文化遗产名录。

历史渊源

针灸是我国一种古老的治疗方法，起源于远古时期人类的生活生产中，历经数千年的发展，形成了较完整的理论和临床体系。《黄帝内经》是我国最早的、内容

“Shi Yi Zhen” Acupuncture (acupuncture therapy for pain in the motor system, also referred to as “exercise acupuncture”) is a treatment method for pain diseases in the motor system. Based on the meridian theory and kinematics principle, it uses traditional acupuncture and combines acupuncture and movement in traditional Chinese medicine to treat a series of diseases with limited function of the motor system, such as stiff neck, cervical spondylosis, lumbar spondylosis, scapulohumeral periarthritis, elbow strain, heel disease, wrist pain, ankle pain, hip pain, muscle strain, rheumatism pain, gout, sports pain and strain.

Its main distribution area is Shiyuxiang Traditional Chinese Medicine (TCM) Clinic in Hailing District, Yangjiang City. It has specific influence in Jiangcheng District, Hailing District, Yangdong District, High Tech Zone, Yangxi County, and Yangchun City in Yangjiang City. It gradually expands to the Pearl River Delta region. In 2018, “Shi Yi Zhen” Acupuncture was selected into the seventh batch of the provincial intangible cultural heritage list in Guangdong Province.

Historical Origin

Acupuncture is an ancient therapeutic method in China. It originated in the life and production of human beings in ancient times. After thousands of years of development, it has formed a relatively complete theoretical and clinical system. *The Yellow Emperor's Canon of Internal Medicine* is the earliest medical work with rich and systematic contents in China, in which the meridian, acupoints, acupuncture methods, and indications are discussed in detail.

A-B Classic of Acupuncture and Moxibustion by Huangfu Mi of the Jin Dynasty is the earliest existing monograph on acupuncture in China, which serves as a link between the past and the future in the development of acupuncture. *The Compendium of Acupuncture and Moxibustion* by Yang Jizhou of the Ming Dynasty is a summary of acupuncture works of previous dynasties.

"Shi Yi Zhen" Acupuncture is based on the experience and lessons of predecessors. This acupuncture went through five reformation and it evolved constantly by continuous exploration and practice. After summarizing and improving the diagnosis and treatment steps, this acupuncture method gradually established a complete system combining theory and practical efficacy, and finally formed the "exercise acupuncture" treatment method.

The first set of acupuncture is electric acupuncture mode, in which acupuncture points are selected based on syndrome differentiation, and the needles are retaining with electricity.

The second set of acupuncture is a combination of three acupuncture points, eliminating electric acupuncture. The second set of acupuncture was influenced by the work of Dr. Jin Rui of Guangzhou University of Traditional Chinese Medicine, and was treated with "Jin's Three-needle Method", which was effective.

The third set of acupuncture is the mode of the multiple matching acupoint with lying position, which is a process of multi-combination to seek curative effect and development.

The fourth set of acupuncture involves combining the sitting mode with a suitable exercise mode, which is the embryonic form of "Shi Yi Zhen" Acupuncture.

The fifth set of acupuncture is "exercise acupuncture", which is acupuncture therapy for pain in the exercise system. It adopts the treatment mode of combining distal point selection with exercise and point assignment at the corresponding point of Ashi point.

So far, the "exercise acupuncture" treatment mode has matured and has been widely applied and promoted.

Basic Content

The treatment process of "Shi Yi Zhen" Acupuncture is divided into three steps. The first step is distal acupoint treatment, which is to select distal acupoint corresponding to the pain at the same meridians of injury place or same side of namesake meridian of hands and feet or opposite side of namesake meridian of hands and feet, and retain the needles for treatment.The second step is fully to activate the affected part so that the affected region can recover its

丰富又系统的医学著作，其中对经络、腧穴、针灸方法及适应证有详细的论述；晋代皇甫谧的《针灸甲乙经》是我国现存最早的针灸专著，对针灸发展史起到了承前启后的作用；明朝杨继洲的《针灸大成》是对历代针灸著作的总结。

在吸取前人经验教训的基础上，“施一针”针法通过不断的探索实践，历经五次针法变革改进，归纳完善其诊治步骤，逐步建立起理论与实际疗效相结合的完整体系，最终形成“运动针法”治疗方法。

第一套针法：电针模式，辨证选穴，留针加电。

第二套针法：三针穴位组合，取消电针。该针法受广州中医药大学靳瑞医生著作影响，用“靳三针”进行治疗，疗效尚可。

第三套针法：以卧位结合多种配穴模式。这是一个多方组合寻求疗效、寻求发展的过程。

第四套针法：坐位结合适当的运动模式，局部运动疗效显著，这一套针法是“运动针法”的雏形。

第五套针法：也就是“运动针法”，即运动系统疼痛针灸治疗法，采用远端取穴结合运动和在阿是穴对应穴取穴的治疗模式。

到目前为止，“运动针法”治疗模式已经成熟，并进行了广泛的应用和推广。

基本内容

“施一针”针法分三步治疗。第一步，远端配穴治疗，即在患处本经远端或者手足同名经同侧远端或者手足同名经对侧远端与疼痛相对应的部位选穴留针。第二步，运动患处，即让患者充分活动患处，使患处恢复正常生理活动功能。第三

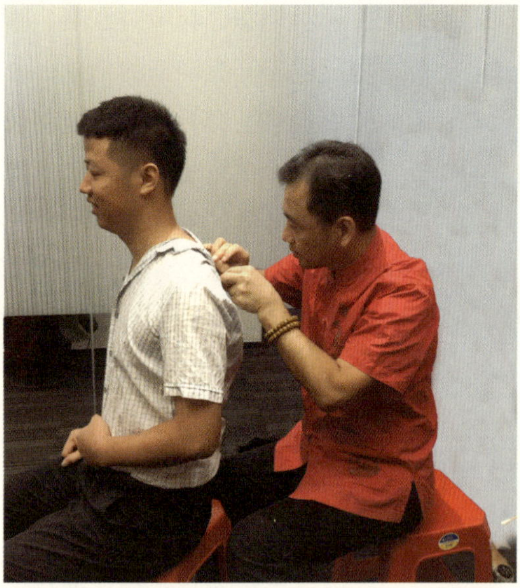

坐位模式针灸治疗
Acupuncture treatment of sitting mode

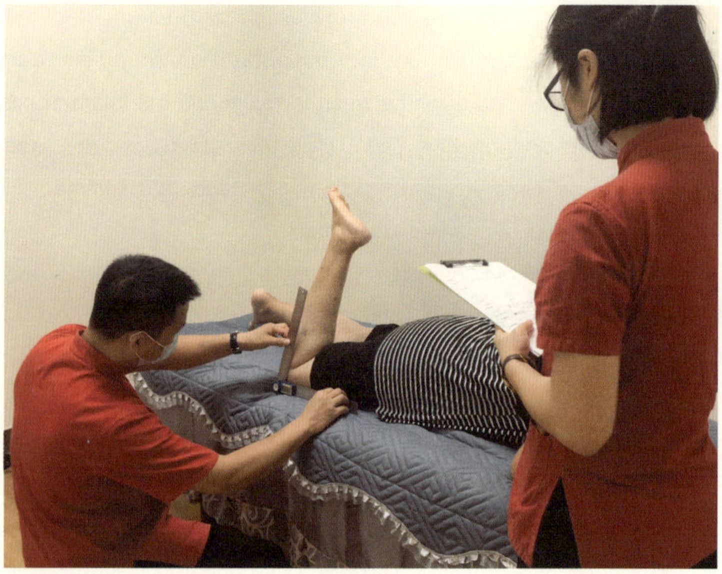

医生为膝关节疾病患者检查膝关节活动度
The doctor is checking the range of motion of knee joint for a patient

步，取“阿是对应穴”治疗，即以正中矢状面把身体分为左右两侧，把阿是穴另一侧的对称部位的穴位命名为“阿是对应穴”，并在该穴位留针治疗。

（1）远端配穴治疗。在患处本经络远端取穴体现了“经脉所过，主治所及”的中医经络理论，也体现了“本经病本经求”的治疗原则。关于在手足同名经上选穴，隋杨上善《黄帝内经·太素》有清晰记载：“手太阴、阳明之上有病，宜疗足太阴、阳明……足太阴、阳明之下有病，宜疗手太阴、阳明。”

（2）运动患处。因经络系统是人体生理综合调控系统，所以恢复身体运动系统正常的生理活动功能是本针法治疗的目的。同时，人体正常生理运动功能恢复程度也是疗效评定标尺。运动穿插整个治疗过程。运动能加速身体气血循环，加快组织之间新陈代谢，也使患处病理产物的代谢进一步加快，起到疏通经脉的作用，从而使患处活动功能正常。

（3）“阿是对应穴”治疗。唐代孙思邈的《备急千金要方》记载：“有阿是之

normal physiological function. The third step is to select the Ashi-corresponding point for treatment, which is to divide the body into left and right sides in the midsagittal plane, name the symmetrical point on the other side of the Ashi point as “Ashi corresponding point”, and leave needles at this point for treatment.

(1) Distal acupoint treatment. The acupoint selection at the far end of the original meridian at the affected area reflects the traditional Chinese meridian theory of “where the meridian passes, the main treatment reaches”, and the treatment principle of “the disease of the original meridian is based on the meridian”. In the Sui Dynasty, Yang Shangshan's *The Yellow Emperor's Canon of Internal Medicine · Taisu* recorded that “if there is a disease above the hand Taiyin or Yangming, it is appropriate to treat the foot Taiyin or Yangming... if there is a disease below the foot Taiyin or Yangming, it is appropriate to treat the hand Taiyin or Yangming”.

(2) Exercise the affected area. As the meridian system is a comprehensive regulation system of human physiology, the purpose of this acupuncture treatment is to restore the normal physiological activity function of the body movement system. At the same time, the degree of recovery of normal human physiological and motor functions is also a standard for efficacy evaluation. The exercise intersperses the whole treatment process. During the training, it speeds up the body's blood circulation, accelerates the metabolism between tissues, and further speeds up the metabolism of pathological products in the affected area, which plays a role in dredging the meridians so that the activation function of the affected area is improved.

(3) Treatment of “Ashi corresponding point”. According to Sun Simiao’s *Essential Recipes for Emergent Use Worth a Thousand Gold* of the Tang Dynasty, “There is Ashi acupoint treatment, which says that when a patient is pressed around the injury place, no matter whether it is an acupoint or not, as long as there is pain or unpleasant sensation, it is an Ashi acupoint.” It is effective to apply acupuncture treatment to Ashi point. However, the patient will experience a painful needle sensation when the needle is inserted into the Ashi point. Patients can’t tell whether it is the pain of the affected part or the pain of acupuncture, which will slow down the healing process and make the treatment less effective.

The meridians of the human body are symmetrically distributed on the left and right. Of course, the stimulation of the acupoints with the same name on the left and right meridians is also projected on the same part in the brain center. The meridian system is a comprehensive regulation system of human physiology, mainly controlled by the nervous system. An acupuncture message is given at the symmetrical part of Ashi point. The message is transmitted from the peripheral afferent nerve pathway to the centers at all levels and then converted into efferent nerve impulses through the central action at all levels. Through the efferent centers at all levels, it is transmitted to the respective effectors along the corresponding somatic motor nerve or autonomic nerve, causing various changes in its functional activities to achieve the therapeutic purpose. Due to the symmetrical distribution of the meridians, the stimulation information of the left and right acupoints of the same name will converge at all levels of the central nervous system. And the efferent nerve impulses will also be transmitted to the left and right acupoints simultaneously, which is a robust basis for treating the left side for curing diseases located on the right side.

Pain, whether it is excess or deficient, is due to improper local circulation of Qi and blood. “You will feel pain when your Qi and blood are blocked, and you won’t when your Qi and blood run smoothly.” Therefore, the treatment purpose of this method is to smooth Qi and blood of the affected area and restore the human body’s normal physiological function. Under pathological conditions, if one side is deficient and insufficient, the other side will appear excess and redundant. On the contrary, if one side is excess and redundant, the other side seems deficient and insufficient. Just as one leg is injured, the other leg assumes to take the function of two legs. One side is excess and redundant due to injury, and the other is deficient and insufficient due to overwork. If the affected part is excess, the opposite side of the affected part is deficient. If

法，言人有病痛，即令捏其上，若里当其处，不问孔穴，既得便快或痛处，既云阿是，灸刺皆验，故曰阿是穴也。”阿是穴的治疗效果得到认可，疗效也是确切的。可是在患者阿是穴上进针会留下疼痛针感，与患处原来的疼痛混淆难以分清，影响治疗速度及治疗效果。

人体经络呈左右对称分布，左右相同经络同名穴位受到的刺激当然也在大脑中枢投射在同一部位。经络系统是人体生理综合调控系统，人体生理调控主要是通过神经系统。在阿是穴对称部位给一个针刺信息，信息由外周传入神经通路传入各级中枢，通过各级中枢作用后转换为传出神经冲动，通过各级传出中枢，再沿相应的躯体运动神经或自主神经传至各自的效应器，引起其功能活动的各种变化以达到治疗目的。由于经脉对称性的分布，左右同名穴位刺激的信息都会在各级中枢汇聚，传出神经冲动也会同时传至左右同一穴位，这是左病右治的一个有力的根据。

不管是实而疼痛还是虚而疼痛，都是因为局部气血循环不畅。“痛则不通，通则不痛”，因此使患处气血通畅、恢复人

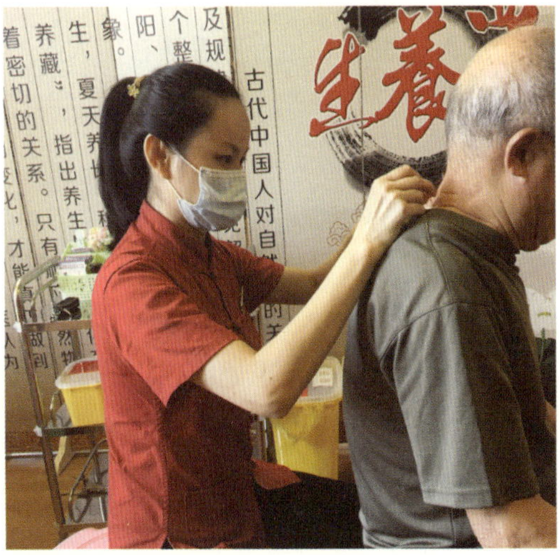

钟银利医生为患者进行针灸治疗
Dr. Zhong Yinli is treating the patient with acupuncture

体正常生理功能是此法的治疗目的。在病理情况下，如果一侧虚而不足，另一侧就显得实而有余。反之，如果一侧实而有余，另一侧就显得虚而不足。正如一条腿受伤，另一条腿就承担两条腿的功能；一侧因为受伤实而有余，另一侧因为过劳虚而不足。患处是实，那患处对侧就虚，虚则在"阿是对应穴"留针补其不足，活动患处乃泻其有余以扶正祛邪，阴阳乃秘。"阿是对应穴"治疗乃是本针法的一个核心内容，该空位既能代替阿是穴，起到治疗作用，又有其特殊治疗内涵。

主要特征

（1）创新的运动针法。"施一针"针法通过三步治疗法充分调动机体的自身能量，把患者从病理状态向生理状态转化，具有医治时间短、疗效好、见效快的特点和优势。

（2）"施一针"针法是从传统中医个体化治疗模式走向集体化治疗模式的一种方法，具有辨证个体化、施治模式化的特点，可缩短治疗时间，提高治疗效果，达到治病治本的目的。

（3）手法独特。"施一针"针法的握针、持针、进针、运针等手法在前人经验基础上作了进一步改进，进针迅速，渗透力强。

（4）独具一格的选穴方式。在传统取穴的基础上，结合临床实践研究，创新命名并使用"阿是对应穴"的选穴方式，其意义有二。一是防止患处的二次伤害，二是不在患处进针留针，让患处灵活活动，能调动机体自身能量加快患处局部血液循环，提高治疗效果。

it is deficient, leaving a needle at the Ashi corresponding point can compensate for its deficiency. Movement of the affected area aims to let out the excess to help support the healthy Qi and expel the pathogenic Qi and balance the Yin and Yang. The Ashi corresponding point treatment is a core content of this acupuncture method. It not only can replace Ashi's point and play a therapeutic role, but also has its particular therapeutic connotation.

Main Features

(1) An innovative method of exercise acupuncture. The three-step treatment method fully mobilizes the body's energy to transform the patient from a pathological state to a physiological condition. It has the characteristics and advantages of high efficiency and good effect within short treatment time.

(2) "Shi Yi Zhen" Acupuncture is a treatment method changing the individualized treatment mode of TCM into collective treatment mode, with the characteristics of individual syndrome differentiation and collective integration treament, which improve the treatment effect, and achieve the purpose of curing the disease.

(3) Unique technique of needling manipulation. The needle holding, insertion, manipulation, and other practices of "Shi Yi Zhen" Acupuncture have been further improved based on previous experiences, with rapid needle insertion and strong penetration.

(4) Unique point selection method. Based on traditional point selection and in combination with clinical practice research, the point selection method of Ashi corresponding point is innovatively named and used. Its significance lies in the followings: Firstly, it can prevent the secondary injury of the affected part. Secondly, it does not inject the needle into the affected area so that the affected area can move flexibly, which can mobilize the body's energy to accelerate the local blood circulation of the affected area and improve the treatment effect.

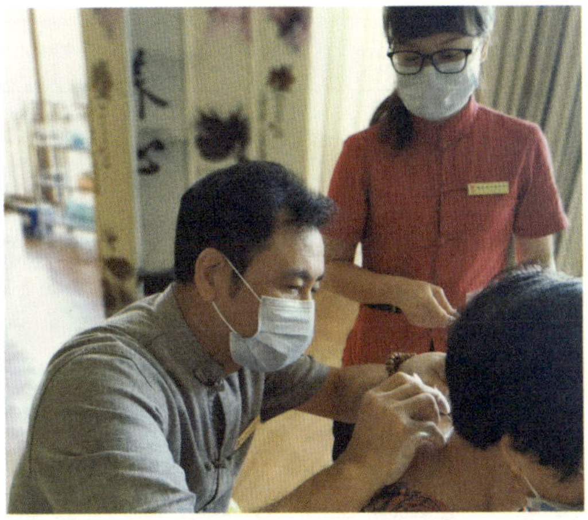

施粤响医生为患者进行针灸治疗

Dr. Shi Yuexiang is treating a patient with acupuncture

施粤响医生在示范针法

Dr. Shi Yuexiang is demonstrating acupuncture

Great Value

· Historical value

For thousands of years, Chinese traditional medicine has been evolving. Acupuncture, a fundamental component of traditional Chinese medicine treatment, has been crucial in helping Chinese people maintain their health. "Shi Yi Zhen" Acupuncture is an innovative development based on the experience of previous acupuncturists, and has the role of carrying on the past and initiating the future.

· Social value

The implementation of this method has significant social impacts. On the one hand, it offers new therapies and new ideas for the development of TCM acupuncture and brings new vitality into modern acupuncture. On the other hand, by promoting this acupuncture method, it can be known and understood by more doctors so that the clinical efficacy of doctors can be improved to some extent, which can help more patients.

重要价值

· 历史价值

中国传统医药传承发展数千年，针灸作为中医的一个重要的治疗方法，在维系国人健康方面起到了重要的作用。“施一针”针法是在前人针灸经验的基础之上创新发展而成，具有承前启后的作用。

· 社会价值

该治疗法的实施有着重要的社会意义，一方面为中医针灸学的发展提供了新的疗法和新的思路，为现代针灸学注入了新的活力；另一方面，通过对该针法的推广，其被更多的医生认识和了解，可以在一定程度上提高医生的临床水平，从而帮助更多的患者。

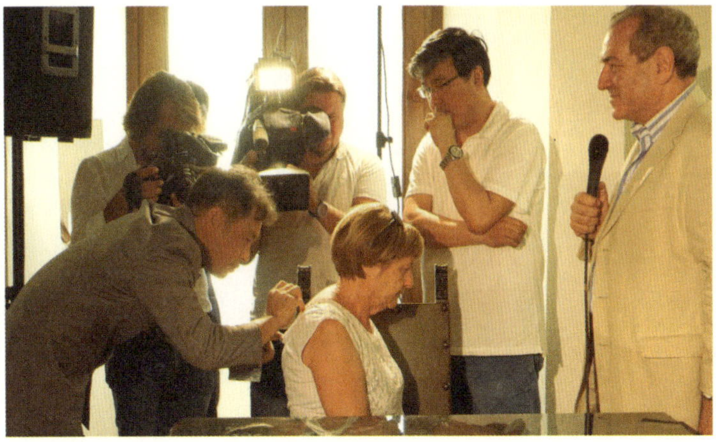

施粤响医生参加意大利第一届中意文化交流周，现场对患者进行针灸治疗，意大利国家电视台全程报道

Dr. Shi Yuexiang participated in the first Sino-Italian Cultural Exchange Week in Italy and conducted acupuncture treatment on the spot. The whole process was reported by Italian state television

主要传承人

Main Inheritor

施粤响，男，生于1968年9月，广东省阳江市人，毕业于广州中医药大学。施粤响自幼生活于中医世家，祖辈几代行医，并有家传医书古籍流传至今。其中外家祖上张宗海为阳江县著名老中医（《阳江县志》有所记载）。施粤响先后跟随外公、岳父研习祖上医学，由此打下了深厚的中医基础。毕业后其跟随阳江市名中医黄昌计学习。施粤响现为广东省第六批省级非物质文化遗产项目代表性传承人。

施粤响（右）
Shi Yuexiang (right)

Shi Yuexiang, male, born in September 1968, was a native of Yangjiang City, Guangdong Province. He graduated from the Guangzhou University of Traditional Chinese Medicine. Shi Yuexiang has lived in a family of traditional Chinese medicine since childhood. His ancestors have practiced medicine for several generations, and there are family ancient medical books handed down to this day. Among them, Zhang Zonghai, an ancestor of his maternal family, is a famous doctor of traditional Chinese medicine in Yangjiang County, which is recorded in *Yangjiang County Annals*. Shi Yuexiang followed his grandfather and father-in-law to study traditional medicine, thus laying a solid foundation in traditional Chinese medicine. After graduating from university, he studied with Huang Changji, a famous doctor of traditional Chinese medicine in Yangjiang City. Shi Yuexiang is now listed as the representative inheritor of the sixth batch of provincial intangible cultural heritage projects in Guangdong Province.

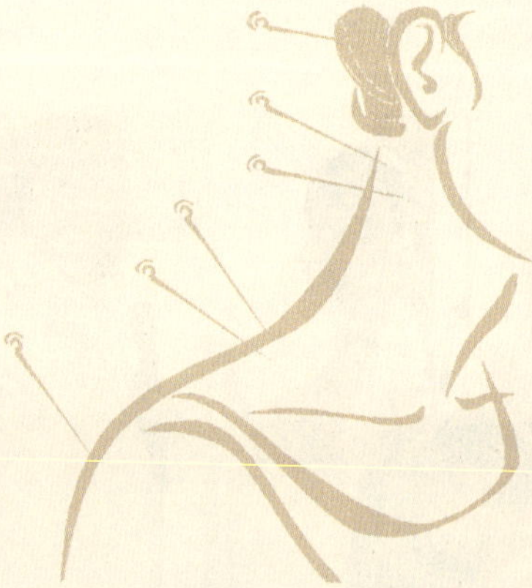

谢氏药摩法

保护单位 阳江江城谢克谦中医诊所

Xie's Medicated Massage Method

Protection Unit Xie Keqian Traditional Chinese Medicine Clinic in Jiangcheng, Yangjiang

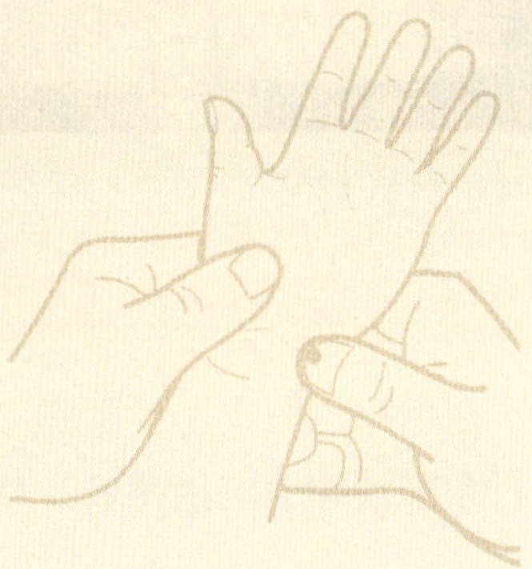

Xie's Medicated Massage Method is an external treatment method that utilizes the Xie family's ancestral secret formula as a medicinal massage medium. This medium, called "Swelling and Pain Relief" or "Swelling and Pain Relief Cream", is applied to the treatment area on the body surface or to the operator's hand. Targeted massage techniques are then used to treat the affected area. This method is distributed in Jiangcheng District, Yangjiang City, Guangdong Province.

This therapy has a unique and practical dual effect, combining both pharmacotherapy and massage therapy. It breaks the restriction that "new injuries can only be treated with cold compresses within 24 hours". This allows for the short-term recovery of injured soft tissues and joints, as well as limited movement and dysfunction caused by other diseases. This therapy is widely used and has high practical value.

Historical Origin

The lineage of Xie's Medicated Massage Method can be traced back more than 100 years. The Xie family has a long history of practicing medicine, and can be traced back to the 11th-generation of the inheritor, Xie Weigen. He practiced medicine in various places including Gangbei Village, and Mashan Village, Baisha, Jiangcheng, Yangjiang. He applied the Xie family's medical techniques and Xie's Medicated Massage Method to treat many patients in the area, earning a good reputation.

Xie Yancheng, the 12th-generation inheritor of the Xie family, followed his father's footsteps and practiced medicine in Gangbei Village, Mashan Village, and other areas. He applied the Xie family's medical techniques and Xie Medicinal Massage Method to help

谢氏药摩法属于中医外治疗法，是将谢家祖传秘方自行研制的药摩介质“肿痛消”或“肿痛消膏”涂抹于治疗部位或操术者手心，并通过有针对性的按摩手法对治疗部位进行治疗。该疗法分布于广东省阳江市江城区等地。

该疗法疗效独特显著，具有药物疗法和按摩疗法的双重效果。它打破了“新伤在24小时内只能冷敷”的限制，可以使损伤软组织和关节活动受限以及功能障碍等病症在短时间内康复。该疗法应用广泛，并具有相当高的实用价值。

历史渊源

谢氏药摩法，其传承脉络可追溯到100多年前，谢氏家族可寻源到第十一代传人谢维根，在阳江江城白沙岗背村、麻汕村等地行医，应用谢家医术和谢氏药摩法治好乡人邻里病患众多，颇有声望。

第十二代传人谢彦成，子承父业，应用谢家医术和谢氏药摩法在岗背村、麻汕村等地行医，愈患无数，颇负盛名。

第十三代传人谢汝进（1911—1982

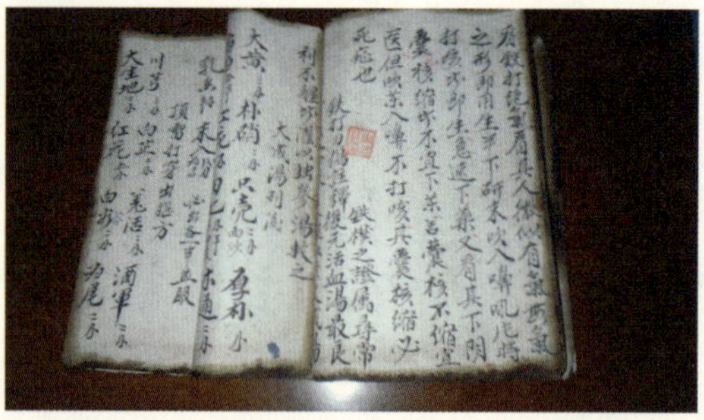

谢家祖传秘方手抄书

The manuscript of the Xie family's ancestral secret formula

年）继承祖传医术，早期随父谢彦成在岗背村和麻汕等地应用谢家医术和谢氏药摩法行医，后独立在阳西沙扒和上洋、书村等地行医，因医术超群得到众多病人和患者亲属的高度赞赏。中华人民共和国成立后，谢汝进被推选为阳江县沙扒镇卫生协会会长，组建卫生院后，又被任命为沙扒镇卫生院院长，继续应用谢家医术和谢氏药摩法愈人无数。

基本内容

谢氏药摩法有疗效独特显著和不受冷敷疗法制约的特点。

其一，该法具有外用药物疗法与按摩疗法的双重作用，比单纯应用外用药物或按摩治疗效果更加显著。该法通过按摩手法和药物作用的有机结合，迅速发挥药物活血化瘀、消肿止痛的治疗功能，改善损伤部位血液循环，促进组织修复，使急性软组织损伤和慢性软组织损伤患者在短时间内消除肿胀、疼痛和功能障碍等症状。

其二，谢氏药摩法不受“新伤在24小时内只能用冷敷疗法”制约。现代医学理论认为，在软组织损伤急性期（受伤24小时内），只能使用冷敷法（如冰块冷敷）进行治疗，否则就会加重皮下软组织周围

numerous patients, earning a good reputation.

Xie Rujin (1911–1982), the 13th-generation inheritor, inherited the ancestral medical techniques and initially practiced Xie's medicine and massage method alongside his father, Xie Yancheng, in Gangbei Village, Mashan Village, and other areas. Later, he worked as an independent practitioner in Shapa, Shangyang and Shucun of Yangxi, earning high praise from many patients and their relatives for his excellent medical skills. After the People's Republic of China was founded, Xie Rujin became the president of the Health Association of Shapa Town in Yangjiang County. Following the establishment of the health center, he was appointed as the president of the health center of Shapa Town, where he continued to apply the Xie family's medical techniques and Xie's Medicated Massage Method to heal numerous people.

Basic Content

Xie's Medicated Massage Method is not limited by cold compress therapy and has been proven to be unique and effective.

Firstly, Xie's Medicated Massage Method has the dual role of external drug therapy and massage therapy, which makes it more effective than simply applying external drugs or massage therapy. By organically combining massage techniques and drug effects, this method rapidly exerts the therapeutic functions of medicines, promoting blood circulation, removing blood stasis, and reducing swelling and pain. Furthermore, it can improve blood circulation in injured areas, promote tissue repair, and quickly relieve patients with acute and chronic soft tissue injuries of swelling, pain, dysfunction, and other symptoms.

Secondly, Xie's Medicated Massage Method is not limited by the restriction "cold compress therapy can only be used for new injuries within 24 hours". According to modern medical theory, during the

谢氏藏书《南雅堂医书全集》

The Complete Collection of Nanyatang Medical Books collected by the Xie family

acute stage of soft tissue injury (within 24 hours of injury), only cold compress (such as ice compress) is recommended for treatment. This is because using other therapies can cause small blood vessels around the subcutaneous soft tissue to break, leading to more blood leakage, more swelling, more pain, and severe consequences. However, Xie's Medicated Massage Method can be applied even after 24 hours of injury. With just 10 minutes of treatment, it can immediately relieve swelling and pain, and reduce inflammation.

Studies have shown that the medicated massage method not only enhances drug permeability but also promotes the reconstruction of the small vascular network in diseased tissues. This results in an increase in diameter of capillaries, which in turn speeds up blood flow in the microcirculation and reduces blood viscosity. Additionally, the method eliminates various inflammatory mediators, such as potassium hydroxide, 5-hydroxytryptamine, bradykinin, and prostaglandin, that are released from local tissues. By reducing high pressure in tissues and clearing meridians, the method promotes blood circulation, relieves muscle spasms, and eliminates blood stasis, swelling, pains, and deformations, such as massiveness, platy and nodules, caused by soft tissue adhesions and degeneration. The ultimate goal is to quickly recover injured soft tissues and joint activity, reducing limitations and dysfunctions.

Main Features

(1) Multiple therapeutic effects. Xie's Medicated Massage Method has multiple therapeutic effects through the organic combination of specific media and corresponding techniques. It rapidly relieves swelling and pain.

(2) Wide application range. The method has a wide application range and can be used to treat soft tissue injuries, whether acute or

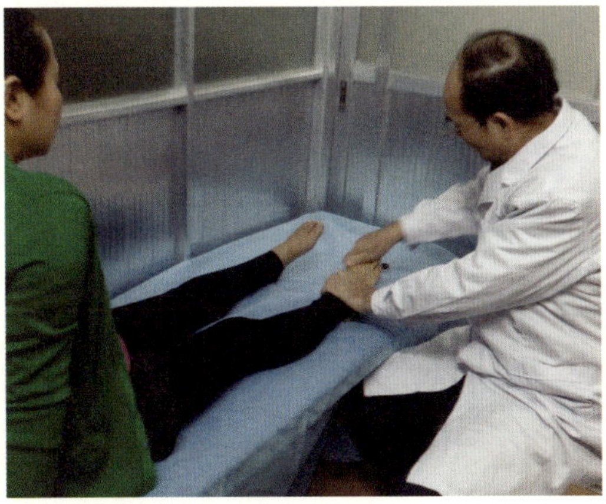

谢克谦医师为患者进行按摩疗法

Dr. Xie Keqian performs massage therapy for patient

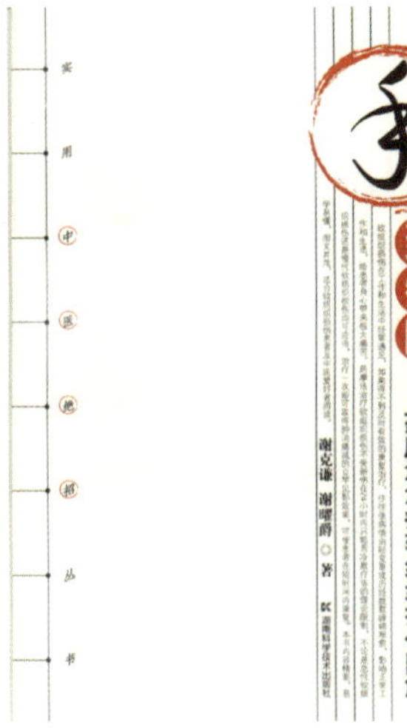

谢克谦与谢曜爵联合撰写的《手到病除：药摩法治疗软组织损伤图解》

Massage Treatment: Illustration of the Treatment of Soft Tissue Injury with Xie's Medicated Massage Method written by Xie Keqian and Xie Yaojue

小血管破裂和局部血液渗出，使肿胀疼痛症状加剧而造成难以想象的后果。谢氏药摩法不仅不受“新伤在24小时内只能用冷敷疗法”的理论限制，而且伤后即可应用，治疗10分钟左右即可取得肿消痛减的立竿见影效果。

相关研究也表明，药摩法通过直接作用于病变组织，可提高药物渗透性能，促进病变组织小血管网的重建，使毛细血管管径增大，加快微循环内血液流动，降低血液黏稠度，排除局部组织释放出的氢钾离子、5-羟色胺、缓激肽、前列腺素等炎症介质，消除组织内高压，达到疏通经络，宣通气血，解除肌肉痉挛，祛除血瘀肿胀疼痛，消除软组织粘连与组织变性产生的块状、片状或结节状等形态改变，使损伤软组织和关节活动受限与功能障碍等病症在短期内康复。

主要特征

（1）多重疗效。谢氏药摩法通过特效介质和相应手法的有机结合，产生多重疗效作用，迅速发挥消肿止痛的治疗作用。

（2）应用范围广。不论是急性还是慢性软组织损伤，不论伤后症状轻重，不论伤后用过何药何法治疗，均可应用治疗。

（3）优势独特。每天只需治疗一次，每次只需治疗10分钟左右，病人无痛苦，疗效立竿见影。

（4）实用性强。平时可快速减轻百姓或运动员伤痛，恢复生产力或竞争力；战时可快速消除损伤战士痛苦，提高战斗力。

（5）使用方便，无令人不适的气味，不会沾污衣物，安全无副作用。

重要价值

· 医疗价值

术简效宏，疗效确切，弥补了现今外治疗法的不足，具有较高的临床应用价值。

· 历史文化价值

药摩之术历史悠久，药摩法绝技在民间数代流传，而谢氏药摩法是民间医药绝活之一，传承了具有地方特色的医药文化。

· 技术价值

谢氏药摩法吸收古代医家药摩治病的经验推陈出新，并使其传承发展。谢氏药摩法的传承为我们提供了活态性的资料，这对我们研究药摩法和探索其治病机理有重要作用，对保护民间传统医药绝技有积极意义。

· 社会经济价值

药摩法治疗生产劳动与生活中常见的急性软组织损伤和慢性软组织损伤，对民众医疗保健可发挥重大作用，药摩法简单方便，经济实惠，可降低治疗费用，减轻国家和患者个人的经济负担。

chronic, regardless of the severity of post-injury symptoms and the of previous medications and treatment techniques.

(3) Unique advantages. It only needs to be treated once a day for about 10 minutes. The patient is painless and the effect is immediate.

(4) High practicability. In daily life, it can quickly reduce pain for individuals or athletes and improve productivity or competitiveness. During times of war, it can rapidly alleviate the pain of wounded soldiers and enhance their combat effectiveness.

(5) It is convenient to use, has no unpleasant smell, will not contaminate clothes, and is safe without side effects.

Great Value

· Medical value

The method has simple treatment process, which brings remarkable effects, making up for the shortcomings of today's external treatment methods, and has high clinical application value.

· Historical and cultural value

The medicated massage methods have a long history, passed down through generations as remarkable folk medicine techniques. Xie's Medicated Massage Method originated from a local medicine culture and is one of the unique techniques.

· Technical value

Xie's Medicated Massage Method builds upon the ancient physicians' experience in medicated massage treatment, incorporating new ideas and methods to further its development. The inheritance of this method has provided us with valuable operational data, which plays a vital role in our research on medicated massage methods and our exploration of their disease-curing mechanisms. It also has a positive significance in preserving traditional folk medical skills.

· Socio-economic value

Xie's Medicated Massage Method can effectively treat both acute and chronic soft tissue injuries commonly seen in daily life and work, making it a valuable tool in public healthcare. The method's simplicity, convenience, and affordability make it a cost-effective treatment option that reduces the economic burden on both patients and the country.

Main Inheritors

Xie Keqian, male, was born in August 1956 and learned traditional Chinese medicine from his father who was a doctor of traditional Chinese medicine. He has shown great intelligence, diligence, and eagerness to learn. Xie's Medicated Massage Method, which he learned from his father, uses a combination of specific massage media— "Swelling and Pain Relief" and "Swelling and Pain Relief Cream" developed by Xie by using an ancestral secret recipe, and techniques such as kneading, pressing, pinching, flicking, and plucking to treat soft tissue injuries with immediate effect. In recent years, Xie has improved and refined his technique, making significant research achievements. The innovative and improved Xie's Medicated Massage Method can be used to treat both new and old soft tissue injuries, breaking the limitation of modern medical theory that suggests new injuries can only be treated with cold compress within 24 hours.

Xie Keqian not only inherited Xie's Medicated Massage Method and medical skills but also actively promoted and applied the technique. He provided treatment at Yangjiang Sports School, Yangjiang Health Inspection Outpatient Department, and Zhuhai Sports Science Research Institute and even trained some students at Yangjiang Sports School in the method. Currently, Xie Keqian is a representative inheritor of the fourth batch of intangible cultural heritage projects in Yangjiang City.

主要传承人

谢克谦，男，1956年8月出生，自幼随身为中医师的父亲习医，由于勤奋好学，聪明能干，悟性强，得父真传，对谢家医术和谢氏药摩法深得要领，应用祖传秘方研制的谢氏药摩介质“肿痛消”与“肿痛消膏”和揉、按、捏、弹、拨等手法，治疗软组织损伤疗效立竿见影，可使急性和慢性软组织损伤患者在短时间内康复。近年来，谢克谦从理论和实践两方面对谢氏药摩法进行总结提升，并取得独有的研究成果。应用经创新提升的谢氏药摩法治疗软组织损伤不仅打破“新伤在24小时内只能用冷敷疗法”的现代医学理论枷锁，而且新旧伤均可应用，即治即见效。

谢克谦在继承谢氏药摩法和谢氏医术的同时，还积极开展传承推广工作，在阳江市体育运动学校、阳江市卫检门诊部和珠海市体育科学研究所等开展应用治疗，并对阳江市体校部分学生进行谢氏药摩法培训。谢克谦现为阳江市第四批非物质文化遗产项目代表性传承人。

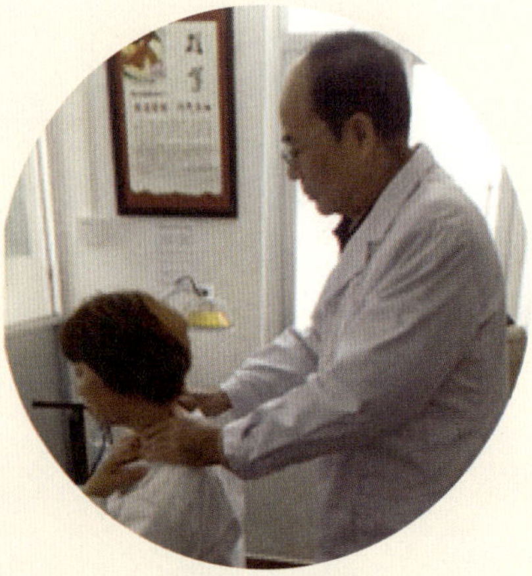

谢克谦（右）
Xie Keqian (right)

谢曜爵，男，1984年1月出生，谢氏药摩法第十五代传承人。中山大学医学博士毕业，主治医师，具有西医处方和中医药饮片处方资格。他积极开展对非遗项目的传承、推广、应用工作。除做好谢氏药摩法的传承工作外，谢曜爵与其父谢克谦根据中医制膏原理和现代膏贴生产技术研制出了“一种药膏贴一体化生产设备”，该设备获得了国家专利证书。谢曜爵现为阳江市第五批非物质文化遗产项目代表性传承人。

Xie Yaojue, male, was born in January 1984 and is the 15th-generation inheritor of Xie's Medicated Massage Method. He obtained his medical doctorate from Zhongshan University and is a practicing physician qualified in both Western medicine prescription and traditional Chinese medicine herbal prescription. He actively promotes and applies intangible cultural heritage projects. Alongside his work on the inheritance of Xie's Medicated Massage Method, Xie Yaojue and his father, Xie Keqian, have developed a “medicinal plaster production equipment” based on the principles of traditional Chinese medicine plaster-making and modern production technology, for which they have received a national patent certificate. Xie Yaojue is currently a representative inheritor of the fifth batch of intangible cultural heritage projects in Yangjiang City.

谢曜爵
Xie Yaojue

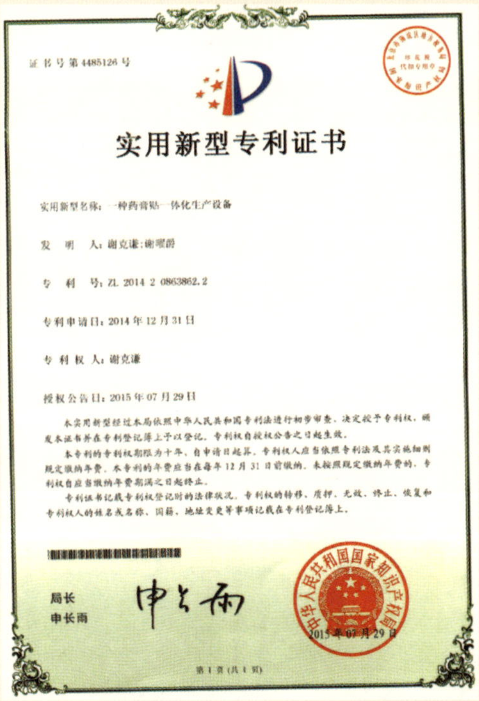

证书号第4485126号

实用新型专利证书

实用新型名称：一种药膏贴一体化生产设备

发　明　人：谢克谦；谢曜爵

专　利　号：ZL 2014 2 0863862.2

专利申请日：2014年12月31日

专利权人：谢克谦

授权公告日：2015年07月29日

本实用新型经过本局依照中华人民共和国专利法进行初步审查，决定授予专利权，颁发本证书并在专利登记簿上予以登记。专利权自授权公告之日起生效。

本专利的专利权期限为十年，自申请日起算。专利权人应当依照专利法及其实施细则规定缴纳年费。本专利的年费应当在每年12月31日前缴纳。未按照规定缴纳年费的，专利权自应当缴纳年费期满之日起终止。

专利证书记载专利权登记时的法律状况。专利权的转移、质押、无效、终止、恢复和专利权人的姓名或名称、国籍、地址变更等事项记载在专利登记簿上。

局长
申长雨

2015年07月29日

第1页（共1页）

谢克谦、谢曜爵“药膏贴一体化生产设备”专利证书
Xie Keqian and Xie Yaojue's patent certificate of “medicinal plaster production equipment”

李氏刮经解穴疗法

保护单位 阳春市杏缘春养生馆

Li's Curettage and Acupoint Relieving Therapy

Protection Unit Yangchun Xingyuanchun Health Preservation Club

Li's Curettage and Acupoint Relieving Therapy was founded by Li Rongke, a native of Yangchun, Guangdong, during the Jiaqing period of the Qing Dynasty, and has a history of more than 200 years. Li's Curettage and Acupoint Relieving Therapy is an ancient and novel treatment method. Its theory integrates traditional Chinese medical thoughts and modern medical views, embodies the essence of Chinese medicine, and is an integral part of traditional Chinese medicine culture.

Historical Origin

Li's Curettage and Acupoint Relieving Therapy is the same as traditional Chinese medicine Guasha (scraping therapy), acupuncture, and massage. They all use simple tools to stimulate the human body to recover its functions. Since ancient times, people have gradually found that pointing, pressing, buttoning, and hitting on the body's surface can reduce or eliminate pain, and some plants can cure diseases. For example, acupoint pressure can be seen many times in the earliest medical document in China, *The Yellow Emperor's Canon of Internal Medicine*. In *Plain Questions · Theory of Lifting Pain*, it records that, "The cold invades between the intestines and the stomach and under the diaphrag part, so the blood cannot be dispersed. The meridian is tense and painful, so it needs to be pressed to stop the pain." This means that the cold coagulation of the spleen and stomach in the middle energizer causes the blood and Qi to run poorly, and the meridian becomes tense, which cause the person to feel painful. So it is necessary to use the pointing and press techniques to make the blood and Qi run smoothly. If the Qi and blood flow smoothly,

"李氏刮经解穴疗法"于清嘉庆年间由广东阳春人李荣科创立，距今已经有200多年的历史。"李氏刮经解穴疗法"是一种既古老而又新颖的治病方法，其融合了中国传统医学思想和现代医学理论，集中体现了中华医学的精髓，是我国中医文化的重要组成部分。

历史渊源

李氏刮经解穴疗法与传统的中医刮痧、针灸、推拿同出一脉，都是利用简单的工具刺激人体从而使其恢复自身的机能。从远古时代开始，人们逐渐发现在体表点、按、扣、打能使疼痛减轻或消失，一些植物可以作为药物治疗疾病。如我国现存最早的医学文献《黄帝内经》可见到多处有关点穴的记载。在《素问·举痛论》中记有"寒气客于肠胃之间，膜原之下，血不得散，小络急引故痛，按之则血气散，故按之痛止"，意思是寒凝中焦脾胃，致使气血运行不畅，脉络拘急而发生疼痛，应用点、按手法，使气血运行畅通，通则不痛，所以可治愈痛证。又如晋

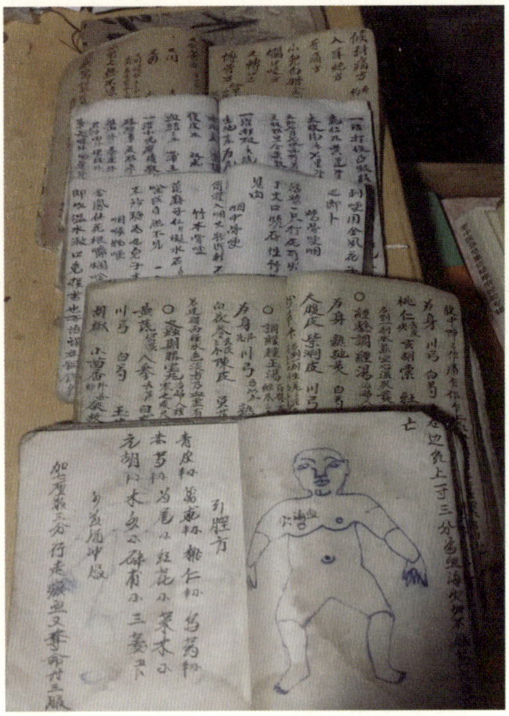

李氏祖传医药古籍手抄本
The Li family' s ancestral medica ancient manuscript

代葛洪《肘后备急方》所言“令爪其病人人中，取醒”，即用手指切按人中穴，以及时苏厥救逆，挽救患者生命。随着医疗经验的积累，人们便把某些特殊的“按之快然”“驱病迅捷”的部位称为“穴”。于是通过对“穴”进行点、按等来治疗疾病的方法也就日益发展，这是刮经解穴疗法的萌芽阶段。

根据史料记载，刮经解穴疗法创始人为张三丰。《明史·方伎传》曰：“张三丰，辽东懿川人，名全一。”《少林拳术秘诀》云：“盖以三丰……能融贯少林宗法……晚年发明七十二穴点按术，为北派中之神功巨子……手法有两指点、一指点、斫点、拍点、掌段点、膝盖撞点、手拐点等法，各有其用，非经亲授，不易于着力……”《穴位数伤秘方》曰：“点穴之妙，在于选中穴位，击中要害，灵在眼疾手快，视其准、点其速，力之雄，无不妙也……”此穴位疗法明代盛行于世，清代

the pain will stop, so the pain can be cured. As also mentioned in Ge Hong's *Handbook of Prescriptions for Emergencies* of the Jin Dynasty, pressing the patient's Renzhong point to wakes the patient up, that is, using the thumbnail to press the Renzhong point in time to save the syncope patient's life. With the accumulation of medical experience, people called certain special points acupuncture points for the pleasure of pressing them and the ability to cure diseases quickly. Thus, the method of treating diseases by pointing and pressing "acupuncture points" was increasingly developed, which was the budding stage of curettage and acupoint relieving therapy.

According to historical records, Zhang Sanfeng was the founder of curettage and acupoint relieving therapy. *The History of the Ming Dynasty · Biography of Fang Ji*: "Zhang Sanfeng, a native of Yichuan, Liaodong, also named Quan Yi." *Secrets of Shaolin Boxing* says, "Zhang Sanfeng, a master of Shaolin Kung Fu, who invented the seventy-two points press method in his later years, was a master of the northern Shaolin school. The hand method has two fingers point, one finger point, hack point, pat point, palm segment point, knee bump point, hand inflection point and other methods, and each point has its own use. It is not easy for a person to learn how to use the right force without being taught..." *Handbook of Acupoint Injuries* says, "The wonder of acupoint pressure lies in the selection of points. To hit the target point, the key lies in the quick eye and hand. The doctor has to see accurately, point accurately, and with enough force. This is what makes it wonderful." This therapy prevailed in the Ming Dynasty, and was widely used and greatly enriched and developed in the Qing Dynasty.

During the Jiaqing period of the Qing Dynasty, Li Rongke, a native of Yangchun, Guangdong, joined Shaolin when he was young. Later, he opened martial arts schools and medical schools, gradually formed his own simple curettage and acupoint relieving therapy, became a famous doctor in western Guangdong, and founded a new school of the curettage and acupoint relieving therapy. So far, it has been passed down five generations in the family.

Li Jialong, the 5th-generation inheritor, took the road of combining clinical practice with scientific research, carried out a series of scientific research on the curettage and acupoint relieving therapy for complicated diseases, further verified the scientificity of the curettage and acupoint relieving therapy, and applied the improved Li's Curettage and Acupoint Relieving Therapy to treat some complex conditions, and achieved apparent effects.

In the 1990s, Li Jialong began cultivating the 6th-generation inheritor.

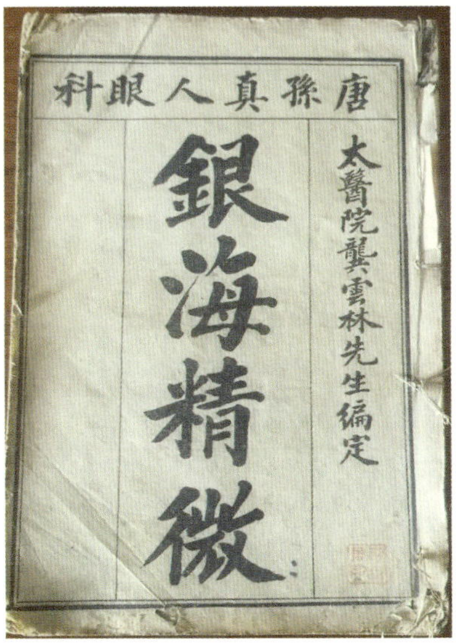

李氏收藏的医学古籍《银海精微》
Li's collection of ancient medical book *Silver Sea Essence*

Basic Content

Li's Curettage and Acupoint Relieving Therapy evolved from traditional Chinese scraping therapy. It is a traditional Chinese medicine therapy based on traditional Chinese medicine's viscera and meridians theory, combining traditional Chinese scraping therapy with Qigong pressing acupoint therapy. It requires that the practitioner, based on mastering the meridians and acupoints of the human body and accurately locating the lesions, use the special ceramic spoon to scrape the diseased area of the patient at high speed of 2-3 times per second. When supplemented with different prescriptions, its power can penetrate the tendons and reach the bones and quickly open the meridians in the diseased areas or unlock the closed acupoint. It is effective for lumbar disc protrusion, lumbar spine hyperplasia, frozen shoulder, lumbar muscle strain, swollen and painful joint growth, limb paralysis, gout, facial paralysis, migraine, etc..

Main Features

(1) It has wide applicability and remarkable curative effect, especially for painful diseases. Li's Curettage and Acupoint Relieving Therapy pays great attention to combination of Qi and force, balancing hardness with softness, and fast scraping speed, which make the patient feel the Qi flows in the meridian and penetrates the tendons and reaches the bones. Once Qi reaches the diseased areas, there will be an immediate therapeutic effect.

(2) The medication is used in vitro, which has no side effects. This method is one kind of physical therapy, which aims to restore the

广泛应用并得到极大的丰富和发展。

清嘉庆年间，广东阳春人李荣科自幼投师少林，后开设武馆和医馆，逐渐形成了一套自己的朴素的刮经解穴疗法，成为当时粤西地区的名医，创立了穴位刮痧治疗的一个新流派。至今已经在家族中传承五代。

第五代传人李嘉龙走临床与科研结合的道路，开展刮经解穴治难疾的系列科研，进一步验证刮经解穴疗法的科学性。应用改进后的李氏刮经解穴疗法治疗一些疑难病症，取得明显疗效。

20世纪90年代，李嘉龙开始培养第六代传人。

基本内容

李氏刮经解穴疗法由传统中医刮痧疗法演化而来，是一门以中医脏腑经络学说为依据、中医刮痧疗法和气功点穴疗法相结合的中医疗法，要求施治者在熟练掌握人体经络穴位和精准定位病灶的基础上，运气至特制的陶瓷调羹，以每秒2～3次的高速刮擦患者致病区域，辅以不同方药后，其力量能透筋达骨，迅速打通病区经络或解开封闭穴位。对腰椎间盘突出、腰椎增生、肩周炎、腰肌劳损、关节增生肿痛、四肢麻痹、痛风、面瘫、偏头痛等疗效显著。

主要特征

（1）适用性广，疗效显著，尤其对痛类疾病有显著疗效。李氏刮经解穴疗法讲究“气”“力”结合、刚柔并济，刮经时速度快，使病人气感大并透筋达骨，使气至病所，疗效立竿见影。

（2）体外用药，无副作用。该疗法为物理治疗，旨在恢复身体正常运转，提高

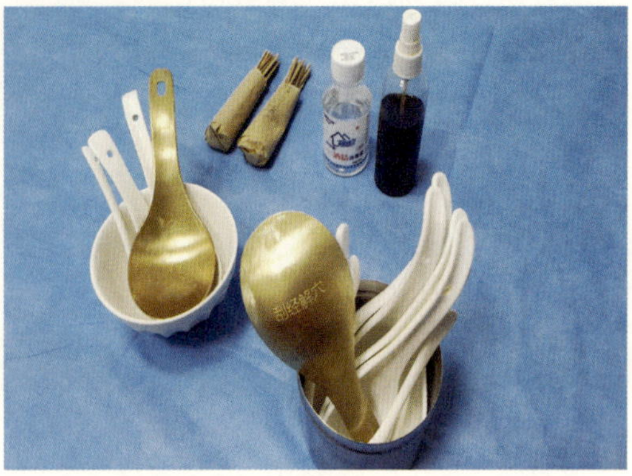

治疗工具是特制的调羹
The treatment tool is tailored spoons

自身免疫力，对内脏功能无毒副作用。

（3）理论系统完整，不断创新。经过李氏几代人的不断探索、积累、创新，使来自民间的刮经解穴疗法由实践上升为理论，形成流派科学的发展基础。

重要价值

· 医学学术价值

李氏刮经解穴法历经200多年的传承，其理论、技艺在中国传统医学中有自身的特点，尤其在痛症类疾病中疗效显著。源于实践的李氏刮经解穴疗法经几代人改进更臻完善，兼具西医疗效见效快的优点，受到了国内外医学界的广泛关注。

· 传统文化价值

李氏刮经解穴法起源于清嘉庆年间，是国内现存为数不多的依靠穴位经络治疗的流派。李氏刮经解穴疗法的理论体现了中华民族自然养生的哲学智慧，是对中华民族几千年的健康养生理念及其实践经验的一种总结，也是中华医药学的重要组成部分。

· 社会和经济价值

通过几代人的努力，尤其是经过李嘉龙的积极推广，李氏刮经解穴治疗法的神奇疗效获得了越来越多患者的肯定和赞

regular operation of the body, improve self-immunity, and has no side effects on visceral functions.

(3) It has complete theoretical system with continuous innovation. Through the constant exploration, accumulation, and creation of several generations of Li family, the folk curettage and acupoint relieving therapy has been upgraded from practice to theory, forming the basis for the development of school science.

Great Value

· Academic value of medicine

After more than 200 years of inheritance, the theories and skills of Li's Curettage and Acupoint Relieving Therapy have their own characteristics in Chinese traditional medicine, especially in relieving pain. Li's Curettage and Acupoint Relieving Therapy originated from practice and has been improved and perfected by several generations. It has the advantages of the rapid efficacy of Western medicine and has received extensive attention from the medical community at home and abroad.

· Traditional cultural value

Li's Curettage and Acupoint Relieving Therapy originated in the Jiaqing period of the Qing Dynasty. It is one of the few schools in China that rely on acupoints and meridians for treatment. Li's Curettage and Acupoint Relieving Therapy embodies the philosophical wisdom of the Chinese nation's natural health preservation, summarizes the nation's thousands of years of health preservation philosophy and practical experience, and is also an essential part of Chinese medicine.

· Social and economic value

Through the efforts of several generations, especially through the active promotion of Li Jialong, the miraculous effect of Li's Curettage and Acupoint Relieving Therapy has been recognized and praised by

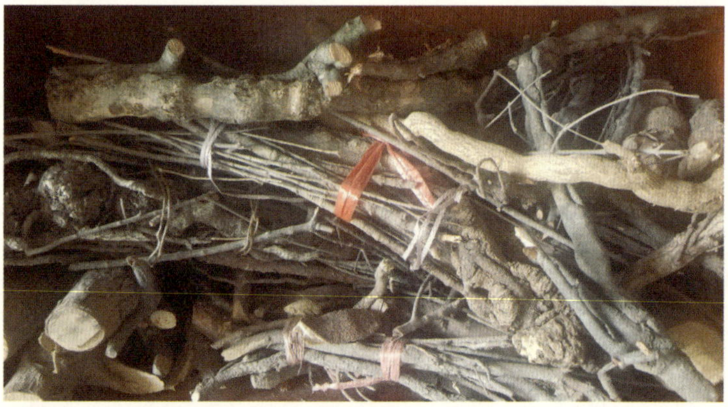

浸酒药材
Medicinal materials to make liquor

more and more patients. It has also attracted the attention of peers at home and abroad. Li Jialong has been invited to Hong Kong and Taiwan of China, even to Vietnam, Malaysia and other countries and regions to give lectures and exchange, bringing good news to local patients. Li's Curettage and Acupoint Relieving Therapy gives full play to the unique advantages of traditional Chinese medicine in "treating both symptoms and root causes". And it has made significant contributions to promoting the modernization of traditional Chinese medicine and promoting traditional Chinese medicine to the world.

誉，也引起了国内外同行的重视。李嘉龙曾受邀到我国台湾和香港地区，甚至是越南、马来西亚等国家和地区讲学与交流，给当地患者带去福音。李氏刮经解穴疗法充分发挥了中医“标本兼治”的独特优势，在推进中医药现代化、推动中医药走向世界方面作出了重要的贡献。

Main Inheritor

Li Jialong, male, born in November 1957 in Yangjiang, Guangdong Province, is the 5th-generation inheritor of Li's Curettage and Acupoint Relieving Therapy. Li Jialong has been practicing medicine for nearly 30 years and has summarized Li's Curettage and Acupoint Relieving Therapy with the leading theory of "unlocking the acupoints, dredging the meridians, promoting blood circulation, removing blood stasis, and nourishing life". He believed that "the blockage of meridians and acupoints is the root of many painful diseases, stasis of Qi and blood in the bones leads to bone pain, stagnation in the epidermis leads to dermatitis, and stagnation in the internal organs leads to multiple diseases". Therefore,he believes that the therapy is after overall judgment, combining manipulative reduction and fumigation therapy, using internal and external medication together, equal emphasis on meridians and acupoints, combining movement and stillness, functional exercise, unblocking acupoints and meridian blockages, to treat various difficults and miscellaneous diseases. Now he is the representative inheritor of the fifth batch of intangible cultural heritage projects in Yangjiang City.

主要传承人

李嘉龙，男，1957年11月生，广东阳江人，是李氏刮经解穴疗法第五代传人。李嘉龙从医至今近30载，总结出了以“解开穴道，疏通经络，活血散瘀，滋补身体，让身体焕发新生活力”为主体理论的李氏刮经解穴疗法。他认为，“经络不畅和穴道堵塞是形成众多痛症的根本，气血淤于骨则骨痛，滞于表皮则易于皮炎，郁于五脏六腑则百病丛生”，因而，他在理论上强调通过整体辨证、手法整复、蒸汽熏蒸、内外用药、经络与穴位并重、动静结合和功能锻炼来解开穴道、疏通经络淤堵，治疗各种疑难杂症。现为阳江市第五批非物质文化遗产项目代表性传承人。

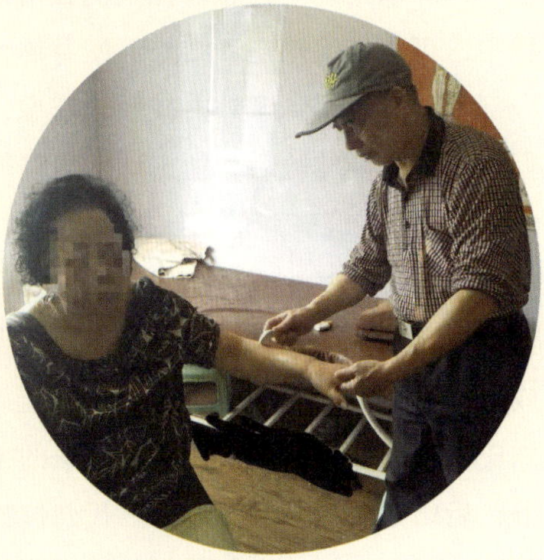

李嘉龙（右）
Li Jialong (right)

中炽药灸疗法

保护单位 阳春市中炽药灸保健有限公司

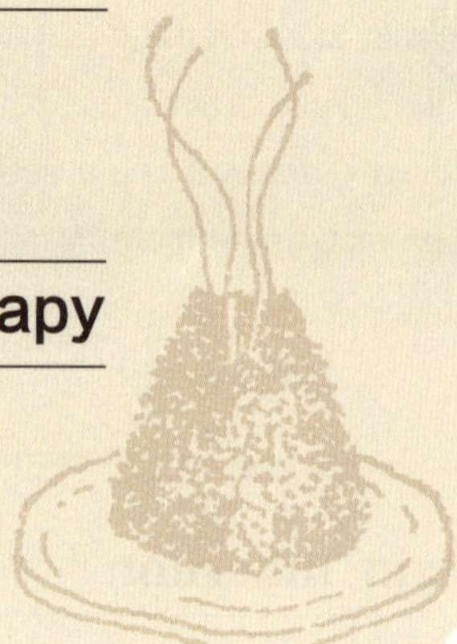

Traditional Chinese Medicine Moxibustion Therapy

Protection Unit Yangchun Zhongchi Medicinal Moxibustion Healthcare Co., Ltd.

中炽药灸疗法流传于广东省阳春市民间。阳春市位于广东省西南部，地处亚热带季风气候区，森林覆盖率66.37%，有650多种野生植物，具有深厚的传统医药文化背景，造就了阳春跌打药行业的兴旺，为中炽药灸疗法的传承提供了物质基础。

历史渊源

中炽药灸疗法是中医学中最古老的疗法之一。近代考古学研究证明，早在北京猿人时期，我们的祖先就已懂得用火来灸患处。《说文解字》将“灸”释为“灼也”，即以火烧灼之意。先人们在用火过程中，可能不慎灼伤，结果却使身体另外一部分的病痛得到意外的减轻或痊愈，他们经多次重复体验后，便主动地以烧灼之法来治疗一些病痛，逐渐产生了炽灸。

中炽药灸疗法项目在阳春地区民间的传承，可追溯到河口镇蝴蝶坡村刘氏家族，有300余年的历史。据刘氏家谱记载，刘氏四世祖刘应达是中炽药灸疗法的祖师爷，后传第二代刘世敬、第三代刘位锜、第四代刘淮、第五代刘英魁、第六代刘德

Traditional Chinese Medicine Moxibustion Therapy is popular among the people in Yangchun City, Guangdong Province. Yangchun City, located in the southwest of Guangdong Province, is in the subtropical monsoon climate zone. The forest coverage rate is 66.37%. There are more than 650 kinds of wild plants. With a profound traditional medical culture background, it has created the prosperity of the Yangchun traumatic injuries-curing industry and provided a material basis for the inheritance of Traditional Chinese Medicine Moxibustion Therapy.

Historical Origin

Traditional Chinese Medicine Moxibustion Therapy is one of the oldest therapies in the traditional Chinese medicine. According to modern archaeological research, our ancestors knew how to use fire as moxibustion to treat the affected area as early as the homoerectus pekinensis period. The Chinese character “zhi” was interpreted as “burning” in *Shuowen Jiezi*. In using fire, ancestors might accidentally be burned, but as a result, the pain of another part of the body was unexpectedly relieved or healed. After repeated experiences, they took the initiative to treat some pain with burning and gradually produced burning moxibustion.

The folk inheritance of the Traditional Chinese Medicine Moxibustion Therapy project in Yangchun can be traced back to the Liu family in Hudiepo Village, Hekou Town, with more than 300 years of history. According to the Liu family’s pedigree, Liu Yingda, the fourth ancestor of the Liu family, was the founder of the Traditional Chinese Medicine Moxibustion Therapy. Later, it was passed down to Liu Shijing (the second generation), Liu Weiqi (the third generation), Liu Huai (the fourth generation), Liu Yingkui (the fifth generation), Liu Dejian (the sixth generation), Liu Yuanyi (the seventh generation), and Liu Chunpu (the eighth generation). Since Liu Xinggao, the ninth generation, both family inheritance and apprenticeship inheritance have existed. It was passed down to the tenth generation, Liu Guangyi, Wei Chenji and Zhang Deguang. From Zhang Deguang, it was passed down to Huang Zhong, (the 11th generation) , and from Huang Zhong to the 12th generation, Huang Weiguo, Xu Yunyan, etc.. It has a long history and an evident pedigree of inheritance. The project has been continued to today due to the patients' affirmation and reputation of the therapeutic effect.

Basic Content

Traditional Chinese Medicine Moxibustion Therapy originated from fire moxibustion therapy in traditional Chinese medicine. The special hot moxibustion therapy introduced by Huang Zhong for many years by clinical exploration, not only makes use of the effect of the hot compress of the meridians of moxibustion, but also combines the application method of traditional Chinese medicine, with the secret medicinal liquor and powder with a unique prescription to treat the patient's spine. Treatment steps: First, evenly spread the medicinal powder on the bamboo pulp and straw paper, wet the powder with medicinal liquor, and apply it to the patient's pain points. Then, place the lighted folded bamboo pulp and straw paper strip above the pain points and burn it slowly. By controlling the amount of the heat, with the help of the operator's hands, let the medicinal liquor's power penetrate the body lesions quickly under the hot compress of the fire, open the Ren and Du veins, cure the patient's disease, and achieve a better effect of hot moxibustion.

After generations of inheritance and innovation, Traditional Chinese Medicine Moxibustion Therapy has gradually formed a more systematic and comprehensive diagnosis and treatment system and procedures with a wide range of treatments. This therapy has the characteristics of accurate symptomatic treatment, high efficacy, immediate effect, strong medicine, intense penetration, external treatment of internal diseases, environmentally friendly medical treatment, and high safety. The inheritance and innovation of Traditional Chinese Medicine Moxibustion Therapy play an essential role in protecting and promoting traditional Chinese medicine culture. It adds a new vitality, new treatments, and new ideas to modern fire moxibustion. It plays a vital role in reducing patients' pain, recovering the sick, and maintaining the health of Chinese people.

健、第七代刘元毅、第八代刘春蒲。自第九代刘杏高起，家族传承和师徒传承兼之，传第十代刘广邑、韦陈计、张德光，张德光传第十一代黄中，黄中传第十二代黄伟国、徐云燕等。其历史渊源久远，传承谱系明朗清晰。该项目凭借患者对该疗法疗效的肯定和口碑，一直延续至今。

基本内容

中炽药灸疗法起源于中国传统医学中的火灸疗法。传承人黄中经多年临床摸索而推出的特殊炽灸疗法，不仅运用了灸疗的经络热敷效应，又综合了中医的贴敷法，再加上秘制的药酒和独特配方的药粉，对患者脊椎进行施疗，具有很好的疗效。疗法步骤：先在竹浆草纸上均匀铺上药粉，淋上药酒浸湿药粉，贴敷在患者痛点上，然后点燃折叠好的竹浆草纸条，放在其疼痛的穴位上方慢慢燃烧，通过控制火的大小和温度的高低，借助施治者的手法让药酒的药力在火的热敷作用下快速渗入体内病灶，打通任督二脉，解决患者痛症，达到较好的炽灸疗效。

中炽药灸疗法经过世代的传承和创新，逐渐形成了较为系统全面、治疗范围较广的诊疗体系和规程。该疗法具有对症准、疗效高、见效快、药物浓、渗透力强、内病外治、绿色医疗、安全性高等特点，其传承和创新，为中华传统中医药文化的保护和弘扬起着承前启后的重要作用，为现代火灸学注入了新的活力、新的疗法和新的思路，为减轻患者的病痛和康复病体、维系国人健康起到了重要的作用。

竹浆草纸条
Bamboo pulp and straw paper

传承人黄中为患者施行药灸
Inheritor Huang Zhong conducts medicinal moxibustion for patients

主要特征

（1）对症准，见效快。中医讲究七经八脉三百六十五络，一经不通久为瘀，瘀久化热而成炎，瘀久不通会导致各关节囊肿、变形或强直。凡瘀血疼痛组织在人体深部的，在人体皮肤表面必然会有1～2个对应的疼痛点，用手指轻压或揉搓进行检查，就能马上找出患处的痛点。直接对痛点进行施灸，一灸即效，弥补了口服药品的药力慢、未能全部到达病灶的缺陷。

（2）药物浓，渗透力强。中炽药灸疗法的药物（药粉、药酒）浓度高于传统药物浓度，在炽灸的作用下迅速渗透进患者的病灶，加强炽灸的效果，帮助患者减轻痛苦。

（3）疗效好，无不良反应。中炽药灸疗法是纯中药无创外敷介入疗法，没有服用西药止痛药可能出现的恶心、便秘、多汗、成瘾，甚至消化性溃疡等副作用，让患者快捷、安全、有效地控制病情。药贴敷在患处治疗30分钟，在药物通过物理加热的作用下，渗透皮下组织间，扩张毛细血管，加速血液循环，使患处得到充分

Main Features

(1) Be accurate and effective. Traditional Chinese medicine focuses on the 365 collaterals of the seven meridians and eight veins. If a meridian has been blocked, then congestion will form. Once congestion has been accumulated for a long time, it will become inflammation, resulting in joint cyst deformation or stiffness. If the congestion tissue is deep inside the body, there will be one or two pain points on the surface of the skin. If you gently press with your finger or rub to check, you will immediately find the pain points in the affected area. Directly apply moxibustion to the pain points, and the effect will be immediate. It makes up for the disadvantage that the effect of the oral medicine is slow and the medicine fails to reach the focus.

(2) The drug is concentrated and has intense penetration. The concentration of drugs (medicinal powder and liquor) used in Traditional Chinese Medicine Moxibustion Therapy is higher than that of traditional medicine. Under the effect of the hot moxibustion, the drugs can quickly penetrate the patient's focus, increase the impact of the hot moxibustion, and help patients to reduce their pain.

(3) It has good therapeutic effect with no adverse reaction. It is a non-invasive external application of pure Chinese medicine intervention therapy which does not have side effects such as nausea, constipation, hyperhidrosis, addiction, or even peptic ulcer that may occur with Western painkillers. It gives patients a quick, safe, and effective treatment to control their condition. The medicine patch is applied to the affected area for 30 minutes, and under the effect of physical heating, the medicine penetrates the subcutaneous

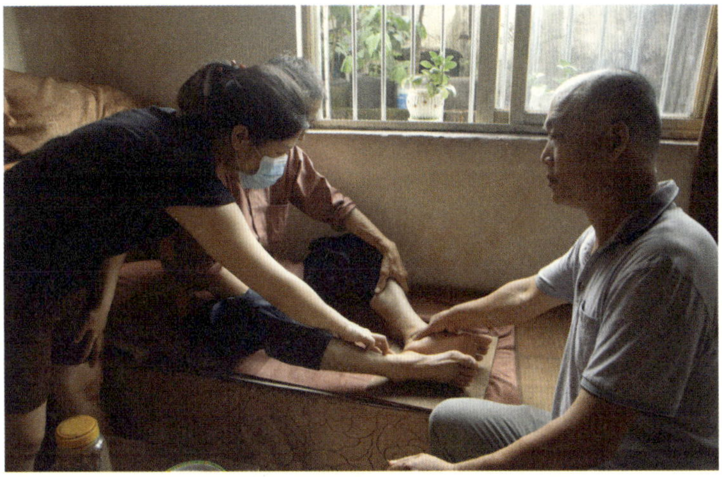

黄中为患者的脚伤作诊断
Huang Zhong is diagnosing the patient' s foot injury

tissues, expands capillaries, accelerates blood circulation, and fully treats the affected area. It can relax tendons, dredge collaterals, activate blood circulation, and remove wind-cold and pathogenic dampness. At the same time, drugs can stimulate acupoints, cause nerve reflexes, stimulate the self-regulation ability of the human body to warm channels and unblock collaterals, promote blood circulation and remove blood stasis, dissipate cold and dehumidify, boost metabolism, improve human immunity. It is safe and harmless with low treatment cost, a short course of treatment, and no pain for patients.

(4) Treat internal diseases with external therapy safely and reliably.

Great Value

Chinese traditional medicine has developed for thousands of years. As a vital treatment method of traditional Chinese medicine,

的治疗，起到舒筋通络、活血化瘀、祛除风寒湿邪的作用。同时药物可刺激腧穴，引起神经反射，激发人体的自我调节能力，从而达到温经通络、活血化瘀、散寒除湿、促进代谢的效果，提高了人体免疫力。该疗法安全无害，治疗费用低，疗程短，患者无任何痛苦。

（4）内病外治，质量可靠。

重要价值

中国传统医药学传承发展数千年，中炽药灸疗法作为中医的一个重要的治疗方法，具有多方面的重要价值和意义。

·社会价值

中炽药灸疗法在维系国人健康方面起到了重要的作用，能减轻患者的病痛，治愈疾病，造福更多的患者。

·医学价值

一方面，中炽药灸疗法为中医火灸学的发展提供了新的疗法和新的思路，为现代火灸学注入新的活力；另一方面，推广中炽药灸疗法，使之被更多的医师认识和应用，可以在一定程度上提高医生的临床疗效，从而帮助更多的患者从痛苦中解脱。

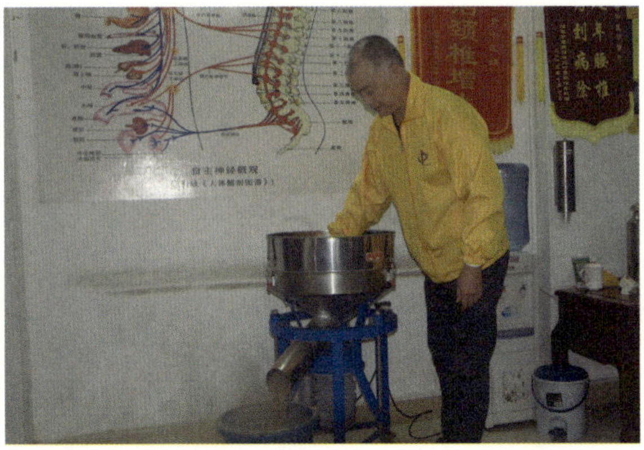

黄中正在制作药灸的药物
Huang Zhong is making medicine for medicinal moxibustion

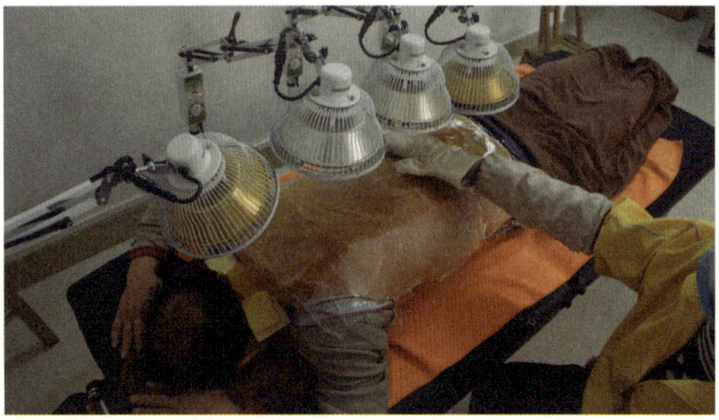

用照灯治疗仪进行物理加热
Heating physically by illuminator therapeutic apparatus

患者康复送锦旗感谢黄中
The patient sends a banner to thank Huang Zhong

·历史文化价值

中华文化源远流长，中医作为中华文化的一部分，一直都是世界文化的重要组成部分，中炽药灸疗法的传承和创新，对中华文化的保护和弘扬起着承前启后的作用。

Traditional Chinese Medicine Moxibustion Therapy has essential values and significance in many aspects.

· Social value

Traditional Chinese Medicine Moxibustion Therapy has played an essential role in maintaining the health of Chinese people, which can reduce the pain of patients, rehabilitate the disease, and benefit more patients.

· Medical value

On the one hand, Traditional Chinese Medicine Moxibustion Therapy provides new treatments and ideas for developing traditional Chinese fire moxibustion and adds new vitality to modern fire moxibustion. On the other hand, the promotion of Traditional Chinese Medicine Moxibustion Therapy makes it possible to be recognized and applied by more doctors, which can improve the clinical efficacy of doctors to a certain extent to help more patients relieve pain.

· Historical and cultural value

Chinese culture has a long history, and traditional Chinese medicine is always an important part of the cultural landscape of the world. The inheritance and innovation of Traditional Chinese Medicine Moxibustion Therapy play a connecting role in protecting and promoting Chinese culture.

主要传承人

黄中，男，生于1968年，广东阳春人。他是传统医药中炽药灸疗法项目第十一代传承人，1978年拜张德光为师，学习中炽药灸疗法。他继承传统，大胆创新，逐渐形成一套独特的中炽药灸疗法。为弘扬祖国医学遗产，他成立了阳春市中炽药灸保健有限公司，并任公司总经理。除父子传承外，还创建传承基地，广招贤徒。目前，黄中弟子开设的医馆或工作室有19间，遍布广东，治病救人，为人民服

Main Inheritors

Huang Zhong, male, was born in 1968 in Yangchun, Guangdong. He is the 11th-generation inheritor of the Traditional Chinese Medicine Moxibustion Therapy project. In 1978, he started to learn Traditional Chinese Medicine Moxibustion Therapy from Zhang Deguang. He inherited the tradition, innovated boldly, and gradually formed a unique Chinese medicine moxibustion therapy. To promote the medical heritage of the motherland, he founded Yangchun Zhongchi Medicinal Moxibustion Healthcare Co., Ltd. and as the company's general manager. In terms of inheritance, he not only passed it on to his son, but also recruited talented individuals. Currently, there are 19 medical halls or studios opened by Huang Zhong's apprentices, and they treat the sick, and serve the people all over the land of Guangdong. Huang Zhong personally led a team to go deep into Yangchun City and the birthplace of the project, looking for traces of ancestors, collecting physical objects, audio-visual materials, pictures and other relevant materials, and sorting out all relevant materials. The historical origin of the project is confirmed by collecting the cultural relics unearthed from Tomb No. 3 of Mawangdui Tombs in Hunan Province and the works of experts and scholars. At ordinary times, he actively participates in public welfare activities and goes to villages and towns to carry out free clinics for patients irregularly. With the assistance of his son Huang Weiguo, he collected and sorted out important medical theories of incandescent moxibustion therapy from ancient and modern medical masterpieces of Chinese (traditional Chinese medicine) and foreign (Western medicine) and foreign famous doctors' academic works through the Internet, so that future generations could better understand, learn and inherit, and promoted the inheritance and development of the project. Huang Zhong had a certain influence in Guangdong Province, and gradually expanded it at home and abroad. He made a lot of efforts to protect, inherit and promote Traditional Chinese Medicine Moxibustion Therapy. Now he is the representative inheritor of the fifth batch of intangible cultural heritage projects in Yangjiang City.

黄中
Huang Zhong

务。黄中曾亲自带队深入阳春民间和项目发源地，寻宗访祖，收集实物、音像、图片等相关资料并记录、整理建档，完善了项目的传承谱系；收集湖南省马王堆三号墓出土的文物资料和专家学者的论著，证实了项目的历史渊源。他平时积极参加社会公益活动，不定期到乡镇为患者义诊。在儿子黄伟国的协助下，他通过网络，从古今中（中医）外（西医）的医学巨著和外国名医学术论著中，收集整理中炽药灸疗法的重要医学理论，深入浅出地传给后人，促进项目的传承和发展。黄中在广东省内具有一定的影响力，并逐步往国内外扩展，为保护、传承和弘扬中炽药灸疗法默默耕耘、无私贡献。黄中现为阳江市第五批非物质文化遗产项目代表性传承人。

阳春市中炽药灸保健有限公司师徒合影
A photo of masters and apprentices of Yangchun Zhongchi Medicinal Moxibustion Healthcare Co., Ltd.

黄伟国
Huang Weiguo

黄伟国，男，1996年生于中炽药灸世家，第十二代传人（家族传承）。从小深受家庭药灸的熏陶，耳濡目染，爱上中炽药灸，能够秘制药粉和药酒，并能熟练地掌握疗法的临床使用，对患者辨证施疗。2015年9月考上江门市中医药学校学习中医学，在校期间，为感师恩，将家族传承的中炽药灸疗法在学校传承和推广，得到师长们的认可和好评，在校曾担任广东省优秀社团之一——针灸推拿社团的副社长。2018年6月毕业后回家乡与父亲并肩传承中炽药灸疗法，全心全意弘扬传统医药。在深圳圆运堂中医馆指导工作时，研发治疗仪，将热疗效应与传统的中炽药灸疗法相结合，反应效果良好，在实践中传承与推广。

他积极收集湖南省马王堆三号墓出土的文物资料和专家学者的论著，证实了项目的历史渊源，并协助父亲黄中深入阳春民间和项目发源地，寻宗访祖，收集实物、音像、图片等相关资料，记录整理建档，完善了项目的传承谱系，并于2019年向地方政府部门及市级非物质文化遗产保护中心申报，使项目于2020年12月被列入阳江市非物质文化遗产项目。黄伟国现为阳江市第五批非物质文化遗产项目代表性传承人。

Huang Weiguo, male, was born in 1996 in the traditional Chinese medicine moxibustion family (family inheritance) as the 12th-generation inheritor. He was deeply influenced by family medicinal moxibustion when he was young and was keen on traditional Chinese medicine moxibustion. He is able to make secret medicinal powder and liquor, master the clinical use of therapy skillfully, and treat patients by pointing their symptoms. In September 2015, he was admitted to Jiangmen City School of Traditional Chinese Medicine to study Chinese medicine. During his school years, he inherited and promoted Traditional Chinese Medicine Moxibustion Therapy inherited from his family in the school, which was recognized and praised by teachers. He once served as the vice president of the Acupuncture and Massage Community, one of the outstanding associations in Guangdong Province. After graduation in June 2018, he returned home to work together with his father, inherited Traditional Chinese Medicine Moxibustion Therapy, and wholeheartedly promoted the definitive medicine cause. When guiding the work in Shenzhen Yuanyuntang Chinese Medical Center, he combined the thermal effect of therapeutic device with the traditional Chinese medicine moxibustion therapy, which yielded good results and was passed down and promoted in practice.

He actively collected the cultural relics unearthed from Tomb No.3 of Mawangdui Tombs in Hunan Province and the works of experts and scholars to confirm to the historical origin of the project, and assisted his father in going deep into Yangchun City and the project's birthplace, searching for traces of ancestors, collecting relevant materials, such as physical objects, audio-visual materials and pictures, and recording, sorting and filing them. The inheritance pedigree of the project was improved, and it was reported to the local government departments and the municipal intangible cultural heritage protection center in 2019. In December 2020, it was Listed in the intangible cultural heritage project of Yangjiang City. Huang Weiguo is the representative inheritor of the fifth batch of intangible cultural heritage projects in Yangjiang City now.

第四部分

传统体育游艺与杂技

Part 4

Traditional Sports, Amusement and Acrobatics

洪拳（梁方伍系）

保护单位 阳春市武术协会

Hong Quan（Liang Fangwu Branch）

Protection Unit Yangchun Martial Arts Association

洪拳，又称作洪家拳，与刘家拳、蔡家拳、李家拳、莫家拳合称为广东省五大名拳。洪拳属于中国传统拳术中的南拳。清康熙十三年（1674）洪门创立，该组织以明太祖朱元璋年号“洪武”的“洪”字立门，故称洪门。反清人士创立洪门，推行和从事洪拳练习，以练习武艺为名，发展组织，实则宣传反清复明思想。洪拳不仅在我国广东、广西、湖南、湖北、香港、澳门、台湾等地流传甚广，在美国、加拿大以及东南亚国家也十分流行。中国民间有“只要有祠堂，就会有狮子、洪拳”之说。

Hung Quan is also known as Hongjia Quan. Hung Quan, Liujia Quan, Caijia Quan, Lijia Quan, and Mojia Quan are called the five famous Chinese boxings in Guangdong Province. Hong Quan is one of the southern boxings in traditional Chinese boxing. Hongmen was founded in the 13th year of the reign of Emperor Kangxi in the Qing Dynasty（1674）. The organization was named Hongmen because the character “Hong” intended to honor the first Ming Emperor, Zhu Yuanzhang. Anti-Qing rebels formed Hongmen, carried out and engaged in Hong Quan, in the name of practicing martial arts. Actually, they developed an organization to promote the idea of rebelling against the Qing and re-establishing the Ming. Hong Quan is famous in Guangdong, Guangxi, Hunan, Hubei, Hong Kong, Macao, Taiwan,and other places in China, and is also famous in the United States, Canada, and in Southeast Asian countries. The Chinese folk saying goes, “As long as there are ancestral temples, there will be lions and Hong Quan.”

历史渊源

洪拳是广东优秀的民间传统武术。在清末广州三元里抗英斗争和湛江市寸金桥抗法斗争中，均有洪拳弟子参与，使洪拳在阶级斗争和民族斗争中的影响力渗透到广东民间的每一个角落。

在广东洪拳的传承中出现了洪熙官、梁方伍等著名人物，他们为洪拳的发展作出了极大的贡献，使洪拳流行于世界各

Historical Origin

Hong Quan is an excellent traditional folk martial art in Guang Dong. Hong Quan's apprentices participated in the anti-British war in Sanyuanli, Guangzhou, and the anti-French war at Cunjin Bridge in Zhanjiang at the end of the Qing Dynasty, making Hong Quan's influence in class and national struggles almost in every corner of Guangdong's folk.

Famous figures, such as Hong Xiguan and Liang Fangwu, have emerged in the heritage of Guangdong Hong Quan. They have contributed significantly to the development of Hong Quan, making it prevalent all over the world. Today, there are not only many Hong Quan practitioners in China but also in the United States, Canada, and in Southeast Asian countries. Hong Quan has become one of the world's most influential martial arts. Based on carrying on the basic techniques of Hong Quan, Liang Fangwu has continuously explored and improved the Hong Quan system and has gradually formed Hong Quan (Liang Fangwu Branch) system.

Liang Fangwu (1877–1972) was born in Tangxiu Village, Shuiwen Town, Cenxi City, Guangxi Zhuang Autonomous Region, in the third year of the reign of Emperor Guangxu in the Qing Dynasty (1877) . His hometown was in Luoding, Guangdong Province. Initially, he learned martial arts at the age of 7, and at the age of 14, he learned Caijia Quan and lion dance with an instructor in Xinyi. At the age of 15, he began to display his talent. After growing up, he visited great masters everywhere to polish his skills and explore his potential from them.

Hong Quan is originated from Hong Xiguan, and Hong Quan (Liang Fangwu Branch) can be traced back to Liang Shaozhuang, the master of Hong Quan in Beiliu County. Had been trained by Liang Shaozhuang for three years, Liang Fangwu was so gifted and brilliant that he integrated the essence of Liujia Quan, Caijia Quan, Lijia Quan, and Mojia Quan and created several sets of Kung Fu styles, such as Eighteen Arhats, and martial arts sets with various weapons, such as the Flying Dragon Stick and Double Knives. In 1927, Liang Fangwu represented Guangdong and Guangxi to participate in the national martial arts tournament where he won the third prize at the age of 50. In such a case, he brought such a huge glory to the people of Guangdong and Guangxi that he attained great fame for his painstaking efforts.The National Government, the Central National Martial Arts Center, and the Central Military Commission of the Republic of China, jointly awarded him a plaque entitled "Wo Wu Wei Yang", which is still preserved at the Sanda Ancestral Temple in Luoding.

In 1933, the folks of Luoding asked Liang Fangwu to return to his hometown to teach martial arts. He readily accepted with the determination to encourage more villagers to practice martial arts and defend the country. During his three years in Luoding, he set up martial arts schools and taught nearly 10,000 apprentices to learn martial arts in Sulong, Tanbu, Henggang, Tanbin, Weidi, Luoping, Taiping, Luojing, Fenjie, Chuanbu and Shaliang in Luoding, Sihe and Zhaigang in Xinyi, and Songbai in Yangchun, etc.. Yan Bingtong was Liang Fangwu's chief apprentice in Songbai, Yangchun. After that, Wu Shengfa became the chief apprentice of Yan Bingtong, who

地。如今，不仅在国内有众多的洪拳练习者，在美国、加拿大以及东南亚等国也有许多人练习洪拳。洪拳已成为国际上最有影响力的武术拳种之一。而梁方伍在传承洪拳基本拳术的基础上，不断开拓创新，完善洪拳体系，并逐渐形成了洪拳（梁方伍系）体系。

梁方伍
Liang Fangwu

梁方伍（1877—1972），清光绪三年（1877年）出生于广西岑溪市水汶镇棠秀村，祖籍广东罗定。他7岁习武，14岁跟随信宜一名教头学习蔡家拳、舞狮，15岁已初露锋芒，长大后云游四海、拜师学艺。

洪拳项目以洪熙官为源头，洪拳（梁方伍系）则可追溯到北流县洪家拳师傅梁少庄。梁方伍拜师梁少庄学习洪拳三年后，经过刻苦磨炼，天资聪颖的他融合了刘家拳、蔡家拳、李家拳、莫家拳的精华，独创十八罗汉等若干套路拳法，以及飞龙棍、双刀等多种兵器的武术套路。1927年，梁方伍代表广东、广西参加全国武术擂台赛，以50岁高龄勇夺第三名，为两广人民争光，一时名声大振。当时的国民政府、中央国术馆、中央军事委员会联合授予他“我武维扬”牌匾。该牌匾至今仍保存在罗定市三达祠。

1933年，罗定的父老乡亲请梁方伍

回故乡设帐授徒，他爽快地答应了，决心让更多的乡人习武健身，保家卫国。他在罗定3年间，先后在罗定的素龙、榃卜、横岗、榃滨、围底、罗平、太平、罗镜、分界、船步、沙两，以及信宜的思贺、寨岗，阳春的松柏等地开武馆教授武术，教过的徒弟有近万人。严炳通就是梁方伍在阳春松柏的首席弟子，之后吴生发又成为严炳通的首席弟子，吴生发又传授给弟子徐耀卓、张少威、林良可、林德戈、李传荣等。经过一代传一代，至今仍有200多人在阳春松柏武馆学武习艺，洪拳（梁方伍系）也在阳春各地得以传播传承至今。

阳春市武术协会在阳春举办洪拳培训班
Yangchun Martial Arts Association held Hung Quan training class in Yangchun

passed on to his apprentices, such as Xu Yaozhuo, Zhang Shaowei, Lin Liangke, Lin Dege, Li Chuanrong, etc.. After passing from generation to generation, more than 200 people still study martial arts at Songbai Martial Arts Center in Yangchun. Hong Quan (Liang Fangwu Branch) has been spread throughout Yangchun.

基本内容

洪拳（梁方伍系）以刚劲为主，刚柔相济，以柔克刚，沉肩坠膊，气沉丹田。手法讲究直中留曲、曲中求直，有“拉弓手，三曲桥”之称。步法追求稳中求活，脚走三角步，善走偏门，避实就虚，顺劲顺势，借力打力。有“逆来顺打，顺来逆取，知黏知放，黏桥引化，离桥飞打”之说。身法讲究沉腰落胯，含胸拔背，子午变换。攻防技术讲究攻则拳脚并用，上

Basic Content

Hong Quan (Liang Fangwu Branch) is based on rigid strength, with characteristics of a combination of hardness with softness, softness overcoming rigidity, lowering shoulders and arms, and lowering Qi into Dantian. The skills of the hands are both direct and roundabout, which makes his hand look like a bow with an arrow and his arm look like a three-bend bridge. The skills of the feet contain a combination of stability and flexibility, with the pace forming a triangle, attacking where others will not notice, and making good use of the force of the opponent's strikes to strike back. It says, “Forces in

阳春学武习艺的人
People study martial arts in Yangchun

opposite directions can convert each other. Knowing how to choose entanglement and release when attacking. When the opponent is entangled with our hands, we should be promptly pulled away, and when the opponent is not entangled we should attack quickly." The skills of the body are to lower the waist and hips, to pull the chest in and stretching the back, and to use Zi and Wu skills interchangeably. When attacking and defending, one can use his fists and feet together to strike up and down at the same time, and use kicking, hitting, holding, and falling together to form a three-dimensional attacking and defending system. When defending, the Zi and Wu skills are used interchangeably, the inner and outer unify as a circle, rigidity and softness are not obvious, and soft defense is used to resist the attack.

The skills of Hong Quan (Liang Fangwu Branch) such as "small bridge", "tiger descending the mountain", "eight immortals crossing the sea", "dragon meeting with tiger", "boxing fight", and other routines are prevalent in Yangchun. The equipment skills include "flying dragon and tiger staff", "double-headed flower staff", "single sabre", "Luocheng's dismounted dun", "Guangong's machete", and "big rake", as well as the attack and defense skills of using machetes, guns, and sticks.

Main Features

Main features of Hong Quan (Liang Fangwu Branch) are as follows:

(1) The hands skill is about the inner and outer unity as a circle, Yin and Yang change into each other.

(2) The body skill is particular about the Zi and Wu skills. One shoulder is Zi, two shoulders are Wu, Zi means defense, and Wu means attack. Zi and Wu are corresponding, with both up and down, and attack and defense.

(3) The gait should not be T-step or with toes pointing outwards. Both feet should be constantly changed, and the body moves and changes in a triangle. The gait is flexible and changeable with stability.

(4) The attack techniques lay emphasis on approaching the opponent from the side with fast and continual attack, and the defense should be combined with the Wu skill, circling hands inside-out skill and moving arms from side to side skill. Beginners learn from simple to complex, from slow to fast then to faster, and then from faster to a state of no selfhood. The skills of the feet are divided into illusory and actual (meaning that the weight of body is placed on one

下相随，踢、打、拿、摔相互兼容，立体兼施；防则子午化身，内外圈圆，劲力不显，阴柔不露，以柔克刚。

洪拳（梁方伍系）的拳术，在阳春区域较为流行的有“小连桥”“猛虎下山”“八仙过海”“龙虎相会”“拳术对打”等套路；器械套路有“飞龙虎棍”“双头花棍”“单刀”“罗成下马枪”“关公大刀”“大钯”以及刀、枪、棍攻防对打等套路技法。

主要特征

洪拳（梁方伍系）的主要特征有如下五点：

（1）手法讲究内外圈圆、阴阳变化。

（2）身法讲究子午身法，单肩为午，双肩为子，子为防，午为攻。子午相应，上下相随，攻防兼备。

（3）步法讲究不丁不八，善走三角马，步法灵活多变，稳中求活。

（4）技击上讲究侧身逼近连环快打，防则以午身法结合内外圈圆、左右挪移桥法而化之。初学者由浅入深，由慢渐快，由快而紧凑至达神明。步法分清虚实，手法明确攻防。达高度熟练之境，浮沉吞吐，内外圈圆，随心所欲，任君施为。

（5）策略上讲究以进为退，以静制动，子午相应，阴阳变化，手、眼、身、法、步、精、神、气、力、功高度协调。拳理说:“心静眼法清,手法快捷步法灵,进退有序左右变,子午沉浮定输赢。”在实践中要重视方位和时机,克敌制胜必先明敌情。拳诀曰:“强敌要巧取,硬碰必难胜;力点勿相碰,避开最高见;四两拨千斤,桥手要看定;桥离知远近,心中算定先;对敌谁得手,近者定占胜;趋避讲眼快,左右见机行;进后避中取,退则虚处生;迈步急似风,变化若游龙;乘势侧峰入,失机宜退缩;撑实即需吐,发声吼惊怪;变化如游龙,快慢见胜败。”练拳须持之以恒,则自然能熟以生巧,千拳一度,万法归宗。

洪拳(梁方伍系)重在精气神,不仅平时练习十分讲究,在实战中更要通过精气神和技术配合运用发挥。同时,也注重人体养生。练拳时,举手投足,动静快慢,呼吸吐纳,心旷神怡,力长千斤,延年益寿。

foot), and the skills of the hands are divided into attack and defense. If one's skills are in a very skillful state, he will switch freely between attack and defense, unifying inside and outside, doing whatever he wants.

(5) The strategy has the following characteristics: Attacking as a means of defense, using a state of immobility to resist dynamic attacks, combining Zi and Wu skills together, and converting *Yin* and *Yang* to each other. Hands, eyes, body, methods, steps, essence, spirit, Qi, force and skills are highly coordinated. Boxing theory says: "The mind is calm, the eyes are clear, the skills are quick, the gaits are flexible, the advance and retreat are orderly and the left and right can be changed, and the skills of Zi and Wu and the means of attack and defense determine victory and defeat". In fighting, one should pay attention to the orientation and timing, and get well know of the combat situation in order to defeat the enemy. The boxing recipe says: "One can take down a strong enemy by using ingenious ways, or he'll be defeated by fighting in a tough way. Do not directly resist the strength of the opponent's attack, and avoid the opponent's strongest moves. Take off the opponent's strong attacks with minimal effort, and focus on the opponent's movements during the forearm entanglement. Use the front arm to measure the distance, and mentally plan your attack in advance.The winner in a battle is the one whose attacking hand is closer to the opponent's body. Move forward or backward quickly, and move left or right with timing. Avoid attacking the front of the opponent when attacking, and retreat away from the opponent when defending. Step as fast as a gust of wind, and change as precise and powerful as a Chinese dragon. Flank

阳春市武术协会举办武术汇演
Yangchun Martial Arts Association held a martial arts performance

attack when on the upper hand during combat, retreat when at a disadvantage in battle. Exhale when the Qi of Dantian accumulated full, accompanied by a roar which can deter the enemy. Movement changes like a Chinese dragon, and speed determines victory or defeat." The practice of boxing must be persistent so that to make it perfect. After a long time of practicing, all skills can be in one theory.

In Hong Quan (Liang Fangwu Branch) , the essence, vigour and spirit are valued, not only in normal practice, but also in actual combat through the combination of the essence, vigour and spirit and skills. At the same time, it also focuses on one's health. When practicing Hong Quan, one can switch between fast and slow, breathe and exhale, have a relaxed mood, grow a thousand pounds of strength, and prolong his life.

Great Value

· Historical and cultural value

Hong Quan (Liang Fangwu Branch), has a deep foundation, a clear historical origin, an evident inheritance pedigree, and numerous exchange activities. Liang Fangwu Branch is brave to innovate, discards the opinions of different branches, and integrates the strengths of various branches. On the premise of keeping the original characteristics of traditional Hong Quan, Liang Fangwu Branch has been developed to a new boxing branch with the characteristics of itself, which is unique and representative. This branch has profound historical and cultural value for the development, promotion, and revitalization of Hong Quan martial arts culture, as well as high academic research value.

· Fitness and defense value

The movement of Hong Quan (Liang Fangwu Branch) is unfolded and generous, simple and unadorned, with a rigid structure, combining hardness with softness and cultivating both inside and outside, practicing Qi of Dantian internally and exercising muscles, bones, and skins externally. The skills of Hong Quan stress more on kicking far, holding closely, and throwing close to the body, with both offensive and defensive capabilities, and has dual value of actual combat and physical fitness.

· Social and educational value

The inheritors of Hong Quan (Liang Fangwu Branch) actively responded to the government's call, adhered to the original intention of "digging, sorting, rescuing, protecting and inheriting" , and cooperated with the "Six Entries" project of Chinese martial arts. Besides, they have promoted and popularized Hong Quan from schools and communities to make Hong Quan spread and

重要价值

· 历史文化价值

洪拳（梁方伍系）底蕴深厚，历史源流明朗，传承谱系清晰，交流活动盛多。梁方伍系勇于创新，摒弃门户之见，融合各门派所长，在不失传统洪拳原有特点的前提下，发展出具有梁方伍系特色的新拳种流派，独具代表性。该流派对洪拳武术文化的发展、弘扬和振兴具有深远的历史和文化价值，也具有很高的学术研究价值。

· 健身防卫价值

洪拳（梁方伍系）动作舒展大方，朴实无华，结构严谨，刚柔相济，内外兼修，既有外家拳的硬，又有内家拳的柔。内练丹田气，外练筋骨皮。技术讲究远踢、近拿、贴身摔，攻防兼备，具有实战和强身健体双重价值。

· 社会、教育价值

洪拳（梁方伍系）传承人积极响应政府号召，秉承“挖掘、整理、抢救、保护、传承”的初心，配合中国武术“六进”工程，从学校、社区开始推广普及，传播、传承，让各个年龄段的人群参与武术活动，了解武术文化，擦亮这面传统文化的品牌匾。对培育中华民族精神、践行社会主义核心价值观、加强精神文明建设、树立健康生活方式新理念、丰富群众文体生活、提高人民身体素质和培养青少年品德意志等方面都起到了巨大的促进作用。

inherited, letting people of all ages participate in martial arts activities, understand martial arts culture, and revive the traditional culture. These activities play a huge role in promoting the cultivation of Chinese national spirit, implementing of core socialist values, strengthening the construction of spiritual civilization, establishing a new concept of a healthy lifestyle, enriching the cultural and sports life of the masses, improving the physical quality of the people and training young people to be better.

阳江青少年参加澳门国际武术套路赛
Yangjiang teenagers took part in Macau International Taolu Competition

主要传承人

吴生发，男，1970年出生于阳春市松柏镇，严炳通首席传承弟子。中国武术四段，阳春市武术协会会长。2010年拜严炳通为师练习梁方伍系洪拳，2016年成立阳春市武术协会并担任会长。2016年参加广东省传统武术锦标赛，获南派拳术套路一等奖；2016年参加澳门国际武林群英会武术比赛，获二等奖；2016年获国家二级社会体育指导员证书和国家二级武术、健身气功裁判员证书；2019年获国家武术职业技能证书。2019年带队参加阳春市粤西地区传统武术（套路）邀请赛，为推动洪拳（梁方伍系）以及其他传统派别武术文化事业发展作出了重要贡献。现为阳江市第五批非物质文化遗产项目代表性传承人。

吴生发
Wu Shengfa

Main Inheritors

Wu Shengfa, male, was born in Songbai Town, Yangchun City in 1970. He is the chief apprentice of Yan Bingtong, and the fourth-stage player of Chinese martial arts. He is the president of the Yangchun Martial Arts Association. In 2010, he took Yan Bingtong as his master to practice Hong Quan (Liang Fang Wu branch) , and in 2016, Yangchun Martial Arts Association was established, and he served as the president. In 2016, he participated in the Guangdong Traditional Martial Arts Championship and won the first prize in the Southern School boxing routine. In 2016, he participated in the Macau International Martial Arts Masters Challenge and won the second prize. In 2016, he acquired the certificate of national secondary social sports instructor and the certificate of national secondary martial arts and fitness Qigong referee. In 2019, he won the national martial arts vocational skill certificate. In 2019, he led the team to participate in Traditional Martial Arts (Routine) Invitational Competition of Western Guangdong in Yangchun. He has made essential contributions to the development of Hong Quan (Liang Fangwu Branch) and other traditional martial arts cultural undertakings. Now he is the representative inheritor of the fifth batch of intangible cultural heritage projects in Yangjiang.

Yan Bingtong, male, was born in 1953 in Songbai Town, Yangchun. He is the chief apprentice of Liang Fangwu. He is now the honorary president and general consultant of the Yangchun Martial Arts Association. In 1967, he started to learn martial arts from Liang Fangwu and mastered the skills of Liang Fangwu Branch. So far, more than 1,000 apprentices have been recruited, and the apprentices are all over Songbai, Yangchun, Enping, Xinxing, and other places. In 1980 and 1981, he participated in the Zhanjiang Martial Arts Observation Competition for two times, in which he both won the second prize. In July 2010, he actively responded to the call of the Songbai Town Party Committee and Government and made significant contributions to the project of building a hometown of martial arts culture in Songbai Town of Yangchun (reported on November 22nd, 2010 by *Yangjiang Daily*) . He made significant contributions to the development of Hong Quan (Liang Fangwu Branch) in Yangchun. Now he is the representative inheritor of the fifth batch of intangible cultural heritage projects in Yangjiang.

严炳通
Yan Bingtong

严炳通，男，1953年出生于阳春市松柏镇，梁方伍首席弟子，现任阳春市武术协会名誉会长兼武术总顾问。于1967年拜梁方伍为师习武，精通梁方伍系拳法。至今共招收徒弟逾千人，门徒遍布松柏、阳春、恩平、新兴等地。1980—1981年，他连续两次参加湛江地区武术观摩比赛，均获二等奖。2010年7月，他积极响应松柏镇委镇政府号召，为打造阳春松柏镇“武术文化之乡”项目立下汗马功劳（2010年11月22日《阳江日报》做过专题报道）。严炳通为阳春市洪拳（梁方伍系）事业发展作出了重要的贡献。现为阳江市第五批非物质文化遗产项目代表性传承人。

潭塘（杨氏）武术

保护单位 阳江市江城区中洲街潭塘村民委员会

Tantang (Yang's) Martial Art

Protection Unit Tangtang Village Committee, Zhongzhou Street, Jiangcheng District, Yangjiang

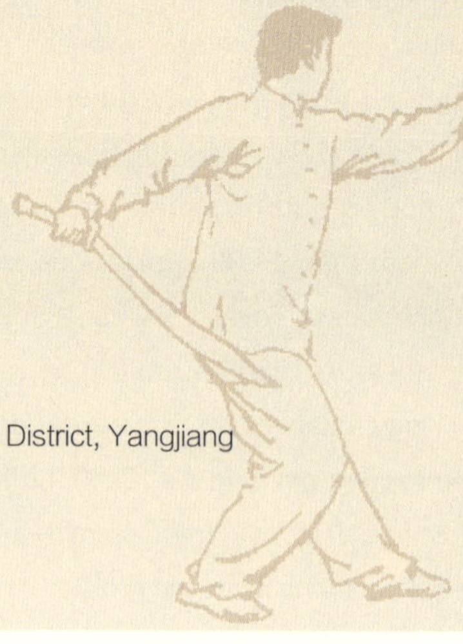

潭塘（杨氏）武术，源于清乾隆末到嘉庆初，雏形是一种体育锻炼形式的简单套路动作，后来经岭南洪拳武术派改良，逐步形成一种规范性章法拳种。在不断革新改进后，潭塘（杨氏）武术初步雏形。从清道光至20世纪90年代的170余年间，经过几代人承前启后的发展，潭塘（杨氏）武术有了一个风靡岭南的武术团队。团队成员有武术精英杨聘三、杨兰芳、杨实夫等人。杨实夫的“鬼脚”有着“岭南两脚称雄”的美誉。“鬼脚”（实名“底脚”）是洪拳中拳谱动作之一，在武林中享有盛名，在福建、广东、广西、香港、澳门等地流传甚广。杨实夫的底脚快、狠，机灵莫测，速度已超出了人心目，快如闪电，神鬼莫测，使人有恐惧的幽感，故杨实夫的绝活得“鬼脚”之美誉，比喻为如鬼的脚打人之意。

历史渊源

根据杨实夫嫡系弟子杨文锦（106岁）口述，潭塘（杨氏）武术起源于清乾隆末到嘉庆初。由于当时政局不稳，时局动荡，时常都会发生兵灾贼劫，村民苦不堪

Tantang (Yang's) Martial Art originated from the end of the Qianlong period to the Jiaqing period in the Qing Dynasty. Its embryonic form was a simple routine movement of a form of physical exercise. Later, it was improved by the Lingnan Hong Quan Martial Arts School and gradually formed a standardized boxing style. After continuously updating and improving, Tantang's (Yang's) Martial Art took initial shape. During the 170 years from the reign of Emperor Daoguang in the Qing Dynasty to the 1990s, Tantang (Yang's) Martial Art has become a famous martial art through the development of several generations in Lingnan area. The team members include the martial art elite Yang Pinsan, Yang Lanfang, Yang Shifu, and others. Yang Shifu's "ghost feet" have the reputation of "being the champion of Lingnan". Ghost feet (the natural name is "low feet") is one of the boxing moves in Hong Quan . It is famous in the Wulin and is widely spread in Fujian, Guangdong, Guangxi, Hong Kong, and Macao etc.. Yang Shifu's bottom kick is quick, hard, and very smart. His speed was beyond people's minds. He was as fast as lightning, and made people feel scared, and was also beyond ghosts' minds, so Yang Shifu's unique skill was known as "ghost feet", which is a metaphor that he attacked the opponent with feet like the ghost' s, fast and invisible.

Historical Origin

According to the dictation of Yang Wenjin (106 years old), a direct apprentice of Yang Shifu,Tantang (Yang's) Martial Art originated in the late of Qianlong and the early of Jiaqing period of the Qing Dynasty. Due to the unstable political situation and turmoil at that time, there were often wars and robberies, causing unbearable suffering for the villagers. The village was crowded and scattered, without any protective equipment and conditions to hide, so the only way to survive was for the men to be strong and to defend themselves by force. Therefore, young men like Yang Beihu, Yang Heng, and Yang Si learned martial arts outside. At that time, an apprentice of Hong Xiguan, the "One-legged Toad" (the nickname of a monk) of Xishan Temple in Fujian Province, taught Yang Si the skills of Hong Quan. Later, Yang Shifu, Yang Beihu and so on were taught by Yang Si about the skills of Hong Quan. After hard practice, they abandoned the bad and preserved the good, and compiled the eleven parts of the Yang family, giving the Yang's martial arts a literary basis, especially the "ghost feet", which was famous and taught in Yangjiang, especially in the villages, towns, and clans of the Yang family. As "ghost feet" became a sensation, no one could compete. It set off an upsurge of martial arts practice among various clans. Because of its vast popularity, continuous passing from generation to generation, and inheritance, Yang's martial arts are the origin of martial arts in Yangjiang. There are seven generations in inheritance in Tantang, and the Yang family clan has more than ten townships still in transmission today.

Later, Yang Si went to the Yangjiang Huahao Society to teach martial arts. He became sworn brothers with Yang Shifu who was from Tantang Village, Zhongzhou Street, Jiangcheng District, Yangjiang. They were as thick as thieves. Yang Si taught Yang Shifu all the skills of Hong Quan he knew. Then Yang Shifu practiced hard, perfected his skills constantly, and succeeded in martial arts. Excelled in Hong

言。村场人多族大且分布零散，没有任何防护设备及躲藏条件，无奈之下只有男儿当自强，以武力自卫抵抗才有生存出路。因此就有青壮之士杨北湖、杨亨、杨四等在外习武。当时福建西山寺洪熙官徒弟"独脚蟾蜍"（和尚化名）传授杨四洪拳之术，后杨实夫、杨北湖等授于杨四之下，经千锤百炼，去劣存优，编纂成杨家的十一路，使杨家武术功夫有文可循，其中尤以"鬼脚"而盛名，并传授于阳江地区，尤其在杨氏村镇族及各村氏族传授。由于"鬼脚"轰动一时，无人匹敌，掀起各氏族的习武热潮。阳江地区武术无不根裔于杨家武术，是因为其普及极广，且各地也不断传承，承袭至今。仅潭塘就有七代之多，杨家氏族有十多个乡镇如今仍在传承。

杨四后来至阳江华濠社授武，与阳江市江城区中洲街道潭塘村杨实夫结拜，拜其为师兄，亲密无间，如同手足，毫无保留地将洪拳之术传授于杨实夫。杨实夫再经苦练，精益求精，终成正果。杨实夫洪拳武术有成之后，脚、爪、拳打田埂，

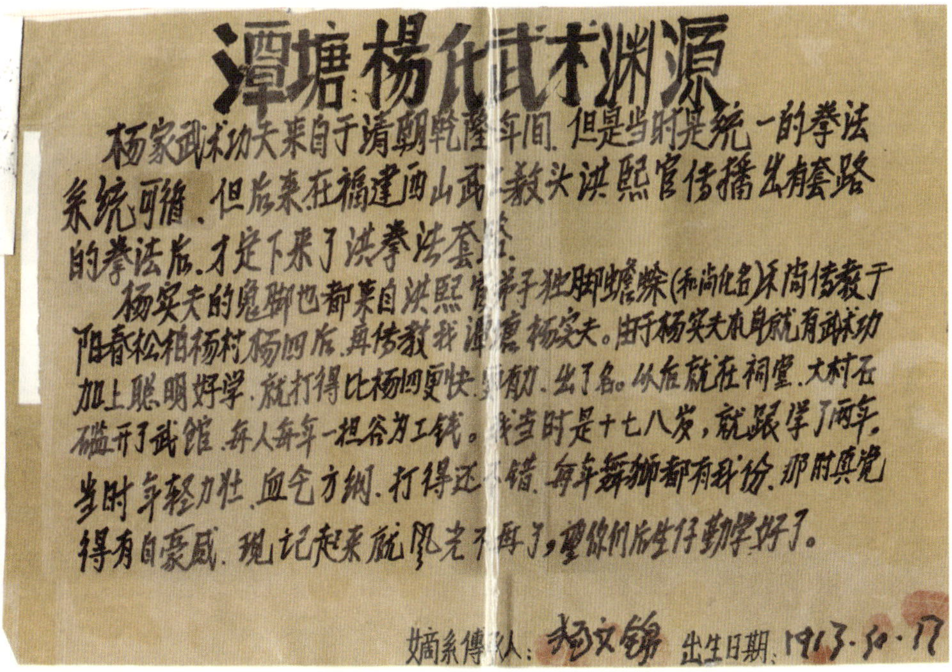
潭塘楊氏武术渊源
杨家武术功夫来自于清朝乾隆年间。但是当时无统一的拳法系统可循。但后来在福建西山武[illegible]教头洪熙官传播出有套路的拳法后，才定下来了洪拳法套路。
杨实夫的鬼脚也都来自洪熙官弟子独脚蟾蜍（和尚化名）和尚传教于阳春松柏杨村杨四后，再传教我潭塘杨实夫。由于杨实夫本身就有武术功加上聪明好学，就打得比杨四更快更有力，出了名。从后就在祠堂、大村石磕开了武馆，每人每年一担谷为工钱。我当时是十七八岁，就跟学了两年。当时年轻力壮，血气方刚，打得还不错，每年舞狮都有我份，那时真觉得有自豪感。现记起来就风光不再了，望你们后生仔勤学好了。
嫡系傳承人：杨文锦 出生日期：1913.10.17

潭塘（杨氏）武术传承人杨文锦关于杨氏武术渊源的口述文字稿
The origin of Yang's Martial Art dictated by Tantang (Yang's) Martial Art inheritor Yang Wenjin

名声卓著，各地武术爱好者纷至沓来，求教、拜访，与之切磋。此后杨实夫走马任教，台山、开平、恩平、电白、海康和阳春等地都留下其足迹，门下弟子不计其数。如其弟子陈成进本已有较高的武术基础，后拜杨实夫为师求学，更是锦上添花，学得其脚、爪、拳法，后成为广东军阀陈济棠麾下军官，军中亦有其“鬼脚”传闻。

中华人民共和国成立后，潭塘武术团队在杨高林、杨文锦、杨运森领衔下曾多次参加武术体育的表演、比赛活动，获湛江地区武术体育运动会第二名，获阳江武术体育运动会演第一名（均在1963年），1995年在广场灯光球声武术表演获优秀奖（不分名次）。潭塘武术团队经常参加节日庆典、助庆活动和醒狮武术活动，现有活动光碟保存。一直到20世纪80年代末，潭塘武术团队在杨高林、杨运森领衔下，一直保持传授徒弟的传统，其中也教授外村徒弟。

潭塘（杨氏）武术世代传承一直保持至今，传至七代之源从未中断，如今仍传承火热。

Quan's martial arts, Yang's fame grew for his feet, claws, and fists on the ridge. Martial arts enthusiasts worldwide came with the intention of consulting, venerating, and competing. Since then, Yang Shifu has been teaching in Taishan, Kaiping, Enping, Dianbai, Haikang, and Yangchun, His apprentices are immeasurable. For example his apprentice, Chen Chengjin had a good foundation in martial arts. After learning from Yang Shifu, his skills were even better. He learned Yang Shifu's feet, claws, and boxing skills. Later, he became an officer of Chen Jitang's army, a Guangdong warlord. There were also rumors of his "ghost feet" in the army.

After the foundation of the People's Republic of China, the Tantang (Yang's) Martial Art Team, led by Yang Gaolin, Yang Wenjin, and Yang Yunsen, participated in many martial arts performances and competitions. They won the second place in Zhanjiang Martial Arts Meeting and the first place in Yangjiang Martial Arts Meeting (both in 1963). In 1995, they won the excellence award (regardless of rank) in the Square Light Ball Sound Martial Arts Performance. They often participate in festival celebrations, festive activities, and lion dance, Which were recorded in CDs. Until the late 1980s, the Tantang (Yang's) Martial Art Team, led by Yang Gaolin and Yang Yunsen, kept passing on apprentices, and also teaching apprentices from the outside of village.

Tantang (Yang's) Martial Art has been passed down from generation to generation, and the source of the seven generations has never been interrupted. Now, the Tantang (Yang's) Martial Art spirit is still moving on.

潭塘村杨氏宗祠
Yang's Ancestral Hall in Tantang Village

Basic Content

Tantang (Yang's) Martial Art boxing skill is divided into 11 parts, each of which is a complete set of performances. The performance is very powerful, just like the meteor that breaks through the night sky, or the river water in the gorge, bravely and over-whelming. During the performance, the moves are clear, the footsteps are flexible, the feet and hands are coordinated, the change is unpredictable, and the attack and defense moves are incredible. Defense is often used as an offensive way, which means to step back in front of the pre-selected protection to prevent the foot from exerting too much force and the back from tilting — The protection can give a support. At the moment, the punching arm will increase the strength, the body will turn to the side 90 degrees, the thigh is raised flat at the hip, the foot will be stretched out like lightning to hit the opponent, the whole body will make the attack greatly strengthened, the force is stronger than the thunder, and the range of action looks small, like only a step forward. The moves are fast and numerous, making the opponent and the audience dazzled and distracted. After finding the right moment, one can attacks again with his feet, catching the opponent off guard. The boxing skill has the characteristics of stability, accuracy, ruthlessness, speediness, cleverness, bravery, secret, and wonder. Its main movements have different effects. For example, Yang Shifu's last ghost feet are fast and shadowless, and the lightning-like kick can knock the opponent out several meters away. He could punch through a field base with one fist, grab a *Cheng* filled with wine with one paw, drill holes in a mud brick wall with one finger, and overthrow an ordinary wall with one palm, etc., all of which are practical manifestations of Yang's martial arts. Yang Shifu has talent for martial arts, and no one has deciphered the last ghost kick.

基本内容

潭塘（杨氏）武术拳法共分十一路，各为一个完整表演套路，演练起来气势磅礴，如划破夜空的流星，又如峡壁中的江水，勇往直前，势不可挡。表演时，招法清晰，步法灵活，脚手协调，变化莫测，攻防、进退招式奇妙，往往是以退为进，即退至其预先选好的身后防护物前，以防止脚发力大而后身倾斜（防护物起到保护作用）。此时出拳的手会加大力度，身体转至侧90度，大腿抬平于臀部，后伸脚闪电般打向对方，全身发力使攻击力度大大加强，力比雷霆，且动作幅度看起来较小，像只向前推进了一步而已。快而多招使对方及旁观者眼花缭乱、心目不定，趁机闪电般出脚后作移码，使人难以识别。其拳法具有稳、准、狠、快、智、勇、隐、奇等特征，主要动作都有不同效果。如杨实夫之最后一“鬼脚”，快且无影无踪，闪电般一脚可将对方踢出数米远，一拳可打穿田基，一爪可抓起一个装满酒的埕，一指能在泥砖墙中钻出孔，一掌可推翻一普通墙体等，以上都是杨氏武术的实际体现。杨实夫拥有武术天赋，其被称为最后一“鬼脚”，无人破解。

潭塘（杨氏）武术中使用的兵器
Weapons used in Tantang (Yang's) Martial Art

重要价值

潭塘（杨氏）武术，是中国武术历史文化的一部分，是中国历史文化遗产，传承弘扬潭塘（杨氏）武术，就是弘扬我国优秀传统文化。如今潭塘（杨氏）武术的传承发展，也必然会促进和充实阳江及各地区的武术巩固、发展，为阳江武术的兴起推波助澜；同时，有助于引导人们积极参与体育锻炼，提高身体素质，推动社会和谐，促进民间武术爱好者的交流。

杨氏武术团队，不但推动了阳江地区的武术发展和推广，而且因为其在阳江及周边地区授徒，所以对阳江与周边的人文、交通、信息交流、物资互通往来的繁荣起到一定作用。杨氏武术的传播、传授、传承延续至今，并无中断，凝聚着和谐、互爱、融合、团结的精神，这是社会上最宝贵的追求，千金不换。

潭塘（杨氏）武术，经过社会实践证明具有重要意义，既可强身健体，亦有防御、修心的功能，又以高、难、精、美等形态特征为外延，是具有鲜明民族特色的传统性体育项目，可以强筋骨、健体魄、长精神、延寿命。

Great Value

Tantang (Yang's) Martial Art is a part of the Chinese martial arts history and culture, and it is Chinese historical and cultural heritages. To inherit and promote Tantang (Yang's) Martial Art is to promote excellent traditional culture of China. Today, the inheritance and development of Tantang (Yang's) Martial Art will certainly promote and enrich the consolidation and development of martial arts in Yangjiang and other regions, which will contribute to the rise of Yangjiang martial arts. At the same time, it will be conductive to guide people to actively participate in physical exercise, improve their physical fitness, promote social harmony, and promote the exchange of folk martial arts enthusiasts.

The Yang's Martial Art Team not only promoted the development and promotion of martial arts in Yangjiang area, but also played a role in the prosperity of the humanities, transportation, and information and material exchange between Yangjiang and its surrounding areas because it taught apprentices in Yangjiang and its surrounding areas. The transmission, teaching and inheritance of Yang's martial arts have continued to this day without interruption. The harmony, mutual love, integration and unity of the people who practice martial arts are the most valuable pursuit in the society.

Tantang (Yang's) Martial Art has proved its importance through social practice. It not only has functions of both strengthening the body, defending against enemies, and keeping a good state of mind, but also characteristics of being high, difficult, precise and beautiful. They are a traditional sport with distinctive national characteristics, which can enhance physical fitness, exercise the body, invigorate the spirit and prolong the life span.

练习潭塘（杨氏）武术的幼儿
Kids are practising Tantang (Yang's) Martial Art

练习潭塘（杨氏）武术的老者
An old man is practising Tantang (Yang's) Martial Art

Main Inheritor

Yang Kunning, male, born in January 1975, is a villager of Xiahe Village, Tantang Village Committee, Zhongzhou Street, Jiangcheng District, Yangjiang. He grew up in the Tantang Village Committee, where Tantang (Yang's) Martial Art was popular. He likes to practice martial arts since childhood. He began to learn Tantang (Yang's) Martial Art from martial art masters such as Yang Yuqing, Yang Yunsen and Yang Huadong in 1985. After years of apprenticeship and research, he has mastered the essence of Tantang (Yang's) Martial Art, and sorted out and preserved the complete boxing manual and other materials of Tantang (Yang's) Martial Art, and participated in Yangjiang Spring Festival Lion Dancing Martial Art Festival Performance for many times. At present, he mainly trains the new generation of inheritors of the Tantang (Yang's) Martial Arts project and devotes himself to teaching the traditional skills of Tantang (Yang's) Martial Art, so that Tantang (Yang's) Martial Art can continue to be inherited and carried forward.

Now he is the representative inheritor of the fifth batch of intangible cultural heritage projects in Yangjiang.

主要传承人

杨昆宁，男，1975年1月出生，阳江市江城区中洲潭塘村委会下禾一村人，其出生、成长及生活都是在潭塘（杨氏）武术盛行的潭塘村委会。他自幼喜欢习武，1985年开始师从杨裕清、杨运森、杨华东等武术师傅学习潭塘（杨氏）武术，经过多年的拜师学艺以及自己潜心研究，熟练掌握潭塘（杨氏）武术的精髓，整理并保存完整的潭塘（杨氏）武术拳谱等资料。他曾多次参加阳江市春节醒狮武术汇演，目前主要致力于培养新一代潭塘（杨氏）武术项目接班人，传授潭塘（杨氏）武术这一传统技艺，使潭塘（杨氏）武术继续传承及发扬光大。现为阳江市第五批非物质文化遗产项目代表性传承人。

潭塘（杨氏）武术协会成员合影

Group photo of Tantang (Yang' s) Martial Art Association

杨昆宁

Yang Kunning

阳江少林武术

保护单位 阳江市阳东区武术协会

Yangjiang Shaolin Martial Art

Protection Unit Yangdong District Martial Arts Association of Yangjiang

阳江少林武术以技击为主要内容，以拳术和器械的舞动为运动形式，是注重内外兼修的一种传统武术技击运动。其主要以武术培训机构、学校、社会团体和师父带徒传承，普遍流传在阳江地区。在阳东区、江城区、阳春市、高新区、滨海新区等各县区及乡镇都有分布，练习者有1000多人。

Yangjiang Shaolin Martial Art is a traditional martial art that focuses on both internal and external cultivation, with the skills of attack and defence as the main content and boxing and wielding apparatus as the form of movement. It is mainly inherited by martial art training institutions, schools, social groups and masters instructing apprentices, and is widely spread in Yangjiang area. There are more than 1,000 trainees in Yangdong District, Jiangcheng District, Yangchun City, High-tech Zone, Binhai New Area and other counties and towns.

历史渊源

少林武术起源于河南嵩山少林寺，始于南北朝，盛于隋、唐、宋、明、清等朝代，距今已有1500多年的历史。少林武术注重强身健体与自卫防身，内容丰富，风格独特，禅武合一，是我国著名的武术流派之一，是中华武术璀璨的明珠。

阳江少林武术（北派南传）源流长远，历史悠久。据年长者介绍，历史上中原人曾经五次大南迁，少林武术也因南迁传承到阳江地区。由于历代战争频繁，少林武术作为一种攻击和防卫的著名武术不断被练习传承。冼夫人（522—602年）和冯盎将军时期，由于诸侯不断争战，战

Historical Origin

Shaolin Martial Art originated from the Shaolin Temple in Songshan Mountain, Henan Province. It dated back to the Northern and Southern Dynasties and flourished in the Sui, Tang, Song, Ming and Qing Dynasties. with a history of more than 1,500 years. It focuses on physical fitness and self-defense with rich content and unique style. The combination of Zen and martial arts is one of the famous martial arts schools in China, and is a very important part of Chinese martial arts.

Yangjiang Shaolin Martial Art（spread from the north to the south of China）has a long history. According to the elders, people in the Central Plains migrated to the south five times in history, and Shaolin Martial Art moved to Yangjiang in the immigrations at that time. Due to the frequent wars in the past dynasties, Shaolin Martial Art, as a kind of famous martial arts of attack and defense, have been continuously practiced and inherited. During the period of Madam Xian（522-602）and General Feng Ang, there were many practicers of Shaolin

Martial Art because of the frequent wars among the vassals. During the Song and Yuan Dynasties, folk martial arts training activities with folk martial arts organizations as the main body rose and martial arts venues flourished, which promoted the development of Yangjiang Shaolin Martial Art. The Ming and Qing Dynasties was a period of great development of Mrtial Art. A dozen schools were set up based on Shaolin Martial Art. The famous martial arts champions include Tan Wei of Yashao Village, Zhong Jinguang of Tangliao Village, etc.. Legends emerged in an endless stream. Zhong Jinguang became famous for practicing martial arts and became a Juren of martial arts, and returned home in glory. After inheritance and improved development of many generations in Yangjiang and the fusion of southern martial arts skills, Yangjiang Shaolin Martial Art has gradually formed. From the end of the Qing Dynasty to the early Republic of China, due to the rampant banditry, practicing martial arts to protect the family became a trend. Martial arts schools were opened at most cities, villages and towns so that people could learn martial arts. Villages and landlords also organized young and strong people to practice martial arts to protect the village and the courtyard, so more than half of the villages have an experience of martial arts, and Shaolin Martial Art was also practiced and inherited by many people at this period. The representative figure at that time is Li Jilin (1910-1986). Later on, Li Zhan (born in 1947) from Liangdong Village learned from Li Jilin to practice Shaolin Martial Art, Yongchun Quan and other traditional martial arts, and finally became one of the famous boxers in Yangdong. In 1992, Tan Zhi'an learned Shaolin Martial Art and Yongchun Quan with Master Li Zhan. After his graduation, in order to learn and develop Yangjiang Shaolin

乱频繁，就出现了众多少林武术练习者。宋元时期，以民间武术组织为主体的民间练武活动兴起，习武场馆蓬勃发展，对阳江少林武术的发展起到了促进作用。明清时期是武术大发展时期，以少林武术创帮立派的有十几家之多。比较出名的武魁有雅韶村的谭谓、塘寮村的钟进光等，传奇人物层出不穷。钟进光因练武成名，高中武举人，衣锦荣归。少林武术在阳江地区经历代传承和改良发展，选取适合于南方人习练的技法，渐渐形成阳江少林武术。清末民初，由于匪患猖獗，练武保家成为一种风气，城、乡、村中大多开设武馆供民众学武，各村庄和地主也都组织青壮年民众习练武术以护村护院。过半数村庄都有习武的历史，少林武术也在此时被较多人练习传承。当时的代表性人物有李计林（1910—1986年）。后来良洞村的李展（1947年出生）师从李计林，习练少林武术、咏春拳等传统拳术，成为阳东区著名拳师之一。1992年谭志安跟随李展习练少林武术、咏春拳。出师后，为更深入学习并发展阳江少林武术，谭志安于1995年再拜师嵩山少林寺首座释永乾法师，成为少林寺第三十四代俗家弟子。艺成后，于2000年1月在家乡阳江创办少林学校，把阳江少林武术发扬光大；在阳江地区经过20多年的传承、沉淀和发展，培养学员近万人，具有一定的规模。现在阳江少林武术在弘扬武术文化、振奋民族精神、强身健体等方面发挥着重要作用，逐步成为现代体育的有机组成部分。

阳江少林武术击技
Function-attack of Yangjiang Shaolin Martial Art

基本内容

阳江少林武术是属于北派南传的武术，是在北派少林武术的基础上，根据南方人体形相对较瘦小、力气较弱、四肢较短等身形特点加以改良，形成的更加适合阳江人练习的一种武术。此武术特别注重远踢近打贴身摔，多出短拳，充分发挥"一寸短，一寸险"的优势，出拳以快取胜。在行拳时注重腰马合一，加强下盘的稳定性。例如少林拳谱中虎拳的身法、步法、腰法、截法等，又如少林单刀中的腰斩刀势、提撩刀势、定膝刀势等。

阳江少林武术通过师父授艺、日常套路练习和实战的方式来传承，主要形式有单练、对练和集体演练。阳江少林武术包括少林拳、长拳、罗汉拳、炮拳、连环拳、七星拳、地躺拳、梅花拳、醉拳、狗拳、蛇拳、虎拳、鹰拳，刀、枪、剑、棍、九节鞭、月牙铲、流星锤、朴刀、双钩、双锤、达摩杖、春秋大刀，少林童子功、少林绝命腿、连环十三腿、散打、拳击、擒拿、格斗及摔跤等。

Martial Art more deeply, in 1995, he became the 34th generation apprentice of the Shaolin Temple under the tutelage of Venerable Shi Yongqian, the head teacher of the Shaolin Temple in Songshan Mountain. After completing his studies, he founded the Shaolin School in his hometown of Yangjiang in January 2000, to carry forward the Yangjiang Shaolin Martial Art. After more than 20 years of inheritance and development in Yangjiang, the school has trained nearly 10,000 students, with a certain scale. Now Yangjiang Shaolin Martial Art plays an important role in promoting martial arts culture, invigorating the national spirit, promoting physical fitness, etc., and gradually becomes an important part of modern sports.

Basic Content

Yangjiang Shaolin Martial Art is a martial art spread from the north to the south, which is more suitable for Yangjiang people to practise, based on the Northern School of Shaolin Martial Art and improved according to the southern people's relatively thinner body shape, weaker strength, shorter limbs and other body characteristics. The martial arts pay special attention to kicking far, hitting close, wrestling close to the body, and more short punches, giving full play to the advantage of "getting an inch closer to the enemy to put him a bit more in danger" and winning with fast punches. Maintain balance in the waist and legs while punching to strengthen the stability of the lower body. For example, in the Shaolin fist manual, the body method, feet method, waist method and interception method of the tiger fist, and the waist chopping knife position, the lifting knife position and the fixed knee knife position in the Shaolin single knife.

Yangjiang Shaolin Martial Art is passed on through master's teaching, daily routine practice and practical combat, mainly including single practice, pair practice and group practice. Yangjiang Shaolin Martial Art includes these contents: Shaolin fist, long fist, Luohan fist, gun fist, revolving fist, seven-star fist, lying down fist, plum blossom fist, drunken fist, dog fist, snake fist, tiger fist, eagle fist; knife, gun, sword, stick, nine-knot whip, crescent shovel, meteor hammer, Podao, double hook, double hammer, Damo staff, spring-autumn machete; Shaolin virgin boy skill, Shaolin fetal leg-attack, thirteen roundhorse kicks, free combat, boxing, capture, fighting and wrestling.

阳江少林武术远踢近打贴身摔

Yangjiang Shaolin Martial Art pays special attention to kicking far, hitting close, and wrestling close to the body

Main Features

According to the southern climate of Yangjiang and the physical characteristics of Yangjiang people, Yangjiang Shaolin Martial Art went through generations of improvement, from the northern school which is unfolded and generous, powerful and vigorous into the Southern School with unique styles which is pay attention to softness, kicking far, hitting close and wrestling close to the body, and flexibility. Northerners are tall and powerful, easy to play pre-emptive attacks, interception techniques, and the upper three-leg techniques, known for the fierce seizure of momentum. Southerners are mostly thin, their boxing is to use softness to overcome hardness, to hit the opponent first but move slower than the opponent, to attack the opponent after defusing his attack, to combine wrestling and fighting, to mislead the opponent that the attack above is actually an attack on the lower place, to keep the moving legs is always below the knees, and to attack after the opponent's attack to break his balance, to hit a short distance but a very strong punch.

(1) Offensive and defensive skills. Yangjiang Shaolin Martial Art, as a means of offensive and defensive training, have obvious characteristics of offensive and defensive skills. In practice, the purpose is to hurt and limit the opponent who is often forced to lose resistance by using the most effective method of attack. The player attacks the target quickly, accurately and ruthlessly, giving full play to the advantage of "getting an inch closer to the enemy to put him a bit more in danger".

(2) The integration of Zen and martial arts. Shaolin Martial Art is taught mainly through the pithy formula, combining with the traditional patriarchal system of Shaolin Temple, integrating Buddhist thoughts into Shaolin Martial Art through the master's words and deeds and the diligent study and hard practice of apprentices. Zen and martial arts are integrated, which makes it less murderous and more defensive.

(3) Unity of internal and external, and combination of form and spirit. Yangjiang Shaolin Martial Art stresses both internal and external cultivation, both physical norms and spiritual transmission. "Practice essence, vigour and spirit inside, and muscles and bones outside." The so-called "internal" refers to the movement of mind, spirit and mind. The so-called "external" refers to physical activities such as the movement of hands, eyes, body and steps. The internal and the external, the form and the spirit are interconnected, which are reflected by the skills.

(4) Characteristics of routine sports. Routine sports are the manifestation of Yangjiang Shaolin Martial Art. A set of movements

阳江少林武术剑术
Art of fencing of Yangjiang Shaolin Martial Art

主要特征

阳江少林武术根据阳江的南方气候环境及阳江人的身体特征，对北派的舒展大方、刚劲有力进行改良，形成南火反柔、远踢近打贴身摔、招法灵活的南派独特风格。北方人高大，力气大，易于抢先攻击，截击技，上三路腿法，以刚猛夺势著称。南方人多体态瘦小，发展的拳术以柔克刚，后发先至，先化再打，跌打结合，上惊下取，腿不过膝，以趁人力后、破坏平衡和发短拳寸劲为主。

（1）攻防技击性。阳江少林武术作为进攻和防卫训练手段，其攻防技击的特性是显而易见的。在实战中，其目的在于杀伤、制限对方，常常以最有效的技击方法迫使对方失去反抗能力。攻击目标快、准、狠，充分发挥“一寸短，一寸险”的优势。

（2）禅武合一。阳江少林武术的传习方式主要以口诀为媒介，与少林寺传统的宗法门头制度相结合，把佛教思想通过师父的言传身教和弟子的勤学苦练融合到少林武术中，禅武合一，少了杀气，多了防守。

（3）内外合一、形神兼备。阳江少林

武术讲究内外兼修，既讲究形体规范，又追求精神传意，“内练精气神，外练筋骨皮。”所谓“内”，指心、神、意等心志运行；所谓“外”，即手、眼、身、步等形体活动。内与外、形与神相联系，通过功法和技法体现。

（4）套路运动特点。套路运动是阳江少林武术的表现形式，一套动作，主要是以踢、打、摔、拿、击、劈诸法为主，其攻防技击特征是通过招式套路来表现的，在行拳时注重腰马合一。此外，套路在技术上要求把内在精气神与外部形体动作紧密结合，做到“心动形随”“形断意连”“势断气连”，以禅武合一的意境来锻炼身心。

重要价值

· 历史价值

阳江少林武术作为一种独立完整的社会文化现象，其起源、传承与发展是同民族文明的产生、发展同步的，并随历史发展不断积累、完善和提高。它适应各历史战争和防卫的特点，反映历史文化特征和各时期历史事件，是一项重要非物质文化遗产。

· 文学价值

阳江少林武术在长期的演进历程中融会了古代哲学、医学、美学、佛学等传统文化的各种要素，构思创作形成独具民族风格的练功方法和套路运动形式，涵盖中国传统文化和佛教思想的精髓，禅武合一，文学内涵丰富。

· 艺术价值

阳江少林武术包含多种拧转、俯仰、收放、折叠、跳跃等身法动作，既柔和轻灵，也刚健有力，协调性艺术较高，有

阳江少林武术枪法
Art of red-tasselled spear playing of Yangjiang Shaolin Martial Art

is mainly based on kicking, hitting, throwing, holding, punching, and chopping. The attack and defense skills are expressed through the whole set of movements, and the combination of the waist and legs is emphasized in boxing. In addition, the technical requirements of the routines are to closely integrate the essence, vigour and spirit with the physical movements, to achieve “the heart moves and the body follows”, “the movement can be broken but not the intention” “the momentum can be broken but not the Qi”, to exercise the body and mind with the combination of Zen and martial arts.

Great Value

· Historical value

As an independent and complete social and cultural phenomenon, Yangjiang Shaolin Martial Art's origin, inheritance and development are synchronized with the emergence and development of national civilization. And it has been accumulated and improved with the development of history, adapted to the characteristics of various historical wars and defense, reflected historical and cultural characteristics and historical events of various periods, and is an important intangible cultural heritage.

· Literary value

Yangjiang Shaolin Martial Art has integrated various elements of ancient philosophy, medicine, aesthetics, Buddhism and other traditional cultures in its long-term evolution process, conceived and created a unique national style of practice methods and routine sports forms, covering the essence of Chinese traditional culture and Buddhist thought, Zen and martial arts are integrated, with rich literary connotation.

· Artistic value

Yangjiang Shaolin Martial Art includes a variety of body

阳江少林武术表演
Yangjiang Shaolin Martial Art performance

movements such as twisting, pitching, retracting, folding, and jumping. It is soft and flexible, but also strong and powerful. It has a high level of coordination art, artistic advantages of "high, difficult, beautiful, and new", and a high artistic and ornamental value.

· Scientific value

Influenced by the traditional culture, Yangjiang Shaolin Martial Art integrates the theories of mechanics, traditional Chinese medicine, anthropology and other traditional disciplines, and scientifically creates technical actions that adapt to the physiological characteristics of the human body for innovation and development, so as to enhance the ability to resist.

· Contemporary cultural significance and social function

The process of inheritance and development of Yangjiang Shaolin Martial Art is a good carrier for social and historical research. It has always been "advocating martial arts and morality". Through long-term practice, confrontation, performance or competitions, it can cultivate people's good habits and will of diligence, hard work, determination, tenacity, modesty, and enterprising. It is of great significance to strengthen physical fitness, fight hard, enrich cultural life, and promote social exchanges and national unity.

"高、难、美、新"的艺术优势，具有较高的艺术和观赏价值。

· 科学价值

阳江少林武术在传统文化的熏陶下，融会了力学、中医学、人体学等传统学科理论，科学地创造了适应人体生理特征的技术动作并加以创新、发展，达到增强对抗能力的作用。

· 当代文化意义和社会功能

阳江少林武术的传承发展会是一部很好的社会历史研究载体。其一贯"尚武崇德"的精神，经过长期练习、对抗或表演比赛，可以培养人们勤奋、刻苦、果敢、顽强、虚心好学、勇于进取的良好习性和意志，对强身健体、奋发斗志，丰富文化生活，增强社会交流和民族团结具有重要意义。

阳江少林武术弟子参加武术大赛
Yangjiang Shaolin Martial Art apprentices participate in martial art competitions

主要传承人

谭志安，男，1977年9月出生，阳江少林武术第三代传承人。2000年1月，在阳江市金山路大放鸡山麓创办阳江少林学校并担任校长。依托阳江少林学校，经过20余年的传承和发展，开展项目的练习、授徒、培训、教学和表演、比赛等，培养传承人的中坚力量，推动阳江少林武术的发展。阳江少林学校建校20余年来，为社会培养了近万名武术爱好者。学员有来自阳江市各县区的，也有来自广州、深圳等省内及广西、湖南等省外各地的，还有来自俄罗斯、美国、法国、爱尔兰等国家的。

谭志安还应邀担任阳江军分区、武警阳江支队、江城区消防大队的武术主教练，通过开展传承授艺活动，推动阳江少林武术的发展，让阳江少林武术一代一代传承下去及发扬光大，对弘扬尚武的民族精神及爱国主义情怀起到积极的作用。现为阳江市第五批非物质文化遗产项目代表性传承人。

Main Inheritors

谭志安（左）
Tan Zhian (left)

Tan Zhian, male, was born in September 1977. He is the third generation inheritor of Yangjiang Shaolin Martial Art. In January 2000, he founded Yangjiang Shaolin School at Dafangji Mountain, Jinshan Road, Yangjiang and served as the principal. He has carried out practice, apprenticeship, training, teaching and performance and competition in Yangjiang Shaolin School. After more than 20 years hard work, he has become the backbone of training inheritors to promote the development of Yangjiang Shaolin Martial Art. Since the establishment, Yangjiang Shaolin School, has trained nearly 10,000 martial arts enthusiasts who are from all counties in Yangjiang, as well as from other cities like Guangzhou, Shenzhen and other provinces like Guangxi, Hunan, as well as other countries like Russia, the United States, France and Ireland.

Tan Zhian was also invited to serve as the martial arts coach of Yangjiang Military Division, Yangjiang Detachment of the Armed Police, and Jiangcheng District Fire Brigade. Through the inheritance and teaching activities, he played a positive role in promoting the development of Yangjiang Shaolin Martial Art, allowing Yangjiang Shaolin Martial Art to be inherited and carried forward from generation to generation, and carrying forward the national spirit and patriotism. Now he is the representative inheritor of the fifth batch of intangible cultural heritage projects in Yangjiang.

Xiang Jiabiao, male, was born in January 1982, and is the fourth generation inheritor of Yangjiang Shaolin Martial Art. Since 2002, he has served as the martial art coach in Yangjiang Shaolin School to teach Yangjiang Shaolin Martial Art, and trained nearly 1,000 students and social masses who are distributed throughout Yangjiang City to practice Yangjiang Shaolin Martial Art. He has always been committed to promoting the martial arts. He undertakes the responsibility of project organization, research, practice, training, exhibition, performance, competition and publicity. Now he is the representative inheritor of the fifth batch of intangible cultural heritage projects in Yangjiang.

项家彪，男，出生于1982年1月，阳江少林武术第四代传承人。2002年至今在阳江少林学校担任武术教练，以教学方式传授阳江少林武术，培养练习阳江少林武术的学员、群众近1000人，习武人群分布在阳江市各地。他一直致力于弘扬武术事业，承担项目的组织、研究、练习、培训、展示、表演、比赛与宣传等传承发展的责任。现为阳江市第五批非物质文化遗产项目代表性传承人。

项家彪
Xiang Jiabiao

Part 5

第五部分

Traditional Fine Art

传统美术

阳春根雕

广东省第二批省级非物质文化遗产名录

保护单位 阳春市根艺雅石协会

Yangchun Root Carving

The Second Batch of the Provincial Intangible Cultural Heritage List of Guangdong Province

Protection Unit Yangchun Root and Stone Art Association

阳春根雕是流传于阳春，使用天然树根（枯根朽木）做素材，通过构思精雕成艺术品的传统艺术表现形式。经人工取舍、简单雕琢后的作品，具有七分天成、三分人工的特点，是“天人合一”的艺术。2007年，阳春根雕被列入广东省第二批省级非物质文化遗产名录。

历史渊源

阳春根雕起源于清代，盛行于民国时期，一直延续至今，其保护、传承和发展情况良好。清代至民国时期，阳春的许多地方文化活动中，均有根雕作品展出，以供民众观赏。《阳春县志》（1996年版）记载：“清代至民国时期，南厢都南在堡高流河回龙寺前、顺阳都高岗堡黑石岗壁笪庙和南乡都岗尾李堡等地，有四十年一度的大型醮会，叫‘万年缘’……化装游街，请粤剧班演戏，还设坛展出古董、雕刻、盆景等工艺品……”那时所说的“雕刻”，即是根雕，当时又叫“木影”。民间人士亦收藏有许多清末民初时期的根雕作品，工艺精湛，足见当时风貌。

Yangchun Root Carving is a traditional form of artistic expression spread in Yangchun, which is carving the materials of natural tree roots (dead roots and rotten wood) into artworks. During the creative process, root carving mostly maintains the natural form of the root along with a little artificial polishing. In other words, root carving is guided by the ancient Chinese wisdom— “unity of nature and humanity”. In 2007, Yangchun Root Carving was listed in the second batch of the provincial intangible cultural heritage list in Guangdong Province.

Historical Origin

Yangchun Root Carving originated in the Qing Dynasty and prevailed in the period of the Republic of China (1912-1949) . In fact, this tradition has carried on all the way through to today with its protection, inheritance and development going well. From the Qing Dynasty to the Republic of China, root carving works were exhibited in many local cultural activities in Yangchun for public viewing. As the *Yangchun County Annals* （1996 edition） records, “From the Qing Dynasty to the Republic of China, there was a 40-year large-scale wedding ceremony in front of the Huilong Temple on the Gaoliu River, Nanzaibao, Nanxiang City; the Bida Temple in Heishigang, Gaogangbao, Shunyang City; Libao in Gangwei, Nanxiang City; which is called ‘Wannian Yuan (Eternal Fate)’ ... People dressed in costumes, invited Cantonese opera troupes to perform, and set up an altar to display antiques, sculptures, potted plants and other handcrafts...” At that time, the so-called “sculpture” was root carving. It was also called “Wood Shadow” at that time. Folk people also collected many root carving works from the late Qing Dynasty to the early Republic of China, which are exquisite in craftsmanship and show the style of that time.

In May 1994, eight people, including Liao Zhengyan, Zhang Yingxiang, Zou Jiyou, Liu Wenshu, participated in the first Guangdong Root and Stone Art Treasure Exhibition with 48 root carving works. Since then, Yangchun Root Carving has begun a new era of communication with the outside world, and the whole industry has well developed. In July of the same year, Yangchun Root and Stone Art Association was established with only 20 registered members. After years of development and growth, it has nearly 300 members now, and more than half of whom are engaged in the root carving business.

1994年5月，廖正炎、张英祥、邹基友、刘文枢等8人携48件根雕作品参展首届广东省雅石根艺珍品展览会，由此打开了阳春根雕与外界交流的新局面，推动了阳春根艺雅石行业的良性发展。同年7月，阳春市根艺雅石协会成立，注册会员仅20余人，经过多年的发展壮大，现已有会员近300人，其中过半从事根雕事业。

阳春市根艺雅石协会收藏的根雕作品
Collection of root carving works of Yangchun Root and Stone Art Association

Basic Content

Yangchun Root Carving works mostly use the original roots of curved ancient wood, with concave and convex texture, scars, and tree holes similar to the horse's eye. The natural shape of the roots is used, with little artificial carving, to highlight the connotation of the theme and retain the original texture. Yangchun Root Carving can be divided into three categories according to function: modeling root art (pictorial, abstract, etc.) , practical root art (furniture, household items, musical instruments, etc.) , and root carving calligraphy. Among them, the root carving calligraphy, as an innovative art form developed on the basis of tradition, is the most characteristic. The creation concept of "made from a single tree root without splicing" is also most reflected in the root carving calligraphy, which integrates art and nature to the fullest extent and has a unique style.

基本内容

阳春根雕作品多运用原根的苍古、弯曲顿挫，凹凸苍劲的肌理、疤痕、马眼，利用天生形状，少施人工制作，突出主题内涵，保留原有肌理纹理。阳春根雕按功能可分为造型根艺（象形类、抽象类等）、实用根艺（家具、生活用品、乐器等）和根书三大类。其中，根书作为传统基础上发展的创新艺术形式，最具特色。根雕“一根成形、不拼不凑”的创作理念也在根书中体现得最为到位，将艺术与自然融合得淋漓尽致，独具风格。

根雕家具
Root carving furniture

主要特征

阳春根雕大都以天然、质坚、古朴、美观、大方和实用为特征。取材于天然的废弃树根，讲究“天人合一”的自然精神。在不改变树根基本形态的基础上，以进行构思创作、雕制成形，一根成形、不拼不凑，是最原生态的。根雕作品对树根天然成形的物象进行取舍，取下的部分便是已天然成形的物象。雕制过程中，尽量减少刀斧痕迹，保留根的弯曲顿挫，如根瘤、马眼、皱褶等。整块天然树根内部藏着某种或多种成形的物象，或字，或人物，或动物，需要斟酌取舍，将有形象的根雕物象提取出来，进行少量的制作后打磨成根雕艺术品。

最具特色的根书不同于一般根字或书法，是更高层次的精神产物，既属根艺，又类书法，形韵并茂，双艺兼优；一根只字，一笔成书，不增不接，气韵生动；根出天然，书沿张素，态比张颠，风若素狂；风格统一，根质统一，颜色统一，主从统一；蟠虬疤曲，根通书圣，玲珑剔透，难窥其巧。从选材开始，就已注入人类的高级智慧。

Main Features

Yangchun Root Carving artworks are mostly characterized by natural, high quality, simplicity, beauty, decency, and practicality. They are made from naturally discarded tree roots, with the spirit of the unity of nature and artificiality, and are conceived and shaped without changing the roots' basic form. Root carvings are made by taking the naturally formed objects of the roots, and the parts that are taken off are the naturally formed objects. In the process of carving, the artists try to minimize the traces of knife and axe, and keep the bending and stumbling of the roots, such as the root tumors, tree holes and the wrinklings. The whole natural root contains one or more kinds of natural objects, such as characters, figures, or animals, so it is necessary to take them out at the discretion and extract the ones that have a shape, and then polish them to become root carving artworks.

The most distinctive root carving calligraphy is different from general root characters or calligraphy, it is a product of higher-level spirit. It is not only a root carving, but also like calligraphic, and the appearance and connotation are very excellent. Using a single root as a stroke, a stroke becomes a character without splicing or cutting the root, making it look very vivid. The roots are natural and shaped like the characters of calligraphers Zhang Xu and Huai Su, however, the shape is more subversive than Zhang Xu's characters and the style is more open than Huaisu's characters. The style of the root carving is unified, the materials and colors of the roots are also unified, and the main body and parts complement each other. The roots are magnificently curved, just like the calligrapher's characters, and the hollowed-out structure is exquisitely made and very delicate. From the beginning of the selection of materials, it has been infused with advanced human wisdom.

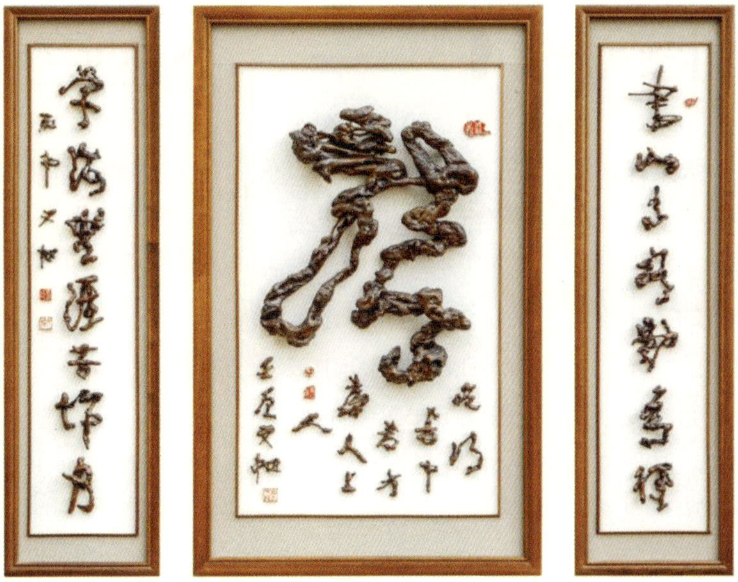

根书
Root carving calligraphy

Great Value

· Historical value

From a few pieces of root carvings inherited from the Qing Dynasty, such as "Mountain" and "Fish", which were referred to "Wood Shadow", the historical style of Yangchun at that time. can be seen. Yangchun's Root Carving plays a positive role in studying Yangchun's history and culture and developing Yangchun's root carving culture.

· Art and collective value

Yangchun Root Carving has become an exquisite art by carving dried roots and decayed wood to impart new meaning to dried and rotted wood, which sublimes the beauty. In particular, the works of root carving calligraphy, with exquisite conception, both spirit and form, and the combination of nature and artificiality, reflect not only the character of calligraphy but also condense the author's understanding and wisdom of art, which has high artistry and collecting value.

· Social and cultural value

The art of root carving has not only enriched the connotation and content of culture. With the popularity of root carving art, people actively participate in root carving creation, collection, appreciation, and communicating activities, forming a kind of cultural entertaining activities that the general public enjoys. At the same time, because of its strong regional representation and artistic ornamental, it has become an important bridge and link for cultural exchange, which has a positive effect on the enhancement of cultural confidence.

重要价值

· 历史价值

从清代留传下来的“山”“鱼”等几件当时称“木影”的根雕作品，可看出阳春当时的历史风貌和阳春根雕文化曾经兴旺的侧影，对研究阳春历史文化和发展阳春根雕文化具有积极的推动作用。

· 艺术、收藏价值

阳春根雕通过雕刻干枯根、朽木，使其成为精美的根雕艺术品，赋予枯根朽木新的意义，从而获得美的升华。尤其是根书作品，构思精巧，神形兼备，天人妙合，不仅体现书法风骨，更凝结了创作者对艺术的感悟和智慧，具有较高的艺术性和收藏价值。

· 社会、文化价值

根雕艺术有丰富高雅的内涵。随着根雕艺术的普及发展，人们积极参与根雕艺术创作、收藏、观赏和交流活动，形成一种广大群众喜闻乐见的文化娱乐活动。同时，也因其较强的地域代表性和艺术观赏性，根雕成为文化交流的重要桥梁和纽带，对文化自信的增强有着积极作用。

主要传承人

张英祥，男，1945年6月出生，广东阳春人，从事根艺创作60余年。张英祥出生于根雕世家，受祖父张奕众和父亲张升构的艺术熏陶，根雕作品仍留着浓郁而抽象的“木影”风格，在融合创新中推动根雕艺术发展，现任阳春市根雕雅石协会会长。其作品注重保留丰富的自然美，并赋予树根以艺术生命。作品《鹏程万里》《侏罗纪雄风》等以雄浑大气的形象，再现天人合一的艺术生命。作品《母子情》《春江水暖》《鹰蛇图》等曾获“全国根艺作品大赛”精品奖、第三届粤港澳台盆景艺术博览会金奖等奖项。张英祥现为广东省第一批省级非物质文化遗产项目代表性传承人。

刘文枢，男，1949年出生，从小对树根造型艺术着迷，虚心向长辈讨教根雕的技术特色、形态、构思及制作等。因摆摊卖过连环画图书，对人物形态、线条表现等有更深刻的认识，为他发展根艺创作进一步奠定了基础。其作品融合自然美和艺术美，自成一格。根艺作品《八骏图》，根书《还我河山》《清风》《马到成功》，根画《八马图》等作品，曾斩获1994年中国书画艺术大赛“王羲之奖”全国一等奖等多个重要奖项。刘文枢现为广东省第一批省级非物质文化遗产项目代表性传承人。

Main Inheritors

Zhang Yingxiang, male, was born in June 1945 in Yangchun, Guangdong Province. He has been engaged in root art for more than 60 years. Born in a family of root carving, Zhang Yingxiang influenced by the art of his grandfather Zhang Yizhong and his father Zhang Shenggou. His root carving works still retain a rich and abstract "Wood Shadow" style and promote the development of root carving art in the process of integration and innovation. Currently, he is the president of the Yangchun Root and Stone Art Association. His works focus on preserving the rich natural beauty and endowing the roots with artistic life. His works, such as *A Thousand Miles of Pengcheng* and *Jurassic Strong Wind*, reproduce the creative life of the unity of nature and artificiality in a powerful image. His works such as *Love of Mother and Child*, *Warm Spring River*, and *Eagle and Snake* have won the excellent production prize of National Root Art Competition and the gold prize of the third Guangdong, Hong Kong, Macao, and Taiwan Potted Plants Art Expo. Zhang Yingxiang is now the representative inheritor of the first batch of provincial intangible cultural heritage projects in Guangdong Province.

Li Wenshu, male, was born in 1949. He was fascinated by the plastic arts of tree roots since childhood. He humbly asked his elders about the technical characteristics, shape, conception and production of root carving. Owing to setting up a bookstall of picture-story books, he has more knowledge of the shape of characters, line expression, etc., which further lay the foundation for his development of root art creation. His works integrate natural beauty and artistic beauty, forming a unique style. The root artworks *The Painting of Eight Steeds*; the root carving calligraphy *Return My River and Mountain*, *Breeze*, and *Success in a Hurry*; the root painting *The Painting of Eight Horses* and other works won many important awards, such as the first prize of the "Wang Xizhi Award" of Chinese Calligraphy and Painting Art Competition in 1994. Now Liu Wenshu is the representative inheritor of the first batch of provincial intangible cultural heritage projects in Guangdong Province.

廖正炎
Liao Zhengyan

张英祥
Zhang Yingxiang

廖正炎，男，1935年11月出生，广东阳春人。15岁时受梁建韶影响爱上书法和根艺。20世纪70年代末，廖正炎另辟蹊径，创造树根书法，使根艺的艺术境界和艺术品位得到进一步升华。多年来，其作品获国内外省级及以上奖项157次，作品《地貌奇观当护本·天然璞玉琢精新》及《江山如画》等被联合国第一届世界地质公园大会甄藏。1994年，他与张英祥、邹基友、刘文枢等四人创建阳春市根艺雅石协会，担任会长15年，现为终身荣誉会长。廖正炎现为广东省第三批省级非物质文化遗产项目代表性传承人。

Liao Zhengyan, male, was born in November 1935 in Yangchun, Guangdong Province. Influenced by Liang Jianshao, he was fascinated by calligraphy and root art at age of 15. At the end of the 1970s, Liao Zhengyan took a different path to create root calligraphy to further sublimate root art's artistic realm and taste. Over the years, his works have won 157 provincial and above awards at home and abroad. His works, including *Landscape Wonders Should Be Preserved · Natural Jade Carved to Be Subtle and Novel* and *Picturesque Rivers and Mountains*, have been collected by the First World Geoparks Congress of the United Nations. In 1994, he established the Yangchun Root and Stone Art Association with Zhang Yingxiang, Zou Jiyou, Liu Wenshu. He served as the president for 15 years and is now the honorary president for life. Now Liao Zhengyan is the representative inheritor of the third batch of provincial intangible cultural heritage projects in Guangdong Province.

刘文枢
Liu Wenshu

邹基友
Zou Jiyou

邹基友，男，1945年生于广东阳春。受父辈们熏陶和言传身教，其作品因材施艺、以形取神，还保留着传统的具象“木影”风格。他积极推动阳春根雕艺术传承，培养根雕人才。其根书作品《中国》入选大型艺术人物史志《中国艺术》，获评“中国艺术成果金奖”，并被授予“中国艺术创作名家”荣誉称号；2008年，他被“中华名人系列丛书”编辑部授予“中华名人杰出成就金奖”和“民族之光”荣誉称号。从艺60余年，邹基友有60多件作品在国内外大展中获得殊荣，为阳春根雕项目的保护传承、发展创新默默耕耘、无私奉献。邹基友现为广东省第五批省级非物质文化遗产项目代表性传承人。

梁其升，男，1974年出生于广东阳春，阳春市根艺雅石协会会员。他从小受到从事根雕艺术的父亲影响，热爱根艺，并得到廖正炎、张英祥、邹基友、刘文枢四位大师的传承。曾创办弘艺根雕厂，作品侧重于实用根艺和造型根艺，产品远销国内外并多次参加各地展览。梁其升现为阳江市第三批非物质文化遗产项目代表性传承人。

Zou Jiyou, male, was born in Yangchun, Guangdong Province, in 1945, As he was influenced by his parents' generation and taught by words and deeds, his works are performed according to the material, and the spirit is taken from the shape, retaining the traditional concrete "Wood Shadow" style. He actively promoted the inheritance of Yangchun Root Carving Art and trained root-cutting talents. His root carving calligraphy work *China* was selected into the historical records of prominent art figures in *Chinese Art*, and won the Gold Award for Chinese Art Achievements. He was awarded the honorary title of "Famous Artist of Chinese Art". In 2008, he won the prize of "Gold Award for Outstanding Achievement of Chinese Celebrities" and the honorary title of "Glory of the Nation" by the editorial department of the "Series of Books about Chinese Celebrities". For more than 60 years, more than 60 pieces of his works have been awarded in domestic and foreign exhibitions. He has devoted himself to the protection, inheritance, development, and creativity of the Yangchun Root Carving project. Now he is the representative inheritor of the fifth batch of provincial intangible cultural heritage projects in Guangdong Province.

Liang Qisheng, male, was born in 1974 in Yangchun, Guangdong Province. He is a member of the Yangchun Root and Stone Art Association. He was influenced by his father who dedicated his entire life to root carving. Since childhood, he has passionate about root carving and polished his skills from four masters, including Liao Zhengyan, Zhang Yingxiang, Zou Jiyou, and Liu Wenshu. He founded Hongyi Root Carving Factory. His works focus on practical root art and modeling root art. Besides, his products have been widely sold at home and abroad and displayed in many exhibitions worldwide. Now he is the representative inheritor of the third batch of intangible cultural heritage projects in Yangjiang City.

梁其升
Liang Qisheng

第六部分

传统技艺

Part 6

Traditional Craftsmanship

漆器髹饰技艺（阳江漆器髹饰技艺）

广东省第一批省级非物质文化遗产名录　　第三批国家级非物质文化遗产名录

保护单位　阳江漆艺院有限公司

Lacquerware Decorating Craftsmanship

（Yangjiang Lacquerware Decorating Craftsmanship）

The First Batch of the Provincial Intangible Cultural Heritage List of Guangdong Province, The Third Batch of the National Intangible Cultural Heritage List

Protection Unit　Yangjiang Lacquer Art Institute Co., Ltd.

阳江漆器工艺制品，早期以私人家庭作坊形式制作。作坊地点集中在阳江市区龙津路、南恩路、太傅路一带，当时已出口东南亚，乃至欧美。1935年为阳江漆器工艺最发达兴盛的时期，产品供不应求，城区主要商业街南恩路西段（西门街）差不多全是做漆器产品的商铺。1958年建立阳江国营漆器工艺厂，漆器产品基本由国营厂生产，产品畅销日本、意大利、德国、法国、东南亚等国家和地区。20世纪80年代末，全市只有寥寥可数的几家私人漆器工艺企业。如今，生产漆器的企业已基本消失，漆艺的另一个种类——漆画，只能靠艺人的爱好和追求苦苦坚守。

2006年漆器髹饰技艺（阳江漆器髹饰技艺）被列入广东省第一批省级非物质文化遗产名录，2011年被列入第三批国家级非物质文化遗产名录。

历史渊源

清代诗人李调元在《南越笔记》中记载：“广中产漆，售行他省，皆称广漆。

In the early days, Yangjiang lacquerware craft products were made in private family workshops that were mainly located in Longjin Road, Nan'en Road, and Taifu Road in the urban area of Yangjiang. At that time, Yangjiang lacquerware craft products were exported to Southeast Asia and even Europe and America. It was the most developed and prosperous period of the Yangjiang lacquerware craft in 1935. Demand for the products is outrunning supply and almost all shops sold lacquerware products in the west of Nan'en Road（Ximen Street）, which was the main business street in the urban area. Yangjiang State-owned Lacquerware Craft Factory was established in 1958, and the lacquerware products were almost exclusively produced by the factory after that. The lacquerware products sold well in many countries and regions like Japan, Italy, Germany, France, Southeast Asia, At the end of the 1980s, there were only a

陈其积作品《金鱼漆屏风》
Chen Qiji's work *Lacquer Screen of Goldfish*

few private lacquerware craft enterprises in Yangjiang. Nowadays, the enterprises producing lacquerware have almost disappeared. Lacquer painting, another kind of lacquer art, grows toughly with the hobbies and pursuits of the artists.

Lacquerware Decorating Craftsmanship (Yangjiang Lacquerware Decorating Craftsmanship) was listed in the first batch of the provincial intangible cultural heritage list of Guangdong Province in 2006 and was listed in the third batch of the national intangible cultural heritage list in 2011.

Historical Origin

The Qing Dynasty poet Li Diaoyuan recorded in his writings *Notes of Nanyue*: "Guangdong lacquerwere, called Guangqi, are sold to other provinces and the side tables, boxes and vessels made by workers in Guangdong are exquisite." As an important component of Guangdong lacquerware, Yangjiang lacquerware has a long history. According to historical records, an emperor of the Sui Dynasty bestowed some jewels and silk clothing on Madam Xian. In order to make later generations always remember the emperor's gift, Madam Xian used a patent-leather suitcase with golden paintings produced in Yangjiang to hold these gifts. Huineng, a monk of the Tang Dynasty, was born in Xinxing next to Gaoliang County which includes most areas of Yangjiang. According to experts' speculation, Huineng's body was protected with lacquer to prevent decay. Yangjiang is located on the coast of the South China and has a long history of wooden shipbuilding. Yangjiang craftsmen often used tung oil or lacquer on wooden boats to prevent moisture and corrosion. These examples confirm the long history of Yangjiang lacquerware, and now it is found that the earliest recorded history can be traced back to the Sui Dynasty.

The Yangjiang lacquerware craft was prosperous during the late Qing Dynasty and the early Republic of China. *Yangjiang Annals* (the edition of 1925) records that lacquer's leather is ordinary, but the lacquer is special and nice. Yangjiang's leather suitcases are well known at home and abroad, and other leather pillows, leather chairs, and leather boxes are also of excellent qualities. But when the same lacquerer made the same lacquer product in the provincial capital, it became lighter in color because the lacquer only suits Yangjiang's soil. During the period of Qianlong in the Qing Dynasty, a Lin family ran a small shoe shop called "Lao Yihe", which had a few workers. Later, due to the bleakness of shoe business, they turned to produce leather suitcases and leather pillows. At that time, Yangjiang lacquerware was limited to the production of leather suitcases and

粤中工人制造几匣器皿，无不精雅……”阳江漆器作为广东漆器的重要组成部分，有着悠久的历史。根据历史记载，隋朝皇帝曾赏赐给冼夫人一些首饰和丝绸宴服，冼夫人为了让后世永远记住皇帝的恩赐，就用了一个金箧来盛装这些赐物，这里的金箧就是阳江生产的描金漆皮箱。唐代六祖惠能是新兴人，与高凉（包括阳江大部分地区）为邻，据专家推测，六祖的金身得以千年不腐就是用漆来保护的。阳江地处南海之滨，造木船业历史悠久，工匠们往往会通过在木船里外刷桐油或油漆的手段来防潮防腐。这些都印证了阳江漆器历史悠久，目前发现有记载的最早可以追溯到隋朝。

阳江漆器工艺，繁盛于清末民初。《阳江志》（1925年版）载：“漆皮器，牛皮亦与他邑同，而漆独佳。故阳江皮箱驰名京省远及外洋，其余皮枕皮椅皮盒各器俱极精良。然同一漆工往省城造之，则减色，盖漆性独与土宜也。”清乾隆年间有林姓人家开办一间名叫老义和的小鞋店，只有几个工人生产。后因做鞋生意淡薄，就转做皮箱、皮枕。当时阳江漆器只限于生产皮箱、皮枕两个产品。当时的皮枕全是真皮做的，里面用谷糠作填充物料，没有生漆，只有桐油，后有安南（现越南）生漆进口，生漆比桐油价低，因此，这间小店就改为在皮枕上刷生漆，阳江漆器从此便开始生产。那时中国的手工业特别发达，因此阳江漆器非常畅销。老义和鞋店便正式转为做皮箱、皮枕的漆器店，并开始大量招收学徒发展漆器生产。在广州、香港均有分厂。

《阳江县志》（2000年版）及《阳江文史》（第8期）载：1919年，“广泰成”老板郑文江在阳江城太傅路开设“广泰成”漆器皮箱庄，附设制作加工厂，招聘名师巧匠、画家到工厂工作，雇用员工70多人，生意兴隆，在香港上环路禧利街12号开设“广泰成”皮箱庄，销售本厂制造的“雄鸡牌”漆器用品，获利颇丰。“广泰成”生产的皮雕“万寿金花漆盒”造型精巧玲珑，浮雕花鸟纹样优美，曾于民国二十五年（1936）在南洋国际货物赛会上荣获金质奖章，令人惊叹不已。阳江漆器声名更显，销路更广。相传在清道光年间，有一个外国商人在中国购买了一批阳江漆皮箱，内装名贵物品乘船回国，途中船沉遇难，虽然船上的旅客获救，但所载运货物却随海水漂流或沉没了。数月后，商人偶在海边拾获自己的漆皮箱，发现箱子外的漆面光泽不损，打开箱子一看，里面所装的物件全部完好无损，既不受海水侵蚀，又不变质，物品光亮如新，商人惊叹不已，并撰写文章登报，传颂于世。从此，阳江漆器更是扬名中外。

20世纪初，阳江的漆皮箱都由私人家庭作坊生产制造，如“老义和”“广泰成”“广隆”“广益成”“利源隆”等。

据《阳江县志》（2000年版）“人物”载：时任阳江县县长李伯振于民国二十二年（1933年）夏创办了“阳江县立改良漆器传习所”（官办，所在地址为县城南路旧关帝庙），力图复兴漆器工业。产销漆器的品种逐渐增多，有首饰盒、印章盒、茶桶、烟盒、茶叶盅、眼镜盒等日常用品，产品上开始有了多种颜色和字画装饰。

1935年为阳江漆器工艺最发达兴盛时期，这时阳江县城南恩路差不多完全是做漆器工艺产品的商店，从业人员达400多人。抗日战争时期，阳江漆器生产一落千丈，许多能工巧匠被迫改行转业，流离失所。据统计，当时全县漆艺工人只剩下40

leather pillows. All leather pillows were then made of genuine leather and filled with grain bran. There was no raw lacquer but only tung oil. Later, raw lacquer imported from Annan (now Vietnam) was less expensive than tung oil. Therefore, this small shop painted leather pillows with raw lacquer, and Yangjiang lacquerware began to produce from then on. China's handicraft industry was particularly developed at that time; thus Yangjiang lacquerware was in great demand. Lao Yihe shoe shop was officially turned into a lacquerware shop for leather cases and leather pillows. It also began recruiting many apprentices to develop lacquerware products. There were branches of “Lao Yihe” in Guangzhou and Hong Kong.

Yangjiang County Annals(the edition of 2000) and *Yangjiang Literary History* (the 8th issue) record that: In 1919, Zheng Wenjiang, the boss of “Guang Taicheng”, ran “Guang Taicheng” lacquerware leather suitcase shop in Taifu Road of Yangjiang, with a manufacturing and processing factory. He recruited famous masters, craftsmen, and painters to work in the factory, employing more than 70 people. Guang Taicheng's business was booming. The “Guang Taicheng” leather suitcase shop was opened at No.12 Xili Street, Shanghuan Road in Hong Kong to sell the “Rooster” lacquerware products manufactured by the factory, making a lot of profits. The leather carved with “Longevity Golden Flower Lacquer Box” produced by “Guang Taicheng” was exquisite, with beautiful relief flower and bird patterns. It won the gold medal at the Nanyang International Goods Competition in the 25th year of the Republic of China(1936), which is amazing. It increased the popularity and sales of Yangjiang lacquerware. It is said that during the period of Daoguang in the Qing Dynasty, a foreign businessman bought a batch of Yangjiang lacquer leather suitcases in China, which contained valuable items. But on the way home, the ship sank. Although the passengers on board were rescued, the goods carried by the ship drifted or sank. A few months later, the businessman occasionally found his lacquer leather suitcases at the seaside. He found that the paint drawn on the suitcases was not damaged. When he opened the suitcases, all the items inside were intact, having neither been corroded by seawater nor deteriorated. The items were as bright as new. The businessman was amazed and then wrote an article in the newspaper to spread it around the world. Since then, Yangjiang lacquerware has become famous both at home and abroad.

At the beginning of the 20th century, all the lacquer leather suitcases of Yangjiang were made in private family workshops such as “Lao Yihe”, “Guang Taicheng”, “Guanglong”, “Guang Yicheng”, “Liyuan Long”, etc..

According to *Yangjiang County Annals*(the edition of 2000), Li

Bozhen, then the county magistrate of Yangjiang County, set up "Yangjiang County Improved Lacquerware Institute" (it is official, and its address was in the old Guandi Temple, South County Road) in the summer of the 22nd year of the Republic of China (1933) to revive the lacquerware industry. The variety of lacquerware has gradually increased, including jewelry boxes, seal boxes, tea barrels, cigarette boxes, tea containers, glass boxes, and other daily necessities, which begun to have a variety of colors and calligraphy and painting decorations.

In 1935, the most developed and prosperous period of Yangjiang lacquerware craft, there were almost entirely lacquerware craft shops in Nan'en Road, Yangjiang County, with more than 400 lacquer practitioners. During the War of Resistance Against Japan, the production of Yangjiang lacquerware fell sharply, and many skilled craftsmen were forced to change their careers. According to statistics, there were only more than 40 lacquer practitioners in the county at that time, and the lacquerware industry was dying. Yangjiang County Lacquerware Production Cooperative was established in 1956, and it was transformed into a local state-owned lacquerware craft factory in 1958, with more than 280 employees originally, increasing to more than 400. Since 1979, its products have been regulated by the Ministry of Light Industry of the People's Republic of China. Yangjiang lacquerware factory has been designated as one of the thirteen key factories of the Ministry of Light Industry in China.

Since the late 1980s, Yangjiang lacquerware craft has gradually declined.

Basic Content

Yangjiang lacquerware crafts

There are many kinds of Yangjiang lacquerware crafts, including leathered-, wooden-, linen-(cloth-), metal-, plastic-, paper-, and porcelain-body lacquerware. In particular, leathered- and paper-body lacquerware products have the most traditional and unique style of Yangjiang lacquerware. Lacquer leather suitcases and lacquer leather pillows are the most famous products. The paintings of traditional lacquer leather suitcases and lacquer leather pillows are monotonous, only in black and vermilion. In the 1950s or 1960s, the lacquer painting craft with Yangjiang characteristics was developed according to the traditional painting craft.

· Manufacturing process of traditional lacquer leather suitcases

First, use wood (fir, camphor, etc.) to make a wooden case.

范高亮脱胎漆器《鹊竹漆盘》
Fan Gaoliang's bodiless lacquerware *Lacquer Plate of Magpie and Bamboo*

余人，漆器行业奄奄一息。1956年成立阳江县漆器生产合作社，1958年转为地方国营漆器工艺厂，原有280多名职工，增加到400多名。其所生产产品从1979年起成为中华人民共和国轻工业部（以下简称“轻工业部”）“部管产品”，阳江漆器厂被指定为轻工业部全国13个重点厂之一。

20世纪80年代末开始，阳江漆器工艺逐渐衰落。

基本内容

· 阳江漆器工艺

阳江漆器工艺的种类很多，从质地上分有皮胎漆器、木胎漆器、麻（布）胎漆器、金属胎漆器、塑料胎漆器、纸胎漆器和瓷胎漆器。尤以皮胎产品、纸胎产品最具阳江漆器的传统和独特风格。皮胎产品又以漆皮箱和漆皮枕最著名。传统漆皮箱、漆皮枕的彩绘比较单调，只有黑色、朱色两种。20世纪五六十年代，根据传统描漆花工艺发展成具有阳江特色的漆画工艺。

· **传统漆皮箱的制作过程**

第一步，先用木材（杉木、樟木等）做成一个木箱壳。

第二步，配皮、裁皮。

①用刨子将牛皮（皮肚，即皮里，一般做皮箱用；皮青，即皮外，做皮枕用）不平整的地方刨平，按木箱壳尺寸将皮肚剪裁好。

②将食用生粉和水煮成稠样的糨糊，用刷子将糨糊涂在裁好的皮肚上。

③将上好浆糊的皮肚裱上木箱壳，箱里裱一层皮，箱面裱一层皮。

④用麻线将接缝用手工缝好，将木箱壳裹实。

⑤再用刨子将裹实的皮肚皮面刨滑。

第三步，髹漆。

①用生粉和生漆调和，按3：7的比例调好稀稠度，用软刷涂在皮面上，晾干。

②用刷子髹一层清漆（底漆）在皮面上，晾干。

③再髹上一层面漆（面漆一般以黑色、朱色为主），晾干。

④用水砂纸（以前用牛筋树叶）抛光打滑皮面，晾干后为成品。

· **传统纸胎漆器工艺产品制作过程（以圆盒为例）**

第一步，做纸盒、盖坯。

①先用糨糊将两张黄板纸（较厚的纸板）粘在一起自然阴干。

②将粘好的双层黄板纸按产品造型需要的尺寸裁剪好，待用。

③将裁剪好的黄板纸放在一个硬木做成的圆柱状模具上定形，预留接口。

④脱开模具取出圆筒状盒坯（又称肚）待用。

⑤再用糨糊将三层黄板纸粘在一起自然阴干，待用。

Then, prepare and cut the leather.

①Use a plane to level the uneven areas of the cowhide (the leather belly, i.e., the inside of the leather which is generally used for making leather suitcases; the outside of the leather which is used for making leather pillows). Cut the leather belly according to the size of the wooden case.

②Mix the edible cornstarch and water, boil them until the mixture become thick paste, and then brush the paste onto the cut leather belly.

③Mount the pasted leather belly on the wooden case shell, with a layer of leather inside and a layer of leather on the case surface.

④Sew the seam by hand with hemp thread and wrap the wooden case tightly.

⑤Then use a plane to smooth the wrapped leather belly.

Last, lacquering.

①Mix the cornstarch with the raw lacquer with the proportion of 3：7. Brush it onto the leather with a soft brush and dry it.

②Paint a layer of varnish (primer) on the leather surface with a brush and dry it.

③Then paint a layer of finish paint (mainly black and vermilion) and dry it.

④Polish the leather surface with water sandpaper (formerly with leaves of lindera glauca) to make it smooth, and dry by airing to make it an end product.

· **Manufacturing process of traditional paper-body lacquerware (taking a round box as an example)**

First, make cartons and cover blanks.

①Glue two pieces of yellow board paper (thicker cardboard) together with paste to dry in the shade.

②Tailor the glued double-layer yellow board paper according to the size required by the product modeling for use.

③Place the cut yellow board paper on a cylindrical mold made of hardwood for shaping, and reserve the joint.

④Detach the paper from the mold and take out the cylindrical box blank (also called belly) for later use.

⑤Then glue the three layers of yellow board paper together to dry in the shade for later use.

⑥Place the dried three-layer yellow board on the drilling machine containing blades, and slice the cardboard paper at the bottom of the round box for later use (the way of making the box cover is the same).

⑦Paste two layers of kraft paper in the finished cylindrical box to the same height as the cylinder. The goal of gluing two layers of kraft paper is to create a small gap between the cylinder and the bonded

范俊漆画《龙虾》
Fan Jun's lacquer painting *Lobster*

kraft paper in order to cover the box cover.

⑧Cover the inside of a cylindrical box (smaller than the previous one) with two layers of pasted yellow board paper. Sandpaper should be used to polish the inner tube's mouth so that the cover can fit easily.

⑨Glue the prepared cylindrical box blank and the cardboard at the bottom of the round box into a round box for later use.

Second, put on the lacquer.

①Use gasoline to mix the lacquer (raw lacquer or cashew nut lacquer can be used). The thickness and consistency are determined by the requirements of the master's construction.

②Soak the finished paper boxes and paper cover blanks into the lacquer bucket, clip and dry them for storage. This process is to shape the paper box and paper cover, strengthen the hardness, and prevent moisture.

③Polish with sandpaper for the first time simply.

④Apply a layer of thick plaster made from priming lacquer and tile ash, and dry it in the air.

⑤Polish with sandpaper.

⑥Apply another layer of lacquer and polish it to make a semi-finished product.

⑦Paint twice or three times, and then polish off some lacquer film with sandpaper.

⑧Various methods can be used for decorating the box.

⑨Paint another layer of finish lacquer, and polish it gently with fine sandpaper after it is dry. Paint the second layer of lacquer and dry it in the air. Finally, the product is finished.

· Manufacturing process of traditional cloth-body lacquer vase

①Make a vase-shaped semi-finished body with clay first.

②Coat the vase body with sticky clay and let it dry.

③Dip the cotton (linen) cloth which cut into triangles (according

⑥将晾干的三层黄板纸放在装有刀片的钻床上，切割出需要的圆盒的底部纸板，待用（盒盖的做法相同）。

⑦在做好的圆筒状盒里以圆筒相同高度粘贴两层牛皮纸。粘贴两层牛皮纸的作用是使圆筒与黏合的牛皮纸之间有一点间隙，以便盖上盒盖。

⑧用已粘贴两层的黄板纸再做一个圆筒状盒坯（要比之前做好的圆筒状盒坯小）套在里面。里筒口要用砂纸打磨光滑，以便盖子易吻合。

⑨将制好的圆筒状盒坯和圆盒的底部纸板粘成圆盒状，待用。

第二步，上漆。

①用汽油调和漆（大漆或腰果漆都可用），稀稠度根据师傅施工需要而定。

②将已做好的纸盒、纸盖坯浸到漆桶里，用夹子夹起，晾干待用。这道工序是使纸盒、纸盖定形，加强硬度，防潮。

③用砂纸第一次简单打磨。

④涂一层用底漆和瓦灰调和的稠样灰浆，晾干。

⑤用砂纸打磨。

⑥再涂一层并再打磨成半成品。

⑦髹两到三次漆，用水砂纸打磨掉一些漆膜。

⑧可采用各种手法在盒外做装饰。

⑨再髹一层面漆，干透后用幼砂纸轻轻打磨一遍；再髹第二层漆，晾干后为成品。

· 传统布胎漆花瓶的制作流程

①先用泥土做一个花瓶状半成品的坯胎。

②将比较有黏性的泥土涂在花瓶坯胎上，晾干。

③用剪成三角形（大小规格根据师傅需要决定）的棉（麻）布浸渍上底漆，裱到花瓶上。裱布时布一定要重叠。裱两层

布后，晾干。

④底漆加水和瓦灰调和，用胶刷把调好的灰浆涂在裱过二层的花瓶上，晾干。

⑤打磨至光滑、平整。

⑥再裱第三层布，晾干。

⑦在花瓶对称的两边用有颜色的笔画上一条垂直线准备切开。

⑧再涂一次调好的瓦灰，涂抹瓦灰时要空出两边的画线。

⑨待干后打磨平滑，再涂第二层调好的瓦灰。

⑩用刀将制作好的花瓶胎沿留出的画线切断，分成两部分脱出布胎。

⑪将脱出的两部分花瓶布胎嵌回泥土花瓶坯胎定形，用绳子把花瓶固定，扎回原样。

⑫三四天后待花瓶布胎全部干透，解开绳子，花瓶定形，布胎可从两边脱开。

⑬用麻线缝合（贴线缝口）补平缝口。

⑭晾干后，整个花瓶涂一遍调好的瓦灰，将剩余的布边修剪整齐。

⑮将调好的瓦灰涂到花瓶里面，涂到厚薄适中为止。

⑯用砂纸打磨瓶内部至平滑，用黑漆或底漆涂两到三遍。

⑰按规格用木板做一个花瓶底，涂上调好的瓦粉，用砂纸打磨好，晾干。

⑱再做花瓶外面（刷瓦粉三次，打磨三次以上）。

⑲涂两层底漆，打磨至平滑，晾干。

⑳装饰、修饰，采用各种描绘手法彩绘瓶身后，髹漆，晾干，做好成品。

· 漆画制作流程

第一步，漆板。

①在作画所需的木板（夹板）上均匀地涂一层底漆，晾干待用。

②在涂了底漆的木板（夹板）上裱布

to the needs of the master to decide the size and specification) with priming lacquer and mount it on the vase. When mounting cloth, the cloth must be overlap. After mounting two layers of cloth, let it dry.

④Mix the priming lacquer with water and tile ash, and then apply the adjusted soupy plaster to the vase mounted with two layers of lacquer and let it dry.

⑤Polish it to be smooth.

⑥Then mount the third layer of cloth and let it dry.

⑦After it is dried, draw a vertical line on the symmetrical sides of the vase with colored strokes to prepare for cutting.

⑧Apply the adjusted plaster once more. When applying the plaster, leave out the lines on both sides.

⑨After it is dried, polish it smoothly, and then apply the second layer of adjusted plaster.

⑩Use a knife to cut the prepared vase body along the reserved line, and separate it into two parts to remove the cloth.

⑪Insert the two disengaged vase bodies back into the clay vase body for shaping, fix the vase with a rope, and tie it back to its original shape.

⑫After three or four days when the cloth of the vase is completely dry, untie the rope. The vase is shaped and the cloth can be detached on both sides.

⑬Sew up (the stitching seam) with ramie thread.

⑭After it is dried, paint the whole vase with the adjusted plaster, and trim the remaining cloth edges in order.

⑮Apply the adjusted plaster to the inside of the vase until the thickness is appropriate.

⑯Polish the inside of the vase with sandpaper until it is smooth, and apply two to three coats of black lacquer or priming lacquer.

⑰Make a vase bottom with wood according to specifications, apply the adjusted plaster, polish it with sandpaper and dry it in air.

⑱Then make the outside of the vase (apply the plaster three times and polish it more than three times) .

⑲Apply two coats of priming lacquer, polish it to be smooth and dry it in air.

⑳Ornament, decorate, use various painting craftsmanship to paint the vase body, lacquer it, dry it in air, and finally finish the products.

· Manufacturing process of lacquer painting

First, lacquer on the plate.

①Paint a coat of priming lacquer on wood (plywood) evenly and dry it for use.

②Then use cloth (cotton, linen) to mount on the primed wood board (plywood) .

③Coat and seal all around the board mounted with cloth (cotton and linen) with priming lacquer by a gum brush (the cloth shall be wet, even, and flat when applying priming lacquer; the paint board shall be dried in the air) .

④After it is dried, cut the edge and scrape the cloth edge.

Second, scraping plaster.

①Allocate the required plaster with priming lacquer, tile ash, and water in proportion.

②Use a gum brush to evenly apply the adjusted tile powder paste to the cloth (cotton and linen) mounted on the board (plywood) which was coated with priming lacquer.Generally two to three layers are required. The tile powder paste shall be applied as evenly and smoothly as possible. The process of applying the first layer of tile ash is important, because the linen (cotton) cloth shall not be wrinkled. Dry it in air.

③Polish with waterproof abrasive dpaper. Polish with coarse sandpaper after applying the first layer of tile powder paste. Polish with fine sandpaper after applying the second layer of tile powder paste. After applying the third layer of tile powder paste, the wood (clamp) board shall be polished with sandpaper, and excess tile powder shall be cleaned.

Third, paint with black lacquer.

Using a soft brush to apply the prepared black lacquer to the wood (clamp) board evenly. The amount of lacquer shall be appropriate. The lacquer on layer shall not be too thick or too thin. Generally, it should be painted twice or three times. When painting, the vertical and horizontal forces must be even. The surrounding

（棉、麻布）。

③在裱了布（棉、麻布）的板上用胶质的刷子将四周涂上底漆封好（涂底漆时布要湿透、均匀、平整；漆板要风干）。

④晾干后，切边，将布边刮平。

第二步，刮瓦灰。

①用底漆、瓦粉和水按比例调配出所需的灰浆。

②用胶刷把调好的瓦粉糊均匀地涂抹到裱在木板（夹板）上涂了底漆的布（棉麻）上，一般需涂两至三层。涂瓦粉糊时用力要均匀，尽量将瓦粉糊抹平，上第一层瓦粉的工序很重要，不要让麻（棉）布起皱褶。晾干。

③用水砂纸打磨。上第一层瓦粉糊后用较粗的砂纸打磨；上第二层瓦粉糊后用较细的砂纸打磨；上第三层瓦粉糊后，用砂纸将木（夹）板打磨平滑，将多余的瓦粉屑扫净。

第三步，髹黑漆。

用软刷将调好的黑漆均匀地涂在木（夹）板上。漆的分量要适当，不要太厚，也不要太薄，一般要涂两到三次，涂漆时纵、横向力度要均匀，将周边也均匀

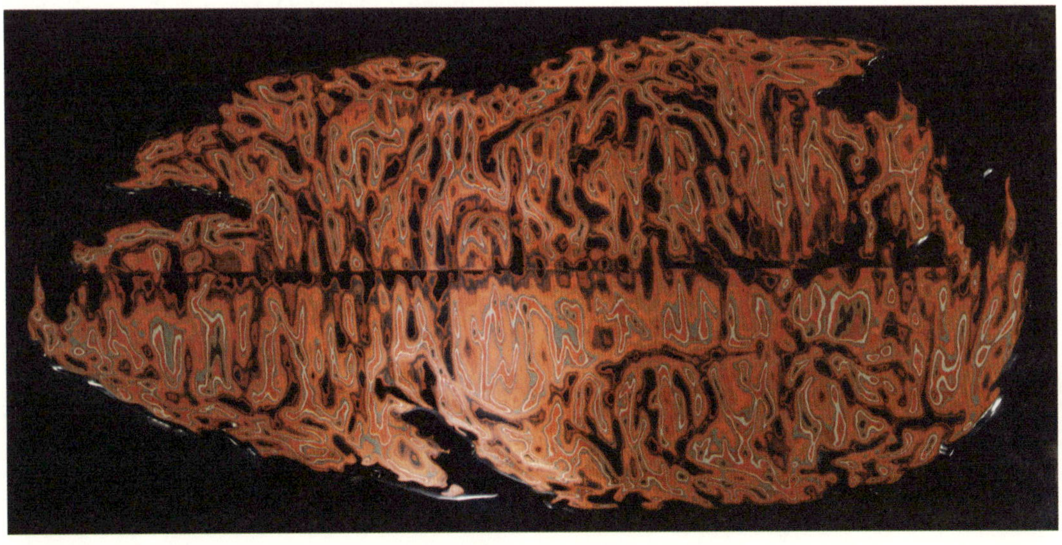

傅以周作品《爻》

Fu Yizhou' s work *Yao*

地涂上黑漆，之后将多余的漆抹去，晾干。晾干后，用砂纸加水打磨至平滑，打磨过程中要向同一个方向打磨，不能纵横方向交错地磨。最后用水擦干净。

第四步，画稿。

①用粉笔在制好的木板上起稿（也可在纸上画好稿再誊到漆板上）。

②贴箔。贴箔要平滑，要晾干，一般贴一至两次箔（箔泛指金箔、银箔、铜箔、铝箔等；贴箔的材料包括金、银箔，蛋壳，蛋壳粉，铝粉，螺钿粉，光漆粉等）。

③将银浆（用底漆或面漆加银粉调制的涂料）、面漆涂于面上。

④晾干。

⑤干燥后彩绘，绘图。先将全部画面彩绘一次，再慢慢调整，用手指把各种颜料（色彩）调和至衔接自然，晾干。

第五步，推光（打磨）。

①彩绘完成后，先用砂纸将画面打磨一次。

②推光，用棉花蘸清水和细瓦粉薄涂一次。

③将画面满满地涂上一遍瓦粉后，用手掌推磨瓦粉，抛光时要顺着一个方向推，要将板面推亮，再用湿布抹干净画面。

④用棉花蘸点食用花生油将画面涂抹一遍。

⑤将食用生粉满满地涂抹在画面上。

⑥用手掌推光，然后用干净的棉花擦掉生粉。

⑦洗干净双手，直接用生粉推磨画面，再用干净棉花全面擦拭一遍清理干净，做好成品。

黎汝汉漆画《灵芝风筝传说》

Li Ruhan's lacquer painting *The Legend of Ganoderma Lucidum Kite*

area shall also be painted evenly with black lacquer. Excess paint must be wiped away and then air-dried. After it is dried, polish it with sandpaper and water. It shall be polished in the same direction, not in a criss-cross direction. Finally, wipe it with water.

Fourth, make a drawing.

①Use chalk to draft on the prepared board (you can also draw the draft on the paper and then pass it to the paint board) .

②Foiling. The foil must be smoothly pasted and dried in the air. Generally, the foil (foil generally refers to gold foil, silver foil, copper foil, aluminum foil, and so on; foil materials include gold and silver foil, eggshell, eggshell powder, aluminum powder, mother-of-pearl powder, varnish powder, etc.) is pasted once or twice.

③Apply the silver paste (coating material made of priming or finish lacquer and silver powder) and finish lacquer on the surface.

④Dry by airing.

⑤Painting and drawing after drying. Paint all the pictures once first, then slowly adjust them. Use fingers to make all kinds of paints (colors) link up naturally and dry them.

Fifth, buff and polish the picture.

①After painting, polish the picture with sandpaper once.

②Buff. Apply it thinly with cotton dipped in water and fine tile powder.

③After painting the picture with tile powder, push the tile powder with palm. When buffing, push it in one direction to brighten the board, and then wipe the picture with a wet cloth.

④Coat the picture once with cotton dipped in edible peanut oil.

⑤Smear the edible cornstarch on the screen.

⑥Use the palm to buff, and then use clean cotton to wipe off the cornstarch.

⑦Wash your hands, grind the picture directly with cornstarch, then fully wipe it with clean cotton. Finally, the product is finished.

· Yangjiang lacquer

Lacquerware products cannot be produced without coating materials. Yangjiang lacquerware craft has always based on raw lacquer. Raw lacquer is made from the sap of lacquer trees. Raw lacquer has excellent performance and is known as the "king of coatings", but the output of raw lacquer in China is far from meeting the demand. Yangjiang ancestors explored and developed a new coating material to replace raw lacquer, that is Yangjiang lacquer, namely cashew nut lacquer.

The manufacturing processes of different Yangjiang lacquer are as follows.

· Manufacturing process of finishing paint

The first step — purification: original cashew nut shell liquid + sulfur + acid + water + turpentine→stirring and heating (adding active clay) →stirring and heating→out of the reacting kettle→stewing and settling→filtering→refined cashew nut shell liquid.

The second step — compounding: refined cashew nut shell liquid + formaldehyde + phenol + tung oil + turpentine + ammonia→stirring and heating (adding drier) →stirring and heating (diluting with turpentine) →out of the reacting kettle→filtering→cooling→storing.

· Manufacturing process of priming paint

Cashew nut shell liquid + rosin + phenol + formaldehyde+ ammonia→stirring and heating (adding drier) →stirring and heating (diluting with 200# paint solvent) →out of the reacting kettle→filtering→cooling→storing.

The advantages of Yangjiang lacquer and traditional lacquer are: ①The paint film is transparent, bright, thick, and has good brushing performance. ②The film is hard, strong, and wear-resistant, and it can be polished. ③The film can prevent corrosion, radiation, water, and organic solvents. Yangjiang lacquer is superior to the traditional lacquer in the following aspects: ①The painting conditions are not harsh. It can be carried out almost all seasons, and the operation is easy to master. However, traditional lacquer should be used under conditions of specific temperature, humidity, and pH value. ②The transparency is better than that of traditional lacquer, making it easy to adjust colors. It can be used to make a variety of colour paints. The

· 阳江漆

漆器产品的生产离不开涂料。阳江漆器工艺向来以生漆为主要涂料。生漆即大漆，是用植物漆树的树液制造而成的。生漆性能精优，素有“涂料之王”的尊称，但我国生漆的产量远不能满足需求，阳江先民们探索研制出代替生漆的新涂料——阳江漆，即腰果漆。

不同的阳江漆的制作流程如下。

· 甲漆（面漆）的制作流程

第一步——提纯：原腰果壳液+硫+酸+水+松节油→搅拌、加温（加活性陶土）→搅拌、加温→出釜→静置沉降→过滤→精腰果壳液。

第二步——合成：精腰果壳液+甲醛+苯酚+桐油+松节油+氨水→搅拌、加温（加催干剂）→搅拌、加温（加松节油稀释）→出釜→过滤→冷却→贮装。

· 乙漆（底漆）制作流程

腰果壳液+松香+苯酚+甲醛+氨水→搅拌、加温（加催干剂）→搅拌、加温（加200号溶剂油稀释）→出釜→过滤→冷却→贮装。

阳江漆与传统的大漆共同的优点是：①漆膜透明，光亮丰厚，涂刷性能好。②漆膜坚硬，耐磨性能强，能抛光。③漆膜能防腐，防辐射，抗水，耐有机溶剂。而阳江漆优于大漆的是：①施工条件不苛刻，几乎一年四季都可以进行，操作容易掌握，但大漆要在特定的温度、湿度以及pH值等条件下方能施工。②透明度比大漆好，易于调色，可以配制多种色漆。漆膜比大漆丰厚光亮，耐碱性优于大漆。③没有毒性，没有臭味，施工中不会发生过敏中毒现象。④制漆原料易获取，价格比大漆便宜。

阳江漆研制成功，使阳江漆器更加多

姿多彩。绘彩工艺改变了过去多半是在黑色底上画上花鸟鱼虫，再用金色勾勒的老款式、老手法，使用了如罩金、镶嵌、推磨等的新技巧，使漆器五彩缤纷，令人叫绝。漆器工艺品表面还采用螺钿、贝壳、玉石等装饰，使其显得雍容华贵、光彩夺目。

主要特征

阳江传统漆器工艺制品有质轻、坚固、耐用、耐水、防潮湿、耐碱、耐大气侵蚀、耐热、耐磨等性能以及硬度高、光亮、漆膜丰富等特点，还有如非强光直照，能长时间不变形、不褪色的优点。使用阳江研制的阳江漆制作的漆器工艺品有以下两种效果：一种叫油光，这种效果的特点是工序流程快、出货快、亮度高，色泽比较浮亮，艺术表现力比较平面；另一种叫推光，这种效果的特点是用砂纸研磨，光暗分明，色泽比较沉实，工序流程慢，艺术表现力更立体、更强。

重要价值

·历史价值

阳江地处沿海，受海洋文化的影响，明末清初始有本地的漆器生产。清嘉庆、道光年间，阳江的漆器在全国已颇具影响。及至清末，不仅产量大，而且具有较高的工艺水平。因阳江的漆器产品多出口东南亚一带，甚至欧美，所以阳江的漆器风格与内陆地区传统的技法、图案都有一些差异，这也就形成了一种地域性极强的、具有广东岭南文化特色的阳江漆器工艺。阳江漆器也成为阳江地区很重要的出口产品。20世纪50年代，阳江国营漆

film is thicker and brighter than the film of traditional lacquer. And the alkali resistance is also better than traditional lacquer. ③Yangjiang lacquer is non-toxic and odorless, preventing allergic reactions and poisoning during construction. ④The raw materials of making Yangjiang lacquer are easy to obtain, and the price is lower than that of the traditional lacquer.

The successful development of Yangjiang lacquer has made Yangjiang lacquerware more colorful. The painting process has changed the old style and method of painting flowers, birds, fish, and insects on a black background and then using gold to outline them. It has used the new craftsmanship of gilding, inlaying, grinding, and so on, which has made the lacquerware colorful and amazing. In addition, the surface of lacquerware handicrafts is decorated with mother-of-pearl, shells, jade, and so on, making them elegant and dazzling.

Main Features

Yangjiang traditional lacquerware handicrafts have functions of lightweight, firm, durability, water resistance, moisture resistance, alkali resistance, atmospheric erosion resistance, heat resistance, abrasion resistance. They also have characteristics of high hardness, brightness, rich film, etc..If it is not directly illuminated by strong light, it has the advantages of no deformation and without fading for a long time. The lacquerware handicrafts made of Yangjiang

戴倩芳漆画《千手观音》
Dai Qianfang's lacquer painting *Thousand-hand Avalokitesvara*

lacquer manufactured in Yangjiang have the following two effects: The first one is called glossy effect, which is characterized by fast process flow, high efficiency, brightness, bright color, and flat artistic expression. The other is called buffing. This effect is characterized by sandpaper polishing to make light and dark clear, with relatively solid color,slow process flow, and a more three-dimension and stronger artistic expression.

Great Value

· Historical value

Yangjiang is located in the coastal area and influenced by the marine culture. There were local lacquerware productions in the late Ming and the early Qing Dynasties. During the period of Jiaqing and Daoguang in the Qing Dynasty, Yangjiang lacquerware had a considerable influence in the country. By the end of the Qing Dynasty, Yangjiang lacquerware had not only a large quantity but also a high technological level. Because most Yangjiang lacquerware products were exported to Southeast Asia, as well as Europe and the United States, there were some differences between Yangjiang lacquerware's style and the traditional craftsmanship and patterns in the mainland, forming a highly regional Yangjiang lacquerware with the characteristics of Lingnan culture in Guangdong. Yangjiang lacquerware has also become a very important export products in the Yangjiang region. In the 1950s, the Yangjiang State-owned Lacquer-ware Craft Factory had been able to produce more than 500 varieties of lacquerware products including practical lacquerware, such as lacquerware furniture and lacquerware supplies, and art lacquerware, such as lacquer ornaments and lacquer paintings, with appreciation and collection value. Back then, only Yangjiang could produce leather lacquer products in larger sizes.

· Cultural value

"A quiet woman's heart is like hair, and a famous master's hands are like gods. Yangjiang's vermilion lacquer is good, leaving the spring of Lingnan behind." This is a poem written by the famous poet Tian Han when he visited the Yangjiang State-owned Lacquerware Craft Factory in 1962.

Yangjiang lacquerware, one of the traditional Chinese arts and crafts, has a long history and is famous both at home and abroad. As early as 1936, a leather lacquer carving called "Longevity Golden Flower Lacquer Box" which won the gold medal at the Nanyang Games was amazing because of its exquisite, ancient simplicity, and beautiful patterns.

范高亮脱胎漆器《四方座海棠瓶》
Fan Gaoliang's bodiless lacquerware
Four-side Begonia Vase

器工艺厂已经能够生产500多个品种的漆器产品，包括实用型漆器工艺品如漆器家具、漆器用品，以及有欣赏、收藏价值的美术工艺品如漆摆件、漆画等。其中较大件的皮制漆艺制品在全国也只有阳江能够生产。

· 文化价值

"静女心如发，名师手有神。阳江朱漆好，留得岭南春。" 这是我国著名诗人田汉在1962年参观阳江国营漆器工艺厂时给阳江漆器题写的诗句。

阳江的漆器制品历史悠久、驰名中外，是中国传统的工艺美术品之一。早在1936年于南洋赛会上荣获金质奖章的一个皮雕"万寿金花漆盒"，就以其精巧玲珑、古朴、花样优美，令人惊叹不已。

1964年由漆艺工人杨华汉创作的漆画《苍鹰》被视为国宝，由外交部赠送给英国女王伊丽莎白。

1978年制作的大型磨漆画《亲切的关怀》，在1978年第二期《人民画报》上发表。

1980年制作的漆壁画《葵乡》，陈列于北京人民大会堂广东厅。

1986年首届中国漆画展上，马文奇的漆画作品《瓜叶梅》被中国美术馆收藏。

1987年，为全国第六届运动会设计木胎“象鼻漆器花瓶”奖杯。

阳江漆器产品作为一种文化载体，它在中外文化艺术交流、艺术品收藏、艺术欣赏中起到了一种桥梁的作用。

·科学价值

因“漆性独与土宜也”，故阳江漆器制作必用阳江漆。阳江漆具有以下特点：没有毒性，没有臭味，在施工中不会发生过敏中毒现象；易于调色，透明度好，可以配制多种色漆，漆膜丰厚光亮、抗碱性强；在施工过程中不受天气、温度、湿度等条件限制；等等。

·经济价值

在20世纪50年代建立的阳江国营漆器工艺厂已经能够生产500多个品种的漆器产品，每年能为国家创汇数十万元，具有很高的经济价值。20世纪80年代之前，阳江漆器产品大多属于出口产品，远销日本、美国、东南亚等国家和地区。

·工艺价值

阳江漆器产品以皮胎、纸胎产品著称，尤以皮胎漆器产品突出，其制作精良，以防潮、耐碱、耐热、耐磨等特点优于其他漆器产品。纸胎漆器产品又以质轻、不易摔碎、耐大气腐蚀等优点在此类产品中独树一帜。

In 1964, the lacquer painting *The Eagle*, created by a lacquer craftsman named Yang Huahan, was presented to Queen Elizabeth by the Ministry of Foreign Affairs as a national treasure.

In 1978, the large-scale polished lacquer painting *Kind Care* was published in the second issue of the *People's Pictorial*.

The lacquer-fresco painting *Kui Xiang*, produced in 1980, is displayed in the Guangdong Hall of the Great Hall of the People in Beijing.

Guayemei, the lacquer painting of Ma Wenqi in the first Chinese lacquer painting exhibition in 1986, is collected by the National Art Museum of China.

The wooden-body “Elephant Nose Lacquerware Vase” trophy was designed for the Sixth National Games in 1987.

As a cultural carrier, Yangjiang lacquerware plays a role as a bridge in fostering cultural and artistic exchanges, art collections, and art appreciation between China and foreign countries.

· Scientific value

Because “the lacquer especially suits Yangjiang's soil”, Yangjiang lacquer must be used in the production of Yangjiang lacquerware products. The Yangjiang lacquer is superior to other lacquers in that it has no toxicity, no odor, no allergy, or poisoning during construction; it is easy to mix with color and could be used to compound multiple color paints, and has good transparency, rich and bright film and strong alkali resistance. In the process of construction, it is not limited by any weather, temperature, humidity, or other conditions.

· Economic value

The Yangjiang State-owned Lacquerware Craft Factory, established in the early 1950s, has been able to produce more than 500 varieties of lacquerware products, earning hundreds of thousands of foreign currency for the country every year with great economic value. Before the 1980s, most of the Yangjiang lacquerware products were exported to Japan, the United States, Southeast Asia, and other countries and regions.

· Craft value

Yangjiang lacquerware products, famous for leathered- and paper-body products, especially for leathered-body lacquerware products, are superior to other lacquerware products in characteristics of well-making, moisture resistance, alkali resistance, heat resistance, wear resistance, etc.. Paper-body lacquerware products are unique among these types of products because of their light weight, resistance to breaking and atmospheric erosion.

Main Inheritors

Fu Yizhou, male, was born in June 1954 in Yangjiang, Guangdong Province. He is now the national representative inheritor of the national intangible cultural heritage list (the fifth batch) "Decorating Craftsmanship of Lacquerware (Yangjiang Decorating Craftsmanship of Lacquerware) " project.

Over the past 50 years of his career, he has devoted himself to the study of traditional lacquer art and has deep attainments in the combination of pottery and lacquer and the Biantu decoration of lacquer art, which forms various decorative patterns based on different materials and tools in a regular manner. He often skillfully uses lacquer art materials and traditional craftsmanship to organically integrate them, so that the works show differences from traditional Chinese painting, oil painting, printmaking, carving, and other art forms. He disproves the narrow perception that lacquer painting is only decorative art and broadens the artistic expression space of lacquer art. His independent or collaborative works have won awards in national and provincial exhibitions numerous times.

傅以周陶胎漆器《漆艺变涂饰纹钵》
Fu Yizhou's pottery-body lacquerware *The Bowl of Lacquer Art with Biantu Decoration Technique*

Chen Qiji (1938–2022) , was born in Yangjiang, Guangdong Province. He was a member of the Guangdong Artists Association and an art and craft artist.

Chen Qiji entered the Yangjiang State-owned Lacquerware Craft Factory in 1962 and founded the Lacquer Ink Garden—Chen Qiji Lacquer Art Studio in 2005. In his lacquer art career with more than 50 years, he was taught by Fu Naibin, Tan Shaoqing, and other old masters in the early stages, skillfully mastering the traditional

主要传承人

傅以周，男，1954年6月生，广东阳江人，现为国家级非物质文化遗产名录“漆器髹饰技艺（阳江漆器髹饰技艺）”项目的国家级代表性传承人（第五批）。

从艺50多年来，傅以周潜心深研传统漆艺，在陶漆结合和漆艺变涂技法等方面有较深的造诣。其漆艺创作常常巧妙运用漆艺材质与传统漆艺技法，使之有机融合，让作品呈现与国、油、版、雕等艺术形式的差异，打破人们对漆画“只属装饰艺术”的狭隘偏见，拓展了漆艺的艺术表现空间。傅以周独立创作或与他人合作的作品多次在国展、省展获奖。

傅以周
Fu Yizhou

陈其积（1938—2022），广东阳江人。广东美术家协会会员，工艺美术师。1962年进入阳江国营漆器工艺厂，2005年创立漆墨苑——陈其积漆艺工作室。50多年的漆艺生涯中，陈其积早期得到傅乃彬、谭绍清等老师傅的亲传，熟练地掌握了漆器传统技艺。他创作的作品融入当代绘画艺术元素，画面富有立体感，而且漆色层次丰富，极致地体现了漆画之美。作品多次在国展、省展获奖或被中国工艺美术馆收藏。为广东省第一批省级非物质文化遗产项目代表性传承人。

craftsmanship of lacquerware. His works were integrated with contemporary painting elements. His works also have stereoscopic screens and rich color, which perfectly reflect the beauty of lacquer painting. His works won awards in national and provincial exhibitions many times or were collected by the China National Arts and Crafts Museum. He was the representative inheritor of the first batch of provincial intangible cultural heritage projects in Guangdong Province.

陈其积
Chen Qiji

陈其积漆画《金龙鱼》
Chen Qiji's lacquer painting *Gold Arowana*

范俊（1938—2013），男，广东阳江人，曾任阳江国营漆器工艺厂设计组组长，中国漆艺家、全国工艺美术学会会员、广东省工艺美术学会理事。1990年10月获中国漆器质量管理协会、漆艺研究中心、中国漆艺家评审委员会"中国漆艺家"称号。为广东省第一批省级非物质文化遗产项目代表性传承人。

范俊一生从事漆艺事业，其漆艺技艺多采用现实主义表现手法，在漆的使用上追求薄、明亮、洁净的艺术效果。他创作、设计过无数漆艺作品，如1962年设计了《四美人台屏》；1965年设计了《荷花折椅》；1982年担任策划，设计制作了广州花园酒店两幅大型（11米×2米）漆画：《百骏图》《百美图》（与山西平遥漆器厂、北京金漆厂等的六位漆艺艺人一起制作完成）；1985年设计制作的《竹型凤纹

Fan Jun (1938-2013), male, was born in Yangjiang, Guangdong Province. He was once the head of the design team of the Yangjiang State-owned Lacquerware Craft Factory. As a Chinese lacquer artist, he was a member of the National Arts and Crafts Society, and a director of the Guangdong Arts and Crafts Society. In October 1990, he was awarded the title of "Chinese Lacquer Artist" by the China Lacquer Quality Management Association, the Lacquer Art Research Center, and the China Lacquer Artist Appraisal Committee. He is the representative inheritor of the first batch of provincial intangible cultural heritage projects in Guangdong Province.

Fan Jun was engaged in lacquer art all his life. His lacquer art features primarily realistic expression craftsmanship, with a focus on thin, bright, and clean artistic effects achieved through the use of lacquer. He created and designed countless lacquer artworks, such as the *Four Beauties Platform Screen* in 1962 and the *Lotus Folding Chair* in 1965. In 1982, he planned, designed, and produced two large lacquer paintings (11 m × 2 m): *The Painting of Hundred Horses* and *The Painting of Hundred Beauties*, cooperating with six lacquer artists from Shanxi Pingyao Lacquerware Factory and Beijing Gold Lacquer Factory, etc. In 1985, he designed and produced the *Bamboo Phoenix Pattern Box*, which won the first prize in Guangdong

Province and was published in *Guangdong Pictorial*; the *Octagon Birthday Box* won the provincial excellent craft award; the *Golden Sleeping Buddha Box* won the third prize of the provincial award.

With the decline of the market for lacquerware, he turned to explore the creation of lacquer painting. His lacquer painting work *Dragon Getting Out of the Sea* was selected in the first national craft exhibition; the *Lighthouse* was selected in the Chinese Lacquer Painting Exhibition; *Begonia* was selected in the 7th National Art Exhibition in 1989; the *Autumn Quail*, created in 2000, was selected in the first lacquer painting exhibition in Guangdong Province; *Group of Chickens* and *Silver Star* and *Begonia* were selected for the second lacquer painting exhibition in Guangdong Province; *As Clean as a New Pin* was published in *Life Magazine*. Fan Jun was interviewed by news media such as Guangdong TV Station and Yangjiang TV Station which reported and broadcasted his works and skills.

范俊脱胎漆器《百子图天球瓶》
Fan Jun's bodiless lacquerware, *Globular Vase with a Cylindrical Neck of Hundred Children's Picture*

Fan Gaoliang, male, was born in August 1972 in a lacquer art family in Yangjiang. Influenced by the lacquer culture in family, he studied traditional lacquerware decoration craftsmanship with his father, Fan Jun (the late provincial inheritor), from childhood. Since graduation from high school, he has been engaged in lacquerware craftsmanship, learning a lot from his father. He is currently the president of the Yangjiang Lacquerware Industry Association, the representative inheritor of the fifth batch of provincial intangible cultural heritage projects in Guangdong Province, a top-notch talent in Yangdong District, Yangjiang and a metrical cultural propagandist in Guangdong Province. Since 2019, he has been invited by Guangdong Lingnan Institute of Technology to give lectures to the students majoring in arts about Yangjiang decorating craftsmanship of lacquerware.

范俊
Fan Jun

盒》，获省一等奖，同时在《广东画报》发表；设计制作的《八角祝寿盒》，获省工艺优秀奖；设计制作的《罩金睡佛盒》，获省三等奖。

随着漆艺工艺品的市场衰退，其转向探索漆画创作，漆画作品《游龙出海》入选第一届全国工艺展；《灯塔》入选中国漆画展；《秋海棠》入选1989年第七届全国美术展；2000年创作的《秋鹑》入选广东省第一届漆画展；《群鸡》《银星海棠》入选广东省第二届漆画展；《一尘不染》则发表在《生活杂志》上。范俊接受过广东电视台、阳江电视台等新闻媒体的采访，其作品和技艺被报道。

范高亮，男，1972年8月出生于阳江一个漆艺家庭，受家庭漆文化氛围的熏陶，自幼跟随父亲范俊（已故省级传承人）研习传统漆器髹饰技艺；高中毕业后开始从事漆器工艺工作至今，深得其父真传。现任阳江市漆艺产业协会会长，为广东省第五批省级非物质文化遗产项目代表性传承人、阳江阳东区区管拔尖人才和广东省基层宣传文化能人。2019年起，受广东岭南职业技术学院聘请，为学院美术专业学生授课，传授阳江漆器髹饰技艺。

范高亮
Fan Gaoliang

曾爱琼，女，生于1956年。1975年至1991年在阳江国营漆器工艺厂工作，师从傅以珍学习漆基础工艺，从事漆器工艺的粉底、油漆两个环节的工作；1991年至1994年任阳江国营漆器工艺厂油漆车间主任；1994年至今，自创漆艺作坊，从事漆器工艺品的粉底、油漆工作。现为阳江市漆艺产业协会会员、阳江市第一批非物质文化遗产项目代表性传承人。

黎安乐，男，生于1974年3月，1996年师从广州美术学院油画系主任袁浩教授学习油画，为日后从事漆艺创作打牢基础，2006年开始专业从事漆艺研究、创作及发展工作。2007年创建黎安乐艺术工作室——漆彩坊，2012年创立黎安乐漆艺馆。在长期的艺术实践与探索中，不断地创新与发展，多次参加全国全省各种漆艺创作大展，屡获殊荣并得到行内专家肯定和认可。现为阳江市第三批非物质文化遗产项目代表性传承人。

Zeng Aiqiong, female, was born in 1956. From 1975 to 1991, she worked at Yangjiang State-owned Lacquerware Craft Factory. She studied basic lacquer craftsmanship from Fu Yizhen and was engaged in the bottom decoration and painting lacquer. From 1991 to 1994, she served as the director of the paint workshop of Yangjiang State-owned Lacquerware Craft Factory. Since 1994, she has created her own lacquer workshop and engaged in bottom decoration and painting lacquer. Now, she is a member of the Yangjiang Lacquerware Art Industry Association and a representative inheritor of the first batch of intangible cultural heritage projects in Yangjiang.

曾爱琼
Zeng Aiqiong

Li An'le, male, was born in March 1974. He studied oil painting under the guidance of Professor Yuan Hao, director of the Oil Painting Department of Guangzhou Academy of Fine Art in 1996, laying a solid foundation for future lacquer art creation. In 2006, he began to specialize in lacquer art research, creation, and development. He founded the Li Anle art studio—Lacquer Shop in 2007 and founded Li Anle Lacquer Art Museum in 2012. In long-term art practice and exploration, he has kept innovating and developing continuously, participating in various national and provincial lacquer art creation exhibitions many times. He has won many awards and has been affirmed and recognized by experts in the industry. Now he is the representative inheritor of the third batch of intangible cultural heritage projects in Yangjiang.

黎安乐
Li An'le

Liang Ruhuan, male, was born in Yangjiang, Guangdong Province in 1940. He is an art and craft artist, a member of the China Lacquer Painting Research Association, a member of the China Arts and Crafts Artists Association, a consultant of the Yangjiang Artists Association Lacquer Painting Art Committee, and an art consultant of the Southeast Art Academy in Yangxi County. In 1978, he served as the design team leader of Yangjiang State-owned Lacquerware Craft Factory, engaging in lacquer art creation until retirement. He is able to skillfully use the traditional skills of lacquer art. In the creation of lacquer painting, he pays attention to the characteristics of the lacquer, and the integration of painting and lacquer, so that the screen can produce a unique random, natural, mysterious, and unique aesthetic feeling. Now he is the representative inheritor of the third batch of intangible cultural heritage projects in Yangjiang.

梁汝欢，男，1940年生，广东阳江人。工艺美术师，中国漆画研究会会员，中国工艺美术家协会会员，阳江市美术家协会漆画艺术委员会顾问，阳西县东南画院艺术顾问。1978年在阳江国营漆器工艺厂任设计组组长，从事漆艺创作至退休。他能娴熟运用漆艺传统技艺。在漆画的创作中，他重视漆材料特性，注重绘画语言和漆艺语言的融合，使画面产生出特有的随意、自然、神秘、独特的美感。现为阳江市第三批非物质文化遗产项目代表性传承人。

梁汝欢
Liang Ruhuan

Zhang Shao, male, was born in a lacquer art family in Yangjiang in 1953. He started to work at Yangjiang State-owned Lacquerware Craft Factory in 1980 and served as the director of the bodiless workshop in 1986. He founded Shaozhai Studio in 2003 to continue to engage in lacquer production. During this period, he participated in the Training Class for Research Talents in the Village of Folk Literature and Art in Guangdong Province, the lacquer painting class held by Yangjiang Federation of Literary and Art Circles and Yangjiang Calligraphy and Painting Academy, and the Chinese painting class held by Yangjiang Artists Association. Now he is the representative inheritor of the fourth batch of intangible cultural heritage projects in Yangjiang.

张韶，男，1953年生于阳江一个漆艺家庭，1980年进入阳江国营漆器工艺厂，1986年任脱胎车间主任，2003年创立韶斋工作室，继续从事漆艺制作。其间参加广东省民间文艺之乡研究人才培训班、阳江市文联和阳江书画院举办的漆画班、阳江市美协举办的国画班学习。现为阳江市第四批非物质文化遗产项目代表性传承人。

张韶
Zhang Shao

黎汝汉，男，生于1961年，1978年高中毕业后开始从事美术相关工作，曾在多家民间漆器作坊从事漆器彩绘工作，1999年师从省级漆艺传承人陈其积老师学习漆画，2013年应邀在叶志豪老师的工作室从事漆艺制作，2014年入职阳江漆艺院，从事漆基础工艺制作，现为阳江市第四批非物质文化遗产项目代表性传承人。

Li Ruhan, male, was born in 1961. He began to work in arts after graduating from high school in 1978. He engaged in painting at many folk lacquerware workshops. In 1999, he learned lacquer painting from Chen Qiji, the provincial lacquer art inheritor. In 2013, he was invited to work at the studio of Ye Zhihao's in making lacquer production. In 2014, he started working in Yangjiang Lacquerware Art Academy in making basic lacquer crafts. Now he is the representative inheritor of the fourth batch of intangible cultural heritage projects in Yangjiang.

黎汝汉
Li Ruhan

黄光，男，生于1962年，1979年高中毕业进入原阳江国营漆器工艺厂脱胎车间工作，师从傅以珍学习漆基础粉底、髹漆、水磨及髹光等技艺，其间还得到何好和黄祖桂等的悉心指导；2003年与同事合作从事漆器产品研制，制作了目前广东最大的脱胎漆器《富贵锦绣漆瓶》等；2014年入职阳江漆艺院，从事漆基础工艺制作；2015年在中国（深圳）国际文化产业博览交易会现场展示阳江漆器制作技艺。现为阳江市第四批非物质文化遗产项目代表性传承人。

Huang Guang, male, was born in 1962. He started working in the bodiless workshop of the Yangjiang State-owned Lacquerware Craft Factory after graduation from high school in 1979. He studied basic craftmanship of bottom decoration, painting lacquer, water polishing, and light painting from Fu Yizhen. Meanwhile, he also received careful guidance from He Hao and Huang Zugui. In 2003, he cooperated with his colleagues in the research and development of lacquerware products, creating the largest bodiless lacquerware in Guangdong as *Rich and Beautiful Lacquer Bottle* and so on. In 2014, he started working in Yangjiang Lacquerware Art Academy and engaged in the production of basic lacquer crafts. In 2015, he demonstrated the manufacturing skills of Yangjiang lacquerware at the China (Shenzhen) International Culture Industries Fair. Now he is the representative inheritor of the fourth batch of intangible cultural heritage projects in Yangjiang.

黄 光
Huang Guang

Luo Jiacheng, male, was born in 1989. He participated in the municipal lacquer art class in 2009, and started working in Yangjiang Lacquerware Art Academy in 2013. In 2016, he graduated from the lacquer art class at Fujian Vocational College of Art. In 2017, he studied in the lacquer art class at China Academy of Art and graduated from the ceramic art class of Fujian Art Vocational College. In 2020, he graduated from the lacquer art class of Beijing City University. His work *Treasure Holding Box* won the silver medal for the first Home Furnishing Exhibition in Guangdong. Many of his works have been collected by governments, enterprises and other organizations. Now he is the representative inheritor of the fourth batch of intangible cultural heritage projects in Yangjiang.

罗嘉诚，男，生于1989年，2009年参加阳江市漆艺班学习，2013年入职阳江漆艺院；2016年结业于福建艺术职业学院漆艺班；2017年在中国美术学院漆艺班进修，结业于福建艺术职业学院陶艺班；2020年结业于北京城市学院漆艺班。作品《百宝捧盒》获广东首届家居展银奖，多件作品被政府和企业机构收藏。现为阳江市第四批非物质文化遗产项目代表性传承人。

罗嘉诚
Luo Jiacheng

Lin Xianjian, male, was born in Yangjiang, Guangdong in October 1988. He graduated from Yangjiang Polytechnic, majoring in art education. In 2008, he began to learn lacquer art from Chen Qiji, the provincial lacquer art inheritor and studied in the Lacquer Ink Garden Studio founded by Chen Qiji for many years. In 2014, he started working in Yangjiang Lacquer Art Institute Co.,Ltd. and engaged in the production of basic lacquerware base, lacquerware, and lacquer painting. Now he is the representative inheritor of the fourth batch of intangible cultural heritage projects in Yangjiang.

林显健，男，1988年10月出生于广东阳江。毕业于阳江职业技术学院美术教育专业。2008年起开始跟随省级漆艺传承人陈其积老师学习漆艺，在陈其积老师创立的漆墨苑工作室学习多年。2014年入职阳江漆艺院有限公司，从事漆艺基础胎底与漆器、漆画的制作。现为阳江市第四批非物质文化遗产项目代表性传承人。

林显健
Lin Xianjian

马文琪，男，1946年出生，从事漆艺工作50多年，为首位被中国美术馆收藏漆画作品的阳江人。现任中国工艺美术家协会会员、首届阳江市民间艺术大师。1966年进入阳江国营漆器工艺厂工作至退休。师从漆艺名师傅乃彬学习漆器的设计、制作。漆画《鹤鸣椰林》《瓜叶梅》入选首届中国漆画展，其中《瓜叶梅》荣获“优秀作品奖”。2006年创立文奇漆艺工作室，开始专职创作和授徒。作品多次在报纸、画刊发表。现为阳江市第五批非物质文化遗产项目代表性传承人。

马文琪
Ma Wenqi

杨国伟，男，1967年出生，从事漆艺工作近40年，自幼跟随父亲杨华汉（阳江漆艺名师）研习漆艺，在漆基础工艺及漆器髹饰技艺方面打下坚实的基础。1984年进入阳江国营漆器工艺厂工作。1995年创立阳江市大成漆器工艺厂，主营漆器出口产品，培养了30多名技术骨干。2004年创立杨氏漆艺工作室。2019年入职阳江漆艺院从事漆艺宣传推广工作。1986年漆画《牛》入选全国漆画展，并荣获优秀作品奖。2014年个人成功研究出新技艺——用

Ma Wenqi, male, was born in 1946, and has engaged in lacquer art for more than 50 years. He is the first Yangjiang person whose lacquer painting has been collected by the National Art Museum of China. Now he is a member of the China Arts and Crafts Association and the Yangjiang folk art master of the first batch. In 1966, he started working in Yangjiang State-owned Lacquerware Craft Factory until retirement. He learned lacquerware design and production from Fu Naibin, a famous lacquer master. His lacquer paintings *Crane Tweeting in Coconut Forest* and *Guayemei* were selected in the first Chinese lacquer painting exhibition, and *Guayemei* won the Excellent Work Award. In 2006, he founded Wenqi Lacquer Art Studio and began full-time creation and teaching apprentices. His works have been published in newspapers and pictorials for many times. Now he is the representative inheritor of the fifth batch of intangible cultural heritage projects in Yangjiang.

Yang Guowei, male, was born in 1967, and has engaged in lacquer art for nearly 40 years. He studied lacquer art with his father Yang Huahan (a famous lacquer artist in Yangjiang) when he was young, and laid a solid foundation in the basic craftsmanship of lacquer and decorating craftsmanship of lacquerware. In 1984, he started working in Yangjing State-owned Lacquerware Craft Factory. In 1995, he founded Yangjiang Dacheng Lacquerware Craft Factory which mainly engaged in exporting lacquerware products and trained more than 30 technical talents. In 2004, he founded the Studio of Yang's Lacquer Art. In 2019, he joined Yangjiang Lacquerware Art Academy to promote lacquer art. In 1986, his lacquer painting *Cow* was selected for the national lacquer painting exhibition and won the excellent work award. In 2014, he successfully developed a new technique—lacquer painting skill with pens, and the representative painting *Narcissus* was displayed in the museum of Yangjiang Lacquerware Art Academy. In November 2020, he won the third prize of the staff group in the final of the National Crafts Making (Lacquerware Painter) Vocational Skills Competition (Practical Operation Competition) . In December 2020, his lacquer painting *Blooming Season* was selected for the 7th provincial lacquer painting exhibition held by Guangdong Artists Association. Now he is the representative inheritor of the fifth batch of intangible cultural heritage projects in Yangjiang.

杨国伟
Yang Guowei

笔堆漆技法，代表作有漆画《水仙花》，作品现在在阳江漆艺院博物馆展示。2020年11月在全国工艺品制作（漆器髹漆工）职业技能竞赛（实操比赛）总决赛中荣获职工组三等奖。2020年12月漆画《花开时节》入选广东省美术家协会举办的全省第七届漆画作品展。现为阳江市第五批非物质文化遗产项目代表性传承人。

Yang Yaozhuo, male, was born in 1963, has engaged in lacquer art for more than 40 years. His grandfather and father engaged in the lacquer art industry. He has inherited from them. After graduating from high school, he began to learn decoration and painting craftsmanship of lacquer. In 1987, he started working in the painting workshop of Yangjiang State-owned Lacquerware Craft Factory. After the dissolution of the factory, he has continued to engage in the lacquer art industry until now. In 2018, he founded the Chaliao Lacquer Art Workshop to teach lacquer skills. In 2013, his lacquer painting *Lotus Pond* was selected for the third Guangdong Lacquer Painting Exhibition. In 2013, he created a large lacquer vase *Flowers Bloom Rich* with a height of 230 cm, which has been kept in Yangjiang Lacquerware Art Academy since then. In 2014, his lacquer painting *Spring Scenery* was selected into the Yangjiang Dragon Boat Culture Festival and won the second prize. Now he is the representative inheritor of the fifth batch of intangible cultural heritage projects in Yangjiang.

杨耀卓，男，1963年出生，从事漆艺工作40多年，祖父与父亲从事漆艺行业，三代家族传承，高中毕业后开始学习漆画装饰和髹饰技艺。1987年进入阳江市国营漆器工艺厂的画花车间工作；企业解散后，继续从事漆艺行业至今。2018年创立茶寮漆艺作坊，收徒传授漆技艺。2013年，漆画作品《荷塘》入选广东省第三届漆画作品展；2013年，创作高230厘米的漆器大花瓶《花开富贵》，并在阳江市漆艺院保存至今；2014年，漆画作品《春色》入选阳江市龙舟文化节并荣获二等奖。现为阳江市第五批非物质文化遗产项目代表性传承人。

杨耀卓
Yang Yaozhuo

阮文峰，男，1988年出生，从艺20多年。2001年师承陈其积（漆器髹饰技艺项目省级传承人）学习漆器髹饰技艺至今。作品多次获国家级奖项。漆画《岁月如歌》获得中国当代漆艺展优秀奖。《筑境·岁月流金》入选第四届全国漆画作品展；《筑境·峥嵘岁月》入选第五届全国漆画作品展；《筑境·红色记忆》入选2017年“中国·厦门漆画作品双年展”，并被福建省美术馆永久收藏。现为阳江市第五批非物质文化遗产项目代表性传承人。

Ruan Wenfeng, male, was born in 1988, and has engaged in lacquer art for more than 20 years. In 2001, he began to learn Yangjiang Lacquerware Decorating Craftsmanship from Chen Qiji (the provincial inheritor of the Lacquerware Decorating Craftsmanship project) . His works have won many national awards. His lacquer painting *Time Like Song* won an excellent award at China contemporary lacquer art exhibition. *Building Scenery · Time Flowing like Gold* was selected for the 4th national lacquer painting exhibition. *Building Scenery · Emergent Years* was selected for the 5th national lacquer painting exhibition. *Building Scenery · Red Memories* was selected for the 2017 China · Xiamen Lacquer Painting Biennale, and permanently collected by Fujian Art Museum. Now he is the representative inheritor of the fifth batch of intangible cultural heritage projects in Yangjiang.

阮文峰
Ruan Wenfeng

林业潮，男，1986年出生，从艺17年，2006年开始跟随陈其积老师（漆器髹饰技艺项目省级传承人）学习漆艺，现供职于阳江市漆墨苑——陈其积漆艺工作室。2011年10月，漆画作品《明清遗迹》被评为阳江市美术作品赴穗调展优秀作品。2013年10月，漆画作品《北山宋塔》入选广东省第十二届美术书法摄影作品联展。2013年10月，漆画作品《韵》荣获广东省第十二届美术书法摄影作品联展银奖。现为阳江市第五批非物质文化遗产项目代表性传承人。

Lin Yechao, male, was born in 1986, and has engaged in lacquer art for 17 years. In 2006, he began to learn Yangjiang Lacquerware Decorating Craftsmanship from Chen Qiji (the provincial inheritor of the Lacquerware Decorating Craftsmanship project). He is now working in Lacquer Ink Garden—Chen Qiji's Lacquer Art Studio in Yangjiang. In October 2011, his lacquer painting *Relics of the Ming and Qing Dynasties* was rated as the outstanding work of the Yangjiang artworks exhibition in Guangzhou. In October 2013, his lacquer painting *Song Tower of the Beishan Mountain* was selected for the 12th Guangdong Fine Arts, Calligraphy, and Photography Joint Exhibition. In October 2013, his lacquer painting *Charm* won the silver award at the 12th Guangdong Fine Arts, Calligraphy, and Photography Joint Exhibition. Now he is the representative inheritor of the fifth batch of intangible cultural heritage projects in Yangjiang.

林业潮
Lin Yechao

阳江风筝

广东省第一批省级非物质文化遗产名录

保护单位 阳江市风筝协会

Yangjiang Kite

The First Batch of the Provincial Intangible Cultural Heritage List of Guangdong Province

Protection Unit Yangjiang Kites Association

As a typical representative of the "Southern Kite" in China's "Northern Kite and Southern Kite", Yangjiang Kite's making and flying skills are unique. Yangjiang is located on the southwest coast of Guangdong Province, which is the key point in the west of Guangdong. It has a subtropical monsoon climate with mostly southeast winds. It faces the sea with mountains behind, with vast wilderness and natural kite-flying grounds. Yangjiang's autumn is cool and dry, and the wind is strong, making it the best season to fly kites. The unique geographical and climatic conditions have nurtured a long history of kite culture in Yangjiang. Because Yangjiang is close to the sea, it has high humidity, diverse climate, and typhoons in the summer. Yangjiang kites have been improved repeatedly under such conditions. The folk craftsmen's skills of making and flying kites were more and more sophisticated. With practice, they can use the wind to aid their works, freely applying the "wind" to them, which is fully reflected in the Yangjiang Kite's representative work, "Ganoderma Lucidum Kite". Even in bad weather, it can fly high and far with good stability, which is also one of the important reasons why Yangjiang Kite has won good awards many times in national kite competitions.

Manufacturing craftsmanship of Yangjiang Kite has spread throughout Yangjiang, among which Jiangcheng District and Yangxi County are the most widespread areas. In Jiangcheng District, kite craftsmen are mainly gathered in the Longjin Road area. In the 1980s or 1990s, dozens of households along Longjin Road specialized in making kites for family maintenance. The kite craftsmen in Yangxi County mostly gathered in coastal areas, represented by Shapa Town. Every year, from the beginning of August of the lunar calendar, hundreds of meters of Hedi Road will be filled with a variety of colorful

阳江风筝是中国“南鹞北鸢”中“南鹞”的典型代表，其制作和放飞技巧自成流派，独具风采。阳江市地处广东西南沿海，扼粤西要冲，属于亚热带季风气候，多吹东南风。其地势背山面海，旷野辽阔，到处都是天然的放飞场。秋季凉爽干燥，风力顺劲，是放飞风筝的最好时节。得天独厚的地理和气候条件孕育了源远流长的风筝文化。因为阳江靠海，其湿度较大，气候变化多样，夏季还有台风侵袭，阳江风筝就是在这样的条件下经过反复改良而制成的。民间艺人的扎制手艺和放飞技能也愈发高超，通过实践能借风扶摇，把“风”自如地运用到自己的作品中，这在阳江风筝代表作“灵芝风筝”中得到充分的体现。即使在恶劣气候下，“灵芝风筝”的稳定性仍非常好，能飞得又高又远，这也是阳江风筝在全国风筝比赛中屡获佳绩的重要原因之一。

阳江风筝的制作技艺流传于整个阳江地区，其中，流传最广的是在江城区和阳西县。在江城区，风筝艺人主要集中在龙津路一带。20世纪八九十年代，龙津路沿街有数十户人家是靠制作风筝来维系生活的专业户。而阳西县的风筝艺人，则多集中在沿海地区，以沙扒镇为代表。每年从农历八月初起，长几百米的河堤路就会摆满千姿百态、五彩缤纷的风筝摊档，市民纷纷来此购买风筝，准备在重阳节期间放飞。在阳江，无论是知识阶层还是普罗大众都十分喜爱此项活动，他们以制作风筝为乐，艺人则以制作出精品风筝为荣，所以阳江地区重阳节放风筝的传统，一直延续至今。

2006年，阳江风筝被列入广东省第一批省级非物质文化遗产名录。

历史渊源

根据史志记载，早于明清时期阳江风筝已兴盛。清《阳江县志》记载，“九月九日重阳节，士人结伴登高，饮菊花酒。童子放纸鸢，或悬藤弓其上，半空嘹亮，响彻云衢”。《阳江志》（民国十四年版）记载，“重阳日结伴携酒选胜登高，士人赋诗儿童放纸鸢较高下，或悬藤弓其上，风激之鸣，响彻云霄，北山尤盛”。明代诗人陈震的《重九偕游翠岩亭次韵》，清代阳西女诗人王若霞的七言律诗《纸鸢》、林葆莹的《竹枝词》、陈芸池的《己巳年重九同人泛棹登高北山有感》、林钟英的《重九登高步韵我佛》和李春元的《风筝》等诗歌辞赋对阳江风筝都有记载。

据冯光、阮加培、梁汝兴等风筝传承人回忆，旧时，每年中秋节过后，家家户户、男女老幼都会亲手制作风筝迎接重阳节的到来。富庶人家还会请名师至家中扎制风筝，筹备重阳祭祀事宜。每逢重阳，全城出动，万人空巷，红男绿女，扶老携幼，经水路、陆路聚集北山等地，放鹞、赋诗、唱弦歌、对山歌和野炊，人山人

龙津路一带的风筝艺人

Kite craftsmen in the Longjin Road area

kite stalls. Citizens will come here to buy kites for flying during the Double Ninth Festival. Both the intellectuals and the general public in Yangjiang are very fond of this activity. People enjoy making kites, while kite craftsmen are proud of making fine kites. Therefore, the tradition of flying kites during the Double Ninth Festival in Yangjiang has continued until now.

In 2006, Yangjiang Kite was listed in the first batch of the provincial intangible cultural heritage list of Guangdong Province.

Historical Origin

According to historical records, flying kites flourished as early as the Ming and Qing Dynasties in Yangjiang. *Yangjiang County Annals* in the Qing Dynasty records that "on the Double Ninth Festival, scholars climb mountains together to drink chrysanthemum wine, and children fly paper kites.The kites make a sound in the wind, resounding in the sky, because of the bamboo framework on the kites". According to *Yangjiang Annals* in the period of the Republic of China, "On the Double Ninth Festival, people climb high together. Scholars compose poems, and children fly kites to compete with each other. Because of the bamboo framework on the kites, the kites make a sound by blowing, resounding to the sky, especially of frequent occurence in the Beishan mountains". *Visiting Cuiyan Pavilion Together on the Double Ninth Festival* written by the poet Chen Zhen of the Ming Dynasty; the seven-character poem *Kites* written by the Yangxi female poet Wang Ruoxia, *Zhuzhi Poem* written by Lin Baoying, *Boating and Climbing Beishan Mountain with Others on the Double Ninth Festival of 1869* written by Chen Yunchi, *Climb*

High on the Double Ninth Festival and Feel the Buddh written by Lin Zhongying, and *Kites* written by Li Chunyuan in the Qing Dynasty are all about Yangjiang kites.

According to Feng Guang, Ruan Jiapei, Liang Ruxing, and other inheritors of kites, in the old days, every family and every person would make kites to welcome the Double Ninth Festival after the Mid-Autumn Festival. Rich families would invite famous kite craftsmen to make kites at home to prepare for the Double Ninth Festival sacrifice. On the Double Ninth Festival, the whole city turned out to fly kites, compose poems, sing string songs and hill songs, and have picnics, gathering in Beishan Mountain and other places by water and land. The activity was very bustling, with huge crowds of people. As a cultural symbol handed down from generation to generation, Yangjiang Kite carries the shared social memory and spiritual feelings of the Yangjiang people.

Because of the deep and extensive mass base of Yangjiang Kite, the government of Yangjiang selected the site on the side of Yuanyang Lake in the urban area in 1991 and planned to build the Southern Kite Competition Field covering 120,000 square meters. In the same year, Yangjiang was named "Hometown of Kites in Guangdong" by the Guangdong Provincial Sports Committee. In 1992, the Standing Committee of Yangjiang Municipal People's Congress adopted a resolution to designate the Double Ninth Festival as "Yangjiang Kite Festival". In 1993, Yangjiang was awarded the title of "Hometown of Kites in China" by China Kites Association. In 2002, the Yangjiang Kite Museum covering 1,500 square meters was built.

Basic Content

Yangjiang Kite is made by hand, combining the four arts of tying, pasting, painting, and flying, which are especially different from northern kites in terms of tying and flying skills. Yangjiang Kite has a wide range of themes. Flowers, grass, vegetables, fruits, birds, fish, insects, and other plants and animals in life, and folk legends, literary stories, and modern commercial advertisements can all be creation themes, full of the rich flavor of life. Kite painting adopts a large area of contrast color, which is bright in color and clear in shape when flying. Representative works include Ganoderma Lucidum Kite, Dragon (Centipede) Kite, Eagle Kite, Stereoscopic Flower and Plant Kite, Advertising Kite.

(1) Ganoderma Lucidum Kite. It is unique in shape, and is the only extant board kite with a complete kite buzzer (rattan bow) and

市民在南国风筝竞赛场放风筝
Citizens fly kites at the Southern Kite Competition Field

海，热闹非凡。阳江风筝作为代代相传的文化符号，承载了阳江人民共同的社会记忆与精神情感。

正是由于阳江风筝深厚广泛的群众基础，阳江市政府于1991年选址于市区鸳鸯湖一侧，规划建设占地12万平方米的南国风筝竞赛场；同年，阳江被广东省体委命名为“广东省风筝之乡”；1992年，阳江市人大常委会通过决议，将重阳节定为“阳江风筝节”；1993年，阳江被中国风筝协会授予“中国风筝之乡”称号；2002年，面积1500平方米的阳江风筝馆建成。

基本内容

阳江风筝纯手工制作，融合了扎、糊、绘、放四艺，尤其在扎、放技巧上与“北鸢”风格迥异。题材种类繁多，生活中的花、草、蔬、果、鸟、鱼、虫、兽等动植物，以及民间传说、文学故事、现代商业广告，均可为创作题材，充满浓郁的生活气息。风筝绘画采用大面积对比色，放飞时色彩鲜艳、外形清晰。阳江风筝的代表作有灵芝风筝、龙（百足）风筝、崖鹰风筝、立体花草鹞和广告风筝。

（1）灵芝风筝。该风筝造型独一无二，是国内唯一存世的带完整筝鸣器（藤

"世界十绝风筝"之一：灵芝风筝，传承人梁汝佳作品
Ganoderma Lucidum Kite, one of the "Top Ten Kites in the World", the work of the inheritor Liang Rujia

传统串飞崖鹰风筝，传承人梁玉泉作品
The traditional Eagle Kite of tandem flying, the work of the inheritor Liang Yuquan

弓）和不带尾巴的板子类风筝，为"世界十绝风筝"之一，有过风筝比赛全国"五连冠"的辉煌纪录。

（2）龙（百足）风筝。该风筝因其独特的制作技艺以及放飞时能表演"龙戏水""龙吐珠""戏鞭炮""龙头吐火"等放飞特技，被誉为"阳江活龙"。

（3）崖鹰风筝。该风筝既可"单飞""双飞"，还可有"竖飞""串飞"和上百只"群飞"的放飞形式，常引真鹰同飞共舞。

（4）立体花草鹞。该风筝用立体扎制工艺表现自然花草，使风筝生活气息浓郁、趣味盎然。

（5）广告风筝。改革开放以来，阳江风筝制作样式与时俱进，出现了各种商业造型和企业广告的新风筝类型。

主要特征

阳江风筝以造型别致、工艺精巧、绘制精美、色彩鲜艳、生动灵活、惟妙惟

without tail in China. It is one of the "Top Ten Kites in the World", and has the glory of "Five Consecutive Championship" in national kite competitions.

(2) Dragon (Centipede) Kite. It is known as the "Yangjiang living dragon" because of its unique manufacturing craftsmanship and the ability to perform flying stunts such as "dragon playing with water", "dragon spitting pearls", "playing with firecrackers", and "spitting fire from the dragon head".

(3) Eagle Kite. It can not only "fly alone", and "fly together", but also fly in the form of "vertical flying", "tandem flying" and "group flying". It often attracts real eagles to fly together.

(4) Stereoscopic Flower and Plant Kite. It shows natural flowers and plants with three-dimension binding technique, making kites rich in vitality and interest.

(5) Advertising Kite. Since the reform and opening-up policy, Yangjiang Kite has developed with the times, emerging new types of kites with a variety of commercial modeling and corporate advertising.

Main Features

Yangjiang Kite is famous for its unique shape, exquisite craftsmanship, delicate painting, bright colors, vividness and flexibility, lifelikeness, and unity of form and spirit.

· Features of manufacturing

Yangjiang kites are purely handmade, and their craftsmanship is mainly embodied in the skeleton binding. Taking the production of dragon head for example, the skeleton binding of ears, eyes, nose, tongue, cheeks, whiskers, horns, and other parts is stereoscopically presented. Take another example of Ganoderma Lucidum Kite, whose "water chestnut meat", "Ganoderma lucidum grass", "orchid leaf", "deer", and other parts are also fully demonstrated. Stereoscopic Flower and Plant Kite shows natural flowers and plants with a three-dimension binding craftsmanship.

· Features of flying

The flying of Yangjiang kites pays attention to flexibility and vividness, such as Dragon Kite, which changes the length and force angle of the kite's connecting line through traction to make it swing flexibly in the air. It can also perform flying stunts such as "dragon playing with water", "dragon spitting pearls", "playing with firecrackers", "spitting fire from the dragon head", and is known as "Yangjiang living dragon". Eagle Kite can not only "fly alone", but also "fly in groups" by "vertical flying" and "tandem flying", often attracting real eagles to fly together. The most characteristic is Ganoderma Lucidum Kite installed with a rattan bow, and it will make a kite sound with the change of airflow when flying, being truly one of the "Top Ten Kites in the World".

龙风筝，被誉为“阳江活龙”
Dragon Kite, Known as "Yangjiang living dragon"

肖、形神兼备而著称。

· 制作特色

阳江风筝为纯手工制作，其工艺主要体现在骨架扎制中。如龙头的制作，在耳、眼、鼻、舌、腮、须、角等部位的骨架扎制上均立体呈现。再如灵芝风筝，其“菱角肉”“灵芝草”“兰花叶”“小鹿”等部位结构也充分彰显。而立体花草鹞则用立体扎制工艺表现自然花草。

· 放飞特色

阳江风筝放飞讲究灵活生动，如龙风筝，通过牵引改变风筝连线长度和受力角度，使其在空中灵活摆动，还能表演“龙戏水”“龙吐珠”“戏鞭炮”“龙头吐火”等放飞特技，被誉为“阳江活龙”；崖鹰风筝既可“单飞”，还可用“树飞”和“串飞”形成“群飞”，常引真鹰同飞共舞；最具特色的灵芝风筝，则安装了“藤弓”，放飞时随气流变化会发出筝鸣声，是名副其实的“世界十绝风筝”。

重要价值

· 历史、文化价值

阳江是“南鹞”的发祥地之一，阳江风筝是具有代表性的南派风筝。风筝作为代代相传的文化符号，承载着阳江人民共同的社会记忆与精神情感，为研究阳江的历史文化、各时代社会状况、生产力发展及文化娱乐生活提供了宝贵的依据。

· 艺术、收藏价值

阳江风筝所创作的各种造型，都追求别致精巧、形神兼备、色彩明亮、生动逼真，其工艺古朴精湛，具有较高的艺术性和收藏价值。

· 科学价值

阳江风筝的制作及放飞包含了空气动

力学、流体力学和飞行等原理，具有科学研究的价值。

·社会、伦理价值

阳江“放鹞”始于邑民自发的重阳登高、祈福习俗，阳江人民将国泰民安、风调雨顺、幸福安康等美好、吉祥的意愿，寄情于高飞的风筝，并逐渐演变为“志存高远、脚踏实地、拼搏向上、锲而不舍、团结合作”的风筝文化精髓和人文精神。其为阳江独特的地方文化的形成和发展，奠定了坚实的文化底蕴，产生了深远的历史影响。

在多元文化交互融合的新时代，阳江风筝成为阳江连接世界的桥梁纽带。以“五湖四海一线牵”为宗旨的阳江国际风筝节，通过“走出去、请进来”的形式开展国际交流，对实施“一带一路”倡议有着积极的促进作用。为阳江独特的地方文化的形成和发展，奠定了坚实的文化底蕴，也为发展中的阳江营造了一个文明、友善、和谐的社会氛围。

阳江凤凰风筝，传承人梁玉泉作品
Yangjiang Phoenix Kite, the work of the inheritor Liang Yuquan

Great Value

· Historical and cultural value

Yangjiang is one of the birthplaces of “Southern Kite” and Yangjiang Kite is the representative of southern kites. As a cultural symbol handed down from generation to generation, Yangjiang Kite carries the social memory and spiritual feelings shared by the people of Yangjiang. It provides a valuable basis for the study of Yangjiang's history and culture, social conditions of various times, productivity development, and cultural and entertainment life.

· Art and collecting value

The various shapes of Yangjiang Kite pursue unique and exquisite design, with both form and spirit, bright colors, and vivid and lifelike appearance. Its craftsmanship is simple and exquisite, with high artistic value and collecting value.

· Scientific value

The manufacturing and flying of Yangjiang Kite include the principles of aerodynamics, hydrodynamics, flight, and so on, providing value for scientific research.

· Social and ethical value

The activity of flying kites in Yangjiang began with the spontaneous custom of climbing high in the Double Ninth Festival and praying for blessings. Yangjiang people place their hopes on flying kites for good and lucky wishes, such as peace and prosperity, good weather, as well as happiness and health. It gradually evolved into the essence of kite culture and the humanistic spirit of “aiming high, doing down-to-earth work, striving upward, perseverance, unity, and cooperation”. It has laid a solid cultural foundation for the formation and development of Yangjiang's unique local culture, having a profound historical impact.

In the new era of multi-cultural integration, Yangjiang Kite has become a bridge connecting Yangjiang to the world. The Yangjiang International Kite Festival, which aims to unite people from different areas and lead the international exchanges in the form of “going out and inviting in”, plays a positive role in promoting the implementation of the “Belt and Road Initiative”. It has laid a solid cultural foundation for the formation and development of Yangjiang's unique local culture and created a civilized, friendly, and harmonious social atmosphere for the developing Yangjiang.

Main Inheritors

Liang Ruxing (1943-2017), whose stage name was Liang Jia, male, was born in November 1943. He began to fly kites with his father when he was young, and learn to make kites from his father when he was a little older. He engaged in the research, inheritance, and development of kites, and enjoyed a high reputation in the kite industry. Three generations of his family have been engaged in kite production and sales, making them truly a "kite family". Liang Ruxing was the representative inheritor of the first batch of the provincial intangible cultural heritage projects in Guangdong Province.

Liang Ruxing was good at making southern kites, including the dragon, board, and hard-wing kites. The kites he made were characterized by exquisite workmanship as follows: bright colors, liveliness, and unity of form and spirit. His works were sold at home and abroad. His representative works include Dragon Kite, Ganoderma Lucidum Kite, Double Phoenix Towards Peony Kite, Rich Cat and Butterfly Kite, Duck Piercing Lotus Kite, Goldfish Kite, and so on. Liang Ruxing served as the captain and coach of the Yangjiang Kite Team, leading the team to win eight team championships and more than 130 single event gold medals. Since 1988, he had participated in various domestic and international kite competitions, including 16 national kite competitions, two kite competitions in the national peasants game, and five international kite competitions.

Liang Ruxing was also committed to the inheritance, protection, and development of kites, promoting kite culture, and excavating and protecting endangered kite species. He traveled to various parts of the country for kite performances and exchanges many times. Under the inheritance and guidance of Liang Ruxing, his younger brother Liang Ruhuan, his son Liang Yuquan, his nephews Liang Yujia and Lin Huan, his daughters Liang Yuyan and Liang Yuqin, and his son-in-law Tan Yiwang, have mastered the craftsmanship of kite manufacturing and can make all kinds of kites. They are also the main members of the Yangjiang Kite Team.

Liang Ruxing also taught the skills earnestly to Hong Kong middle school students who came to Yangjiang to learn kite making during their holidays. During the Double Ninth Festival (Yangjiang Kite Festival), he went to kindergartens to give lectures on kites and organize kite-making competitions and other activities, making outstanding contributions to the inheritance and development of Yangjiang Kite.

主要传承人

梁汝兴

Liang Ruxing

梁汝兴（1943—2017），艺名梁佳，男，1943年11月出生，自幼随父放飞风筝，稍大后开始随父亲学习制作风筝，几十年以来一直从事风筝的研究和传承发展工作，在风筝界享有很高的声誉。梁汝兴一家三代都是从事风筝制作和销售的阳江风筝专业户，是名副其实的“风筝世家”。梁汝兴为广东省第一批省级非物质文化遗产项目代表性传承人。

梁汝兴擅长制作南派风筝，即龙类、板子类和硬翅类风筝，他制作的风筝有如下技艺特点：做工精湛、色彩鲜艳、生动活泼、形神兼备。其作品远销国内外。代表性作品有龙风筝、灵芝风筝，以及双凤朝牡丹、富贵猫蝶、宝鸭穿莲、金鱼风筝等。梁汝兴曾任阳江风筝队队长和教练，带领阳江风筝队共取得8次团体冠军，收获130多枚单项金牌。他自1988年开始参加国内、国际各类风筝赛事，其中包括16次全国风筝比赛、2次全国农民运动会风筝比赛、5次国际风筝比赛。

梁汝兴还致力于风筝的传承、保护、发展工作，弘扬风筝文化，挖掘保护濒临绝迹的风筝种类。他多次到全国各地进行风筝表演和交流。在梁汝兴的传承、指导下，小弟梁汝欢、儿子梁玉泉、侄子梁玉家、外甥林焕、女儿梁玉燕和梁玉琴、女婿谭亦旺已掌握了风筝的制作技术，能制作各类风筝，亦是阳江风筝队的主力队员。

梁汝兴还悉心将技艺传授给利用假期来阳江学习风筝制作的香港中学师生，在重阳节（即阳江风筝节）期间到各幼儿园举办风筝讲座，组织风筝制作比赛等活动，为阳江风筝的传承、发展不遗余力，作出突出贡献。

阮加培（1929—2018），男，1929年10月出生，其祖父阮鸿才十分喜爱放风筝，后自己动手制作风筝。父亲阮凤杨从事篾器工艺，扎制风筝可谓轻车熟路、得心应手。阮加培自7岁开始随祖父、父亲学习扎制、放飞风筝，制作了大量精美的风筝，最拿手的是龙类风筝和宫灯风筝。阮加培为广东省第一批省级非物质文化遗产项目代表性传承人。

自1986年参加山东潍坊举行的全国第一届风筝比赛开始，阮加培获得数十枚奖牌和数个奖杯。其中，1992年，他代表中国风筝队到美国参加风筝比赛，获得第一名。2000年制作了龙类风筝“七彩巨龙”，长达200米，堪称阳江龙类风筝第一。在制作中，他突破传统，大胆创新，龙身长度超出传统风筝数倍；在绘制上，他改变过去龙类风筝着色“一片绿，一片红”的单调色彩，采用了赤、橙、黄、绿、青、蓝、紫七种颜色来搭配。龙身的制作与

Ruan Jiapei (1929–2018), male, was born in October 1929. His grandfather, Ruan Hongcai, loved flying kites very much and later made kites himself. His father, Ruan Fengyang, was engaged in the craft of bamboo stripware which made him familiar with making kites. Ruan Jiapei had been learning to make and fly kites with his grandfather and father since he was 7 years old. He had made a large number of exquisite kites. The best ones were dragon kites and palace lantern kites. He was the representative inheritor of the first batch of provincial intangible cultural heritage projects in Guangdong Province.

He had won dozens of medals and trophies since he participated in the first national kite competition held in Weifang, Shandong Province in 1986. In 1992, on behalf of the Chinese kite team, he participated in a kite competition in the United States and won the first prize. In 2000, he produced the 200-meter-long dragon kite "Colorful Dragon", which could be called the best one of Yangjiang dragon kites. He broke through the tradition and made bold innovations in production. The length of the "Colorful Dragon" was several times longer than that of traditional kites. The painting of the dragon kite used seven colors such as red, orange, yellow, green, blue, indigo and purple, changing the monotonous colors of the past with green and red. The body of the dragon kite was similar to that of traditional southern kites but incorporated some techniques of northern kites. The 200-meter-long dragon kite rose into the sky and flew in the air, which was very spectacular. The colorful dragon kite was particularly eye-catching in the sunlight. When the autumn wind passed, the dragon kite sometimes raised its head to the sky, sometimes turned over and moved, being lifelike and vivid, which caused a stir in the whole of Yangjiang City. In the same year, the kite won the international

阳江宫灯风筝，传承人阮加培作品
Yangjiang Palace Lantern Kite, the work of Ruan Jiapei

阮加培
Ruan Jiapei

gold medal in the kite competition held in Hong Kong, China.

The palace lantern kite made by Ruan Jiapei had elegant modeling and exquisite manufacturing, with the characteristics of stable flying and strong wind induction. He participated in domestic and foreign kite competitions on behalf of Yangjiang for many times and won three national championships. *Yangjiang Daily* praised Ruan Jiapei's kites as "palace lanterns hanging in the sky and dragon swimming in the clouds".

Ruan Jiapei's another unique skill was making a kind of special kite called "Flying Moth", which enjoyed a certain reputation in the kite industry in Yangjiang and even in the whole country. The kite was shaped like a butterfly. It could cause a big stir in the sky, set off firecrackers, scatter ribbons, and perform other stunts.

Ruan Jiapei devotedly trained inheritors as well. His three sons and one daughter can also make and fly kites. His eldest son, Ruan Quan, is a key member of the Yangjiang Kite Team. Ruan Jiapei was never tired of teaching kite enthusiasts who came to him for advice.

Feng Guang (1928-2013), male, was born in Yangjiang, Guangdong Province, in February 1928. He began to learn the making and flying of kites from his grandfather, Feng Yuchi, when he was 10 years old, and formally studied under Yang Maozhi when he was 13 years old. In more than 70 years, he always insisted on making kites. On the basis of tradition, he had developed a school of his own. His Ganoderma Lucidum Kite was vivid, lively, reasonable in structure, skillful in wind exposure, and able to make a loud sound spreading throughout a radius of ten miles. Feng Guang was the representative inheritor of the second batch of the provincial intangible cultural heritage projects in Guangdong Province.

传统的南派风筝差不多，但又融入了北派风筝的一些技法。200米长的巨龙腾空而起，在空中十分壮观。七彩的龙身在阳光的映照下分外夺目。秋风过处，巨龙时而昂首向天，时而翻转腾挪，其形栩栩，其魂神似，当时轰动了整个阳江市。同年，该风筝在我国香港举行的风筝比赛中荣获国际金奖。

阮加培制作的宫灯风筝，其造型雍容大度，制作上精致华丽，具有放飞稳定、风流感应力强等特点，曾多次代表阳江参加国内外风筝赛事，并获得过三次全国冠军。《阳江日报》赞誉阮加培的风筝“宫灯天上挂，巨龙云中游”。

阮加培还有一手绝活，就是制作特技风筝“吹蛾”，在阳江乃至全国风筝界都享有一定的声誉。该风筝造型形似蝴蝶，能在天上来一场“大闹天宫”，可以完成“燃放鞭炮”“飞撒彩带”等特技动作。

阮加培还悉心培养传承人，他的三子一女都能制作、放飞风筝，长子阮权更是一把好手，也是阳江风筝队的主力队员之一。对上门求教的风筝爱好者，阮加培更是不厌其烦地传授技艺。

冯光（1928—2013），男，1928年2月生，广东阳江人，自10岁开始随祖父冯玉池学习扎制、放飞风筝，13岁时正式师从杨茂芝。在70多年中，一直坚持风筝制作，在继承传统的基础上，独树一帜，自成一派。其制作的灵芝风筝形象生动、活泼灵巧、结构合理，受风面巧妙，弓响之声传遍方圆十里。冯光为广东省第二批省级非物质文化遗产项目代表性传承人。

冯光以制作灵芝风筝为主。1986年后，他制作的灵芝风筝多次代表省、市参加国内外风筝大赛，曾有过全国“五连冠”的辉煌纪录，被称为“灵芝风筝大王”。冯光还具有丰富的调校经验，因为灵芝风筝的放飞和其他风筝不同，其他风筝放飞时基本会直上，而灵芝风筝一放飞便左右摇摆难以控制，要根据风力的大小和风筝摇摆程度来调整放飞线，才能顺利升空。而经冯光精心调校后的灵芝风筝，不仅能顺利放飞，还可在空中作“横8字”形飞行，令人叫绝，且在放飞后收回时能完好地回到手中。1990年，在潍坊第七届国际风筝赛会上，他制作的灵芝风筝被评选为“世界十绝风筝”之一，这也是阳江风筝迄今获得的最高殊荣。

冯光
Feng Guang

Feng Guang had mainly made Ganoderma Lucidum Kite. After 1986, his Ganoderma Lucidum Kite participated in domestic and international kite competitions on behalf of provinces and cities many times and won the national “Five Consecutive Championship”. He was called the “King of Ganoderma Lucidum Kite”. Feng Guang also had rich experience in adjustment, because the flying of Ganoderma Lucidum Kite is different from that of other kites which basically fly straight while Ganoderma Lucidum Kite is difficult to be controlled due to the swing from side to side. The flying line must be adjusted according to the strength of the wind and the extent of the kite swing so that the kite can be lifted off successfully. The Ganoderma Lucidum Kite, carefully adjusted by Feng Guang, could not only fly successfully but also fly in a horizontal figure-of-eight loop in the air. Its posture was amazing, and it could return after flying. In 1990, Ganoderma Lucidum Kite was selected as one of the “Top Ten Kites in the World” in the 7th Weifang International Kite Competition, which was the highest honor Yangjiang Kite has ever won.

梁玉泉
Liang Yuquan

梁玉泉，男，1967年1月出生，现任阳江市风筝协会副会长兼训练部主任，阳江职业技术学院外聘教师，为广东省第四批省级非物质文化遗产项目代表性传承人。

梁玉泉成长在风筝制作世家，从小跟随其父梁汝兴学习风筝制作和放飞技艺，熟练掌握制作阳江传统风筝的各种技艺要领，并掌握一套过硬的放飞技巧。在长期的风筝制作艺术实践过程中，为了使传统技艺得以发扬光大，梁玉泉在掌握传统风筝制作技艺的基础上，对花草类风筝进行

Liang Yuquan, male, was born in January 1967, and is now the vice president of the Yangjiang Kites Association and director of the training department. He is an external teacher at Yangjiang Polytechnic and a representative inheritor of the fourth batch of provincial intangible cultural heritage projects in Guangdong Province.

Liang Yuquan grew up in a kite-making family. From childhood, he followed his father Liang Ruxing to learn kite making and flying skills. He mastered various techniques for making Yangjiang traditional kites and a set of excellent flying skills. In the long-term practice of kite manufacturing craftsmanship, in order to carry forward the traditional techniques, he made bold attempts, reforms, and innovations on flower and grass kites on the basis of mastering traditional kite-making techniques. He has made breakthroughs and accumulated decades of kite-making experience. He is good at making southern kites such as dragon, board, and hard-wing kites. As the main member, he has participated in national and international kite competitions on behalf of the Yangjiang Kite Team and Guangdong Kite Team many times, winning honors for his hometown and the country.

Liang Zhi'ang, male, was born in November 1973, and is the deputy secretary-general of the Guangdong Kite Association, the secretary-general of the Yangjiang Kites Association, national first-grade referee of kites, Guangdong model worker, and part-time teacher at Yangjiang Polytechnic. He is the representative inheritor of the fifth batch of provincial intangible cultural heritage projects in Guangdong Province.

In 2003, he started to learn the traditional kite-making craftsmanship from Liang Ruxing. He has made great efforts to study the making techniques of various stereoscopic kites and soft kites. He is especially good at making and flying dragon-string kites and sports kites. His representative work, "Fireworks Dragon Glowing in the Dark", combines tradition with modernity to create new effects that can emit light and fire. It is highly praised by the seniors in the kite industry and the public. On behalf of Yangjiang City and Guangdong Province, he has participated in kite competitions at various levels at home and abroad many times and won more than 80 medals, making outstanding contributions to the inheritance, promotion, and development of Yangjiang Kite culture.

大胆尝试和改革创新，并取得突破。梁玉泉已积累几十年的风筝制作经验，擅长制作龙类、板子类、硬翅类等南派风筝，作为风筝代表队的主力队员，他多次代表阳江市和广东省风筝队参加全国和国际风筝比赛并屡获殊荣，为家乡、为国家争得荣誉。

梁治昂，男，1973年11月出生，为广东省风筝协会副秘书长，阳江市风筝协会秘书长，风筝类国家一级裁判员，广东省劳动模范，阳江职业技术学院兼职教师，广东省第五批省级非物质文化遗产项目代表性传承人。

2003年，梁治昂拜梁汝兴为师，学习传统风筝制作技艺，着力研究各种立体风筝和软体风筝的制作技艺。他尤其擅长龙串风筝、运动风筝的制作与放飞，代表性作品“夜光烟火龙”，将传统与现代相结合，创新出可以发光、喷火的效果，深受风筝界前辈的赞许和大众的好评。多次代表阳江及广东省参加国内外各级别风筝比赛，获奖牌80多枚，为传承、弘扬、发展阳江风筝文化作出突出贡献。

梁治昂
Liang Zhi'ang

梁治昂2010年在台北石门放飞阳江巨龙风筝，获最佳放飞奖
Liang Zhi'ang flew the Yangjiang Dragon Kite in Shimen, Taipei, and won the Best Flying Award in 2010

阮权
Ruan Quan

阮权，男，出生于1954年2月，1986年加入阳江县体育委员会风筝队，1991年加入阳江市风筝协会。现为广东省第六批省级非物质文化遗产项目代表性传承人。

阮权出生于阳江风筝世家，祖辈都是阳江著名的风筝制作艺人，从小耳濡目染，跟随父辈制作和放飞风筝，深得父亲阮加培的真传，继承了阮氏祖辈的技术精髓，数十年如一日地不断钻研，累积了50多年的风筝制作及放飞经验。阮权擅长制作龙类风筝、仿真类风筝、各类阳江特色传统风筝、立体风筝等，在制作风筝过程中不断实践新工艺，不断推出新作品，如在阳江传统硬翅类风筝的基础上融入国画元素和结合立体工艺制作出的“蝶恋花风筝”，还有阮权独创的“宫灯风筝”，也是其非常具有代表性的作品之一，这些风筝都一并受到邀请，代表阳江风筝文化在潍坊世界风筝博物馆永久展示。

郑荣发，男，1951年生，从小喜欢放风筝，七八岁时开始自己学做风筝，擅长制作阳江龙、软翅、软体、盘鹰等风筝，也制作各种样式的其他类风筝，在风筝界有着“风筝制作多面手”之称。其代表作

Ruan Quan, male, was born in February 1954. He joined the kite team of the Yangjiang County Sports Committee in 1986 and the Yangjiang Kite Association in 1991. He is the representative inheritor of the sixth batch of provincial intangible cultural heritage projects in Guangdong Province.

Ruan Quan was born in a family of making kites in Yangjiang. His ancestors were famous kite makers in Yangjiang, and he learned the manufacturing craftsmanship and flying skills of kites from his parents' generation, especially from his father Ruan Jiapei, when he was young. He inherited the technical essence of Ruan's ancestors' technique. He has been studying for decades and has accumulated more than 50 years of kite making and flying experience. He is good at making dragon kites, simulation kites, various traditional kites with Yangjiang characteristics, stereoscopic kites, and so on. In the process of making kites, he constantly uses new techniques and produces new works. For example, the “Butterfly Loving Flowers Kite”, which is based on Yangjiang's traditional hard-wing kites and combined with the element of Chinese painting and stereoscopic techniques, is one of the representative works of his kites. “The Palace Lantern Kite” created by him is also a very representative work. These kites are permanently displayed in the Weifang World Kite Museum to represent Yangjiang Kite culture.

Zheng Rongfa, male, was born in 1951, and liked flying kites when he was young. He began to learn how to make kites on his own when he was 7 or 8 years old. He is good at making kites such as Yangjiang Dragon Kite, soft-wing kites, soft-body kites, and Eagle Kite. He also makes other kinds of kites in various styles. He is known as a “versatile kite maker” in the kite industry. His representative works include Eagle Kite, dragonfly kites, butterfly kites, cicada kites, phoenix kites, peacock kites, and other kites. He has participated in kite competitions on behalf of the Yangjiang Kite Team and Guangdong Kite Team many times and won numerous awards. Now he is the representative inheritor of the first batch of intangible cultural heritage projects in Yangjiang.

郑荣发
Zheng Rongfa

有崖鹰、蜻蜓、蝴蝶、蝉、凤凰、孔雀等风筝，曾多次代表阳江市队、广东省队参加风筝比赛，获得无数殊荣。现为阳江市第一批非物质文化遗产项目代表性传承人。

Liang Yuqin, female, was born in 1968 in a kite family, and is the daughter of the provincial representative inheritor Liang Ruxing and the fourth-generation inheritor of the Liang family. She learned how to cut bamboo, whittle bamboo, make kites, and other skills from her grandfather, father, and brother when she was young. With the guidance of her parents' generation and her own efforts, she is skilled in various techniques for making Yangjiang traditional kites such as dragon kites. She has won various awards in domestic and international competitions as a professional kite craftsman. Liang Yuqin made bold attempts, reforms, and innovations on flower and fruit kites, which made huge breakthroughs. She also excavated and protected the ancient and endangered traditional kite varieties, such as Rich Cat and Butterfly Kite, Wild Goose Kite, and Moth Kite. She comprehensively compared the different schools, sizes, and shapes of Yangjiang Ganoderma Lucidum Kite and Dragon Kite. She also studied the characteristics of each craftsman so as to further improve and develop Yangjiang kite-making skills. Now she is the representative inheritor of the fourth batch of intangible cultural heritage projects in Yangjiang.

梁玉琴，女，1968年出生在风筝世家，省级非物质文化遗产项目代表性传承人梁汝兴之女，梁氏第四代风筝传承人。自幼跟祖父、父亲和哥哥学习开竹、削竹、扎制风筝等技艺，在父辈的教导和自己的努力下，熟练掌握制作阳江传统风筝的各种技艺要领，擅长制作传统龙类风筝，并多次在国内和国际比赛中获得各类奖项，现为风筝专业户。梁玉琴对花果类风筝进行大胆尝试和改革创新，并取得突破。她还对古老濒危的传统风筝品种如富贵猫蝶、雁子、吹蛾等风筝进行挖掘和保护，并对阳江灵芝风筝、龙风筝的不同流派、尺寸、造型进行综合比较，对各个手艺人的特点进行研究，扬长避短，使阳江风筝制作技艺得到进一步提高和发展。现为阳江市第四批非物质文化遗产项目代表性传承人。

梁玉琴
Liang Yuqin

黎应光，男，1971年出生， 2018年师从梁玉泉学习阳江传统风筝制作。2009—2020年，他代表广东省及阳江风筝协会到世界各地参加风筝节。2007年至今，多次走进当地校园、企业做阳江风筝推广活动，参加南粤古驿道定向大赛风筝展示宣传活动，致力于推广阳江南派风筝，让世界认识阳江传统特色风筝。现为阳江市第五批非物质文化遗产项目代表性传承人。

黎应光
Li Yingguang

Li Yingguang, male, was born in 1971. He learned manufacturing craftsmanship of Yangjiang traditional kites in 2018 from Liang Yuquan. From 2009 to 2020, he represented Guangdong Province and Yangjiang Kite Association to participate in kite festivals around the world. Since 2007, he has joined in various activities of local campuses and enterprises to promote Yangjiang kites. He participated in display and publicity activities of Yangjiang kites in the Ancient Post Road Orientation Competition in South Guangdong. He is committed to promoting Yangjiang kites of the Southern School so that the world can know about Yangjiang traditional kites. Now he is the representative inheritor of the fifth batch of intangible cultural heritage projects in Yangjiang City.

曾晓全，男，1981年出生，2011年起师从梁治昂学习阳江传统风筝的基本技艺。2019年参加国家艺术基金“阳江风筝技艺传承与创新人才培养”项目培训，并凭风筝作品“我的中国心”成为优秀结业代表。多次参加各类风筝比赛，获得无数奖项。他常在风筝馆向参观和游学的群众介绍、推广阳江的风筝文化，多次参加粤港澳大湾区非遗展的阳江风筝技艺展示活动。现为阳江市第五批非物质文化遗产项目代表性传承人。

曾晓全（右）
Zeng Xiaoquan（right）

Zeng Xiaoquan, male, was born in 1981. He has studied the basic craftsmanship of Yangjiang traditional kites from Liang Zhi'ang since 2011. In 2019, he participated in the “Yangjiang Kite Skill Inheritance and Innovative Talent Training” project of the National Art Fund and his kite work “My Chinese Heart” was chosen as an excellent graduation representative. He has participated in various kite competitions for many times and won numerous awards. In terms of inheritance and promotion, he introduces and promotes Yangjiang Kite's culture to visitors and students in the kite pavilion. He participated in the Yangjiang kite skills exhibition activities of the Guangdong-Hong Kong-Marco Greater Bay Area (GBA) Intangible Cultural Heritage Exhibition for many times. Now he is the representative inheritor of the fifth batch of intangible cultural heritage projects in Yangjiang City.

Huang Yongyang, male, was born in 1981. He has studied the basic craftsmanship of Yangjiang traditional kites from Liang Zhi'ang since 2011. In December 2018, he participated in the training of kite referees in Guangdong Province and successfully completed the course. In 2019, he studied in the "Yangjiang Kite Skill Inheritance and Innovative Talent Training" project of the National Arts Fund. He has participated in kite competitions all over the country and won numerous awards. Now he is the representative inheritor of the fifth batch of the intangible cultural heritage projects in Yangjiang City.

黄永杨，男，1981年出生， 2011年起师从梁治昂学习阳江传统风筝的基本技艺。2018年12月参加广东省风筝裁判员培训并顺利结业。2019年参加国家艺术基金“阳江风筝技艺传承与创新人才培养”项目学习进修。多次参加各地的风筝比赛，获得无数奖项。现为阳江市第五批非物质文化遗产项目代表性传承人。

黄永杨
Huang Yongyang

李远云
Li Yuanyun

Li Yuanyun, male, was born in 1966. His father Li Pei was a craftsman who made kites for a living. He learned from his father to make simple Yangjiang kites when he was in primary school in 1974. In 1998, he studied the manufacturing craftsmanship of Yangjiang kites systematically from Zheng Rongfa. He was committed to studying the kite making and flying skills of Yangjiang Dragon Kite and Ganoderma Lucidum Kite. He has participated in kite competitions all over the country and won numerous awards. In 2006, Yangjiang Museum collected 3 pieces of works, including "Double-fish Kite" made by Li Yuanyun. He has trained some young kite lovers such as Wu Shixiong, Ma Hao, and Huang Haiyang. Now he is the representative inheritor of the fifth batch of intangible cultural heritage projects in Yangjiang City.

李远云，男，1966年出生，其父亲李培是以做风筝为生的手艺人，1974年李远云读小学时跟随父亲学做简易的阳江风筝。1998年师从郑荣发系统性学习阳江风筝制作技艺。他致力于研究阳江长龙及灵芝风筝的制作和放飞技艺。多次参加全国各地的风筝比赛，获得无数奖项。2006年阳江博物馆收藏李远云制作的“双鱼风筝”等3件作品。李远云培养出年轻的风筝爱好者吴世雄、马好、黄海洋等。现为阳江市第五批非物质文化遗产项目代表性传承人。

梁飞杰
Liang Feijie

梁飞杰，男，1985年出生，读初中时就跟随父辈学做简单的阳江风筝。2019年起，师从梁治昂学习阳江传统风筝的基本技艺与文化。多次参加县、市、国家级各类风筝比赛，获得无数奖项。现为阳江市第五批非物质文化遗产项目代表性传承人。

梁世官，男，1979年出生，1989年起跟随父亲梁太西学习制作传统风筝如灵芝风筝的技术，展现现代灵芝风筝的动态与色彩。2019年起师从梁治昂，系统性学习阳江风筝“扎、糊、绘、放”四艺。他积极参加各类风筝比赛，获得无数奖项。梁世官收学生杨元生、黄美元、陈志豪、崔文静等人，学生都能独立制作风筝。现为阳江市第五批非物质文化遗产项目代表性传承人。

Liang Feijie, male, was born in 1985. He learned to make simple Yangjiang kites from his parents' generation when he was in junior high school. In 2019, he started to learn the basic skills and culture of Yangjiang traditional kites from Liang Zhi'ang. He has participated in county-, municipal- and national-level kite competitions for many times and won numerous awards. Now he is the representative inheritor of the fifth batch of intangible cultural heritage projects in Yangjiang.

Liang Shiguan, male, was born in 1979. He has learned the skills of making traditional kites such as Ganoderma Lucidum Kite from his father Liang Taixi since 1989, which embodied the dynamics and colors of modern Ganoderma Lucidum Kite. In 2019, he began to learn from Liang Zhi'ang and since then he has systematically learned the four skills of "tying, pasting, painting, and flying" of Yangjiang Kite. He actively participated in various kite competitions and won numerous awards. He taught students such as Yang Yuansheng, Huang Meiyuan, Chen Zhihao, and Cui Wenjing who are able to make kites independently. Now he is the representative inheritor of the fifth batch of intangible cultural heritage projects in Yangjiang City.

梁世官
Liang Shiguan

Liang Shuxian, female, was born in 1995. She has been inherited from five generations of families. From childhood, she followed her grandfather Liang Ruxing, father Liang Yuquan, and aunt Liang Yuqin to systematically learn Yangjiang Kite making skills. In 2019, as a member of the Yangjiang Kite Team, she participated in the 3rd National "Xingren Terrace" Camping Kite Competition in Guizhou and won the Best Craft Award, the First Place of Soft Kites, the Best Team Fashion Award, and the Individual Sports Ethics Award. Her representative work "Sunflower" won the third prize in the First National Online Traditional Kite Making Competition in 2020 and was exhibited at the 38th China International Sporting Goods Expo in Shanghai in 2020. From 2018 to 2020, she joined more than 60 research sessions held in universities, primary and middle schools, kindergartens, communities, and enterprises in Guangdong Province, teaching the manufacturing process of Yangjiang Kite to promote it. Now she is the representative inheritor of the fifth batch of intangible cultural heritage projects in Yangjiang City.

梁淑娴
Liang Shuxian

梁淑娴，女，1995年出生，五代家族传承，自幼跟随祖父梁汝兴、父亲梁玉泉、姑姑梁玉琴系统性学习阳江风筝的制作技艺。2019年作为阳江代表队成员参加了贵州第三届全国“兴仁放马坪”露营风筝赛，荣获最佳工艺奖、软体风筝第一名、团体最佳风尚奖、个人体育道德风尚奖。她的代表作“向日葵”在2020年首届全国网络传统风筝制作大赛中荣获三等奖，并在上海2020年第38届中国国际体育用品博览会上展出。2018—2020年，梁淑娴在广东省内的大中小学、幼儿园、社区、企业进行60多场研学，讲授阳江风筝制作过程，对阳江风筝进行推广宣传。现为阳江市第五批非物质文化遗产项目代表性传承人。

豆豉酿制技艺（阳江豆豉酿制技艺）

广东省第四批省级非物质文化遗产名录

保护单位 广东阳帆食品有限公司

Fermented Soybean Brewing Craftsmanship

(Yangjiang Fermented Soybean Brewing Craftsmanship)

The Forth Batch of the Provincial Intangible Cultural Heritage List of Guangdong Province

Protection Unit Guangdong Yangfan Food Co., Ltd.

阳江市地处广东西南沿海，依山傍海，多山地和丘陵，当地的土质是由赤红壤和潮沙泥土组成的丘陵红土地，一条富含微量元素和矿物质的母亲河——漠阳江贯穿全市，其特有的土质和水质为豆类的生长提供了有利的水土基础。阳江市属亚热带气候，具有充足的光、热、水等气候资源，为阳江豆豉的酿制提供有利的地理、气候条件，从而生产出独具风味的阳江豆豉。

“阳江豆豉酿制技艺”主要盛行在广东省阳江市，现有生产阳江豆豉的工厂30多家，这些工厂主要分布在江城、阳东、阳西、阳春等县（区），尤其是所属的白沙、平岗、麻汕、双捷、北惯、新洲、三甲、合水等镇。以前，生产规模比较大的作坊多分布在阳江城内，如晚清时产量最大的“三德豆豉”，就在阳江县城甜酒巷里设坊制作，产品远销四邑、广州、澳门和香港。现在，因生产规模不断扩大，各大厂家纷纷把工厂转移到劳动力比较集中的城郊各大工业开发区，产销量逐年上升。据2018年统计，全市豆豉酿制产量共约1.5万吨、销售额共约1.2亿元。该项目的

Yangjiang City is located on the southwest coast of Guangdong Province, near the mountains and the sea, with many mountains and hills. It has hilly red soil with lateritic red soil and tidal sand soil. The mother river, Moyang River which runs through the city, is rich in trace elements and minerals. Its unique soil and water quality provide a favorable water and soil foundation for the growth of beans. Yangjiang's climate is subtropical. It has sufficient climate resources, such as light, heat, and water, which provide favorable geographical and climatic conditions for the brewing of Yangjiang Fermented Soybean, so as to produce the unique flavor of Yangjiang Fermented Soybean.

Yangjiang Fermented Soybean Brewing Craftsmanship is mainly distributed in Yangjiang, Guangdong Province. There are more than 30 factories producing Yangjiang Fermented Soybean, which are mainly distributed in Jiangcheng, Yangdong, Yangxi, Yangchun, and other counties (districts), especially at Baisha, Pinggang, Mashan, Shuangjie, Beiguan, Xinzhou, Sanjia, Heshui, and other towns of these counties(districts). Previously, the workshops with large production scales were mostly distributed inside the city. For example, Sande Fermented Soybean, Yangjiang Fermented Soybean by the largest production in the late Qing Dynasty, was made in the Tianjiu Lane in Yangjiang County and sold to Siyi, Guangzhou, Macao and Hong Kong. Now, due to the continuous expansion of production scale, major manufacturers have transferred their factories to industrial development zones in the suburbs with a relatively concentrated labor force. The production and sales volume have increased year over year. According to the statistics in 2018, the output of Yangjiang fermented soybeans was about 15,000 tons, and the sales volume

广东阳帆食品有限公司晒场
Drying yard of Guangdong Yangfan Food Co., Ltd.

was about 120 million *yuan*. The protection unit of the project, Guangdong Yangfan Food Co., Ltd., is located in the Yangdong District.

In 2012, Fermented Soybean Brewing Craftsmanship (Yangjiang Fermented Soybean Brewing Craftsmanship) was listed in the fourth batch of provincial intangible cultural heritage in Guangdong Province.

Historical Origin

According to *Yangjiang Annals* of the period of Republic of China, "Soybeans are grown from soil, and black beans are staple, which can be used to make fermented soybeans, soy sauce and soybean wine."

According to *Yangjiang County Annals* in the Qing Dynasty, the brewing technique of fermented soybeans prevailed in the late Qing Dynasty. Wang Tingshu, a native of Pinggang, Yangjiang, created a distinctive Sande Fermented Soybean with the largest output. The products were not only popular in the local market but also sold to Siyi, Guangzhou, Macao, and Hong Kong.

In 1954, the local state-owned fermented soybean factory in Yangjiang County was established. At the beginning, there were only 6 employees, with an annual output of 7 tons. In 1958, the number of employees increased to 76, with an annual output of 100 tons. In 1982, the annual output exceeded 2,000 tons, and now the output has reached 3,600 tons. The fermented soybeans of Yangjiang Bridge Brand produced by the factory are sold well in 38 countries and regions.

After the reform and opening-up, a large number of private enterprises producing fermented soybeans have sprung up, among which Guangdong Yangfan Food Co., Ltd. is the most representative,

保护单位"广东阳帆食品有限公司"设址在阳东区。

2012年，豆豉酿制技艺（阳江豆豉酿制技艺）被列入广东省第四批省级非物质文化遗产名录。

历史渊源

民国《阳江志》中关于豆豉酿制技艺的记载为："豆，菽也，土产，以黑豆为大宗，可作豉造酱酿酒。"

清《阳江县志》中有关于豆豉酿制技艺的最早记载，这一技艺在晚清时盛行，此时产量最大的是阳江平冈人王庭恕创建的别具风味的"三德豆豉"，产品除畅销本地外，还远销四邑、广州、澳门和香港。

1954年，阳江县地方国营豆豉厂成立，刚开始职工只有6人，年产豆豉7吨；1958年，职工增至76人，年产量100吨；1982年，年产量突破2000吨；现在产量已达3600吨。该厂生产的阳江桥牌豆豉，畅销38个国家和地区。

改革开放后，大批豆豉民营企业如雨后春笋般涌现，其中广东阳帆食品有限公司最具代表性，现年产量达6000吨。该公司十分注重企业生产发展和品牌的建设，在保持传统的基础上，致力于新产品研发，先后推出葱味、蒜蓉味等各种营养型豆豉和风味型豆豉。

经统计，目前全市共有生产豆豉的厂家30多家，生产人员1500多人。2018年全市酿制豆豉产量共约1.5万吨，销售额共约1.2亿元，其中豆豉酿制项目保护单位——广东阳帆食品有限公司年产量达6000吨，年销售额约5200万元（含税金额）。

经过祖祖辈辈的努力与经营，阳江豆豉酿制技艺现在已经得到很好的保护、传

第四代传承人谢维富（左）和第五代传承人冯一森（右）在凉豆

Xie Weifu (left), the fourth generation inheritor, and Feng Yisen (right), the fifth generation inheritor, were cooling beans

承和发展，产品在国内外的声誉和影响也越来越大，阳江豆豉已经成为阳江地区对外宣传的一张地理名片。

with an annual output of 6,000 tons. The company attaches great importance to the development of enterprise production and brand building. On the basis of keeping the tradition, it has committed to the research and development of new products, successively producing various nutritious and flavored fermented soybeans, such as scallion flavor and garlic flavor.

According to statistics, there are more than 30 manufacturers and more than 1,500 employees producing fermented soybeans in Yangjiang. In 2018, the output of fermented soybeans in Yangjiang was about 15,000 tons and the sales volume was about 120 million *yuan*, of which the protection unit Guangdong Yangfan Food Co., Ltd. had an annual output of 6,000 tons and a sales volume of 52 million *yuan* (tax included).

Through the efforts and management of generations, the brewing technique of Yangjiang Fermented Soybean has been well protected, inherited, and developed. The reputation and influence of the products at home and abroad are also growing. Yangjiang Fermented Soybean has become a geographic symbol for the publicity of the Yangjiang region.

基本内容

阳江豆豉酿制历史悠久，工艺讲究。酿制时要选用优质黑豆，以漠阳江的水及本地的生晒粗颗粒海盐为原材料，结合阳江得天独厚的空气、气温、湿度、阳光等因素，经过选豆、浸泡、蒸煮、米曲霉制曲、固态有盐发酵、晒干、冷却回油等20余道工序，历时40余天，方能酿制出风味独特的阳江豆豉。尤其是在蒸豆、米曲霉制曲、固态有盐发酵等关键工序中，均须由掌握核心技术的师傅操作，其火候、温度、湿度的把握要恰到好处，还要利用阳江得天独厚的地理环境和温度高、湿度大、光照时间长的自然气候优势。阳江的自然气候非常适合米曲霉制曲。制作时，以6天为一个周期完成霉菌的生长和固态有盐发酵，以30天为一个周期完成酶的分解（按全年平均计算，现代工艺与传统工艺的时间完全一样），只有这样才能生产出

Basic Content

Yangjiang Fermented Soybean has a long history of brewing and exquisite technique. During brewing, high-quality black soybeans should be selected, with water from Moyang River and local sun-dried coarse-grain sea salt as raw materials. Combined with the unique air, temperature, humidity, sunlight, and other factors of Yangjiang, it takes more than 40 days to brew Yangjiang Fermented Soybean with a unique flavor through more than 20 processes, such as bean selection, soaking, steaming, koji-making by Aspergillus oryzae, solid-state fermentation with salt, drying and oil returning. Especially in the key processes such as bean steaming, koji-making by Aspergillus oryzae, and solid-state fermentation with salt, the masters who have mastered the core technique should have a proper grasp of the heating degree, temperature, and humidity. The masters should also take advantage of Yangjiang's unique geographical environment and natural climates, such as its high temperature, high humidity, and long lighting time. This climate is very suitable for koji-making by Aspergillus oryzae. When brewing, it takes 6 days as a cycle to complete mold growth and solid-state fermentation with salt, and 30 days as a cycle to complete enzyme decomposition (calculated by the annual average, the time is exactly the same between the current process and the traditional process). Only in this way can the unique

制曲师傅和员工翻曲
Master and the staff were turning koji

flavor of Yangjiang Fermented Soybean be produced, becoming a brand food with strong local characteristics.

Yangjiang Fermented Soybean is a truly pure, natural, healthy food with no additives or pigments. It contains 27.5g of protein, 10.7g of fat, 19.9g of carbohydrate, and other nutrients with different contents per 100g.

Main Features

The core technique of brewing Yangjiang Fermented Soybean is mainly shown in the following aspects.

· The selection of raw materials

(1) Selection of soybeans: Selecting black soybeans with thin skin and high oil and protein content.

(2) Selection of water: Selecting water from Moyang River rich in trace elements and minerals.

(3) Selection of salt: Selecting local sun-dried coarse-grain sea salt.

· Fine and unique brewing technique

There are more than 20 processes for the production of Yangjiang Fermented Soybean, each of which has specific operation requirements and standardized processes. In particular, the key processes of the core technique, such as koji-making by Aspergillus oryzae and solid-state fermentation with salt, require experienced masters to operate and use the unique natural environment and climate conditions to complete.

Yangjiang Fermented Soybean is famous for its complete appearance, with black color, loose beans, rich and mellow flavor, long aftertaste, rich nutrition and unique flavor. It is unique among similar products in China.

风味独特的阳江豆豉，阳江豆豉才能成为具有浓郁地方特色的招牌食品。

阳江豆豉没有任何添加剂、色素等成分，是真正的纯天然健康食品。每100克阳江豆豉含27.5克蛋白质、10.7克脂肪、19.9克碳水化合物等多种含量不同的营养成分。

主要特征

阳江豆豉酿制技艺的核心要素主要表现在如下几方面。

· 原料选用讲究

（1）豆的选择。选用皮薄肉厚、油分和蛋白质含量高的黑豆。

（2）水的选择。选用富含微量元素和矿物质的漠阳江水。

（3）食盐的选择。选用本地的生晒粗颗粒海盐。

· 酿制技术精细独特

阳江豆豉酿制程序有20多道，每道工序都有具体的操作要求和规范流程，特别是米曲霉制曲、固态有盐发酵等关键工序，需要经验丰富的师傅操作，并利用得天独厚的自然环境和气候条件才能完成。

阳江豆豉以外观颗粒完整、色泽乌黑油润、豉肉松化、豉香味浓郁醇厚、余味绵长、营养丰富、风味独特等优点而在国内同类产品中独树一帜，久负盛名。

重要价值

· 历史文化价值

阳江豆豉被誉为“阳江三宝”之一，几百年来一直深受人民群众的喜爱，成为阳江人民引以为傲的文化符号。豆豉文化已经融入每一位阳江人生活当中。用阳江

师傅（中）和员工在检查豆豉发酵的质量情况
The master (in the middle) and staffs were checking the quality of fermented soybeans

豆豉烹煮家乡菜，始终贯穿在阳江人世代传承的过程中。

·科学价值

阳江豆豉酿制的核心技艺是，采用微生物制曲和发酵的科学原理，并结合当地的自然环境与气候特征，具有科学研究价值。

·经济价值

据统计，2018年阳江豆豉年销量约1.5万吨，销售金额约1.2亿元，产品销往全国各地，还远销日本、美国、东南亚等30多个国家和地区，阳江豆豉产业的发展对推动阳江经济的发展起着重要的作用。

·药用价值

《本草纲目》中记载：豆豉具开胃增食、消食化滞、发汗解表、除烦喘等疗效。相关研究成果显示，阳江豆豉含蛋白质、脂肪、碳水化合物以及多种矿物质和维生素，适当食用豆豉还有预防脑血栓等保健作用。

广东阳帆食品有限公司副总经理2017年9月在广东湛江参加东盟农产品交易博览会
In September 2017, the deputy general manager of Guangdong Yangfan Food Co., Ltd. participated in the ASEAN Agricultural Products Trade Expo in Zhanjiang, Guangdong

Great Value

· Historical and cultural value

Yangjiang Fermented Soybean is known as one of the "Three Treasures of Yangjiang". It has been loved by the people for hundreds of years and has become a cultural symbol that the Yangjiang people are proud of. The culture of fermented soybeans has been integrated into every Yangjiang person's life. Hometown dishes cooked with Yangjiang Fermented Soybean have always been passed down from generation to generation by the Yangjiang people.

· Scientific value

The core technique of brewing Yangjiang Fermented Soybean is to use the scientific principles of koji-making by microbes and fermentation, combining with the local natural environment and climate characteristics, which have scientific research value.

· Economic value

According to statistics, the annual sales volume of Yangjiang Fermented Soybean was approximately 15,000 tons in 2018, with a sales value of approximately 120 million *yuan*. The products are sold all over the country and also sold well in over 30 countries and regions, including Japan, the United States and Southeast Asia. The development of the Yangjiang Fermented Soybean industry plays an important role in promoting the economic development of Yangjiang.

· Medicinal value

It is recorded in the *Compendium of Materia Medica* that the fermented soybean has the effects of appetizing and increasing food intake, resolving food stagnancy, relieving exterior syndrome, and relieving asthma. According to the research results, Yangjiang Fermented Soybean contains proteins, fats, carbohydrates, minerals, and vitamins. Proper consumption of fermented soybeans can also prevent cerebral thrombosis.

Main Inheritors

Feng Kang, male, was born in 1966. He took Feng Duo as his master in 1990 and inherited from his family and by apprenticeship. Since December 1994, he has worked for Guangdong Yangfan Food Co., Ltd. as the general manager. The company has been devoted to improving the production process of fermented soybeans and expanded the scale of production, becoming the largest fermented soybean production base in Yangjiang and even in China. Feng Kang has spent many years studying product process transformation and new product development. The scientific research team led by Feng Kang has made remarkable achievements in the production and management of fermented soybeans, achieving rapid development. Over the years, the company has been awarded the titles of "Guangdong (Agricultural) Brand Product", "Guangdong Famous Brand", "Green Food", etc.. The company's brewing technique of Yangjiang Fermented Soybean has been selected into the list of Guangdong provincial intangible cultural heritage. The company's operating plant has been rated as the demonstration base for the productive protection of intangible cultural heritage in Guangdong Province. The company's Yangjiang Fermented Soybean and Yangjiang Ginger-flavored Fermented Soybean have been protected by the National Geographical Indication. Now Feng Kang is the representative inheritor of the third batch of provincial intangible cultural heritage projects in Guangdong Province.

主要传承人

冯康，男，生于1966年，1990年拜冯铎为师，经家族、师徒传承。1994年12月至今，任职于广东阳帆食品有限公司，任公司总经理。该公司致力于改良豆豉的生产工艺和扩大豆豉生产规模，成为阳江乃至全国最大的豆豉生产基地。多年来，冯康一直从事产品工艺改造研究和新产品开发的工作，带领科研团队在豆豉生产管理工作做出显著成绩，使公司获得了飞速的发展。多年来，公司生产的豆豉分别获得“广东省（农业类）名牌产品”“广东省著名商标”“绿色食品”等称号，公司的阳江豆豉酿制技艺入选广东省省级非物质文化遗产名录，公司的生产厂区被评为广东省非物质文化遗产生产性保护传承基地，公司的阳江豆豉、阳江姜豉均获国家地理标志产品保护。冯康现为广东省第三批省级非物质文化遗产项目代表性传承人。

冯康（中）在工厂给员工传授豆豉酿制技艺

Feng Kang (in the middle) was showing the employees the brewing technique of fermented soybeans in the factory

冯一森，男，生于1944年4月，1960年在阳江县国营豆豉厂参加工作后，即师从豆豉老师傅林善喜学艺，学习阳江豆豉的酿制技术。1974年至1977年到华南理工大学就读工业发酵专业，进一步提高技术理论水平。回厂后，全面负责阳江豆豉的生产技术工作，任工程师。

几十年来，冯一森全面地掌握了阳江豆豉的酿制技术，在传统经验式管理的基础上，结合科学技术进行技术管理，使阳江豆豉的制作技术得到更进一步的提高和发展，豆豉品质也得到提高。从1996年开始，冯一森培养林泳斌为其助手，向他传授豆豉各个生产工序的制作技术和理论知识，并且教授相关的生产技术，林泳斌现已全面掌握了豆豉的制作技术，能够独立负责豆豉的生产工作。冯一森现为阳江市第二批非物质文化遗产项目代表性传承人。

冯高锋，男，生于1988年11月，2007年就读于广东外语外贸大学南国商学院，2011年进入广东阳帆食品有限公司，现任公司副总经理。2009年拜冯康为师，经

冯康（右）将阳江豆豉酿制技艺传授给第六代传承人冯高锋（左）
Feng Kang (right) is teaching the brewing technique of Yangjiang Fermented Soybean to Feng Gaofeng (left) , the sixth generation inheritor

Feng Yisen, male, was born in April 1944. After joining the state-owned fermented soybean factory in Yangjiang County in 1960, he learned the brewing technique of Yangjiang fermented soybeans from the experienced worker Lin Xishan. From 1974 to 1977, he studied at South China University of Technology and majored in industrial fermentation, which further improved his technical and theoretical level. After returning to the factory, he took full charge of the production technique of Yangjiang Fermented Soybean as an engineer.

For decades, Feng Yisen has comprehensively mastered the brewing technique of Yangjiang Fermented Soybean. On the basis of traditional empirical management, he conducted technical management combined with science and technique, making the brewing technique of Yangjiang Fermented Soybean further improved and developed, and the quality of fermented soybeans further improved. Since 1996, he has trained Lin Yongbin as his assistant and taught him not only the production technique and theoretical knowledge of various production processes of fermented soybeans, but also related production technology. Now Lin Yongbin has fully mastered the brewing technique of fermented soybeans and can independently take charge of the production. Now Feng Yisen is the representative inheritor of the second batch of intangible cultural heritage projects in Yangjiang City.

冯一森（左）
Feng Yisen (left)

Feng Gaofeng, male, was born in November 1988. He started to study at Nanguo Business School of Guangdong University of Foreign Studies in 2007. He started to work in Guangdong Yangfan Food Co., Ltd. in 2011 and serves as the deputy general manager of the company now. In 2009, Feng Gaofeng took Feng Kang as his master and inherited from his family and by apprenticeship. Feng Gaofeng was born in a family producing fermented soybeans. His family started producing fermented soybeans from his great-great-grandfather. Because he has had a strong interest in food processing, he inherited his father's business after graduation, and has studied diligently and strived for innovation, and made remarkable achievements in product research, production, and enterprise management. Over the years, on the basis of inheriting the traditional fermented soybean brewing technique, Feng Gaofeng has added new equipment, new technique, which has further carried forward the Yangjiang Fermented Soybean hand-made technique and expanded the production scale. At the same time, he has continued to innovate in product process transformation, new product development, enterprise standard management, and other aspects, making contributions to the development and growth of Yangjiang Fermented Soybean. Now Feng Gaofeng is the representative inheritor of the third batch of intangible cultural heritage projects in Yangjiang City.

Ye Qilu, male, learned the brewing technique of Yangjiang fermented soybeans from Master Lin Yongbin after joining the State-owned Fermented Soybean Factory in Yangjiang County in 1997. On the basis of comprehensively mastering the traditional technique of brewing Yangjiang Fermented Soybean, Ye Qilu carried out technical management in combination with modern science and technology, so that the traditional production technique of Yangjiang Fermented Soybean was inherited and developed; established and improved various operating technical procedures and technical management system of Yangjiang Fermented Soybean production. He designed and purchased mechanical equipment and reduce the labor intensity of workers. Yangjiang Fermented Soybean and Yangjiang Ginger-flavored Fermented Soybean of Yefenghua Brand produced by the company have acquired the export record registration of Yangjiang Entry-Exit Inspection and Quarantine Bureau due to their excellent product quality, winning the title of "Guangdong Famous Brand Product". The company is also Yangjiang Fermented Soybean of the Zhujiang River Bridge Brand production base of Guangdong Food Import and Export Corporation. Ye Qilu is the representative inheritor of the fourth batch of intangible cultural heritage projects in Yangjiang City.

家族、师徒传承，冯高锋出身于豆豉酿制世家，其高祖父一辈就开始豆豉的酿制生产。因对食品加工有浓厚兴趣，冯高锋大学毕业后子承父业。他平时勤恳研习，力求创新，在产品科研、生产和企业管理等方面都做出了显著成绩。多年来，冯高锋在继承传统豆豉酿制技艺的基础上，添加了新设备、新技术，扩大了生产规模，使阳江豆豉手工制作技艺发扬光大，同时在产品工艺改造、新产品开发、企业规范管理等方面不断创新，为阳江豆豉的发展壮大不断添砖加瓦。冯高锋现为阳江市第三批非物质文化遗产项目代表性传承人。

叶其禄，男，1997年进入阳江县国营豆豉厂工作后，即师从老师傅林泳斌，学习阳江豆豉的酿制技术。叶其禄在全面掌握阳江豆豉的酿制传统技术的基础上，结合现代科学技术进行技术管理，使传统的阳江豆豉酿制技术得到继承和发展；建立并完善了阳江豆豉生产的各种操作规程和技术管理体系。他设计并

叶其禄（左）
Ye Qilu (left)

购买机械设备，减轻豆豉工人的劳动强度。其公司生产的叶丰华牌阳江豆豉、阳江姜豉，由于产品质量优良，获得阳江出入境检验检疫局出口备案注册，荣获“广东省名牌产品”称号。该厂也是广东省食品进出口公司珠江桥牌阳江豆豉生产基地。叶其禄现为阳江市第四批非物质文化遗产项目代表性传承人。

姚发柱，男，1983年出生，2000年初中毕业后，正式跟外婆和母亲学习传统豆豉的全过程酿制技艺。2016—2019年，在和鲜食品科技集团兼职指导豆豉生产工作，其间也跟随曾经在阳江市国营豆豉厂做豆豉师傅的阮奕文和阳江和鲜食品有限公司董事长黄德满学习传统豆豉的酿制技艺，把个人学到的技艺融会贯通，指导建设豆豉生产车间和自动化生产线，使传统豆豉酿制核心技艺和现代技术相结合。2019年入职阳江和鲜食品有限公司，任豆豉和调味酱事业部中级工程师，配合公司的和鲜中央研究院、工程设备中心及设备供应商，推动阳江豆豉工艺生产环节机械化、自动化改造，最终建成国内首条年产5000吨阳江豆豉的自动化生产线，生产出来的阳江豆豉不仅符合国家标准，而且达到欧洲、美国、日本的出口标准。结合现代人追求健康的理念，姚发柱参与了有机阳江豆豉的创新制作，该项目已获得有机认证证书。2020年，姚发柱代表和鲜食品有限公司到阳江市食品协会参与研讨阳江豆豉（地理标志产品）地方标准的制定。姚发柱现为阳江市第五批非物质文化遗产项目代表性传承人。

Yao Fazhu, male, was born in 1983. After graduating from junior high school in 2000, he formally learned the whole process of brewing traditional fermented soybeans from his grandmother and mother. From 2016 to 2019, he assisted part-time in Hexian Food Technique Group to guide the production of fermented soybeans. During this period, he also followed Ruan Yiwen, who once worked as a master of fermented soybeans at Yangjiang State-owned Fermented Soybean Factory, and Huang Deman, the chairman of Yangjiang Hexian Food Co., Ltd., to learn the traditional brewing techniques of fermented soybeans. He integrated the skills learned by himself and guided the construction of fermented soybean production workshops and automated production lines, combining the core skills of traditional fermented soybean brewing techniques with modernization. In 2019, he joined Yangjiang Hexian Food Co., Ltd. as an intermediate engineer in the Fermented Soybean and Sauce Business Department. He cooperated with the company's Hexian Central Research Institute, Engineering Equipment Center, and equipment suppliers, to promote the mechanization and automation of the production process of Yangjiang Fermented Soybean. Finally, the first domestic automatic production line with an annual output of 5,000 tons of Yangjiang Fermented Soybean was built. The produced Yangjiang Fermented Soybean not only met the national standards but also met the export standards of Europe, America, and Japan. In combination with the health concept pursued by modern people, Yao Fazhu participated in the innovative production of organic Yangjiang Fermented Soybean, which has obtained organic certification. In 2020, on behalf of Hexian Food Co., Ltd., he went to Yangjiang Food Association to discuss the formulation of local standards for Yangjiang Fermented Soybean (geographical indication product). Now he is the representative inheritor of the fifth batch of intangible cultural heritage projects in Yangjiang City.

姚发柱
Yao Fazhu

Xie Guanxian, female, was born in 1965. She has been engaged in the fermented soybean industry for more than 30 years and studied under Lin Zhan (master of the local state-owned fermented soybean factory in Yangjiang County). In 1989, she established Taojinniang Fermented Soybean Factory to produce Yangjiang Fermented Soybean. She has continuously studied and developed the production of fermented soybeans. She used the unique flavor of Yangjiang Fermented Soybean, and combined with secondary fermentation of bean curd in pottery made from soybeans and wheat flour, to make the produced soy sauce a rich flavor. Xie Guanxian has cooperated with *Yangjiang Daily*, Yangjiang TV Station, Guangdong Satellite TV, and other media many times to publicize and promote Yangjiang Fermented Soybean at different levels. She has given lectures about the fermented soybean to young people many times, which makes young people interested in Yangjiang Fermented Soybean, preparing for the growing pedigree of future Yangjiang Fermented Soybean intangible cultural heritage project, and making contributions to inheriting, promoting and developing the brewing technique of Yangjiang Fermented Soybean. Now she is the representative inheritor of the fifth batch of intangible cultural heritage projects in Yangjiang City.

Wu Guanfeng, male, was born in 1986. He learned from Wu Xin. Since childhood, he has learned the brewing technique of fermented soybeans from his family and inherited the ancestral method of Yangjiang Fermented Soybean brewing technique. He has mastered the core processes of selecting beans, soaking, cooking, koji-making, natural fermenting, drying, cooling and oil returning. Since January 2009, he has worked as the director of Yangjiang Yangchun Fermented Soybean Factory of Guangdong Ruiqidun Food Co., Ltd. and served as the technical team leader of fermented soybean brewing. After taking over the factory, he has continued to carry out product research and development on the basis of inheriting the brewing technique of fermented soybeans, to adapt to the consumption habits and taste choices of modern people. On the basis of the unchanged core brewing technique, he has developed sauced fermented soybeans, canned fermented soybeans, and fermented soybeans with different flavors. From 2013 to 2019, he participated in Guangzhou Food Trade Fair, Fuzhou Sugar and Wine Expo, Guangzhou Seasoning Fair, and Chengdu Food Expo to promote Yangjiang Fermented Soybean. *Yangjiang Daily* and Yangjiang TV

谢观献，女，1965年出生，从事豆豉行业30多年，师从林湛（阳江县地方国营豆豉厂师傅）学艺。1989年创立桃金娘豆豉工厂生产阳江豆豉。她不断研发，利用阳江豆豉特有的豉香味，结合黄豆和小麦粉制成的豆曲在陶缸里二次发酵，制成豉香浓郁的豉油。谢观献多次与《阳江日报》、阳江电视台、广东卫视等媒体合作，在不同层面宣传和推广阳江豆豉，多次给青少年讲解豆豉相关课程，使青少年对阳江豆豉产生兴趣，为未来壮大阳江豆豉非遗项目传承谱系做准备，为传承、弘扬、发展阳江豆豉酿制技艺作出贡献。谢观献现为阳江市第五批非物质文化遗产项目代表性传承人。

谢观献
Xie Guanxian

吴冠锋，男，1986年出生，师承吴信，自小在家族学习豆豉酿制技艺，传承阳江豆豉酿制技艺的祖传方法，熟练掌握豆豉制作中选豆、浸泡、蒸煮、制曲、天然发酵、晒干、冷却回油等工序。2009年1月至今，在广东瑞其顿食品有限公司阳江市阳醇豆豉厂当厂长并任豆豉酿制技术组组长。接手豆豉厂经营工作后，吴冠锋在继承豆豉酿制技艺的基础上不断进行产品研发，以使豆豉产品满足现代人的消费习惯和口味。在核心酿制技艺不变的基础上研发酱态豆豉、罐装豆豉和不同风味的豆豉。2013—2019年，他参加了广州市食品交易会、福州市糖酒博览会、广州市调味品展销会和成都市食品博览会，推广阳江豆豉。《阳江日报》、阳江电视台对阳醇豆豉厂生产的豆豉进行了报道。为配合国家级非遗项目申报工作，他组织人员拍摄豆豉生产过程，并积极宣传推广豆豉酿制技艺。吴冠锋现为阳江市第五批非物质文化遗产项目代表性传承人。

梁登庭，男，生于1987年2月，在酿造豆豉的环境中长大，从小就受阳江豆豉酿造工艺的耳濡目染。2009年大学毕业后师从母亲谢观献学习传承豆豉酿制工艺，熟练地掌握传统的豆豉酿制技艺，同时致力于宣传和推广阳江豆豉。现为阳江市第五批非物质文化遗产项目代表性传承人。

梁登庭
Liang Dengting

吴冠锋（左）
Wu Guanfeng (left)

Station reported on the fermented soybean produced by Yangjiang Yangchun Fermented Soybean Factory. To cooperate in applying for the national intangible cultural heritage project, he organized people to shoot the production process of fermented soybeans and promoted the brewing technique. Now he is the representative inheritor of the fifth batch of intangible cultural heritage projects in Yangjiang.

Liang Dengting, male, was born in February 1987. He grew up in a family of brewing fermented soybeans. He has heard about and seen the brewing process of Yangjiang Fermented Soybean since childhood. After graduating from college in 2009, he learned the brewing technique of fermented soybeans from his mother, Xie Guanxian. He has mastered the traditional brewing technique of fermented soybeans and devoted himself to publicizing and promoting Yangjiang Fermented Soybean. Now he is the representative inheritor of the fifth batch of intangible cultural heritage projects in Yangjiang City.

Li Sheng, male, was born in 1956. He has been engaged in the fermented soybean industry for nearly 30 years and learned from Lin Shanxi (master of Yangjiang Fermented Soybean) . In 1996, he served as the director of Yangdong Fermented Soybean Factory. Since 1999, he has served as the director of the Fermented Soybean Factory in Yangjiang Yuesheng Food Co., Ltd.. The company has two series, Zhujiang River Bridge and Moyang River, which enjoy a certain popularity in the industry of Yangjiang Fermented Soybean. Li Sheng constantly summarized his experience and innovated the brewing technique of fermented soybeans to produce products with unique flavors. The handbook of the origin of Yangjiang Fermented Soybean written by Li Sheng recorded the details of the traditional brewing techniques, geographical environment, climate, water and soil, history, as well as social and cultural factors. It provides a written record with certain industry references and guidance value for the development of Yangjiang Fermented Soybean. Li Sheng carried out various publicity and promotion of fermented soybean brewing, making fermented soybeans become global. Now he is the representative inheritor of the fifth batch of intangible cultural heritage projects in Yangjiang City.

李生，男，1956年出生，从事豆豉行业近30年，师承林善喜（阳江豆豉师傅）。1996年，在阳东县豆豉厂任厂长；1999年至今，在阳江市粤生食品有限公司任豆豉厂厂长。公司旗下有“珠江桥”与“漠阳江”两个系列，在阳江豆豉行业享有一定知名度。李生不断总结经验和创新豆豉酿制技艺，生产出风味独特的产品。他编写的阳江豆豉原产地手册，详细记录了阳江豆豉传统酿制技艺、地理环境、气候、水土、历史等，以及社会人文因素，为该项目发展提供了有一定行业参考及指导价值的文字记载。李生对豆豉酿制进行各种宣传推广，使豆豉走向全球。李生为阳江市第五批非物质文化遗产项目代表性传承人。

李生
Li Sheng

传统刀剑制作技艺

保护单位 阳江市阳东区竹本五金制品厂

Traditional Sword Manufacturing Craftsmanship

Protection Unit Zhuben Hardware Factory in Yangdong District, Yangjiang City

传统的刀和剑作为冷兵器出现于人类社会发展的早期，由耕作、狩猎等劳动工具演变而成。传统刀剑制作技艺在清末民初流传于整个阳江地区，其制作作坊主要分布在江城、阳东、阳西、阳春等地的城区以及城郊各墟镇。

Traditional knives and swords appeared as cold weapons in the early stage of human society and evolved from labor tools such as farming tools and hunting tools. Traditional Sword Manufacturing Craftsmanship has spread throughout Yangjiang in the late Qing Dynasty and the early Republic of China. Its workshops are mainly distributed in the urban areas of Jiangcheng, Yangdong, Yangxi, Yangchun and other places, as well as in the suburban towns.

"打铁铺"内
The scene in a forge

历史渊源

阳江靠山面海，海洋渔猎与农耕采集兼备，原居住民是以俚、僚、瑶族为主的少数民族。所谓"靠山吃山，靠海吃海"，独特的地理环境造就了阳江海洋渔业的发展，海洋渔业的发展又成就了发达的造船业，发达的造船业又派生出许多附属行业，打铁制刀就是其中一个行业。这是因为刀、斧、凿、锯都是造船的主要工具，铁钉也是造船不可缺少的重要材料，船上的用具如铁锚、铁链等，全都是要用打铁工艺制成；而北面靠山的农耕采集生活，所需的犁、耙、锄头、镰刀、柴刀等用具也要经打铁工艺才能制成。据《隋书·列女传》卷八十列传第四十五有关谯国夫人的记载，"至陈永定二年（558），

Historical Origin

Yangjiang, facing the sea, is close to the mountains. It has both marine fishing and hunting, farming and gathering. The original residents are ethnic minorities mainly composed of Li, Liao and Yao. They make good use of local resources, and the unique geographical environment has created development of Yangjiang marine fishery. The development of marine fishery has led to the development of the advanced shipbuilding industry which has derived many ancillary industries, among which forging iron and making swords is one of them, because knives, axes, chisels and saws are the main tools for shipbuilding, and iron nails are also indispensable important materials for shipbuilding. The tools on the ship, such as iron anchors and iron chains, are all made by iron forging process. In the north of Yangjiang, the tools such as ploughs, rakes, hoes, sickles, and firewood knives needed for farming and gathering life in the mountains are also made by iron forging process. According to the *Biography of Virtuous Women* in the *Sui Shu*, record about Madam Qiaoguo says that "In the second year of Chen Yongding in the Southern Dynasty, when her son Feng Pu was nine years old, she sent Feng Pu to lead the leaders of all departments to pay homage to the emperor in Danyang. Later, Ouyang He, the governor of Guangzhou, conspired against the emperor and called Feng Pu to Gaoan, luring him to rebel together. Feng sent an envoy to report to Madam Qiaoguo. Madam Qiaoguo replied that, 'I am loyal and have lived through the two dynasties. I can't betray the country just because I care about you.' So she sent troops to the border to resist the enemy, and led the chiefs of the Baiyue ministries to cooperate with General Zhang Zhaoda." It is proved that the heroine of Lingnan, Madam Xian, once sent troops in Yangjiang in the second year of Chen Yongding. The weapons needed in war must be made with the help of the iron forging technique. These factors have promoted the development of Yangjiang's iron forging industry. Therefore, one of the most developed industries in Yangjiang at that time was the iron forging industry. The small Yangjiang City was full of forges. "The red stove with smudging and the loud hammering" was a scene of Yangjiang at that time. The structure and layout of the old Yangjiang is said to be "9 streets and 12 lanes" , one of which is called "Forges Lane" . A map of "9 streets and 12 lanes" .is recorded in *Yangjiang Annals*. Now the old site is still there, and renamed Hebi Street.

The *Yangjiang Annals* also records that "bronzeware, knives and scissors are excellent, and goods are sold far and near" . It proves that Yangjiang Knife has become very famous in the era of making knives with copper. It is recording in *Pedigee of Feng Clan* of the Qing Dynasty that "The eighty-two horned Xuanjin broadsword decorated in the shape of goose nose, used in his life was included in the tomb of General Feng" . General Feng, who was named Feng Ang, the grandson of Madam Xian, was buried at the foot of the Bei Mountain in Yangjiang after his death in 646 AD (the twentieth year of Zhenguan period in Tang Dynasty). The "Emei Xuanjin Broadsword" was commonly known as the "killing broadsword" in Yangjiang, which

其子仆年九岁，遣帅诸首领朝于丹阳，起家拜阳春郡守。后广州刺史欧阳纥谋反，召仆至高安，诱与为乱。仆遣使归告夫人，夫人曰：'我为忠贞，经今两代，不能惜汝，辄负国家。'遂发兵拒境，帅百越酋长迎章昭达。"证明岭南巾帼英雄冼夫人于陈永定二年曾在阳江地区发兵，而打仗所需的兵器，也要经打铁工艺才能制成。这些因素都推动了阳江打铁业的发展，因此，当时阳江最发达的行业之一就是打铁业，小小的阳江城遍布打铁铺，"炉红烟熏，锤声叮当"是当时的阳江城貌。古阳江城的架构布局有"九街十二巷"之说，其中的一巷就被称为"打铁巷"，《阳江志》（民国十四年版）第51页有地图记载，如今旧址仍存，改名为"合碧街"。

《阳江志》（民国十四年版）还记载有"铜器、小刀、花剪俱佳，货行远近"，这证明还在用铜制作小刀的年代，阳江小刀就已经很有名气了。又据清《冯氏族谱》记载："……冯大将军之墓将生平所用八十二角鹅眉宣锦大刀纳于冢中"。冯大将军即冯盎，是冼夫人的孙子，646年（唐贞观二十年）病逝，葬于阳江城内北山脚下，这"鹅眉宣锦大刀"即阳江俗称的"大杀刀"，由此也可看出当时的刀具制作工艺水平之高。

其后，制刀业日趋发展，生产出各种刀具。阳江小刀最初就是由打铁衍生而来的，在打铁技艺的基础上逐渐发展出阳江小刀的专属制作工艺，奠定了阳江小刀发展的基础。清同治年间，阳江城工商业日渐兴旺，手工业异常繁荣，广东有10多个县的客商云集阳江县城进行多种商贸买卖活动，刀具、豆豉、漆器、海产等阳江传统产品成了各地商家争相采购的货物，大大

小规模生产作坊的锅炉工具
Boiler tools in small-scale forging workshops

促进了当时阳江的经济发展，阳江小刀也从此逐渐外销，大大提升其知名度。

1949年前，阳江小刀主要以小作坊（打铁铺）模式生产，产量较小，其主要分布在阳江城与城郊农村，如城里的打铁巷、平冈镇的良朝村、北惯镇的那霍村、中洲街道的潭塘村等地。后随着从事小刀制造的人数逐渐增多，出现了一些新的小刀作坊，比较集中的有那格村和观过村。

20世纪50年代初，为了满足市场的需求，小作坊模式开始逐渐向群体化过渡，一些刀匠自己组织起来成立小刀厂。位于石觉寺附近的合群小刀厂便是当时最早成立的第一家小刀厂，当时有100多个工人。此后还陆续成立了国光小刀厂、百合小刀厂、和平小刀厂、前进小刀厂、风行小刀厂等，但规模都不大。

1955年，政府牵头，把全县分散的小刀制造工人集中起来，组建了4个小刀生产合作社，以一、二、三、四排行，小刀生产已颇具规模。1958年，又将4个小刀

also showed the high level of sword making craftsmanship at that time.

Since then, the sword industry has developed day by day, producing various kinds of cutting tools. Yangjiang Knife was originally derived from iron forging. On the basis of iron forging craftsmanship, it gradually developed its exclusive manufacturing craftsmanship, laying the foundation for the development of Yangjiang Knife. During the reign of Tongzhi period of the Qing Dynasty, the industry and commerce of Yangjiang City became increasingly prosperous, and the handicraft industry was exceptionally prosperous. There were many merchants from more than ten counties in Guangdong Province gathering in Yangjiang County to carry out a variety of business activities. The traditional products of Yangjiang, such as knives, fermented soy beans, lacquerware and seafood, became the goods that merchants from other places scrambled to purchase, greatly promoting the economic development of Yangjiang at that time. The Yangjiang Knife was gradually exported and its popularity was greatly expanded.

Before 1949, Yangjiang Knife was mainly produced in small workshops (forges), with a small output. They were mainly distributed in Yangjiang City and suburban areas, such as Forges Lane in the city, Liangchao Village in Pinggang Town, Nahuo Village in Beiguan Town, Tantang Village in Zhongzhou Street and other places. Later, with the increasing number of people engaged in knife manufacturing, some new knife workshops appeared in many places. They are more concentrated in Nage Village and Guanguo Village.

In the early 1950s, in order to meet the needs of the market, the small workshop mode began to gradually transition to the group mode. Some knife craftmen organized to set up small knife factories. Hequn Knife Factory, located near Shijue Temple, was the first knife factory established at that time with more than 100 workers. Since

打铁
Forge iron

then, Guoguang Knife Factory, Baihe Knife Factory, Heping Knife Factory, Qianjin Knife Factory and Fengxing Knife Factory have been established, but with not large scale.

In 1955, under the leadership of the government, the scattered knife manufacturing workers in the county were gathered and four knife cooperatives were set up, ranking first, second, third and fourth. The knife production has reached a considerable scale. In 1958, the government merged the four knife cooperatives to establish the Yangjiang County Local State-owned Knife Factory. It was located at No.1 of Daza Cooperative, in the fourth district of Yangjiang County with about 500 employees, and became the largest knife factory in Yangjiang County. The government officially invited Liang Jifu from countryside to work in the Yangjiang County Local State-owned Knife Factory, specially to control the heat treatment and check the quality of products. He was awarded the title of "Old Craftsman". During the Great Leap Forward period from 1958 to 1960, the Yangjiang County Local State-owned Knife Factory was renamed the Youth Motor Factory, mainly engaged in steelmaking and motor production. In 1962, by the proposal of Wen Minsheng, the deputy secretary of the Guangdong Provincial Committee, the factory was renamed Yangjiang County Local State-owned Jifu Knife Factory, and was renamed Yangjiang City State-owned Knife General Factory in 1963.

In addition to the Yangjiang City State-owned Knife General Factory, there were also Second Light Industry Hardware Knife Factory, Second Light Industry Hardware Knife No.2 Factory, Jiangcheng Hardware Products Factory, Jiangcheng Knife Factory and nearly ten knife production communes established by street office engaged in knife production in Yangjiang at that time.

After the reform and opening-up policy, the pattern of dominance of the Yangjiang City State-owned Knife General Factory has broken due to institutional limitations, management failure and overstaffing in organizations. With the deepening of reform and opening-up, the individual and private knife and scissors enterprises in Yangjiang have developed rapidly. The state-owned enterprises have gradually lost their advantages and gradually declined. The Yangjiang County Local State-owned Knife Factory began to stop producing knives in 1992 and officially went bankrupt in 1997, which ends a glorious history of the development of Yangjiang Knife.

Private enterprises, such as "Yangjiang Shibazi" "Shengda" "Yinying" "Yongguang" "Hongfeng" "Good Wife" and "Jinhui", grew up during the reform and opening-up, creating a new era of Yangjiang knife and scissors industry. On the basis of inheriting the manufacturing craftsmanship of traditional cutting tools, the

生产合作社合并，成立了阳江县地方国营小刀厂，地点在阳江县城第四区大闸社一号，约有职工500人，成为阳江县规模最大的小刀厂。政府正式把梁季芙从农村请到地方国营小刀厂工作，专门为工厂进行热处理控制和产品质量把关，并授予“老艺人”称号。1958—1960年“大跃进”运动期间，国营小刀厂被改名为五四青年电机厂，主要从事炼钢和生产电机工作；1962年经中共广东省委副书记文敏生提议，工厂改名为阳江县地方国营季芙小刀厂，1963年又改名为阳江市国营小刀总厂。

除了阳江市国营小刀总厂外，当时阳江还有二轻五金小刀厂、二轻五金小刀二厂、江城五金制品厂、江城小刀厂和近10家的街道办的刀具生产社从事小刀生产。

改革开放后，阳江市国营小刀总厂由于体制局限、管理落后、机构臃肿等原因，其独占鳌头的格局被打破。随着改革开放的不断深入，阳江个体、私营刀剪企业迅速发展，国营企业逐渐失去了往日的优势，渐显衰败。工厂于1992年开始停止生产，至1997年正式破产倒闭，结束了阳江小刀发展的一段光辉历史。

在改革开放大潮中成长起来的“阳江十八子”“盛达”“银鹰”“永光”“鸿丰”“巧媳妇”“金辉”等民营企业，开创了阳江刀剪业的新时代。在继承传统刀具制作技艺的基础上，各民企创立的各个品牌产品不仅流行于国内市场，还以前所未有的气势把阳江刀剪业的盛名推向世界。随着这些知名刀剪品牌的树立，“中国菜刀中心”“中国剪刀中心”“中国小刀中心”均先后落户阳江，使阳江被誉为“中国刀剪之都”。

使用传统刀剑制作技艺制作的剑
A sword made with traditional sword making techniques

使用传统刀剑制作技艺制作的小刀
A knife made with traditional sword making techniques

基本内容

由传承人陈荣梁恢复的传统刀剑制作技艺，采用的是十字折叠法方式折叠锻打，其制作流程要经过选材、积沸、折打、下锻、排列、上锻、素延、火造、敷土、烧刃、研磨等工序，且每道工序环环相扣，缺一不可，最值得一提的是它解决了长期困扰五金制造业的热处理工序。

主要特征

用铁砂提炼出来的含碳量10%以上的基础钢材被称为“玉钢”，将“玉钢”采用古传统折叠锻打法打出的刀剑，其主要特征如下：

（1）结构属性优异。在结构上，不论

热处理工序
The process of heat treatment

various brand products created by enterprises in Yangjiang are not only popular in the domestic market, but also promote the reputation of Yangjiang knife and scissors industry to the world with unprecedented momentum. With the establishment of these famous knife and scissors brands, the title of Chinese Kitchen Knife Center, Chinese Scissors Center and Chinese Knife Center have successively confered to Yangjiang, making Yangjiang known as “the capital of Chinese knives and scissors”.

Basic Content

The traditional sword manufacturing craftsmanship restored by Chen Rongliang is the cross forging method for folding and forging. The manufacturing process includes material selection, boiling, hammering, down forging, arranging, up forging, plain stretching, pyrogenesis, soil coating, burning the edge, grinding and other processes. Each process is closely linked and cannot be separated. It is worth mentioning that it solves the heat treatment process which has long troubled the hardware manufacturing industry.

Main Features

The basic steel with carbon content of more than 10% extracted from iron sand is called “jade steel”. The main characteristics of the sword made from “jade steel” by ancient traditional folding forging method are as follows:

(1) Excellent structural properties. In structure, both hardness and toughness can be improved to the highest equilibrium point.

(2) The cutting resistance is super strong. The swords' performance is far better than that of the sword made of modern steel. It feels like that the edge is not sharp and even won't cut your hand when touching the edge of the sword. But the sword can cut paper after cutting the hemp rope with a diameter of 2.7 cm for more than 10,000 times.

(3) High shock absorption. Clamping the strike point with a vise and then bending and letting go, it can be seen that the swing is not in the pendulum way, but in the cycle law, which improves the shock absorption of swords.

(4) It has “memory”. If the new sword is bent due to improper use, it will straighten naturally after two or three days without

烧烫的钢具有韧性，放进工具中可塑造为刀剑的形状
The burned steel is tough and can be shaped into a sword when put into a tool

adjustment.

(5) Hard and flexible. Although the carbon content of the folded forged steel is only 0.6%, it can reach HRC65 by quenching. When the edge is placed flat on the iron round bar and pressed, it protrudes an arc without cracking.

Great Value

Chen Rongliang has spared no effort to rediscover the "Chinese Traditional Sword Manufacturing Craftsmanship" from the extensive and profound traditional Chinese culture, which is not easy and is an outstanding contribution to the inheritance of intangible cultural heritage. He had taken his actions to assume the responsibility of restoring the ancient Chinese art. He also reminded the Chinese people that we should pay attention to the inheritance, promotion and protection of the excellent traditional Chinese culture. The Traditional Sword Manufacturing Craftsmanship is the fruit of wisdom of ancient Chinese people, and a precious intangible cultural heritage. Restoring and inheriting the Traditional Sword Manufacturing Craftsmanship has important significance for us to protect and defend national cultural sovereignty.

In addition, after the craftsmanship is widely used, it can comprehensively improve the quality of the Yangjiang knife and scissors industry, enhance the technical connotation of core technique to support the sustainable development of the brand, and make rich economic profits and benefit the general public.

硬度、韧性都能提高到最高平衡点。

（2）耐割性超强。其性能远超现代钢铁所做之刀剑，刀锋用手摸不感觉锋利，甚至不会割手，但砍断直径2.7厘米的麻绳一万余次后还可以削纸。

（3）减震性优。将物打区用老虎钳夹住，然后扳弯放手，可以看到刀的摆动不是以钟摆形式，而是周波形式，提高了刀剑的减震性。

（4）具有记忆性。新刀剑如使用不当拍弯了，不必调整，放两三天后其会自然回直。

（5）兼具硬度和柔韧性。折叠锻打后的钢虽然含碳量只有0.6%，但能通过淬火使其洛氏硬度达到HRC65，且将刃口平放在铁圆棒上面压，会看到刃口突出一个圆弧形而不会脆裂。

重要价值

传承人陈荣梁不遗余力地从博大精深的中华传统文化中重新挖掘出“中国古法锻造刀剑技艺”，实属不易，也是对传承非遗作出的杰出贡献。他用自己的实际行动担当起复原中国古老技艺的重任，并提醒广大国人注重中华优秀传统文化的继承、弘扬和保护。古法制刀是中国古人智慧的结晶，是宝贵的非物质文化遗产，恢复并传承古法制刀技艺对我们保护、捍卫国家文化主权具有深远的意义。

此外，该技术得到广泛应用后，可以全面改善阳江五金刀剪行业的质量，提升核心技艺对支撑品牌可持续发展的技术内涵，创造丰厚的经济利润，造福广大民众。

主要传承人

陈荣梁，男，1956年6月出生，台湾台中人，1997年开始学习传统刀剑制作技艺，在500多次的失败过程中克服了长久以来困扰古今中外刀匠的热处理问题，最终觅得成功之果，打造出了刚柔并济的刀剑，掌握古法锻造刀剑技艺。陈荣梁采用传统刀剑制作技艺生产出的刀剑，结构属性优异，耐割性超强、减震性高，且具有记忆性。陈荣梁现为阳江市第四批非物质文化遗产项目代表性传承人。

Main Inheritor

陈荣梁
Chen Rongliang

Chen Rongliang, male, was born in Taichung, Taiwan, in June 1956. He began to learn the Traditional Sword Manufacturing Craftsmanship in 1997. In the process of more than 500 failures, he overcame the heat treatment problems that have plagued the swordsmen at home and abroad for a long time, and finally succeed. He created strong and soft swords and mastered the Traditional Sword Manufacturing Craftsmanship. The sword produced by Chen Rongliang with the traditional manufacturing craftsmanship has excellent structural properties. And it has super cutting resistance and high shock absorption as well as the function of memory. Chen Rongliang is the representative inheritor of the fourth batch of intangible cultural heritage projects in Yangjiang now.

阳江小刀制作技艺

广东省第四批省级非物质文化遗产名录

保护单位 阳江十八子集团有限公司

Yangjiang Knife Manufacturing Craftsmanship

The Fourth Batch of the Provincial Intangible Cultural Heritage List of Guangdong Province

Protection Unit Yangjiang Shibazi Group Co., Ltd.

Yangjiang Knife Manufacturing Craftsmanship has spread throughout Yangjiang, and its workshops are mainly distributed in Jiangcheng, Yangdong, Yangxi, Yangchun, and other urban areas, as well as various suburban towns. The widespread forges are characterized by dispersion and concentration. The famous ones are Forges Lane in Yangjiang urban area, and other forges in Pinggang Town, Guanguo Village, Naluo Village, and Tantang Village in Ganglie Town, Jiangcheng District, Zhilong Town in Yangxi County, Nahuo Village in Beiguan Town, Yangdong District, Gangmei Town in Yangchun City, etc.. And other towns also have iron shops of different sizes.

In 2012, Yangjiang Knife Manufacturing Craftsmanship was listed in the fourth batch of provincial intangible cultural heritage list in Guangdong Province.

打铁
Forge iron

阳江小刀制作技艺流传于整个阳江地区，其制作作坊主要分布在江城、阳东、阳西、阳春等地的城区以及城郊各墟镇。遍布的打铁铺有既分散又集中的特点。名气较大的有阳江城区的打铁巷，江城区的平冈镇，岗列镇的观过村、那洛村、潭塘州等，阳西的织篢镇，阳东的北惯镇那霍村，阳春的岗美镇等，其他各乡镇也有不同大小规模的打铁铺。

2012年，阳江小刀制作技艺被列入广东省第四批省级非物质文化遗产名录。

历史渊源

《阳江志》（民国十四年版）有地图记载：古阳江城架构布局称“九街十二巷”，其中一巷因主营打铁铺而得名“打铁巷”；又载：“小刀、花剪俱佳，货行远近”。这证明阳江小刀在清代就已经很有名气了。《隋书·列女传》卷八十列传第四十五有关谯国夫人的记载：冼夫人于陈永定二年曾在阳江地区发兵；清《冯氏族谱》记载，“冯大将军之墓将生平所用八十二角鹅眉宣锦大刀纳于冢中”，冯大将

阳江古代手工刀具
Yangjiang ancient handmade knife

军即冼大人的孙子冯盎，逝世后葬于阳江城内北山脚下，“鹅眉宣锦大刀”即阳江俗称的“大杀刀”，属兵器。

在20世纪以来的近代发展史中，阳江小刀大致经历了以下4个时期：第一个时期是20世纪初以何全利（文武刀）为代表的打铁铺时代；第二个时期是1939年至1958年以梁季芙（季芙小刀）为代表的集体作坊、合作社时代；第三个时期是1958年至1997年的阳江国营小刀厂时代；第四个时期是1988年至今的民营企业时代。

基本内容

长期以来，五金小刀一直是阳江的支柱产业，在阳江经济发展中扮演着重要角色，“中国菜刀中心”“中国剪刀中心”“中国小刀中心”均先后落户阳江。至2012年，阳江市五金刀剪企业已发展到2000多家，主营业务收入2000万元以上的企业有229家，年总产值341.81亿元，销售产值338.39亿元，占全市工业总值的30%；产品产量居全国首位，占全国总产量的70%，占全国出口量的85%以上，产品行销全球40多个国家和地区，阳江被誉为“中国刀剪之都”，引领着中国刀具行业的发展前进方向。

Historical Origin

A map was recorded in The *Yangjiang Annals* that the structure and layout of the ancient Yangjiang City are called “9 streets and 12 lanes”, and one lane is named Forges Lane because it mainly engages in forges; the *Yangjiang Annals* recorded that “knives and scissors are excellent, and goods are sold far and near”, which proves that Yangjiang Knives were already famous in the Qing Dynasty. In the *Biography of Virtuous Women* in the *Sui Shu* recorded that Madam Xian had sent troops to the Yangjiang area in the second year of Chen Yongding; according to *Pedigee of Feng Clan* of the Qing Dynasty, “the eighty-two horned Xuanjin broadsword decorated in the shape of goose nose, used in his life was included in the tomb of General Feng”. General Feng, named Feng Ang, the grandson of Madam Xian, was buried at the foot of the Bei Mountain in Yangjiang City after his death. The “Emei Xuanjin broadsword”, commonly known as the “killing broadsword” in Yangjiang, is a weapon.

In the modern development history of the Yangjiang Knife since the 20th century, it has roughly experienced the following four periods. The first period represented by He Quanli (Wenwu machete), was the era of the blacksmith of the early 20th century. The second period was the era of collective workshops and cooperatives represented by Liang Jifu (Jifu Knife) from 1939 to 1958. The third period was the era of Yangjiang State-owned Knife Factory from 1958 to 1997. The fourth period is the era of private enterprises since 1988.

Basic Content

For a long time, hardware knives have been the pillar industry of Yangjiang, playing an important role in the economic development of Yangjiang. The title of China Kitchen Knife Center, China Scissors Center, and China Knife Center have all confered to Yangjiang. By 2012, there were more than 2,000 knife and scissors enterprises in Yangjiang City and 229 enterprises with a main business income of more than 20 million *yuan*. The total annual output value of them is 34.181 billion *yuan*, and the sales output value is 33.839 billion *yuan*, accounting for 30% of the city's total industrial value; the product output ranks first in the country, accounting for 70% of the total output of the country and more than 85% of the national export volume. The products are sold in more than 40 countries and regions around the world. Yangjiang is known as the “capital of knives and scissors in China”, leading the development of Chinese knives.

工人在手工锻制小刀

The worker is forging knives by hand

Main Features

Yangjiang Knife belongs to hardware. "Knife" here is a general term. It includes all knife products.

The most remarkable feature of the traditional Yangjiang Knife is that it is purely handmade, and it is famous for its high quality and performance, such as its thin and non-rolling blade, sharpness, rustproofing, versatility, and with various styles, etc.. Its main features are as follows:

(1) Sharpness. Yangjiang Knife is famous for its sharpness. In daily life, people can use Yangjiang Knife to cut vegetables or bones, shave, cut firewood, rice or bamboo.

(2) Durability. Yangjiang Knife is not easy to roll or crack, and generally can be used for more than 10 years with good quality.

(3) Beauty and practicality. A variety of unique shapes of Yangjiang Knife make the perfect combination of beauty and practicality, catering to Yangjiang people's aesthetic pursuit of high-quality knives with the improvement of life quality.

Great Value

Yangjiang Knife Manufacturing Craftsmanship has a long history and is famous at home and abroad. Yangjiang Knife is not only the first choice for Yangjiang citizens to present gifts to relatives and friends, but also one of the necessary specialties for tourists. The knife culture has deeply influenced the Yangjiang people, and always runs through the Yangjiang people's generation-to-generation inheritance, becoming a unique cultural symbol of Yangjiang and the pride of the Yangjiang people.

The traditional craftsmanship of the Yangjiang Knife has its own core and unique craft, which are mainly embodied in the processes of steel entry, heat treatment, etc.. It is the crystallization of wisdom

主要特征

阳江小刀属五金类。“小刀”在这里是一个泛指，它包含了所有的刀类产品。

阳江传统小刀最显著的特点是纯手工制作，并以薄不卷刃、锋可刮须、不生锈、一刀多用、款式多样等高品质性能称雄于世，其主要特点如下：

（1）锋利好用。阳江小刀素以锋利著称。人们可以在日常生活中将阳江小刀用于切菜、砍骨、刮须、砍柴、割稻和削竹等。

（2）坚固耐用。阳江小刀不易卷口、崩口，一般都能使用10年以上，品质上乘。

（3）美观实用。阳江小刀的各种造型达到了美观实用的完美结合，迎合了阳江人民随着生活品质的提高对高品质刀具的审美追求。

重要价值

阳江的制刀技艺历史悠久，驰名中外。阳江小刀既是阳江市民馈赠亲友的首选礼品，也是外地游客来阳江的必选特产之一。小刀文化已流淌在阳江人的血液里，贯穿在阳江人民世代传承的过程中，成为阳江特有的文化符号，也是阳江人的自豪和骄傲。

阳江小刀的传统制作技艺，有其专属的核心技艺和独特的工艺绝技，着重表现在入钢、热处理等工序，它是阳江打铁工匠经过长期实践积累的智慧结晶，也是阳江地域文化的具体体现，它的发展历程为研究阳江的历史、文化、民俗、生产力发展等情况提供了宝贵的真实依据。阳江小刀作为支柱产业，在阳江的地方经济发展中发挥着举足轻重的作用，培养了成百上千名制刀技术人才，提供了成千上万个就业

热处理工序
The process of heat treatment

工人正在对加热后具有延展性的小刀进行敲打塑型
Workers are beating and shaping the malleable knife after heating

岗位，创造了可观的经济效益，推动了民族工业的发展，振兴了中国品牌的威望。

accumulated by Yangjiang ironsmiths through long-term practice and is also the specific embodiment of Yangjiang regional culture. Its development process provides a valuable real basis for the study of Yangjiang's history, culture, folk customs, product development, etc.. As a pillar industry, Yangjiang Knife plays an important role in the development of the local economy. It has trained hundreds of knife-making technicians, provided thousands of jobs, created considerable economic benefits, promoted the development of national industries, and revitalized the prestige of Chinese brands.

主要传承人

李良辉，男，生于1937年12月，阳江十八子集团的创始人，现任该公司董事长。1949年，他跟随一位刘姓师傅学习打铁技艺，后又拜梁季芙为师深造制刀技术。12岁时，他与打铁、锻制刀剪结缘，此后一生从事与制刀相关的行业。李良辉追求工艺技术不断进步，将毕生精力都投入为“做一把好刀”的技术钻研中。他将传统打铁制刀的技艺思想与现代制刀技术相结合，形成了精益求精的工匠精神。他在传承中创新，以产品质量成就了一个民族刀具品牌。李良辉革新了传统打铁制刀的刃口入钢技术，创新地用现代优质钢材作刃部焊接制成厨刀，体现“好钢用在刀刃上”的理念；勇于运用新材料及对标国际先进产品

Main Inheritors

Li Lianghui, male, was born in December 1937. He is the founder of Yangjiang Shibazi Group and the current chairman of the company. In 1949, he studied forging skills with a master surnamed Liu, and he pursued further study in knife-making skills from Liang Jifu. At the age of 12, he became attached to forging and making knives and scissors. Since then, Li Lianghui has been engaged in the industry related to knife making all his life, pursuing continuous progress in technique and devoting himself to the technical research of "making a good knife". By combining the idea of traditional forging techniques with the application of modern technique to knife making, he has formed an unwavering and excellent craftsmanship spirit. He innovated from his inheritance, and created a national brand of knives with high quality products. Li Lianghui innovated traditional forging techniques of making knife blades from steel to weld the blade for making modern kitchen knives by using modern high-quality steel, reflecting the concept of "good steel is used on the blade". Also, he had the courage to apply new materials and benchmark international

李良辉
Li Lianghui

advanced production technique to improve his own knife making technique, and he created a precedent for domestic stainless steel knife making. At the same time, he innovatively applied mechanized wet-type cutting edge grinding to ensure that the material of the knife edge won't change due to the heat during grinding, thereby ensuring the sharpness of the knife.

Li Lianghui invested in independent steel making, realized the "integration of steel making and knife making", and formed the business model of the entire industrial chain guarantee to pursue the product quality of knives to catch up with the international advanced level and advance the R&D and preparation process of knife materials. He is the representative inheritor of the third batch of provincial intangible cultural heritage projects in Guangdong Province now.

Li Youwei, male, was born in January 1964. He is the general manager of Yangjiang Shibazi Knife and Scissors Products Co., Ltd. now. Li Youwei is the eldest son of Li Lianghui. In 1980, he learned traditional knife-making skills from his father Li Lianghui, inherited his father's craftsmanship spirit of "making a good knife", actively carried forward the culture of Yangjiang Knife Manufacturing Craftsmanship, and had taken the lead in establishing the learning institute of Yangjiang Knife Manufacturing Craftsmanship, which created conditions for extensive publicity and promotion of Yangjiang Knife culture.

Li Youwei has a good command of the technological process of manufacturing knives. He applies various technologies of modern industrial manufacturing to implement special heat treatment for steel, gives full play to the technique contained in the traditional process by combining theory with practice, effectively develops targeted heat treatment process for knives with different performance requirements, and promotes the sustainable development of the enterprise with the cultural heritage. He is the representative inheritor of the fourth batch of provincial intangible cultural heritage projects in Guangdong Province now.

技术来提高自己的制刀技术水平，开创国内不锈钢制刀的先河；同时创新性地运用机械化的湿式开刃法磨削，保证了刃口的材质不会在磨削时受热影响而发生变化，从而保证刀具的锋利性能得以体现。

为追求刀具产品质量追赶国际先进水平，李良辉向刀用材料的研发和制备工艺迈进，他投资自主制钢，实现"炼钢制刀一体化"，形成全产业链保障的经营模式。李良辉现为广东省第三批省级非物质文化遗产项目代表性传承人。

李有维，男，生于1964年1月，现任阳江十八子刀剪制品有限公司总经理。李有维是李良辉的长子；1980年，他跟随父亲李良辉学习传统小刀制作技艺，传承父亲"做一把好刀"的工匠精神，积极发扬阳江小刀制作技艺的文化，主导打造阳江小刀制作技艺传习所，为广泛宣传推广阳江小刀文化创造条件。

李有维熟练掌握刀具的制作工艺流程，运用现代工业制造的各种技术对钢材实施特殊热处理，通过理论结合实际，充分发挥出传统工艺中蕴含的科技，有效地对不同性能需求的刀具进行针对性

李有维（前）
Li Youwei (front)

的热处理工艺开发，用非遗传承的文化底蕴促进企业实现持续发展。李有维现为广东省第四批省级非物质文化遗产项目代表性传承人。

李积回，男，生于1967年5月，现任阳江十八子集团有限公司总经理。李积回是李良辉次子，1986年跟随父亲学习传统小刀制作技艺，掌握传统制刀技术，深入领会传统制刀文化与创新内涵并融于企业经营中，不断挖掘阳江制刀文化的历史渊源，传承父亲为“做一把好刀”而大胆创新的精神，主导公司融入现代管理模式，提出高质量、高标准传承阳江小刀制作技艺的精髓，在传承中创新，在不断创新中超越。他改善各类刀具的性能与结构以丰富厨刀产品种类，首创出富有中国特色的各类刀具产品，提倡厨刀必须符合现代人体工程学及力学性能的原理，推动现代工业设计技术运用于刀具生产中，并进行系统性的创新设计，与时俱进地丰富刀具产品以满足消费市场的需求。李积回现为阳江市第三批非物质文化遗产项目代表性传承人。

郑业存，男，1973年出生，从事小刀制作技艺27年，师承袁日祥（冠成五金的创始人）。1994—2004年，开始学习制作小刀的技艺；2004年—2011年，开办五金小刀加工厂；2011—2013年，为小刀制作技艺的深造走访各个传统小刀制作工坊，了解传统制刀技艺；2014—2018年，在烨田工贸公司当小刀制作技术主管；2018年至今，在冠成五金工贸公司小刀厂担任技术主管。为了更好地了解阳江小刀，郑业存向老工匠学习阳江小刀制作技艺，开展系统性的调查研究，并把研究做成文字

李积回
Li Jihui

Li Jihui, male, was born in May 1967. He is the general manager of Yangjiang Shibazi Group Co., Ltd. now. He is the second son of Li Lianghui. He followed his father to learn the traditional knife making technique from 1986. He mastered the traditional knife making technique, deeply understood the traditional knife manufacturing culture and innovation connotation, and integrated them into the enterprise operation, constantly excavated and carried forward the historical origin of Yangjiang Knife manufacturing culture, and inherited his father's spirit of bold innovation for “making a good knife” . He led the company to integrate into the modern management mode, put forward high quality and high standards to inherit the essence of Yangjiang Knife manufacturing technique, innovate from inheritance, and surpass through continuous innovation. He improved the performance and structure of various knives to enrich the types of kitchen knife products, pioneered various knife products with Chinese characteristics, and advocated that the craftsmanship of kitchen knives must conform to the principles of modern ergonomics and mechanical properties. He promoted the systematic innovative design and modern industrial design technique of knives, and enriched knife products to meet the needs of the consumer market of the times. He is the representative inheritor of the third batch of intangible cultural heritage projects in Yangjiang City now.

Zheng Yecun, male, was born in 1973. He has been engaged in knife-making for 27 years, learning from Yuan Rixiang (the founder of Guancheng Hardware) . From 1994 to 2004, he began to learn how to make knives. From 2004 to 2011, he ran a knife processing factory. From 2011 to 2013, he further studied the craftsmanship of manufacturing knives, visited various traditional knife-manufacturing workshops, and learned about the traditional craftsmanship of manufacturing knives. From 2014 to 2018, he worked as the technical

郑业存（左二）
Zheng Yecun

supervisor of knife manufacturing in the Yetian Industry and Trade Company. Since 2018, he has served as the technical supervisor in the knife manufacturing factory of Guancheng Hardware Industry and Trade Company. In order to understand Yangjiang Knife better, he learned the craftsmanship of Yangjiang Knife from old craftsmen, carried out systematic investigation and research, and made them into text files. Zheng Yecun believes that the most important thing about a good knife is to do two things: first, it should be practical, and second, it should be beautiful. In order to achieve the best of these two things, he constantly seeks the source and asks for advice with an open mind. During his period serving as the technical supervisor in the knife manufacturing factory of Guancheng Hardware Industry and Trade Company,he taught apprentices Zeng Qingqiang, Huang Jinjun, Liang Daopei, Ao Qingzhi, Chen Xuehua, Gu Yufen, etc.. Each of them mastered the special technique in their own processes. He is the representative inheritor of the fifth batch of intangible cultural heritage projects in Yangjiang City now.

Hu Ziqin, male, was born in January 1951. Inheriting from his family and learning from Hu Hai (who ran the "Haili Forge"), he has been engaged in knife making for 56 years. From 1965 to 1973, he worked in the Stainless Steel Products Factory Co., Ltd. as the workshop director, managing the production of knives and sharp tools. From 1973 to 1978, he worked as a quality inspector to inspect the quality of knives. Since 1978, he has produced and manufactured knives independently, dealt with the heat treatment of process molds, sharpened knives, etc. at home. At present, he retains the workshop manufacturing of traditional Yangjiang Knife, and his son continues to inherit the craftsmanship learning from his family. Hu Ziqin is the representative inheritor of the fifth batch of intangible cultural heritage projects in Yangjiang City now.

档案。郑业存认为，一把好刀最主要的是要做到两点，一要实用，二要美观。为了把这两点做到极致，他不断寻根求源，虚心求教。在冠成五金工贸公司小刀厂担任技术主管期间，他教有徒弟曾庆强、黄锦均、梁道培、敖青志、陈雪花、古玉芬等，他们均熟练掌握各自所处理的工序当中的专项技术。郑业存现为阳江市第五批非物质文化遗产项目代表性传承人。

胡子钦，男，生于1951年1月，从事小刀制作56年，家族传承，师承胡海（创办海利打铁铺）。1965—1973年，在不锈钢制品厂有限公司上班，担任车间主任，管理生产刀具利器制作；1973—1978年，担任质检员，从事刀具质量检测工作；1978年至今，在家自主从事刀具生产制造、加工模具热处理、磨刀等工作。目前其保留传统阳江刀具制作作坊形式，其儿子继续传承家族技艺。胡子钦现为阳江市第五批非物质文化遗产项目代表性传承人。

胡子钦
Hu Ziqin

阳江剪刀锻制技艺

广东省第五批省级非物质文化遗产名录

保护单位 永光刀剪集团有限公司

Yangjiang Scissors Forging Craftsmanship

The Fifth Provincial Intangible Cultural Heritage List of Guangdong Province

Protection Unit Yongguang Knife and Scissors Group Co., Ltd.

剪刀作为民用生活工具，很早就走进了千家万户，它是发明创造者在生产生活劳动过程中的智慧结晶，在漫长的产品培育过程中，又发展性地创造了各类专用工具，不仅减轻了劳动强度，也大大提高了工效，还衍生出相关的诗词、剪纸等艺术，现已成为家家必备、户户都有的一般生活用具了。

阳江剪刀的生产区域主要分布在阳江县城、城郊和阳江各墟镇，包括岗列街道、城西街道、白沙街道、平冈镇、双捷镇、埠场镇、北惯镇、合山镇、织篢镇等，其中尤以织篢镇旧墟的织篢河沿岸剪刀生产作坊分布较密集。

2013年，阳江剪刀锻制技艺被列入广东省第五批省级非物质文化遗产名录。

历史渊源

阳江古为百越地，据《阳江志》（民国十四年版）记载，“恩州秦属南海郡”，说明自秦开始阳江地区已有居民。阳江自隋大业二年（606）得名阳江县以后，郡治长期设置在阳江县城，古城位于

As a tool for civil life, scissors have been used by thousands of households for a long time. It is the wisdom of the inventors in the processes of production, life, and labor. In the long process of product cultivation, the craftsmen have also created various special tools developmentally. They not only reduced labor intensity but also greatly improved work efficiency. In the meantime arts such as related poetries, paper-cuts, and so on were generated. Now, it has become a necessary and common daily tool for every household.

Yangjiang Scissors' production areas are mainly distributed in Yangjiang County, the suburbs, and various market towns in Yangjiang, including Ganglie Subdistrict, Chengxi Subdistrict, Baisha Subdistrict, Pinggang Town, Shuangjie Town, Buchang Town, Beiguan Town, Heshan Town, Zhilong Town, and so on, among which the scissors workshops along the Zhilong River in the old market are especially concentrated.

In 2013, Yangjiang Scissors Forging Craftsmanship was listed

精美的阳江剪刀

Exquisite Yangjiang scissors

in the fifth batch of the provincial intangible cultural heritage list in Guangdong Province.

Historical Origin

Yangjiang was a place in the Baiyue area in ancient times. According to *Yangjiang Annals*, "Enzhou belongs to Nanhai Prefecture in the Qin Dynasty" indicating that there had been residents in Yangjiang since the Qin Dynasty. Since the name Yangjiang County was obtained in the second year of Daye of the Sui Dynasty (606 AD), the county government has been set up in Yangjiang County for a long time. The ancient city was located in the middle and lower reaches of the Moyang River. During the Tang and Song dynasties, Yangjiang County developed into a political, economic, and cultural center. In the Song Dynasty, Yangjiang carried out economic and trade exchanges with Jiangsu and Zhejiang regions, especially coastal areas. Silk cloth and other products were transported to the Yangjiang region by water way, which accelerated the development of the handicraft industry in Yangjiang. Scissors gradually played a significant role as living goods and for commercial purposes. In 1953, archaeologists unearthed iron scissors from the Western Han Dynasty Tomb in Shaogou, Luoyang, Henan Province, indicating that scissors first appeared in the central plains. Scissors were called "Jiaodao" in ancient times, also known as "Bingdao" or "Bingzhou Dao", which indicating that the most famous place in the ancient Chinese scissors making industry was Bingzhou (now Taiyuan, Shanxi Province). As for the forging history of Yangjiang Scissors, the *Yangjiang Annals* records that "bronze-ware, knives and scissors are excellent, and goods are sold far and near". "Excellent" means beautiful and good, which shows that the forging technique of Yangjiang Scissors at that time had reached a high level and had a good reputation in terms of product quality, appearance and design. "Goods are sold far and near" indicates the sales volume and scope of scissors at that time. Since ancient times, Yangjiang people have called scissors *"Jiaojian"*, which also proves the long history of forging and using Yangjiang Scissors.

The development history of Yangjiang Scissors Forging Craftsmanship has roughly experienced the stage of family handicraft workshops before the Qing Dynasty and the period of Republic of China, the stage of cooperative, collective and state-owned enterprises after 1949, and the stage of private enterprises since the reform and opening-up.

Before the end of the Qing Dynasty, the making of knives and

漠阳江中下游。唐宋时期，阳江县城发展成为政治经济文化中心。在宋代，阳江与江浙地区尤其沿海地区有贸易往来，丝绸布匹等产品经水路运至阳江地区，加速了阳江手工业的发展，剪刀作为生活用品逐步发挥其商业用途。1953年，考古学家在河南洛阳烧沟西汉墓中发掘出土了铁剪实物，说明剪刀最早出现在中原地区。剪刀古时称“铰刀”，又被称为“并刀”或“并州刀”，说明中国古代制剪业最负盛名者当数并州（今山西太原）。阳江剪刀的锻造历史，据《阳江志》（民国十四年版）记载：“铜器、小刀、花剪俱佳，货行远近”。“佳”乃“美、好的”之意，说明了阳江当时的剪刀锻制技艺已经具有相当的水平，在产品质量、外观造型等方面都有好口碑；“货行远近”则说明了当时剪刀产品的销量和销售范围。而从阳江人自古至今都将剪刀称呼为“铰剪”，也佐证了阳江剪刀锻制、使用的历史悠久。

阳江剪刀锻制技艺，大致经历了如下三个发展阶段：清代之前和民国时期以家庭手工作坊为主的阶段，1949年后以合作社、集体企业和国营企业为主的阶段，改革开放后至今以私营企业为主的阶段。

清末以前，刀剪制作已成为传统产业，阳江剪刀的锻造以家庭手工作坊为主，主要分布在阳江县城、城郊，比如邻近华濠涌的坝岸，就有两间锻打裁缝剪的打铁铺，名为“美利”和“新有利”。阳江各墟镇中，织篢旧墟的织篢河沿岸剪刀生产作坊分布较为密集，产品以普通民用剪为主。民国时期，剪刀生产制作仍以家庭手工作坊为主，但已有商号标志和店铺，据接受采访的“老义栈”皮箱铺老板张悌清（86岁）回忆，当年的阳江县城西门街（今南恩路西段）何屋祠门前就有

"义兴""昌记"两间专门销售铜铰（指皮箱专用配件，如铜合页、铜箱耳、铜锁牌等）、铜柄小刀、铜制剪刀等小五金的店铺，两店既生产又销售，产品均为手工制作，张悌清的"老义栈"漆皮箱配件就是委托"义兴"加工专制的。又据阳江商界老前辈谢彦伦生前回忆，20世纪20年代（民国初期），"义兴""昌记"手工制作的专门用来修剪花枝的花剪，就被销往美国市场，名扬"美利坚"。所产花剪由"水客"带到香港，再上货船运抵美国，因花剪锋利好用，深受美国花农欢迎，产品相当畅销，一度供不应求。

而阳江西部的织篢镇，是阳江剪刀锻制发祥地之一。据《阳西县志》记载，早在明清时期，织篢镇的刀剪制作已成为传统产业，以织篢河为中心，沿岸两边分布着很多制作刀剪的家庭手工作坊。民国时期，织篢镇有张世伦、毛连、郑水生、郭伦、冯众、何辉等著名的刀剪师傅，其中尤以张世伦的刀剪铺最为著名。织篢镇制造的理发系列工具，名驰南路，产品包括理发剪、剃刀、理发推剪、理发转盘椅等专业理发系列产品，在阳江地区是独一无二的。

新中国成立后，政府组织成立了生产刀剪的合作社，体制以集体企业和国营企业为主，如1955年成立阳江县地方国营小刀厂，厂址设在阳江县城南的禾村仔，除生产小刀外，还生产怀剪、折叠剪、裁缝剪、旅游剪、修饰剪等品种，款式达数百种。其间还成立了隶属阳江县二轻系统的织篢镇五金厂、阳江市二轻五金小刀一厂、阳江市二轻五金小刀二厂、江城小刀厂、超美人民公社农具刀剪厂等。成立于1956年的织篢镇五金铁器社，下设五金修理组和农具组，五金修理组由张世伦、张

scissors had become a traditional industry. The forging of Yangjiang Scissors was mainly done in family workshops, which were mainly distributed in Yangjiang County and its suburbs. For example, near the dam bank of Huahao Chong, there were two forges forging tailor's scissors, namely "Meili" and "Xinyouli". In the market towns of Yangjiang, the scissors workshops, especially along the Zhilong River in the Zhilong old market, are relatively intensive, and their products are mainly ordinary household scissors. During the period of Republic of China, the production of scissors was still dominated by family handicraft workshops, but there were trademarks and stores. According to an interview with Zhang Tiqing (86 years old), the owner of the leather suitcase shop "Laoyizhan", there were two shops called "Yixing" and "Changji" in front of Hewuci Gate, Ximen Street, Yangjiang County (now the west section of Nan'en Road), which were dedicated to selling copper hinges (referring to special accessories for leather suitcases, such as copper hinges, copper case rings, copper lock plates, etc.), small knives with copper handles, copper scissors, and other hardware. The two shops are both produced and sold, and the products are all handmade. The lacquered leather case accessories of Zhang Tiqing's "Laoyizhan" are exclusively processed by "Yixing". According to the memory of Xie Yanlun, an old senior in Yangjiang business circles, in the 1920s (the early years of the period of Republic of China), "Yixing" and "Changji" handmade flower scissors specialized in pruning flowers entered the American market and became famous in the America. The scissors were brought to Hong Kong by the "itinerant trader" and then transported to the United States by cargo ship. Because the flower scissors were sharp, they are welcomed by American flower farmers. The products were very popular and out of stock.

Zhilong town, which is in the west of Yangjiang, is one of the birthplaces of scissors forging in Yangjiang. According to *Yangxi County Annals*, the production of knives and scissors in Zhilong town has been a traditional industry since the Ming and Qing dynasties. With the Zhilong River as the center, there were many family handicraft workshops of knives and scissors on both sides of the river. During the period of Republic of China, there were many famous knife and scissors-making craftsmen such as Zhang Shilun, Mao Lian, Zheng Shuisheng, Guo Lun, Feng Zhong, and He Hui in Zhilong Town, among whom Zhang Shilun's knife and scissors shop was the most famous. The barber series tools made in Zhilong are famous in the south. The products include barber scissors, razors, hair clippers, barber swivel chairs, and other professional barber products, which are unique in the Yangjiang area.

After 1949, the government organized cooperatives for the production of knives and scissors. The system is dominated by collective enterprises and state-owned enterprises. For example, the Local State-owned Knife Factory in Yangjiang County was established in 1955. The factory is located in Hecunzai, the south of Yangjiang County. In addition to producing knives, it has also produced pocket scissors, folding scissors, sewing scissors, tourist scissors, decorative scissors, and other varieties with hundreds of styles. During the period, Zhilong Hardware Factory, which was subordinated to the Second Light Industry System of Yangjiang County, Yangjiang Second Light Industry Hardware Knife No.1 Factory, Yangjiang Second Light Industry Hardware Knife No.2 Factory, Jiangcheng Knife Factory, Chaomei People's Commune Farm Tools Knife and Scissors Factory, etc., were also established. The Hardware and Ironware Commune in Zhilong Town, founded in 1956, had a hardware repair group and a farm tool group. And the hardware repair group consists of 13 people, including Zhang Shilun, Zhang Fengxin, Liang Lifeng, Jiang Bang, Chen Xingxiu, Liu Changfu, Liu Xingyao, Deng De, He Yuanjie, Liang Jiasheng, Xu Kaizheng, Jiang Jinyun, and Ye Guicou. The workshop of the commune covers an area of more than 380 square meters. At that time, the plant and equipment were simple and crude, but the craftsmen had developed many products such as razors, barber scissors, barber swivel chairs, and so on. There are more than 1,000 barber scissors and more than 100 barber swivel chairs produced by hand and sold all over the country. In September 1958, the Hardware and Ironware Commune in Zhilong Town was under the management of the Yangjiang Second Light Handicraft Industry Association and renamed the Central Machinery Factory of Zhilong People's Commune. At that time, the whole factory had 108 workers and was located in the original Mazu Temple in Xinqing Street, Zhilong Town. It mainly produced scissors, knives, razors, kitchen knives, and other products. In 1960, the Central Machinery Factory was divided into four communes: the iron tool commune, the plough commune, the wood tool commune, and the hardware commune. The division of products was more professional. The main product of the hardware club was scissors. In 1963, the four communes were merged by the government and renamed the Yangjiang County Zhilong Farm Tool Factory. More than 80 workers were employed at this time in the large-scale production of barber tools such as barber scissors, razors, barber swivel chairs (50 pieces per month) , and household scissors.

From the late 1950s to the 1960s, the main production areas of

逢新、梁立锋、江邦、陈幸修、刘昌符、刘幸尧、邓德、何元杰、梁家胜、徐开正、江金允、叶桂凑等13人组成，工厂占地面积380多平方米，当时工厂厂房及设备虽简陋，但师傅们研发出剃刀、理发剪、理发转盘椅等多个产品，年产理发刀剪1000多把、理发转椅100多张，全是手工制作，产品销往全国各地。1958年9月，织篢镇五金铁器社隶属阳江二轻手工业联社管理，改名为织篢人民公社中心机械厂，当时全厂工人有108人，厂址设在织篢镇新庆街原妈祖庙内，主要生产剪刀、小刀、剃刀、菜刀等产品；1960年，中心机械厂被分为4个社，即铁器社、犁头社、木器社、五金社，产品分工更加专业，五金社的主打产品为剪刀。1963年，4个社又被政府合并，改名为阳江县织篢农具厂，大规模生产理发用具，包括理发剪刀、剃刀、理发转盘椅（每月生产50张）、民用剪刀等，全厂工人有80多人。

20世纪50年代后期至60年代，全国生产理发剪的主要产地为上海、天津、广州、织篢，“世伦发剪”占有一席之地，其质量及名声堪与上海等地名牌理发剪媲美。1964年，织篢农具厂被再次分为铁器厂、铸造厂、木器厂、五金厂。1978年8月，织篢五金厂厂址搬到织篢镇东堡街1号（现奋兴路5号），职工有100多人，厂房占地面积11 000平方米，建筑面积3000平方米，生产刀剪和理发用具等，年产刀剪10万把。1979年，该厂被湛江地区轻工业品进出口公司指定为出口产品生产基地，年产刀剪20万把，年产值达50多万元。1981年，阳江县政府将织篢五金厂定为县唯一剪刀出口基地，为加快发展，阳江轻工业品进出口公司与织篢五金厂建立联营关系，成为湛江地区第一家工贸联营商品出口基地，投入资金30万元，为发展阳江剪刀出口打下基础，并将原织篢五金厂改名为阳江工贸联营织篢五金厂，厂房建筑面积第一期扩大至6000平方米，从原来生产理发剪、民用剪，增加了文具剪、厨房剪、园林剪等系列产品，年产量达100多万把，年产值达200多万元。

改革开放的春风吹来时，张逢新等人敢为人先、抢占先机，率先注册成立了民营企业，之后国营、集体企业纷纷改制，阳江刀剪业进入了以民营为主的时代。张逢新于1981年最早成立了阳江第一家刀剪民营企业——阳江织篢刀剪厂。他把握机遇，寻求发展，1985年与香港永光铰剪厂有限公司达成合作，大胆引入外资，实行股份制，扩大生产规模，并找到一条将产品打入国际市场的销路，使企业得到发展的空间，并在民营企业中起到带头和示范作用。经过三年的发展，“永光”刀剪产品在国际市场上供不应求。1988年阳西建县后，在县委县政府及有关部门的大力支持下，企业又一次把握机遇，从“阳江织篢刀剪厂”发展成为“织篢光阳刀剪厂”，再发展为“阳西县光阳刀剪厂”。1993年，张逢新果断地创办了“阳西县张氏永光刀剪厂有限公司”，其长子张锐宗出任董事长，扩大了企业规模和生产规模，奠定了阳西县刀剪业的发展基础。1988—1998年，仅阳西县就先后创建了阳西县金徽五金工业有限公司、阳西县光阳刀剪有限公司（前身是织篢光阳刀剪厂）、阳西县光达餐厨具制造有限公司、阳西县华星五金有限公司、阳西县业诚工业有限公司、阳西县锋达刀剪厂、阳西县永丰五金制品厂、阳西县科达刀剪厂等17家刀剪生产企业。此外，还有为数不少的家庭作坊式装配加工场点也加入织篢生产

barber scissors in China were Shanghai, Tianjin, Guangzhou, and Zhilong. “Shilun Hair Scissors” had a place, and their quality and reputation were almost equal to those famous barber scissors in Shanghai and other places. In 1964, the Zhilong Farm Tool Factory was divided into an ironware factory, a foundry factory, a woodwork factory, and a hardware factory again. In August 1978, the Zhilong Hardware Factory moved to No. 1, Dongbao Street, Zhilong Town (now No. 5, Fenxing Road) , with more than 100 employees. The factory covers 11,000 square meters, with a building area of 3,000 square meters. It produced scissors and barber tools, with an annual output of 100,000 knives and scissors. In 1979, the factory was designated as the production base for export products by the Light Industrial Products Import and Export Company in Zhanjiang, with an annual output of 200,000 knives and scissors and an annual output value of more than 500,000 *yuan*. In 1981, the Yangjiang County Government designated the Zhilong Hardware Factory as the only scissors export base in the county. In order to speed up development, Yangjiang Light Industrial Products Import and Export Company established a joint venture relationship with the Zhilong Hardware Factory, which became the first industry and trade joint commodity export base in Zhanjiang with an investment of 300,000 *yuan* to lay the foundation for the development of Yangjiang scissors export. It renamed the Zhilong Hardware Factory as Yangjiang Industry and Trade Joint Zhilong Hardware Factory. The building area of the factory was expanded to 6,000 square meters in the first phase. Besides the original production of barber scissors and civil scissors, a series of products such as stationery scissors, kitchen scissors, and garden scissors have been added, with an annual output of more than 1 million and an annual output value of more than 2 million *yuan*.

When the reform and opening-up policy started, Zhang Fengxin and others had the courage to preempt the opportunity and took the lead in registering and establishing private enterprises. After that, state-owned and collective enterprises were restructured in succession, and the knife and scissors industry of Yangjiang entered an era dominated by private enterprises.In 1981, Zhang Fengxin established the first private enterprise of knife and scissors in Yangjiang, Yangjiang Zhilong Knife and Scissors Factory. He seized the opportunity and sought development. In 1985, he reached a cooperation with Hong Kong Yongguang Scissors Factory Co., Ltd., introducing overseas investment boldly, implementing shareholding system, expanding production scale, and helping to sell products in the international market, so that the enterprise can develop and play a leading role in private enterprises. After three years of development, the "Yongguang" knife and scissors products were in short supply in the international market. After the establishment of Yangxi County in 1988, with the strong support of the county party committee and government and relevant departments, the enterprise seized the opportunity once again to develop from Yangjiang Zhilong Knife and Scissors Factory to Zhilong Guangyang Knife and Scissors Factory, and then to Guangyang Knife and Scissors Factory of Yangxi County. In 1993, Zhang Fengxin decisively established Yangxi County Zhang's Yongguang Knife and Scissors Factory Co., Ltd. His eldest son, Zhang Ruizong, served as the chairman of the board, expanded the enterprise scale and production scale, and laid the foundation for the development of the knife and scissors industry in Yangxi County. Between 1988 and 1998, Yangxi County has successively established 17 enterprises of knife and scissors, including Yangxi County Jinhui Hardware Industry Co., Ltd., Yangxi County Guangyang Knife and Scissors Co., Ltd. (formerly known as Zhilong Guangyang Knife and Scissors Factory), Yangxi County Guangda Kitchen Utensils Manufacturing Co., Ltd., Yangxi County Huaxing Hardware Co., Ltd., Yangxi County Yecheng Industry Co., Ltd., Yangxi County Fengda Knife and Scissors Factory, Yangxi County Yongfeng Hardware Products Factory, Yangxi County Keda Knife and Scissors Factory, etc.. In addition, there are a large number of assembling and processing family workshops also joining in the production of knives and scissors. Until 2000, there were 8 enterprises of knife and scissors industry with an output value of more than 5 million and 9 enterprises with an output value of more than 2 million. There were 5 manufacturers of scissors accessories, 5 workshops for processing and assembling, and 12 family handicraft workshops, making Yangxi County become the largest production base of knife and scissors in the country at that time, which played a positive role in promoting the vigorous development of the knife and scissors industry in Yangjiang City and made great contributions. In the time of reform and opening-up, Zhang Fengxin and his son Zhang Ruizong followed the trend and seized the opportunity to develop the enterprise into Guangdong Yongguang Knife and Scissors Group Co., Ltd. in 2002. In April 2009, with the approval of the State Administration for Industry and Commerce of the People's Republic of China, they integrated resources and upgraded the enterprise to Yongguang Knife and Scissors Group Co., Ltd. The former small workshop was developed into a large enterprise in the domestic knife and scissors industry, which is currently the largest in the national knife and scissors industry with the strongest technical power. Its production and sales volume and export volume of knives and scissors ranks the first in

刀剪的行列。至2000年，织篢产值规模超500万元的刀剪企业有8家、超200万元的有9家，制作剪刀配件的厂家、加工装配的加工场点有5个，家庭手工作坊有12个，使阳西县成为当时全国最大的刀剪生产基地，这对推动阳江市刀剪业的蓬勃发展起到积极作用，立下了汗马功劳。在改革开放的浪潮中，张逢新、张锐宗父子顺应潮流，抓住机遇，2002年将企业发展为广东永光刀剪集团有限公司。2009年4月，经国家工商总局批准，他们整合资源，又将企业升格发展成为永光刀剪集团有限公司，将最初的一个小作坊发展成为国内刀剪行业的一艘“航母”。永光刀剪集团有限公司是目前全国刀剪行业规模最大、技术力量最雄厚的大型企业，刀剪产销量、出口额均居全国首位，在行业内举足轻重，成为带动当地乃至全国刀剪行业发展的龙头企业。

截至2012年，阳江市五金刀剪企业已发展到1500多家，主营业务收入达2000万元以上的企业有229家，五金刀剪业年总产值341.81亿元，年销售额338.39亿元，占全市工业总值的30%；产品产量居全国首位，占全国总产量的70%，出口量占全国出口量的85%以上。阳江市是名副其实的“中国刀剪之都”。

基本内容

阳江剪刀锻制技艺工艺流程如下：

（1）选材。选择原钢，包括铁、弹簧钢、碳钢、废钢等。

（2）试钢、试铁。就是将小部分材料放入炉火中烧红，见水后用铁锤锻打，会断就是钢，不会断就是铁；断口粗糙度细是好钢，反之，断口粗糙度粗则说明钢材质量不够好，并以此分辨材料与产品的质量要求是否相符。

（3）开料。根据产品的要求确定用料尺寸和数量。

（4）裁切。按产品所需规格用铁锤和錾子将原材料裁切成粗坯。

（5）熔火。将裁切好的粗坯放入炭火中加热。

（6）入钢。这是剪刀锻制的核心技艺之一，将粗坯加热到一定火候后用铁锤和錾子在刀口处起槽，起槽后将钢芯嵌入，趁热用铁锤锻打熔合，把好钢用在刀刃上。

（7）锻打。将粗坯放入炭火中加热，达到一定温度时用铁钳钳出，放在铁砧上按照剪刀的形状用铁锤进行锻打。锻打也是剪刀锻制的核心技艺之一，更是评价师傅的一个标准，火色看得准，是剪刀锻制的基本功夫。

（8）整形、成型。按照产品形状、厚薄、大小的不同要求，特别是几何角度（也称折弯度）的成型，反复多次进行熔火锻打。剪刀刃口的角度大小是根据所剪物体和使用要求的不同设置的，如剪布、剪纸、剪树枝、剪铁皮，它们所需的刃口折弯度就不同。千锤百炼既能使剪体的金相组织进一步细密，更能增加钢的硬度和韧性。

（9）退火。退火就是将工件退出

the country, playing an important role in the industry. It has become the leading enterprise driving the local and even national knife and scissors industry. By 2012, the number of hardware knife and scissors enterprises in Yangjiang has grown to more than 1,500, among which 229 enterprises had a main business income of more than 20 million *yuan*. The hardware knife and scissors industry had a total annual output value of 34.181 billion *yuan* and a sales output value of 33.839 billion *yuan*, accounting for 30% of the city's total industrial value. The product output ranked the first in the country, accounting for 70% of the country's total output. The export volume of knife and scissors accounted for more than 85% of the country's export volume. Yangjiang is worthy of the name of "the capital of knives and scissors in China".

Basic Content

The processes of Yangjiang Scissors Forging Craftsmanship are as follows:

(1) Material selection. Select raw steel, including iron, spring steel, carbon steel, scrap steel, etc..

(2) Steel and iron test. Put a small part of the material into the furnace fire and burn it. After putting it into water, forge it with an iron hammer. If it breaks, it is steel. If it does not break, it is iron. If the fracture roughness is fine, it is good steel. On the contrary, if the fracture roughness is coarse, it indicates that the quality of the steel is not good enough. It helps distinguish whether the material meets the quality requirements of the product.

(3) Material determining. Determine the size and quantity of materials according to the product requirements.

(4) Cutting. Use the hammer and chisel to cut the raw materials into rough billets according to the required specifications of the product.

(5) Melting. Put the rough billets into the charcoal fire for heating.

(6) Steel entry. This is one of the core craftsmanship of scissors forging. After heating the rough billets to a certain temperature, use a hammer and chisel to slot at the edge of the knife, insert the steel core into the slot, and forge and fuse it with a hammer while it is hot, so that the steel can be used on the blade.

(7) Hammering. Then put the rough billet into the charcoal fire for heating. When it reaches a certain temperature, clamp it out with iron tongs, and put it on the anvil to forge it with iron hammer according to the shape of the scissors. Hammering is also one of

the core craftsmanship of scissors forging. It is also a standard for evaluating the blacksmith. Hammering at accurate temperature is the basic skill of scissors forging.

(8) Shaping and forming. Repeatedly melt and forge according to the requirements of different shapes, thicknesses and sizes of products, especially the forming of geometric angles (also known as bending degrees). The angle size of the blade of the scissors is set according to the different objects to be cut and the use requirements, such as cloth cutting, paper cutting, tree cutting, iron sheet cutting, which requires different bending degrees of the blade. Through repeated melting and forging, the metallographic structure of the scissors body can be further refined and it can also increase the hardness and toughness of steel.

(9) Annealing. Annealing is to take the workpiece out of the furnace but keep it at a certain temperature. The purpose of annealing is to reduce the hardness of the raw material, refine the grain, eliminate the stress, and make it soft for the next process operation. The specific method is to put the hammered, shaped and formed scissors into the furnace again and heat them to about 700–800 degrees. When the color is dark cherry red, clamp the workpiece out and insert it into the lime powder or rice husk ash filled in buckets, and cover it all, to achieve the effect of slow cooling. Generally, it should be put in the furnace for one night (more than ten hours). When the temperature is reduced to not hot, it can be taken out for the next process.

(10) Cliping. Fix the annealed scissors on the dedicated table, and clip the scissors belly and the scissors margin with the scraper for rough processing.

(11) Filing. Then fix the scraped scissors on the dedicated table, and fine process each part of the scissors with a file.

(12) Punching. Punch a hole at a specified position under the left and right scissors blade for connecting the left and right scissors blade.

(13) Chiseling. Use a hammer and chisel to chisel the product's brand or mark at some part of the scissors.

(14) Heat treatment. The function of heat treatment is to improve the mechanical properties of materials, eliminate residual stress and improve the machinability of metals. In short, it is a method to change the physical properties of metals by heating and cooling. Heat treatment can improve the microstructure of steel and iron. The necessary toughness, hardness and wear resistance of scissors can be obtained through heat treatment.

Heat treatment includes quenching, tempering, and annealing.

火炉，但又要使之保有一定的温度。退火的目的是降低原材料的硬度、细化晶粒，消除应力，使之变得柔软，便于下一步工序操作。具体做法是：将经锻打整形、成型后的剪片再次放入火炉加热至700～800℃，火候呈暗樱红色，然后钳出插放到用桶盛装的石灰粉或谷壳灰中，并全部覆盖，达到缓慢冷却的效果，一般要放一整夜（10小时以上），温度降至不烫手时可取出进行下一步工序。

（10）铲。将退好火的剪刀固定在专用铲台上，用铲刀铲削剪肚和剪口余量，进行粗加工。

（11）锉。将铲削好的剪刀固定在专用锉刀台上，用锉刀在剪刀各部位进行细加工。

（12）冲孔。此步骤也称“打眼”，在左右剪片下方设置规定的部位冲出一个孔，用于左右两爿剪刀的连接。

（13）凿字。在剪刀的某个部位用铁锤和錾子凿出产品字号或标记。

（14）热处理。热处理的作用就是提高材料的机械性能、消除残余应力和改善金属的切削加工性。简言之，就是利用加热和冷却改变金属的物理性质。热处理能改善钢、铁的显微结构，剪刀必须具备的韧性、硬度和耐磨等特性都要通过热处理获得。

热处理包括淬火、回火、退火工序。

淬火要经过加热、保温和冷却这三道流程。加热的目的是要使剪片达到一定的温度指标。加热有两种方法，一是将经过整形工序已成型的剪片重新放入炭炉中加热，如碳钢产品温度要达到830～870℃，火候至橘黄或微红色；不锈钢产品温度要达到1000～1050℃，火候至黄色。二是将剪片放入用高温熔成水的硝盐中加热（也称盐浴），使其温度和在炭炉中加热的温度一样。盐浴的优点是可以防止钢材脱碳和表面被氧化。保温就是将剪片放在加热时所达到的温度中持续一段时间，使产品表里的温度达到一致，根据不同的材质和产品要求，持续时间为3～10分钟。最后是冷却（也称“见水”），冷却有三种方法，即水冷、油冷（水冷、油冷也称为淬水或淬油）、风冷，即将保温后的剪片钳出后垂直浸入水中或油中，或直接利用风进行冷却。碳钢产品一般要进行水冷或油冷处理，不锈钢则要采用油冷或风冷处理。

经淬火后的剪片还要经过回火工序，回火是将温度降低至180～200℃，火候呈稻黄色。回火的目的是要使剪片达到一定的韧性和弹性指标，但如果硬度超标，还要经过退火工序，降低剪片的硬度和强度，以达到最佳的韧性和硬度要求。

热处理是剪刀锻制流程的重要工序，也是剪刀锻制的核心技艺，更是一个好师傅的衡量标准。热处理得好不好将直接影响产品质量。为了准确把握和控制钢材的含碳量，一般来说，碳质量分数高于0.5%的碳钢，为降低其硬度使其易于切削，常采用退火处理；碳质量分数低于0.5%的碳钢，为避免其硬度过低，则要采用淬火处理，要达到一定的韧性和弹性指标，则要经过回火处理。淬火、退火和回火后，通过锻打，均能细化晶粒、均匀组织。一般来讲，硬度（HRC）为48～52就较为合适，但这完全要靠师傅对钢材的认知和了解以及丰富的操作经验，既要考虑剪片的材质，又要考虑剪片的厚薄，还要注意火候的颜色，正所谓“打铁要看火色”。剪片见水后师傅还会采取较原始的方法对剪刀进行硬度检验，即用钢锯片无齿的一端在剪片上来回划几下，如无划痕出现，表

Quenching goes through three processes: heating, heat preservation and cooling. The purpose of heating is to make the scissors reach a certain temperature index. There are two methods of heating. One is to put the shaped scissors after the shaping process into the furnace again for heating. For example, the temperature of carbon steel products should reach 830-870 degrees, and the color of fire should be orange and reddish, while the temperature of stainless steel products should reach 1,000-1,050 degrees, and the color of fire should be yellow. The second is to heat the scissors in molten nitrate (also known as salt bath) and make the temperature the same as it in the furnace. The advantage of salt bath is that it can prevent steel decarbonization and surface oxidation. The process of heat preservation is that the scissors is placed in the heating temperature for a sustained period of time, so that the temperature of the product surface and inside are consistent. According to different materials and product requirements, the duration varies from 3 to 10 minutes. And the last process is cooling. There are three methods of cooling, namely water cooling, oil cooling (also known as water or oil quenching) , and air cooling. That is to say, after the heat preserved scissors are pulled out, they are vertically immersed in water or oil, or directly cooled by wind. Carbon steel products are generally subject to water or oil cooling, while stainless steel products are subject to oil cooling or air cooling.

The quenched scissors also need to go through the tempering process. Tempering is to reduce the temperature to 180-200 degrees, when the color of fire is rice-yellow. The purpose of tempering is to make the scissors reach a certain toughness and elasticity index. If the hardness index exceeds the standard, it also needs to go through the annealing process to reduce some hardness and strength of the scissors for achieving the best toughness and hardness requirements.

Heat treatment is not only an important process in the processes of scissors forging, but also the core craftsmanship of scissors forging, and is the standard of measuring a good blacksmith. Good or bad heat treatment will directly affect the quality of products. Generally, in order to accurately control the carbon content of steel, carbon steel with carbon content higher than 0.5% is often annealed to reduce its hardness for cutting easily. If carbon steel with carbon content lower than 0.5%, in order to avoid low hardness, quenching treatment should be adopted. Tempering treatment should be adopted to achieve certain toughness and elasticity indexes. After quenching, annealing and tempering, crystalline grains and uniform structure can be refined through forging. Generally speaking, when the hardness (HRC) reaches 48–52, it is more appropriate, but this depends entirely on the blacksmith's knowledge and understanding of steel and rich operating experience. It is necessary to consider not only the material and the thickness of the scissors, but also the color of the fire, which is so-called "forging depends on the color of fire". After putting the scissors into water, the blacksmith will also take a more primitive method to test the hardness of the scissors, that is, use the end of the hacksaw blade without serration to scratch the scissors back and forth. If there isn't scratch, it indicates that the hardness of the product meets the requirements and standards, and if the hardness is not enough, there will be scratches.

(15) Cleaning. After heat treatment, while the scissors are still warm, rub it in the furnace ash for a few times to clean the surface. In the case of large quantities, oil quenching products should be washed in boiling water.

(16) Sharpening. Place and fix the whetstone in two wooden basins made of cedar about 30 cm in diameter, one place rough whetstone (also known as red stone and rough stone) , and the other place fine whetstone (also known as blue stone and pink stone) . The whetstone should be 6–10 cm higher than the wooden basins for sharpening. The basins should be filled with appropriate amount of water. First, rough sharpening should be carried out in the rough whetstone basin for shape sharpening, and a little water should be poured by hand while sharpening, which makes the scissors and whetstones lubricated during sharpening. Then sharpen them in the fine whetstone basin for sharpening blade, and water should also be poured while sharpening to make the scissors bright and sharp.

(17) Assembling. To put the screws in the punched hole and forge to connect so that the scissors become real scissors which can open and close freely.

(18) Trimming the tip of the scissors. Use a file to trim the length of the two pieces of scissors to make them consistent, beautiful and safe.

(19) Bending. After the two pieces of scissors are connected and combined by screws, in order to make the two blades of the scissors meet closely and achieve the ideal cutting effect, it is necessary to make the blade slightly curved. This bending depends on the experience and feeling of the blacksmith to beat it by hammer, that is, press the back part of inside edge of the scissors down, raise the blade part of inside edge of the scissors, and keep the end of the inside edge horizontal, so that when the two pieces of scissors are combined, a small gap will be formed in the middle. The cutting effect is better. Therefore, bending is particularly important.

热处理环节
The process of heat treatment

明该产品的硬度达到了要求和标准，而硬度不够的，则会出现划痕。

（15）清洗。热处理后趁剪刀还有温度，在炉灰中蹭几下，达到使表面清洁干净的效果。在量大的时候，淬油的产品要放到沸水中清洗。

（16）磨削。在两个直径为30厘米左右用杉木制作的木盆中分别安放并固定好磨刀石，一个安放粗磨刀石（也称红石、粗石），另一个安放细磨刀石（也称青石、粉石），磨刀石要高于木盆6～10厘米以方便磨削。盆中盛装适量的水，先在粗磨刀石盆中进行粗磨，主要是磨形状，边磨边用手浇洒少许水，使剪片和磨刀石在打磨时得以润滑。然后在细磨刀石盆中进行细磨，主要是开刃口，也要边磨边洒水，使剪片光亮并具有锋利度。

（17）装配。用螺丝钉放在冲好的孔内，锻打连接，使剪刀成为真正意义上的剪刀，并能够开合自如。

（18）齐剪尾。用锉刀对两爿剪片的长短进行修正，使之长短一致、美观、安全。

（19）调弯。两爿剪片被螺丝钉连接合拢后，要使剪刀双刃相交时能密切配合，达到理想的剪切效果，必须使剪刃稍有弯度，这个弯度全靠师傅的经验和感觉用手工敲打，即把剪刀里口靠背部分压下去，剪刀里口刃部抬高，里口尾部保持水平，这样当两爿剪刀合在一起时就会在中间形成一条很小的空隙，剪切效果更佳，所以调弯尤为重要。

（20）检验。检验剪刀的外观，要求剪面平整、对称、光洁，不能有瑕疵。

（21）试剪。用一块棉布，一剪刀剪下去，剪痕要平整，不咬口，不挂丝，开合自如，得心应手，才是一把质检合格的剪刀。

（22）上油。保持剪刀的润滑度，并起防锈作用。

（23）包装。将产品入盒、入箱、入库，准备出厂。

剪刀能剪切，主要是通过连接的螺丝钉以及被手控制的剪柄，使两爿剪片的两个刃口交叉开合，以刃口接触物体从而剪断物体。要使剪刀剪开的物体剪口平整、光滑、不咬口，对剪刀锻制提出很高的工艺要求，第一，两爿刃口之间相交点的接触不能间断；第二，除剪刃外，其他部位不能与剪刃有接触；第三，根据产品的不同要求，锻打出合理的剪刀刃口几何角度；第四，要使两爿剪刀的大小、厚薄、硬度一致；第五，要使剪刀两刃的锋利度一致。所以，锻制剪刀较之一般刀具，工艺更加复杂和更具有难度。

主要特征

阳江传统剪刀，具有钢火好、比例匀称、外形美观、工艺精美、锋利耐用、松紧适度、开合自如、线条自然流畅、剪口平整光滑等特点，还具有款式新颖、品种齐全等优势，因此深受广大消费者的青睐和好评。

(20) Check. Check the appearance of the scissors. The cutting surface is required to be flat, symmetrical, clean and flawless.

(21) Cutting test. Use a pair of scissors to cut off a piece of cotton cloth once. The cut marks should be flat, without pressing edges when two pieces of scissors are assembled together and hanging thread. The scissors should be opened and closed freely, which can be considered a pair of scissors with good quality.

(22) Oiling. Maintain the lubricity of the scissors and act as rust prevention.

(23) Packaging. Pack the products by boxes and cases. Put them in storage, preparing for delivery.

Scissors can cut things mainly by connected screw and manually controlled scissors handle, so that the two blades of the two pieces of scissors can be crossed and closed, so as to contact the object with the blades and cut the object. The scissors should be able to make the cut of the cut object flat, smooth and the two pieces of scissors will not press each other's edges when they are assembled together, which puts forward high technological requirements for the scissors forging. First, the contact between the intersection points of the two blades should not be interrupted. Second, no part other than the blade should be in contact with the other blade. Third, according to the different requirements of the product, the geometric angle of the scissors blade should be set reasonably. Fourth, the size, thickness and hardness of the two pieces of scissors should be consistent. Fifth, the sharpness of the two blades of the scissors should be consistent. Therefore, forging scissors is more complex and difficult than forging general cutting tools.

Main Features

Yangjiang traditional scissors have the characteristics of high hardness, being well-proportioned, beautiful appearance, exquisite craftsmanship, sharp and durable, moderate tightness, smoothly opening, smooth shape, smooth cutting edge, etc., and also have the advantages of novel style and complete variety, so they are favored and praised by the majority of consumers.

阳江剪刀锻制技艺项目代表性传承人张锐宗（右）在检查剪刀品质

Zhang Ruizong, the representative inheritor of the project of Yangjiang Scissors Forging Craftsmanship, is checking the quality of scissors

Great Value

· Historical value

Only from the scissors unearthed in the ancient tombs of the Western Han Dynasty, the history of forging and using scissors has been thousands of years in China. Whether recorded in historical materials or traced back from the lineage of the representative inheritor Zhang Ruizong, scissors forging in Yangjiang has a long history. In the long process of production and labor, the craftsmen maintain tradition and keep innovating, and pass down through the long years. Although the craftsmanship has been developing and changing through the ages, it has been handed down in various forms, showing its lasting and dynamic vitality, becoming an existing phenomenon in the process of historical development, and also a witness to the process of historical development, and providing valuable historical basis for the study of Yangjiang's history, folk customs, productivity development in various times and people's living conditions from one aspect.

· Cultural and artistic value

Since the scissors entered the public life, people have a deep connection with scissors. The scissors culture is deeply rooted in the thoughts and feelings of our nation, and has produced many famous classical sentences. For example, in the *Book of Songs*, "Zhaonan Gantang", there are sentences like "don't scissor, don't fell, don't scissor, don't destroy, don't cut, don't break". Du Fu's poem "Song of Scenery and Landscape Paintings by the Wang Zhai" says, "How can I get the sharp scissors of Bingzhou to cut half of Wusong River." He Zhizhang's poem "Intoning the Willow" says, "I don't know who cut the thin leaves. The spring

重要价值

· 历史价值

仅从西汉古墓中出土的剪刀算起，剪刀的锻制、使用在我国已有上千年历史。无论是史料记载，抑或从代表性传承人张锐宗的传承谱系追溯，阳江锻制剪刀的历史都源远流长。在长期的生产劳动过程中，手工艺人们保持传统且不断创新，在漫长的岁月中薪火相传。该技艺在历史的长河中不断发展，历经沧海桑田，以其独特的功能和魅力，通过各种形式传承至今，显示出其持久的、充满活力的生命力，成为历史发展过程中存在的现象，也成为历史发展进程的见证，更从一个侧面为研究阳江的历史、民俗、各时代生产力发展情况以及民众生活状况提供了宝贵的历史依据。

· 文化和艺术价值

剪刀自走进大众生活后，人与剪刀就结下了深深的情缘，剪刀文化深深植根于我们民族的思想情感之中，并衍生出了脍炙人口的经典名句，如《诗经》中《召南·甘棠》篇里有“勿翦[①]勿伐、勿翦勿败、勿翦勿拜”之句，唐代诗人杜甫《戏题王宰画山水图歌》中有“焉得并州快剪刀，剪取吴淞半江水”，贺知章《咏柳》中有“不知细叶谁裁出，二月春风似剪刀”，李商隐《夜雨寄北》中有“何当共剪西窗烛，却话巴山夜雨时”，宋代陆游《秋思》中有“诗情也似并刀快，剪得春光入卷来”，黄孝迈《湘春夜月》中有：

①翦同剪。

“这次第，算人间没个并刀，剪断心上愁痕”，元代杨维桢《庐山瀑布谣》中有“便欲手把并州剪，剪取一幅玻璃烟”，南唐李煜《相见欢》中有“剪不断，理还乱，是离愁”。在我国的词牌中，有“一剪梅”的词牌，源于北宋词人周邦彦所作的“一剪梅花万样娇”。此外，剪刀还衍生了剪纸艺术，剪纸艺人以纸张为载体，使用剪刀剪出栩栩如生的人物、动物、植物形象以及各种图案如窗花、门笺、墙花、顶棚花、灯花等。而这种艺术的产生和流传与中国农村的节日风俗有着密切关系，逢年过节或举办婚嫁喜事时，人们把美丽鲜艳的剪纸贴在雪白的窗纸或玻璃窗上、墙上、门上、灯笼上，既使人们欣赏到剪纸的艺术魅力，也将节日的气氛渲染得浓郁喜庆。剪纸因此成为民间艺术的一朵奇葩。

·民俗价值

从古代直至民国时期，剪刀在民间被视作吉祥物，还作为馈赠亲友的礼品或订婚的信物。男婚女嫁时，剪刀可作为婚嫁礼品；女子出嫁时，剪刀是必备嫁妆之一，用红绸包裹后放在小礼品盒中，寓意情思剪不断，夫妻恩爱，白头到老；婴儿出生时，人们用剪刀剪断婴儿脐带，昭示新生命从此开始了其人生征程；在人百年之后，出殡时，巫师会用剪刀将挂在竹竿上的黑色幡带剪断，以示和已逝之人今生情缘已断，从此阴阳两隔。在民间，人们还视剪刀为镇恶辟邪的法宝。在乡间，人们将剪刀挂在家宅门口上方以辟邪镇宅。在阳江江城端午逆水赛龙舟民俗活动中，在其中的三角白旗龙舟“旺龙”出征仪式上，巫师的托盘里就会放一把剪刀，作为镇邪和梳妆之物，以示期望在龙舟比赛中旗开得胜。在民间习俗中，常在煎熬

breeze in February is like scissors.” Li Shangyin’s poem “The Night Rain Sends to the North” says, “When we cut the candles in the west window, it’s at the night raining in Bashan.” Lu You’s poem “Autumn Thoughts” says, “The poetry is also like a sharp scissors, and the spring light can be cut into a volume.” Huang Xiaomai’s Ci “The Moon on the Spring Night of the Xiangjiang River” says, “This scene is really sad, there is no scissors in the world to cut the sorrows in the heart.” Yang Weizhen’s poem “The Ballad of Lushan Falls” says, “I want to get a pair of Bingzhou quick scissors to cut the satin open.” Li Yu’s Ci “Happy Meeting” says “the thing can not be cut and sorted is the sadness of separation”. Among China’s names of the tunes of Ci, there is name of the tunes of Ci called “A Spray of Plum Blossoms”, which are derived from the sentence “A spray of plum blossoms makes all kinds of beautiful” of Zhou Bangyan, a poet of the Northern Song Dynasty. In addition, the scissors have also derived the paper-cut art. The paper-cut artists use the paper as the carrier to cut out the images like figures, animals, plant and various patterns such as window flowers, door flowers, wall flowers, ceiling flowers, lanterns flowers, etc.. The emergence and spread of this art is closely related to the festival customs in rural China. During the festivals or the weddings, people paste beautiful and bright paper-cuts on the snow-white window paper or glass windows, walls, doors, and lanterns, which not only makes people appreciate the artistic charm of paper-cut, but also renders the festival atmosphere very rich and festive. Therefore, paper cutting becomes a unique branch of folk art.

· Folk value

From ancient times to the period of Republic of China, people regarded scissors as mascots, and also as gifts to relatives and friends or keepsakes of engagement. During marriage, scissors can be used as a wedding gift. When a woman marries, scissors are one of the necessary dowries. They are wrapped in red silk and put in a small gift box, implying that the husband and wife will live happily together till old. After the baby is born, people use scissors to cut the baby’s umbilical cord, indicating that a journey of a new life has begun. When someone is died, the wizard will use scissors to cut the black flag band hanging on the bamboo pole at the funeral to show that the relationship with the deceased has been broken, and from then on, the living and the dead are separated. In the folk, people also regard scissors as the magic weapon to ward off evil. In the countryside, the scissors will be hung above the entrance of the house to ward off evil and protect the house. In the folk activities of the upstream dragon boat race at the Dragon Boat Festival in Jiangcheng District, Yangjiang, a pair of scissors will placed in the tray of the wizard at the expedition ceremony "Wanglong" of the Triangular White Flag Dragon Boat to ward off evil and dressing, hoping to win in the dragon boat race. Also, in the folk custom, when boiling traditional Chinese medicine, a pair of scissors is put on the lid of the medicine pot, which is intended to suppress the ghost of disease and plague and hope to cure the disease after taking the medicine.

· Craft and technical value

Traditional Yangjiang Scissors Forging Craftsmanship has complex processes, with very high technical requirements and unique craftsmanship. It is the achievement accumulated by Yangjiang scissors craftsmen through long-term practice, and is a valuable traditional craftsmanship. It has the value for scientific research.

· Practical value

Thanks to the invention and widespread use of scissors, especially after they have been professionally classified, scissors have become indispensable daily tools in people's production and life. A small pair of scissors has inadvertently changed the quality of people's lives, satisfying their needs and improving their working efficiency. Scissors are quietly integrated into people's daily lives, making them enjoying lives with ease.

· Economic and employment value

For a long time, the hardware industry has been the pillar industry of Yangjiang and played an important role in the economic development of Yangjiang. From the middle of the Qing Dynasty to the 1940s, knife and scissors products have created considerable economic benefits. In various historical stages after 1949, the production of knife and scissors has played a leading role in the local economic development of Yangjiang. Only the export of products can earn millions of *yuan* of foreign exchange for the country every year. With the rise of private enterprises, the hardware industry has developed and expanded. By 2021, the annual industrial output value of Yangjiang Knife and Scissors has reached more than 55 billion *yuan*, accounting for about 75% of the total output of national production, with nearly 200,000 employees. It not only solved the employment problem of a considerable number of local people, but also doubled the total tax revenue. The products are exported to more than 160 countries and regions. The total export volume accounts for about 85% of the total national export volume, which has made great contributions to the economic development of Yangjiang.

中药时，将一把剪刀放在药煲的盖上面，意为镇伏疫鬼病魔，期盼病人服药后能药到病除。

·工艺和技术价值

阳江剪刀的传统锻制技艺工序繁复，技术要求非常高，并有其独特的工艺绝技，它是阳江制剪工匠经过长期实践积累的智慧结晶，是一项相当宝贵的传统技艺，具有进行科学研究的价值。

·实用价值

由于剪刀的发明和普遍使用，特别是剪刀已按专业分类后，剪刀已成为人们生产生活中不可或缺的日用工具。一把小小的剪刀在不经意间改变了人们的生活品质，满足了人们对生活的需求，提高了劳作的工效。剪刀悄悄地融入了人们的日常生活，使人们在得心应手间享受生活。

·经济和就业价值

长期以来，五金业一直是阳江的支柱产业，在阳江的经济发展中扮演着重要角色。从清代中期到20世纪40年代，刀剪产品创造了可观的经济效益。在1949年后的各个历史阶段中，刀剪生产在阳江地方经济发展中更是起到了主导作用，仅产品出口一项，每年都能为国家创汇数百万元。随着民营企业的崛起，阳江五金行业也在逐渐发展、壮大。至2021年，阳江刀剪工业产值超550亿元，约占全国刀剪总产量的75%，相应的从业人员近20万人，其不仅解决了当地相当数量人员的就业问题，税收总额也成倍递增，产品远销160多个国家和地区，剪刀出口总量约占全国剪刀出口总量的85%，为阳江的经济发展作出了重大贡献。

主要传承人

张锐宗，男，生于1954年8月，出身于五金世家。其祖父张世伦为织篢一代刀剪名匠；父亲张逢新子承父业，在业界久负盛名，创立了阳江第一家民营专业刀剪生产厂——阳江织篢刀剪厂，成为远近闻名的“刀剪张”，也是全国有名的乡镇企业家。成长于刀剪世家的张锐宗从小耳濡目染，与刀剪结下不解之缘。1968年，张锐宗进入织篢五金厂工作，成为一名学徒工，开始了他的刀剪生涯。在祖父张世伦、父亲张逢新的悉心传授下，凭着虚心好学的态度和刻苦钻研的精神，熟练掌握了传统阳江剪刀锻制技艺。从学徒工到技术员，张锐宗不断积累经验，为日后的发展打下了坚实的基础。1983年，张锐宗开始担任阳江工贸联营织篢五金厂副厂长，主管厂里的业务与技术，成为刀剪专家。1993年，成立阳西县张氏永光刀剪厂有限公司。2002年，整合资源，又组建了广东永光刀剪集团有限公司。2009年4月，张锐宗将企业升格为永光刀剪集团有限公司，使企业登上国家级平台，获得更大的发展空间。张锐宗现为广东省第四批省级非物质文化遗产项目代表性传承人。

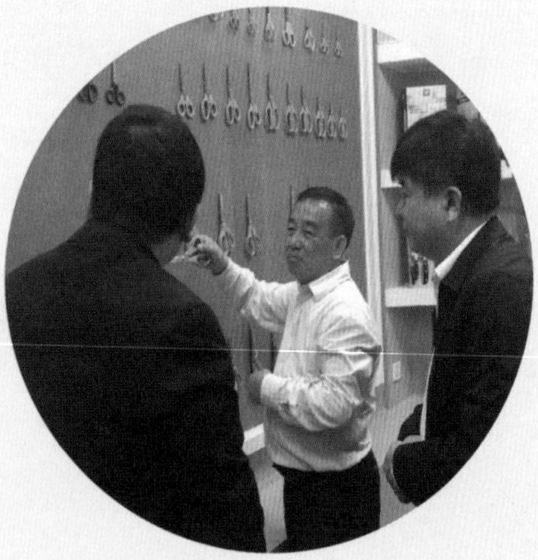

张锐宗（中）
Zhang Ruizong (middle)

Main Inheritor

Zhang Ruizong, male, was born in a hardware family in August 1954. His grandfather, Zhang Shilun, was a famous knife and scissors craftsman of the generation in Zhilong Town. Zhang Ruizong's father, Zhang Fengxin, inherited his father's business and enjoyed a long reputation in the industry. He founded the first private manufacturer of knife and scissors in Yangjiang, Yangjiang Zhilong Knife and Scissors Factory, and became famous with his nickname "knife and scissors Zhang". He is also a famous township entrepreneur nationwide. Growing up in a family of knife and scissors, Zhang Ruizong was influenced from childhood, and inextricably bound to knife and scissors. Zhang Ruizong entered the Zhilong Hardware Factory where he began his knife and scissors career in 1968 and became an apprentice. With an modest and studious attitude and the spirit of assiduous study, he mastered the traditional Yangjiang scissors forging craftsmanship, by the careful instruction of his grandfather Zhang Shilun and father Zhang Fengxin. From apprentice to technician, he has accumulated work experience and laid a solid foundation for future development. In 1983, Zhang Ruizong began to serve as the deputy director of the Zhilong Hardware Factory of Yangjiang Industry and Trade Joint Venture, in charge of the business and technique in the factory, and became an expert in knife and scissors. In 1993, he established the Zhang's Yongguang Knife and Scissors Factory Co., Ltd. of Yangxi County. On this basis, in 2002, he integrated resources and established the Guangdong Yongguang Knife and Scissors Group Co., Ltd. In April 2009, Zhang Ruizong upgraded the enterprise to Yongguang Knife and Scissors Group Co., Ltd., so that the enterprise can get on the national platform and gain greater space for development. He is the representative inheritor of the fourth batch of provincial intangible cultural heritage projects in Guangdong Province now.

闸坡蔡家木帆船模型制作技艺

保护单位 阳江市海陵岛经济开发试验区蔡家船艺馆

Manufacturing Craftsmanship of Zhapo Cai Family Wooden Sailboat Model

Protection Unit Cai Family Boat Art Hall of Hailing Island Economic Development Pilot Zone, Yangjiang City

Yangjiang is an important passing place, transit port and supply port of the ancient maritime silk road in China. It has deep connotation of marine culture. Its superior geographical environment, long sailing history, rich fishery resources and leading Guang Chuan shipbuilding technique established a unique cultural geographical coordinate for Yangjiang in the history of the ancient maritime silk road. The wooden wind sailboat model is characterized by delicate materials, beautiful shape, exquisite workmanship and craftsmanship. It shows the basic structure and shape of the original style of wooden sailboat, condenses all the characteristics of the Zhapo wooden sailboat, embodies the painstaking efforts and wisdom of the shipbuilders of all generations. It truly and comprehensively retains and inherits the ancient South China Sea Guang Chuan shipbuilding culture and skills.

阳江是中国古代海上丝绸之路重要的途经地和中转港、补给港，深蕴海洋文化内涵。优越的地理环境、悠久的航海历史、丰富的渔业资源和领先的广船造船技术，为阳江在古代海上丝绸之路史中确立了独特的文化地理坐标。木质风帆船模以选料精致、造型精美、做工精巧、技艺精湛为主要特征，复原展示了木帆船原始风貌的基本结构和形态，浓缩了闸坡木帆船的所有特质，凝聚了历代造船工匠的心血和智慧，真实、全面地保留和传承了古代南海广船造船文化和技艺。

闸坡蔡家木帆船模型
Zhapo Cai family wooden sailboat model

历史渊源

据《阳江县志》（2000年版）记载，“阳江县的造船业是一个古老的和规模较大的行业。唐代，恩州已能建造较大的运输船和渔船。明代，阳江县是广东有名的造船中心之一。清代，阳江县的造船业有较大的发展……”。《民国时期广东两阳史》也记录了阳江造船业和闸坡渔业情况。前清时期，作为西南沿海港口船舶避风补给之处，闸坡镇开始建制。独特的地理位置和资源使海洋捕捞成为当地的支柱产业，渔船就是海上重要的交通和捕捞工具。蔡氏家族可追溯至高祖（清光绪年间）开始投身造船业，后举家由阳江北惯迁徙至闸坡，专事造船业。祖父蔡日生继承曾祖技艺，后又传给儿子蔡黑和蔡有才。作为闸坡造船世家，蔡家以制造闸坡七艕船在当地颇有声望，并拥有名号为“茂利”的私营造船厂。1952年，船厂被政府改制为集体所有制闸坡造船厂后，蔡有才、蔡黑将技艺传给蔡保、蔡皮、蔡根、蔡浩、蔡数（蔡有才的五个儿子）、蔡安（蔡黑的儿子）等，他们后来都成为厂中重量级专业技术人才。蔡家装造的七艕船因美观大方、适航平稳、坚固耐用，成为风帆动力时代渔业先进生产力的代表，为当地的经济发展作出过巨大的贡献，更为渔业现代化发展奠定了坚实的基础。但随着时代的飞速进步，风帆动力木船已不能适应现代海洋捕捞业的发展需求。2006年，阳江钢船、玻璃钢船相继问世，木帆船慢慢淡出了历史舞台。如今，造船人选择了以另一种方式来演绎和传承造船技艺。在蔡家第四代传承人蔡数的带领下，在继承祖传技艺的基础上，蔡氏家族进行了创新，发展出闸坡蔡家木帆船模

Historical Origin

According to the *Yangjiang County Annals*, “the shipbuilding industry in Yangjiang County is an ancient and large-scale industry. In the Tang Dynasty, it was able to build large transport ships and fishing boats in Enzhou. In the Ming Dynasty, Yangjiang County was one of the famous shipbuilding centers in Guangdong. The shipbuilding industry in Yangjiang County in the Qing Dynasty had a great development...”. *The History of Guangdong Yangjiang and Yangchun in the period of Republic of China* also records the shipbuilding industry and Zhapo fishery in Yangjiang. In the early Qing Dynasty, as a ship shelter and replenishment place in southwest coastal ports, Zhapo Town began to be set up. The unique geographical location and resources made marine fishing a local pillar industry, and fishing boats were important transportation and fishing tools on the sea. The Cai family can be traced back to the great ancestors (during the period of the reign of Emperor Guangxu in the Qing Dynasty) that began to devote themselves to the shipbuilding industry. Later, the whole family moved from Yangjiang Beiguan Town to Zhapo Town to specialize in shipbuilding. The grandfather Cai Risheng inherited from family and passed on the skills to his sons Cai Hei and Cai Youcai. As a family of Zhapo Shipbuilders, Cai family was most famous for manufacturing Zhapo Qibang Ship, and was quite prestigious in the local area and had a private shipyard named Maoli Shipyard. After Maoli shipyard being transformed into a collectively owned Zhapo Shipyard by the government in 1952, Cai Youcai and Cai Hei passed on their skills to Cai Bao, Cai Pi, Cai Gen, Cai Hao, Cai Shu (Cai Youcai's five sons) and Cai An (Cai Hei's son). They became professional technicians in the factory. Because of its beautiful appearance, stable seaworthiness, sturdiness and durability, Zhapo Qibang Ship became the representative of advanced fishery productivity in the era of wind sail power. It has made great contributions to the local economic development and laid a solid foundation for the modern development of fishery. However, with the rapid progress of the times, sail powered wooden boats can no longer meet the development needs of modern marine fishing industry. In 2006, Yangjiang steel boats and glass fiber reinforced plastic boats appeared one after another, and wooden boats had faded out of the historical stage. Nowadays, shipbuilders choose another way to express and inherit shipbuilding skills. Under the leadership of Cai Shu, the fourth generation inheritor of the Cai family, and on the basis of inheriting the ancestral skills, Cai family made further innovation and developed the Manufacturing Craftsmanship of Zhapo Cai Family Wooden Sailboat Model, which has its own style. Now the fifth generation inheritors, Cai Minhui and Cai Minjin, have handed down the craftsmanship.

Basic Content

The Manufacturing Craftsmanship of Zhapo Cai Family Wooden Sailboat Model is based on the creative materials of Qibang Ship, tail ship, round stern ship, Suogu ship, cargo ship, sampan tugboat, Pazai ship, and ocean fishing boats in eastern Guangdong and Hainan produced in Zhapo. It is developed and extended on the basis of the ancestral traditional shipbuilding technique of the Cai family. As one of the most representative ship types of Guangchuan, the Qibang Ship pioneered deep-sea operations and was the fruit of the unique ingenuity and wisdom of Zhapo shipbuilders. The distribution, retention and inheritance of Qibang Ship are mainly in Zhapo fishing port. The ship models of Cai family are sold to both inside and outside the province as well as overseas.

Main Features

(1) Delicate materials. All the wooden sailboat models are made of high-quality hard wood, such as black sandalwood, purple sandalwood, teakwood, merbau, etc..

(2) Beautiful shape. It is unique in the characteristics of the Guang Chuan, especially the Qibang Ship. Because of the high waves and strong wind at sea, the long distance of the voyage, the high probability of the ship in dangerous situations, the ship has characteristics of slender shape, low head and high tail, U-shaped

闸坡蔡家木帆船模型
Zhapo Cai family wooden sailboat model

七艕船船模
Model of Qibang Ship

型制作技艺，并自成风格。现第五代传承人蔡敏慧、蔡敏劲又接棒相传。

基本内容

闸坡蔡家木帆船模型制作技艺以闸坡装造出产的七艕船、开尾船、圆尾船、索姑船、货运船、舢拖船、扒仔船及粤东、海南海洋捕捞作业船等为创作素材，在蔡氏家族祖传传统造船技术基础上发展延伸而来。七艕船作为广船最具代表性的船型之一，开深海作业之先河，是闸坡造船工匠独具匠心的智慧结晶。七艕船的分布、保留与传承主要在闸坡渔港。蔡家制作的船模作品畅销省内外乃至远销海外。

主要特征

（1）选料精致。制船木材全部采用上等木材，如黑、紫檀木，柚木，菠萝格等，材优质硬。

（2）造型精美。其独具广船之海船特点，尤以七膀船为突出代表。海船因海上风大浪高、航行距离远、船遇险境的概率较高等特殊航行环境，在建造上具有船型瘦长、首低尾高、船底呈U形、船体为流线型等特点，以及有扇形帆、开孔舵等造型，其结构坚固，有较好的适航性能和续航能力。

（3）做工精巧。涉及的工种广、技术全，有木工、捻工（灰工）、帆作、缆索作、旋作、铁作等，桅杆、舵、插等船的任何部位及船上所有用具都与实船实物用同样工序制作。

（4）技艺精湛。闸坡蔡家木帆船船模根据实船数值按照比例缩小制作而成，形象地展示了木帆船的基本结构和形态。在"技"方面，真实地再现了木帆船制作的全过程及其特征、性能、用途等，如真船般锚可抛、舵能纵、帆可升降、舱门可开关、舱内可储物、救生艇可吊可卸等；在"艺"方面，追求美观、完整、细腻、自然、光顺、流畅、规范，精准地反映出木帆船的特点和韵味，彰显蔡家风格，使作品人见人赞，可观赏，可收藏。

bottom, streamlined hull, and beautiful shapes like fan sail, perforated rudder in its construction. It has a solid structure, good seaworthiness and endurance.

(3) Exquisite workmanship. It involves a wide range of work types and technologies, including woodwork, the work of repairing ship seams, sail work, cable work, metal-cutting work, iron work, etc.. Any part such as mast, rudder, plug and all appliances on the ship are made by the same process as the real ship.

(4) Exquisite craftsmanship. Zhapo Cai Family Wooden Sailboat Model is made according to the actual ship data with reduced scale. It vividly shows the basic structure and shape of the wooden sailboat. In terms of craftsmanship, it truly represents the whole process of making the wooden sailboat and its characteristics, performance and uses. It shows that how the anchor dropped, how the rudder pitched, how the sail raised and lowered, how the cabin door opened and closed, how the cabin stored, how the lifeboat lifted and unloaded. In terms of art, it pursues beauty, integrity, delicacy, naturalness, smoothness, fluency and standardization, accurately reflecting the characteristics and charm of wooden sailboats. It highlights the style of Cai family and makes the works viewable and collectable and admired by people.

闸坡蔡家木帆船模型制作

Manufacturing of Zhapo Cai family wooden sailboat model

Great Value

· Historical and cultural value

Manufacturing Craftsmanship of Zhapo Cai Family Wooden Sailboat Model is based on the historical facts of traditional sailing wooden sail shipbuilding, and integrates Cai family's ancestral shipbuilding experience and practice, forming the craftsmanship spirit that embodies the wisdom of generations of shipbuilders. This kind of ship model is not only a handicraft, decoration and collection, but also an unforgettable memory of the older generation of fishermen and shipbuilders in the South China Sea. It also carries a section of history and culture of ocean boats and is a precious intangible cultural heritage. The ship model is made according to the traditional shipbuilding structure with reduced scale. The production processes of keel, watertight compartment, side plate, mast sail and other parts of the traditional shipbuilding are implemented synchronously. It not only covers the shipbuilding structure, technical skills, aesthetic pursuit, customs and other comprehensive traditional navigation and shipbuilding culture of the ancient South China Sea, but also remains technique entity for inheriting and studying the historical era, social style and features, production and life style of traditional sail powered wooden shipbuilding. It provides real materials and historical basis for presenting and recording the ancient shipbuilding history, and is a living inheritance of the ancient sail power shipbuilding technique.

· Academic and scientific value

In China's history of navigation with historical records, the representative wind sail powered wooden sailboat, Guang Chuan, which connects the East and the West on the main channel of the ancient Maritime Silk Road, is the physical carrier of China's ancient people's navigation operations. Like many traditional skills, ancient navigation and shipbuilding skills have been passed down by families and apprenticeship. Manufacturing Craftsmanship of Zhapo Cai Family Wooden Sailboat makes ship models according to the actual shipbuilding bearing structure and hull proportion. It analyzes and restores the ancient Cantonese shipbuilding skills, exploring the deep marine cultural connotation of the Maritime Silk Road. It witnesses the marine fishery development process of Zhapo, an important town of the ancient Maritime Silk Road. It also provides living research materials for the research and restoration of the history of shipbuilding of Guang Chuan, the history of ancient maritime science and technique, as well as the Tanka folk customs and religious beliefs in the South China Sea, and so on. The wooden wind sailing boat, which conforms to the mechanical structure and principles of safety and

重要价值

· 历史和文化价值

闸坡蔡家木帆船模型制作技艺，基于传统航海木质风帆造船史实，融会蔡家祖传造船技术经验和实践，凝聚了几代造船人的智慧。该类船模不仅是工艺品、装饰品、收藏品，还是南海老一辈渔民、造船师傅挥之不去的记忆，更承载着一段海洋舟船历史和文化，是宝贵的非物质文化遗产。依照传统造船结构和缩小比例制作的船模，从龙骨、水密隔舱、侧板到桅杆风帆等传统造船的部位，工序制作流程均同步实施，既涵盖了造船结构、技术技巧、审美追求、风俗习惯等古代南中国海传统航海造船文化，也为传承和研究传统风帆动力木质造船的历史时代、社会风貌、生产生活方式存留了技艺实体，更为呈现和记录古代造船历史提供了真实的素材和历史依据，是古代风帆动力造船技艺的活态传承。

· 学术和科学价值

在中国有历史记载的航海史中，连接东西方古代海上丝绸之路主航道的代表性风帆动力木帆船——广船，是中国古代人民航海作业的实物载体。与诸多传统技艺一样，古代航海造船技艺亦通过家族、师承等方式传承至今。闸坡蔡家木帆船模型制作技艺依据实际造船承载结构和船体比例制作，解析并复原了古代粤海人耕海造船技艺，探究了海上丝绸之路深蕴的海洋文化内涵，见证了古代海上丝绸之路重镇——闸坡的海洋渔业发展历程，也为研究和复原广船造船史、古代航海科技史以及南海区域疍家民俗、宗教信仰等提供了活态研究素材。符合古代航海造船力学结构和安全稳定性原理的木质风帆船，不仅见证了阳江海洋渔业繁荣的历史，为新时代航海远洋作业和渔业现代化发展奠定了基础，也为现代造船技术改良、科技应用提供了重要的启示参考。

· 艺术欣赏和收藏价值

随着20世纪70年代机械动力航海船舶的推广运用，传统风帆动力木帆船已濒临消亡，广船建造所需的高密度硬木质材料难以为继，大量钢、玻璃钢、铝合金材料运用于造船，至今仍在南中国海留存使用的木质船舶，亦早已更新安装了大功率机械提供动力。遵循古代造船结构和装饰技艺制作的木质风帆船模，以一种新的表现形式，再现特殊的传统历史记忆，复原了古代广船的形制和技艺，为南海传统造船技艺赋予了新的生命。依据古代造船工序，通过精致选料、精巧手工、精湛技艺制作的独具匠心的木质风帆船模，既展示了古代传统造船技艺，也是研究古代海洋文化的重要载体，成为蕴含丰富现代美学意趣的精美木制工艺品。这一独具特色的传统工艺珍品，已被国内多家知名博物馆和社会各界有识之士收藏，用于陈列展览和学术研究等。

stability of ancient navigation and shipbuilding, not only witnessed the history of the prosperity of Yangjiang's marine fishery, and laid a foundation for the development of ocean navigation operations and fishery modernization in the new era, but also provided an important reference for the improvement of modern shipbuilding technique and the application of technology.

· Art appreciation and collection value

With the promotion and application of mechanical powered navigation ships in the 1970s, the traditional wind sail powered wooden sailboats were on the verge of extinction. The high-density hardwood materials required for the construction of Guang Chuan were difficult to sustain. A large number of steel, glass fiber reinforced plastics and aluminum alloy materials are used in shipbuilding. The wooden ships still used in the South China Sea have been updated and installed high-power mechanical power. The making of wooden sail ship model according to the ancient shipbuilding structure and decoration techniques is a special representation of traditional historical memory in a new form of expression. It restores the ancient Guang Chuan's shape and technique, giving new life to the traditional shipbuilding techniques in the South China Sea.The unique wooden sail boat model, based on the ancient shipbuilding process, is made by delicate material, exquisite workmanship and craftsmanship. It not only shows the ancient traditional shipbuilding skills, but also is an important carrier for studying the ancient traditional marine culture, becoming a beautiful wooden handicraft with rich modern aesthetic interest. This unique traditional craft treasure has been collected by many well-known museums and people from all walks of life in society for exhibition and academic research.

Main Inheritor

Cai Shu, male, was born in 1956. He is the fourth generation of Cai family's shipbuilding craftsmanship. The Manufacturing Craftsmanship of Zhapo Cai Family Wooden Sailboat Model was summarized and refined from Zhapo Cai family's long-term engagement in wooden sailboat production. It is an artistic expression form based on ship models. Zhapo Cai family began to build ships in the late Qing Dynasty and its shipbuilding craftsmanship began in the first generation of great-great-grandfather. It was handed down to the second generation of great grandfather and to the third generation of grandfather Cai Youcai when they struck out a new line for themselves. It was handed down to the 4th generation of Cai Bao, Cai Pi, Cai Gen, Cai Hao, Cai Shu and Cai An, becoming an important shipbuilding technical force in Zhapo. Now the 5th generation of Cai Minjin and Cai Minhui have handed down the craftsmanship.

Influenced by family shipbuilding culture since childhood, Cai Shu has been working independently since he was 15 years old. From 1971 to 1990, he worked as a worker in Zhapo Xiongou Fishery Fleet and Zhapo Shipyard respectively. After the dissolution of the enterprise, he engaged in individual shipbuilding and inherited Cai family's shipbuilding craftsmanship. Since 2000, he has been specialized in ship model making. He is the representative inheritor of the fourth batch of intangible cultural heritage projects in Yangjiang now.

主要传承人

蔡数
Cai Shu

蔡数，男，生于1956年，蔡家造船技艺第四代传人。闸坡蔡家木帆船模型制作技艺是闸坡蔡氏家族在长期从事木质帆船生产的过程中总结提炼出来的民间技艺，是以船模为载体的艺术表现形式。闸坡蔡氏造船始于晚清，造船技术始于高祖第一代；传于二代（曾祖父），及至第三代（祖父蔡有才），已自成一家；再传至第四代（蔡保、蔡皮、蔡根、蔡浩、蔡数、蔡安等），这一代已成为闸坡一支重要的造船技术力量；现有第五代蔡敏劲、蔡敏慧接棒相传。

蔡数自幼受家庭造船文化熏陶，15岁起独立从业，1971—1990年，分别在闸坡雄鸥渔业大队和闸坡造船厂当工人，企业解体后，从事个体修造船业，传承蔡家造船技艺。2000年起，专业从事船模制作。蔡数现为阳江市第四批非物质文化遗产项目代表性传承人。

阳江粉酥焙制技艺

保护单位 阳江市莲香食品有限公司
阳江市阳东奇香园食品有限公司等

Baking Technique of Yangjiang Fried Rice Biscuit

Protection Unit Yangjiang Lianxiang Food Co., Ltd.,
Yangjiang Yangdong Qixiangyuan Food Co., Ltd., etc.

阳江粉酥焙制技艺是流传在阳江地区的一种民间传统手工制作技艺，主要分布在江城区、阳东区、阳西县、阳春市、海陵区、高新区、滨海新区等各县区及其乡镇村庄。

历史渊源

阳江市莲香食品有限公司从民间搜集到的、经广东省文物鉴定委员会专家鉴定的清末至民初的文物“茂祥黄金万两”木饼模和“茂祥添丁吉兆”木饼模，证明阳江粉酥焙制技艺在清末民初就已在阳江地区商铺和家庭中流传。当时家家户户都有做粉酥过年的习俗，以家庭作坊生产为主，风气盛行，颇具规模，这种习俗一直延续至今。

阳江是古代南海海上丝绸之路的补给港和货物中转站，因此外出做生意、打工的阳江人很多，从陆路走的，经水上走的，都免不了风餐露宿。那时候餐馆不多，所以人人都得带上粉酥作干粮。在当时，生产粉酥在阳江已经是一个发展得比较成熟的产业，阳江城里已有专门生产粉

Baking Technique of Yangjiang Fried Rice Biscuit is a traditional folk handicraft technique spread in Yangjiang area, mainly distributed in Jiangcheng District, Yangdong District, Yangxi County, Yangchun City, Hailing District, Gaoxin District, Binhai New Area and other towns and villages.

Historical Origin

“Maoxiang Ten Thousand Taels of Gold” wooden biscuit mold and “Maoxiang Auspicious Omen of Begeting Son” wooden biscuit mold from the late Qing Dynasty to the early Republic of China, which were collected by Yangjiang Lianxiang Food Co., Ltd. from the folk and identified by experts from the Guangdong Cultural Relics Appraisal Committee, proved that the baking technique of Yangjiang Fried Rice Biscuit has been spread in shops and families in Yangjiang area since the late Qing Dynasty and the early Republic of China. At that time, every family had the custom of making fried rice biscuits for the Spring Festival, which was produced mostly by family workshops. The custom was very popular and had a large scale, continuing to this day.

Yangjiang was the supply port and cargo transfer station of the ancient Maritime Silk Road in the South China Sea, so many Yangjiang people out-migrated for business and work. Those who travelled by land or by water went through the rigors of living in the wilderness. There were not many restaurants, so they had to bring fried rice biscuits as food. At that time, the production of fried rice biscuits was a mature industry in Yangjiang. There were more than 20 bakeries specializing in fried rice biscuits in Yangjiang City. In the

阳江粉酥非常受市民热爱
Yangjiang Fried Rice Biscuit has been very popular with citizens

late 1940s, Su Mingxi, a native of Hengshan, Yangxi County, opened a cake shop named "Heshuian" in Yangjiang City, specializing in the production of various gifts based on fried rice biscuits, which pushed the production to a peak. After 1949, the three bakeries, "Heshuian", "Tianxing" and "Lizhang", jointly operated by the public and private, and became the famous Hetianli Pastry Factory at that time (Su Lianzhou, the descendant of Su Mingxi, as the factory director). Later, Yangjiang County Food Factory was formed by Hetianli Pastry Factory and other factories, and later renamed as "Yangjiang City Food Company". Before and after the establishment of Yangjiang City, private enterprises have developed rapidly and there were many manufacturers producing fried rice biscuits. With the development of tourism in Yangjiang, Yangjiang Fried Rice Biscuit has made great progress in recent years. It is no longer a special festival food for the Spring Festival, but a daily snack with more and more varieties. In addition, a large number of manufacturers have embarked on large-scale production, distributing Yangjiang Fried Rice Biscuit throughout the country and even Southeast Asia. Now, even far away from home, Yangjiang people can buy hometown fried rice biscuit from the online shops of these manufacturers.

Basic Content

Baking processes of Yangjiang Fried Rice Biscuit include: selecting materials, frying rice, milling, mixing ingredients, pressing with molds, baking and wrapping up. Each process adopts traditional techniques and is meticulous. There are various patterns made by molds, including auspicious patterns such as "mandarin ducks playing in water" "dragons and phoenixes presenting good luck" "auspicious animals" "flowers, plants and trees", as well as

酥的饼铺20多间。20世纪40年代后期，阳西县横山人苏名溪在阳江城开设了“河水安”糕饼铺，专门生产以粉酥为主的各种礼品，使粉酥生产业进入了一个鼎盛时期。新中国成立后，“河水安”“天兴”“丽章”三家饼铺公私合营，成为当时有名的河天丽饼面厂（苏名溪的后人苏莲舟任厂长）。后来，河天丽饼面厂及其他厂组合成阳江县食品厂，改名为阳江市食品公司。阳江建市前后，民营企业迅猛发展，生产粉酥的大小厂商作坊较多。随着阳江旅游业的发展，近几年来，阳江粉酥有了较大发展，阳江粉酥不再是春节独有的应节食品，而是日常小吃零食，品种越来越多，而且大批厂家已经走上规模化生产之路，使阳江粉酥销往全国各地及远销至东南亚地区。现在，阳江人即使远在他乡，也可以从这些厂家的电商店铺买到家乡的粉酥。

基本内容

阳江粉酥制作过程分为选料、炒米、磨粉、配料拌和、上印制作、烘焙、起烘装缸。每道工序采用传统技法，精工细作。粉酥经印模印出的图案多种多样，有“鸳鸯戏水”“龙凤呈祥”“祥禽瑞兽”“花草树木”等吉祥图案，还有“福禄”“平安”之类的文字，意为“吉祥如意”“福禄平安”等。

阳江粉酥制作技艺由阳江劳动人民在日常生活中创造、传承和发展。百年来，阳江人都有打粉酥过年的习俗，春节几乎家家户户都做粉酥，人们把粉酥作为春节节庆食品之一，用于充饥、招待客人以及春节探亲送礼。如果家里没现钱，还可将粉酥作为春节醒狮拜年、舞龙、舞鲤鱼、做喜事的酬劳。因此，人们在逢年过节、婚嫁、祝寿、小孩满月酒、开灯、入伙等的喜庆日子，都喜欢将粉酥作为祭品和喜庆食品。

主要特征

阳江粉酥采用民间传统的手工制作技艺，经炭火的烘焙处理，讲究色、香、味，成品甘香可口，松化酥脆，容易携带保存，地方性特征明显。

（1）制作过程复杂。经选料、炒米、磨粉、配料拌和、上印制作、烘焙、起焙装缸工序精心焙制而成，制作工艺最为复杂讲究。

（2）制作技术独特。阳江粉酥用炒熟的米粉经印模压制，用炭火烘焙而成，还要随时掌握好火候及色泽的变化，工艺精细，工具简单，易就地取材。

（3）风味独特。阳江粉酥入口松化、酥脆，口感甜而不腻。

（4）样式多样。阳江粉酥样式非常多，有圆饼状、鲤鱼状、鸡仔状等，外形

阳江粉酥制作所需原料
Raw materials for making Yangjiang Fried Rice Biscuit

粉酥印制模具
Yangjiang Fried Rice Biscuit mold

words such as "Fulu" "Pingan", meaning good luck and well.

Baking technique of Yangjiang Fried Rice Biscuit was created, inherited and developed by Yangjiang people in their daily life. For hundreds of years, Yangjiang people have the custom of making fried rice biscuits for the Spring Festival. Almost every family makes fried rice biscuits during the Spring Festival. They regard it as a favorite festival food for the Spring Festival, which is used to eat, serve to guests, and send gifts for visiting relatives during the Spring Festival. If people don't have cash at home, fried rice biscuits can also be used as a reward for lion dance, dragon dance, carp dance and other celebrating events during the Spring Festival. Therefore, people prefer to use fried rice biscuit as sacrifices and festival food on festivals, wedding, birthday celebration, feast of celebrating the first month of a newborn baby, lighting festival, and new residence admission ceremony.

Main Features

Yangjiang Fried Rice Biscuit is made by traditional folk handcrafts. It is baked by charcoal fire and is particular about color, fragrance and taste. The finished product is sweet and delicious, loose and crisp, easy to carry and preserve, having obvious local characteristics.

(1) Complexity of the production process. It is carefully made by the processes of material selection, rice frying, milling, mixing ingredient, pressing with molds, baking and wrapping up. The production process is very complex.

(2) Specificity of production technique. Yangjiang Fried Rice

阳江粉酥制作技艺项目代表性传承人吴瑞莲（左）在制作粉酥
Wu Ruilian（left）, the representative inheritor, is making Yangjiang Fried Rice Biscuit

印模压制炒熟的米粉
Press the fried rice flour with mold

Biscuit is made by pressing the fried rice flour with mold and baking with charcoal fire. It also needs to control the change of heat and color at any time. The process is fine with simple tools and it is easy to obtain raw material locally.

（3）Specificity of flavor. Yangjiang Fried Rice Biscuit is loose, crisp and tastes sweet but not greasy.

（4）Diversity of style. Yangjiang Fried Rice Biscuit has many styles, including round biscuit, carp-shaped biscuit, chicken-shaped biscuit and so on with exquisite shape. The patterns include dragon and phoenix presenting good luck, all kinds of flowers and birds, and decorative patterns. Most of the flowers are plum, orchid, chrysanthemum, and bamboo. The characters are mostly of blessing, wealth, longevity, and happiness, implying good luck.

（5）Strong local characteristics. Yangjiang households make fried rice biscuits during the Spring Festival, forming a tradition with local and regional characteristics.

Great Value

Yangjiang Fried Rice Biscuit, one of the famous cookies of the Han nationality in Guangdong Province, is known as “the first biscuit of Yangjiang”. It is a special festival food for the Spring Festival. Foshan Manggong Biscuits, Zhongshan Almond Biscuits, Nanhai Xiqiao Biscuits, and Yangjiang Fried Rice Biscuit are called Guangdong four famous biscuits. It is a famous traditional food in the local area.

· Historical value

The baking technique of Yangjiang Fried Rice Biscuit has been passed on for a hundred years. In the process of the inheritance, it

精致玲珑。图案有龙凤呈祥、各式各样花鸟及图案花纹，花大多取梅、兰、菊、竹，字多为福、禄、寿、喜，寓意吉祥。

（5）地方性浓郁。阳江人家家户户都在春节做粉酥，形成传统，具有本土特色。

重要价值

阳江粉酥，广东省汉族名点之一，有“阳江第一饼”之美称，是春节独有的应节食品，与佛山盲公饼、中山杏仁饼、南海西樵大饼合称广东四大名饼，在当地是著名的传统食品。

· 历史价值

阳江粉酥焙制技艺传承上百年，在传承过程中融合当地历史人物和事件，清末至民初的“茂祥黄金万两”木饼模和“茂祥添丁吉兆”木饼模具有重要的历史考证价值。

· 文化价值

阳江粉酥图案多种多样，有龙凤呈祥，各种花鸟图案及纹饰，有寓意吉祥的福、禄、寿、喜字，文化内涵丰富，富含想象力。

· 艺术价值

阳江粉酥焙制技艺是一门传统手工艺术，塑造的形状图案有丰富的艺术价值。

· 社会价值

阳江粉酥焙制技艺在传承过程中，形成春节做粉酥的习俗，寄托美好愿望，增进团结，营造欢乐和谐的社会氛围，是研究阳江传统文化和民俗的一个重要载体。

一家人一起制作粉酥
The family made Yangjiang Fried Rice Biscuit together

integrates local historical figures and events. The "Maoxiang Ten Thousand Taels of Gold" wooden biscuit mold and "Maoxiang Auspicious Omen of Begeting Son" wooden biscuit mold from the late Qing Dynasty to the early Republic of China also have important historical research value.

· Cultural value

Yangjiang Fried Rice Biscuit has a variety of patterns, including dragon and phoenix pattern, various flower and bird patterns, decorative patterns, and words implying good fortune, wealth, longevity and happiness. It is rich in cultural connotation and imagination.

· Artistic value

The baking technique of Yangjiang Fried Rice Biscuit is a traditional handicraft art and the shapes and patterns have rich artistic value.

· Social value

In the process of inheriting the baking technique of Yangjiang Fried Rice Biscuit, the custom of making fried rice biscuits during the Spring Festival has been formed. It gathers blessings and wishes, enhances unity and builds a happy and harmonious society, which is an important carrier for studying Yangjiang traditional culture and folk customs.

主要传承人

岑定昌，男，出生于1972年，广东阳江市阳东人，是阳江粉酥焙制技艺第三代传承人。岑定昌师从利国良，熟练掌握阳江粉酥焙制传统技艺。其从事阳江粉酥焙制行业30多年，技艺娴熟，经验丰富，是阳江粉酥焙制技艺的代表性传承人和阳江粉酥行业的领头人之一，其创立的阳江市阳东奇香园食品有限公司也被评为“阳东县农业龙头企业”。岑定昌制作的阳江粉酥香脆可口，传统风味十足，并创新研制出黑芝麻大夹肉粉酥。岑定昌致力于阳江粉酥焙制技艺的传承和发展，收有林超卓、韦之柯、李少龙、陈后访4名徒弟，

Main Inheritors

Cen Dingchang, male, was born in Yangdong District, Yangjiang City, Guangdong Province in 1972. He is the third-generation inheritor of the baking technique of Yangjiang Fried Rice Biscuit. He learned from Li Guoliang and mastered the traditional baking technique of Yangjiang Fried Rice Biscuit. He has been engaged in the baking industry of Yangjiang Fried Rice Biscuit for more than 30 years, and is skilled and experienced, He is the representative inheritor of the baking technique of Yangjiang Fried Rice Biscuit and one of the leaders of Yangjiang Fried Rice Biscuit industry. The Yangjiang Yangdong Qixiangyuan Food Co., Ltd. founded by him has also been rated as the Leading Agricultural Enterprise in Yangdong County. The Yangjiang Fried Rice Biscuit made by Cen Dingchang is crispy, delicious, and full of traditional flavor, and he has innovatively developed the black sesame fried rice biscuit with meat. Cen Dingchang devotes himself to the inheritance and development of

岑定昌（右）
Cen Dingchang (right)

the baking technique of Yangjiang Fried Rice Biscuit. He has four apprentices including Lin Chaozhuo, Wei Zhike, Li Shaolong and Chen Houfang. He has continuously passed on to the company's workers the baking technique, cultivated many apprentices and performed the duties of inheritors. He is the representative inheritor of the fifth batch of intangible cultural heritage projects in Yangjiang City now.

Wu Ruilian, female, was born in Yangjiang, Guangdong Province in September 1956. She is the fourth-generation inheritor of the baking technique of Yangjiang Fried Rice Biscuit. Wu Ruilian has mastered the traditional skills of baking Yangjiang Fried Rice Biscuit, becoming the main inheritor of the baking technique of Yangjiang Fried Rice Biscuit and the leader of Yangjiang Fried Rice Biscuit industry. Yangjiang Lianxiang Food Co., Ltd., founded by Wu Ruilian was awarded the title of "The Most Influential Brand in Guangdong Bakery Industry in the Thirty-Year Period of Reform and Opening-up" by Guangdong Food Industry Association in 2008. Wu Ruilian has made positive contributions to the inheritance and development of Yangjiang Fried Rice Biscuit and has won more than ten honors. She is the representative inheritor of the fifth batch of intangible cultural heritage projects in Yangjiang now.

并将阳江粉酥焙制技艺不断传授给公司员工，培养众多学徒，履行传承人职责。岑定昌现为阳江市第五批非物质文化遗产项目代表性传承人。

吴瑞莲，女，出生于1956年9月，广东省阳江人，是阳江粉酥焙制技艺第四代传承人。吴瑞莲掌握阳江粉酥制作的传统技艺，成为阳江粉酥焙制技艺的主要传承人和阳江粉酥行业的领头人。吴瑞莲创建的阳江市莲香食品有限公司在2008年被广东省食品行业协会评为“改革开放三十年广东省烘焙产业最具影响力品牌”。吴瑞莲为阳江粉酥的传承和发展作出了积极贡献，她先后获得十多项荣誉。吴瑞莲现为阳江市第五批非物质文化遗产项目代表性传承人。

吴瑞莲（左）
Wu Ruilian (left)

陈静婷，女，出生于1980年10月，广东省阳江人，是阳江粉酥焙制技艺第五代传承人。陈静婷深得母亲吴瑞莲真传，熟练掌握阳江粉酥焙制传统技艺。在创业过程中和母亲一起将阳江粉酥焙制技艺不断传承发展，将所学的阳江粉酥焙制技艺不断传授给公司生产技术工人。陈静婷现为阳江市第五批非物质文化遗产项目代表性传承人。

Chen Jingting, female, was born in Yangjiang, Guangdong Province in October 1980. She is the fifth-generation inheritor of the baking technique of Yangjiang Fried Rice Biscuit. Chen Jingting has inherited from her mother, Wu Ruilian, and has mastered the traditional baking techniques of Yangjiang Fried Rice Biscuit. In the process of entrepreneurship, she continued to inherit and develop the baking technique of Yangjiang Fried Rice Biscuit with her mother. They passed on to the company's technical workers the baking technique. She is the representative inheritor of the fifth batch of intangible cultural heritage projects in Yangjiang now.

陈静婷
Chen Jingting

新洲腊味制作技艺

保护单位 阳江市阳东娥姐食品有限公司

Xinzhou Cured Meat Making Craftsmanship

Protection Unit Yangjiang Yangdong Ejie Food Co., Ltd.

Xinzhou Cured Meat Making Craftsmanship has a long history and is widely spread in Xinzhou Town, Yangdong District. It is mainly distributed in Xinzhou Town and surrounding villages by small businesses, small workshops, shops and family production, and also spread to Yangjiang downtown within a small range, and radiates to all parts of Guangdong province.

新洲腊味制作技艺历史悠久，在阳东区新洲镇广泛流传。其主要以小企业、小手工作坊、店铺经营生产及家庭制作等形式集中分布在新洲镇内及周围村庄，也在较小范围内流传到阳江市区，并辐射省内各地。

Historical Origin

According to the introduction of the elderly and the textual research of *Pedigree of Tan Clan*, the ancestors of Xinzhou people migrated to Xinzhou from Zhuji Lane 400 years ago to settle down. Since then, Xinzhou people have made simple cured meat for their own use.In the Qing Dynasty, Xinzhou Market and Nadu Market were prosperous. Tan Shihong (born in 1834) , the ancestor of Tan family in Xinzhou, learned to make cured meat from his father when he was young. When he grew up, he made a living by selling cured meat, fermented soybean, preserved fruits, dried bean milk cream in tight rolls and so on. Later, his son Tan Shitai (born in 1865) inherited from him and ran a shop in Xinzhou to sell cured meat, fermented soybean, preserved fruits and dried bean milk cream in tight rolls. He developed and improved the technique of making cured meat, which can be used to make sausage, cured pork, cured duck and other cured foods, mainly for local sales. At that time, the output was not much because meat was precious food and common people could not afford it. Tan Shitai's three sons, Tan Hanqing, Tan Lianqing, and Tan Tianqing inherited Tan Shitai's skills, and then opened three stores to make dried cured meat, fermented soybean, etc., inheriting

历史渊源

据老人口述及《谭氏族谱》考证，新洲人祖先在400多年前从珠玑巷迁徙至新洲定居，从那时起便有新洲人制作简单腊肉自用。到清代，新洲墟及那笃墟较为兴旺，新洲谭氏祖先谭士宏（1834年生）从小跟父亲学做腊味，成年后做腊味、豆豉、凉果、腐竹等，以走墟贩卖为生。后其子谭时泰（1865年生）子承父业，在新洲开店，做摆卖腊味、豆豉、凉果、腐竹生意，将腊味制作技艺发展完善，能做腊肠、腊肉、腊鸭等腊味，以销往本地为主。由于当时肉类是贵重食品，百姓消费不起，故产量不多。谭时泰有谭瀚清、谭涟清、谭添清三子，三子继承谭时泰技艺，分家后开三间店铺做腊味、豆豉等，将腊味制作技艺传承和发展。民国时期，新洲墟墟场兴旺，恩平、台山、开平人也到此购物、贩卖，腊味由于品质独特、浓香可口，也得到外地人喜爱，声名远扬，新洲腊味在当时就由开平销往香港等地。谭瀚清次子谭世安成年后子承父业。1949年后，因废私营企业，公私合营，谭世安以技术入股新洲供销社做腊味，统一销售。腊味制作曾经一度低迷。改革开放后的20世纪80年代，谭世安退休，带领家人开饭店做腊味销售，腊味制作技艺重获发展。当时新洲也有几家人做腊味销售生意，郑素娥也是在此时向家公谭世安学做腊味。2012年，郑素娥开店以小作坊形式做腊味销售，由于手工制作供应不上，2016年开厂扩大生产，发展传统技艺。受其影响，新洲先后建立的腊味制作企业有15家，镇内及各村庄也有家庭制作，在阳江全市销售，也销往省内各市及全国，名声远扬。

and developing the craft of cured meat making. During the period of Republic of China, Xinzhou Market was prosperous, and people from Enping, Taishan, and Kaiping also go there to shop and sell. Because of its unique quality and delicious flavor, Xinzhou Cured Meat was also loved by people from other places and became famous. Xinzhou Cured Meat was sold from Kaiping to Hong Kong and other places at that time. Tan Shi'an, the second son of Tan Hanqing, inherited his father's skills when he was an adult. After 1949, because of the abolition of private enterprises and the public-private joint management, he became a shareholder by his craft in Xinzhou Supply and Marketing Cooperative to make cured meat for unified sales. The production of cured meat was once in a downturn. In the 1980s after the reform and opening-up, Tan Shi'an retired and led his family to run a restaurant to sell cured meat. Xinzhou Cured Meat Making Craftsmanship was gradually developed again. At that time, there were several families in Xinzhou who also sold cured meat. Zheng Su'e also learned how to make cured meat from her father-in-law Tan Shi'an at that time. In 2012, Zheng Su'e ran a shop to sell cured meat in the form of small workshops. Since the supply of handmade products was not available, the factory was established to expand production and develop traditional techniques in 2016. Under its influence, Xinzhou has successively established 15 enterprises for the production of cured meat, and there are also family workshops in the town and villages. The cured meat is sold in Yangjiang City and sold to many cities in the province and the country, which gained a reputation for Xinzhou Cured Meat.

基本内容

新洲腊味制作技艺主要以手工制作为主，一直以来都以师徒和家族方式传承。新洲腊味主要以腊肠、腊肉、腊鸭为主，也有制作腊鱼、腊鸟等腊味，制作最佳时间一般为秋冬季北风起时节。新洲腊肠的制作技艺分为选料、洗料、切肉、腌制、拌料、制肠衣、灌肠、挂沥、烘干、生（腊）晒等工序。制好后的生肠在晾晒一个星期后，待腊肠的瘦肉变为暗红色，肥肉呈乳白色，肠体硬挺干爽呈圆柱形，肠衣表面有自然皱纹，腊肠香味明显时，即可完成晾晒。腊肉和腊鸭分别是以新鲜五花猪腩肉和本地鸭鸭肉为主要原料，经选料、洗料、切料、腌制、生晒而成。腊肉

Basic Content

Xinzhou Cured Meat Making Craftsmanship is mainly made by hand. The craft has always been inherited by apprentices and families. Xinzhou Cured Meat mainly consists of cured sausages, cured pork and cured ducks. It also makes cured fish, cured birds and other cured foods. The best time to make cured meat is autumn and winter when the north wind blows. The production of cured meat is made through the processes of material selecting, washing, cutting, curing, mixing, casing making, sausage making, drip drying, drying, and airing. After the prepared sausages have been dried for a week, the processes are finished when the lean meat of the sausages turns dark red, the fat is milky white, the sausages are hard, dry and cylindrical, the surface of the casings has natural wrinkles, and the sausages smell good. The cured pork and cured duck are made of fresh streaky pork and local duck as the main raw materials, through

腊鸭
Cured duck

material selecting, washing, cutting, curing and drying. The cured meat can be divided into meat with bone and meat without bone, most of which is meat without bone.

There are many varieties of Xinzhou Cured Meat, and the production craft is sophisticated. The main processes are marinating, baking and curing. Each process should be well controlled in terms of time and color change. The dried cured meat is crystal clear and moist with good smell and taste, which is loved by people.

Main Features

Xinzhou Cured Meat Making Craftsmanship has the characteristics of sophisticated craft, unique flavor, diverse content, unique production, and obvious regional characteristics.

(1) Elaborateness of production technique. The production of cured meat is made through the processes of material selecting, washing, cutting, curing, mixing, casing making, sausage making, drip drying, drying, and airing. It is important to master the time, temperature, and color changes. The processes are delicate and complex. There is a saying in the industry that "one night decides everything". It means that, the key to make a good sausage is the charcoal baking on the first night.

(2) Uniqueness of flavor. The cured meat produced by this method is mainly dried in air with dark red in color, crystal clear, and has the characteristics of good smell and taste. The sausage dried by charcoal fire is not easy to stink. The sausage flavor is loved by people.

(3) Diversity of products. Xinzhou Cured Meat mainly consists of cured sausage, cured pork, and cured duck, while it also includes cured fish, cured birds, and other cured foods. The cured meat can be divided into meat with bone and meat without bone. There are

腊肉
Cured Meat

分带骨肉和不带骨肉两种，多为不带骨肉。

新洲腊味品种较多，制作技艺精细复杂，工艺以腌、烘和腊为主，每道工艺要掌握好时间及关注色泽变化。晒好的腊味晶莹润透，具有香、脆、爽的特点，深受人们喜爱。

主要特征

新洲腊味制作技艺具有制作技术精巧、风味独特、内容多样、制作独特、地域特色明显等特征。

（1）制作技术精巧。腊味的制作经选料、洗料、切肉、腌制、拌料、制肠衣、灌肠、挂沥、烘干、生（腊）晒工序而成，每道工艺要掌握好时间、温度及关注色泽变化，工艺精细复杂。行内有“一夜定乾坤”之说，即要晒出好腊肠，关键在于第一晚的炭烘。

（2）风味独特。此法制作的腊味主要以自然腊晒为主，色泽暗红，晶莹润透，具有香、脆、爽的味道特点。经过炭火烘干的腊肠不易发臭，特别有腊肠香味，深受人们喜爱。

（3）种类多样。新洲腊味以腊肠、腊肉、腊鸭为主，同时也有制作腊鱼、腊鸟等腊味，腊肉又可分为带骨肉和不带骨肉，腊种丰富多样。

（4）制作独特。新洲腊味制作技艺的主要工艺是腌、烘、腊，制作工艺讲究，工具简单，易就地取材。

（5）地域特色明显。新洲腊味与其他地区腊味相比，具有形状细长、表面干爽、不带油的特点，容易携带保存，乡土传统风味浓郁，地域特色明显。

重要价值

以新洲腊味制作技艺制作的腊味，是在当地知名度高的传统食品，彰显地方特色美食文化，实现地方品牌效应价值。

·历史价值

新洲腊味制作技艺在新洲传承数百年，它的产生、传承和发展都经历了一定的历史过程，融入当地人民的智慧和思想，反映了阳江历史时代的特点。

·艺术价值

新洲腊味制作技艺经选料、洗料、切肉、腌制、拌料、制肠衣、灌肠、挂沥、烘干、生（腊）晒工序而成，每道工序的侧重点不同，艺术手法不同，是一门传统手工艺术，有丰富的艺术价值。

·科学价值

新洲腊味制作技艺融合了美食、工艺等方面的物理过程和化学反应的科学理论，科学地制作出适应人们味觉的美食品种，具有一定的科学价值。

·文化和社会价值

新洲腊味制作技艺是随着农耕文明、商贸文明、手工技艺文明的发展而产生和发展的，是一种独特的地方历史文化的积淀，对打响地方文化品牌、维系社会关系、丰富社会物质生活具有重要意义。新

新洲腊味制作技艺中的挂沥工序

Drip drying process of Xinzhou Cured Meat production technology

diverse kinds of cured meat.

(4) Uniqueness of production. Xinzhou Cured Meat Making Craftsmanship is mainly based on marinating, baking and curing. The production process is exquisite. The tools are simple, and the materials are easy to obtained.

(5) Obvious regional characteristics. Compared with cured foods in other regions, Xinzhou Cured Meat have the characteristics of being long and thin, dry surface, not greasy, easy to carry and preserve. It has strong local traditional flavor and obvious regional characteristics.

Great Value

The cured meat making by Xinzhou Cured Meat Making Craftsmanship is a traditional food with high popularity in the local area, highlighting the local characteristic food culture and realizing the local brand effect value.

· Historical value

Xinzhou Cured Meat Making Craftsmanship has been passed down in Xinzhou for hundreds of years. Its emergence, inheritance and development have all gone through a certain historical process. It integrates the wisdom and ideas of local people, reflecting the characteristics of Yangjiang's history.

· Artistic value

Xinzhou Cured Meat Making Craftsmanship is formed through the processes of material selecting, material washing, meat cutting, curing, mixing, casing making, sausage making, drip drying, drying, and airing. Each process has different emphasis and artistic craft. It is a traditional handicraft art with rich artistic value.

· Scientific value

Xinzhou Cured Meat Making Craftsmanship integrates the

scientific theory of physical process and chemical reaction in food, craft, etc.. It has scientific value of scientifically creating food varieties that adapt to people's taste.

· Cultural and social value

Xinzhou Cured Meat Making Craftsmanship is produced and developed with the development of agricultural civilization, commercial civilization and handicraft civilization, which is a unique accumulation of local history and culture. It is of great significance for building a local cultural brand, maintaining social relations, and enriching social material life. Xinzhou Cured Meat is loved by many people because of its unique flavor, which affects many people's lives. It plays an important role in promoting social material and spiritual civilization, placing good wishes, enhancing unity and building a happy and harmonious society.

洲腊味以其独有的腊香味道受到众多人民的喜爱，影响较多人的生活，对促进社会物质文明、精神文明建设，寄托美好愿望，增进团结，营造欢乐和谐社会有重要作用。

Main Inheritors

Zheng Su'e, female, was born in Xinzhou Town, Yangdong District in May 1963. She is the fifth generation inheritor of Xinzhou Cured Meat Making Craftsmanship. Zheng Su'e has been engaged in the production of Xinzhou Cured Meat for 37 years. During the process from learning to starting her own business, she has constantly investigated and studied the making craft of Xinzhou Cured Meat, accumulating rich experience. She has passed on her skills to workers and the masses for inheritance. She is the representative inheritor of the fifth batch of intangible cultural heritage projects in Yangjiang City now.

郑素娥
Zheng Su'e

主要传承人

郑素娥，女，出生于1963年5月，阳东区新洲镇人，是新洲腊味第五代传承人。郑素娥从事新洲腊味制作37年，从学艺到创业的过程中不断对新洲腊味制作技艺进行调查研究，积累了丰富的经验，并把技艺的心得领会传授给工人和群众，进行技艺传承。郑素娥现为阳江市第五批非物质文化遗产项目代表性传承人。

赵重明，男，出生于1984年2月，阳东区新洲镇人，是新洲腊味第三代传承人。赵重明从小跟随祖父、父亲学习新洲腊味制作技艺。在2000年，父亲赵必华在传统的新洲腊味制作技艺基础上首创了一门工艺，生产出的腊肠肥而不腻、香脆可口，受到群众广泛好评。赵重明当年跟随父亲习得这一门工艺，熟练掌握新洲腊味制作技艺。赵重明的宗旨是把家族产品做精做美，按传统工艺规范生产，传承传统风味，以质取胜，回馈客户，为客户提供绿色食品，不断传承和发展新洲腊味制作技艺。赵重明现为阳江市第五批非物质文化遗产项目代表性传承人。

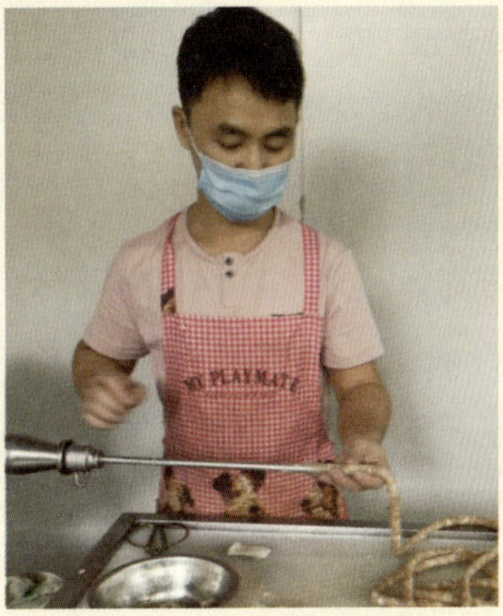

赵重明
Zhao Chongming

Zhao Chongming, male, was born in Xinzhou Town, Yangdong District in February 1984. He is the third generation inheritor of Xinzhou Cured Meat. Zhao Chongming followed his grandfather and father to learn Xinzhou Cured Meat Making Craftsmanship when he was young. In 2000, his father Zhao Bihua pioneered a process based on the traditional skills of making Xinzhou Cured Meat. The sausage was fat but not greasy, crisp and delicious, and the taste was praised by the masses. Zhao Chongming learned this process from his father, and mastered the skills of making Xinzhou Cured Meat. Zhao Chongming's tenet is to make the family products perfectly. He produces the products according to the traditional process specifications, inherits the traditional flavor with high quality, and offers customers green food. He has constantly inherited and developed the production skills of Xinzhou Cured Meat. He is the representative inheritor of the fifth batch of intangible cultural heritage projects in Yangjiang now.

江城传统逆水龙舟制作技艺

保护单位　阳江市江城船业有限公司

Jiangcheng Traditional Upstream Dragon Boat Manufacturing Craftsmanship

Protection Unit Yangjiang Jiangcheng Shipbuilding Co., Ltd.

Jiangcheng Traditional Upstream Dragon Boat Manufacturing Craftsmanship is distributed in Yuzhou Community and Mafu Community of Chengnan Street, Dongbo Village and Naxi Village of Chengxi Street, Mayan Village and Xi'an Village of Zhongzhou Street, Zhouwei Community and Zhoutou Community of Nanen Street, etc.. It spreads to Dongping Town, Linwu Village, Nahuo Village, Danzai Village, Jincun Village, Duantao Village and other villages in Beiguan Town, Yangdong District, and Xiadian Village, Chengcun Town, Yangxi County.

江城传统逆水龙舟制作技艺分布于阳江市江城区城南街道渔洲社区、马福社区，城西街道东钵村、那西村，中洲街道麻演村、西岸村，南恩街道洲尾社区、洲头社区等，并辐射到阳东区东平镇，北惯镇的林屋、那霍、丹载、金村、端陶等村，以及阳西县程村镇下店村等地。

Historical Origin

Jiangcheng Traditional Upstream Dragon Boat Manufacturing Craftsmanship began in the early Qing Dynasty, and the most representative maker is the Zhou Family of shipbuilding. The fifth ancestor of the Zhou family, Zhou Guozhu, originally lived in Dongguan County. In the early Qing Dynasty, he moved from Dongguan County to Baotanbu Village in Jiangcheng, Yangjiang County. He has a career in shipbuilding and engaged in trade operation. He was the ancestor of the Zhou family of making Jiangcheng Dragon Boat and Beiguan Dragon Boat, and had fifteen generations of descendants until now. The Zhou Family of shipbuilding has inherited the ingenious data measures (including the length of the entire boat, the crosstie, and the bilge-plate of Jiangcheng Traditional Upstream Dragon Boat, etc.) and exquisite craftsmanship (including structure of Jiangcheng Traditional Upstream Dragon Boat) from generation to generation. The dragon boat has been praised by the people and still continues to spread.

历史渊源

江城传统逆水龙舟制作技艺始于清初，最具代表性的制作者是造船世家周氏家族。周氏家族第五世祖周国柱原居东莞县，在清初由东莞县迁居于阳江县江城西岸堡炭埠村，以造船为业，贸易经营。周国柱是周氏家族装造江城龙舟及北惯龙舟的始祖，至今已有十五代传人。周氏造船世家祖传造龙舟的奇巧数度（江城逆水龙舟的长度、龙舟的枕长、龙舟的大艕长等）及精湛技艺（江城逆水龙舟的结构）世代相传。周氏家族制作的龙舟得到民众的称赞，至今还继续传扬。

周氏造船世家第十一代传人周作柽（1837—1895），是清道光年间江城传统逆水龙舟制作技艺传人，在漠阳江边下濑洲尾开设阳江县最早的造船厂——“祥盛”船厂。周作柽传承祖业，造船及造龙船有过硬功夫，技艺超群，可“以斧代刨”，船板接缝，不用“挣灰”而不漏水，当时江城在漠阳江竞渡的逆水龙舟不少是他带领晚辈制作的。

周氏造船世家第十二代传人周成禧（1878—1969），别号“老周康”，承袭了前人造龙舟的工艺并加以改进，把前人用尺量度各构件数据的方法改为采用先进的“用样条（样板）取值画样”的方法取形，提高了数据的准确度，做出的龙舟线型光顺、流畅、美观，行舟阻力小，成为当时名声显赫的龙舟制作大师。民国时期初到中华人民共和国成立之初，在江城漠阳江竞渡的龙舟“三角白旗”“华濠”“下濑”“东砵红须”“东砵白须”“东砵龙乸”“七星旗”及北惯部分龙舟都是由“老周康”带领他的儿子周合义（1909—1987）精心制作的代表作。“三角白旗”“下濑”都是当时龙舟竞渡的“常胜将军”。

周氏造船世家第十三代传人周合义，早期跟随父亲学艺几十年，掌握了一整套龙舟制作技艺。民国后期，他自己开船厂（安记船厂）继承祖业。1957年他加入国营船厂。20世纪80年代，“单白旗”“双白旗”“华濠”“上濑”等一大批制作工艺堪称阳江一绝的逆水龙舟都是由他言传身教指导儿子及晚辈建造的。

周氏造船世家第十四代传人周世赏，1948年生，六七岁开始跟祖父、父亲学做木船及龙舟。1968—1976年，在阳江各造船厂从事木工工作，1977年至现在，在江城船厂负责生产、技术管理工作，1984年，开始主持负责制作各种龙舟，1988年

Zhou Zuocheng（1837–1895）, the 11th-generation inheritor of Zhou family of boat making, was an inheritor of Jiangcheng Traditional Upstream Dragon Boat Manufacturing Craftsmanship during the Daoguang period of Qing Dynasty. The earliest shipyard in Yangjiang County— "Xiangsheng" shipyard, was opened by him at the end of the Xiala area, near Moyang River. He inherited his ancestors' heritage, and had excellent skills in shipbuilding and dragon boat making. He could "use an axe instead of a plane" to make the seams of the boat board without ash and without water leakage. At that time, many of upstream dragon boats competing in Moyang River in Jiangcheng were made by the younger generation under his leadership.

Zhou Chengxi（1878–1969）, the 12th-generation inheritor of the Zhou Family of boat making, nicknamed "Old Zhoukang", inherited and improved the craft of predecessors in building dragon boats. He changed the method of measuring the data of each component with a ruler by predecessors into advanced method of drawing with spline（template）for taking shape to improve the accuracy of the data. The dragon boat line made by this method is fairing, smooth, beautiful and has little resistance, and he became a famous master of dragon boat making at that time. From the beginning of the Republic of China to the beginning of the founding of the People's Republic of China, the "Triangular White Flag" "Huahao" "Xialai" "Dongbo Red Beard" "Dongbo White Beard" "Dongbo Female Dragon" "Seven Star Flag" and some of the dragon boats in Beiguan Town that ferried across Moyang River in Jiangcheng were elaborately produced by "Old Zhoukang" with his son Zhou Heyi（1909–1987）under his leadership. "Triangular White Flag" and "Xialai" were the "ever-victorious generals" of the dragon boat races at that time.

Zhou Heyi, the 13th-generation inheritor of the Zhou Family of boat making, learned from his father for decades and mastered the whole set of dragon boat making skills. In the late Republic of China, he established his own shipyard（Anji Shipyard）to inherit his ancestral business. He joined the state-owned shipyard in 1957. In the 1980s, "Single White Flag" "Double White Flag" "Huahao" "Shanglai" and a large number of upstream dragon boats with excellent craftsmanship were built by his son and the younger generation under the guidance of him.

Zhou Shishang, the 14th-generation inheritor of the Zhou Family of boat making, was born in 1948. At the age of six or seven, he began to learn from his grandfather and father to make wooden boats and dragon boats. From 1968 to 1976, he worked as a carpenter in various shipyards in Yangjiang. From 1977, he has been responsible for production and technical management in Jiangcheng Shipyard.

In 1984, he began to take charge of the production of various dragon boats. In 1988, he was awarded as assistant engineer of hull design. From 1997 to 1999, he was a member of the professional title review of Jiangcheng District.

Basic Content

Jiangcheng Traditional Upstream Dragon Boat Manufacturing Craftsmanship, from design to production, is passed down by words and in experience from generation to generation. Making a dragon boat requires nearly 30 complex processes which are done by hand. Traditional production processes of Jiangcheng traditional dragon boat are as follows.

Selecting materials–cutting materials–splicing the bottom plates–taking shape of the bottom plates–making the crosstie–binding the bottom plate–ditching on the bottom plate–making the baffle plates–splicing the bilge-plates–taking shape of the bilge-plates–nailing the bilge-plates–processing the thickened shell–nailing the sitting plates–nailing the outer pallets–nailing the inner pallets–making the keel–nailing the golden top–shaping and polishing the whole ship–installing the bailing bucket–installing the dragon head and tail–launching the dragon boat.

Selecting materials: Select big timber with high strength, small specific gravity, long length and large diameter. Imported Kundian wood or imported sapwood with a length of 14 meters shall be selected for the keel and thickened shell. The imported teak or sapwood with a length of 14 meters and a diameter of more than 70 cm shall be used for the bilge-plate, bottom plate and pallets. The dragon head is made of mothproof camphor wood with small proportion.

Cutting materials: Before cutting, the material positions of each component must be arranged reasonably on the whole wood according to the primary and secondary order of the dragon boat components. After positioning and snapping the line, the plate can be cut and then processed into various components.

Splicing bottom plate: It is the basic process of making Jiangcheng traditional upstream dragon boat. The width of the bottom plate is spliced by one or two whole materials. In this way, the bottom plate has few joints, without water seepage and with high strength.

Taking shape of the bottom: The center line of the bottom plate and whether the shape of both sides of the bottom plate are symmetrical will affect the orientation of the dragon boat's rowing. Especially the specifications of the front and rear positions of the force points of the full-load waterline on the bow must be taken according to the design offset data, otherwise it is unfavorable to the wave-

被评为船体设计助理工程师，1997—1999年为江城区工程系列职称评审委员会成员。

基本内容

江城传统逆水龙舟制作技艺，从设计到制作都是由祖辈口头代代传授和经验代代相传的。制作一艘龙舟需要20多道复杂工序，全部都由纯手工完成。江城传统龙舟的制作流程如下：

选料—开料—拼接底板—底板取形—打枕—扎底—底板开柳沟—做挡板—拼接大膀—大膀取形—钉大膀—加工甲筋—钉坐板—钉外花膀—钉里花膀—做龙骨—钉金顶—整条船整形打磨光滑—安装戽斗—安装龙头龙尾—龙舟进水。

选料：选用强度高、比重小、长度长、直径大的长木材。龙骨甲筋要选用14米长的进口坤甸木或进口梢木。做大膀、底板、花膀选用长14米、直径70厘米以上的进口柚木或进口梢木。龙头选用防虫蛀、比重小的樟木。

开料：开料前，必须按龙舟构件的主次顺序在整条木上合理地划分各构件的用材位置。定好位置，弹好线，才开介成板材，再由板材加工成各构件。

龙舟制作工具
Tools for making dragon boat

拼接底板：拼接底板是制造江城传统逆水龙舟的基础工序，底板选用一整材或两整材拼接而成。这样用材的底板接缝少，不渗水，强度高。

底板取形：底板的中心线及底板两边的取形是否对称，会影响龙舟划行的定向程度，特别是船头满载水线的着力点前后位置的规格一定要按设计的型值取值，否则对龙舟的兴波阻力不利。所以在弹中线及修正底板两边形状时要进行多次的反复取形修正加工。底板取形完成后，就要在底板面上进行底板的枕位及挡板定位、编号等工作。

扎底：扎底是制作江城新龙舟的隆重工序，它表示新龙舟开始动工，要选择良辰吉日进行。“扎底”前把已取好形的底板放在预先根据设计配置好弧度的中枕上，校好布枕。枕面上，龙搽用两根上等木料做成，并上红色漆油，周围扎着红色彩绸带、插上金花，中间装上插香用的小香案，分别支撑底板的头、尾枕处。校正底板的中心线及各个设计位置的弧度后，把底板固定在各枕面上。到“扎底”的吉时，制作工匠把点燃的香插到“龙搽”的香案上，地面周围烧银宝、蜡烛、香等祭品，口中念着一些象征着吉祥如意的话，然后放鞭炮。“扎底”完成后，龙舟制作工匠要等待三四个小时才能在龙舟底板面工作。

底板开柳沟：该工序是制造江城龙舟最严格、最细致的工作。如果柳沟不小心被弄裂了，装好的龙舟就会变软及渗水，整块底板就要更换或补换。

做挡板：龙舟的隔舱板（挡板）加工及安装好坏也会影响龙舟的流线形状，所以在加工时两端的角度必须准确。挡板底部长度与相应位置的船底板的宽度必须吻合。安装

making resistance of the dragon boat. Therefore, when snapping the center line and correcting the shape on both sides of the bottom plate, it is necessary to make repeated shape correction processing. After the bottom plate is shaped, it is necessary to locate the position for installing bottom plates, baffles, and numbering, and other work on the bottom plate.

Binding the bottom plate：It is a grand process to make a new Jiangcheng dragon boat. It means the starting of the construction of the new dragon boat, which should be proceeded on a auspicious day. Before binding the bottom plate, the shaped bottom plate should be placed on the middle crosstie with camber configured according to the design in advance, and the position of crosstie should be corrected. On the surface of bottom plate, the Longbeng (wooden bar) supporting the dragon boat is made of two superior timbers, painted with red paint, tied with red colored silk ribbon and inserted with gold flowers around. The Longbeng supporting the dragon boat with a small incense table is inserted in the middle to support the front and behind position of the bottom plate. After correcting the center line of the bottom plate and the radian of each design position, the bottom plate should be fixed on each correct position. At the auspicious time of binding the bottom plate, the craftsman puts the lighted incense in the censer of the Longbeng supporting the dragon boat, burns special paper for sacrifice, candles, incense and other sacrificial offerings around the ground, and says some auspicious words and sets off firecrackers. After the completion of binding the bottom plate, the craftsmen have to wait three or four hours before working on the bottom plate of the dragon boat.

The work of making groove on the bottom plate: It is the most rigorous and meticulous work for building Jiangcheng dragon boats. If the groove is accidentally cracked, the installed dragon boat will become soft and seep, and the entire bottom plate has to be replaced. The processing and installation of the bulkhead（baffle）of the dragon boat will also affect the streamlined shape of the dragon boat, so the angles at both ends must be accurate during processing.

Making the baffle plate: The length of the bottom of the baffle plate must match the width of the bottom plate at the corresponding position. When installing the baffle plate, 4 mm × 50 mm hook square nail should be used to fasten the bottom and baffle, and the nail distance is generally 7 cm（the length of the nails used for Jiangcheng dragon boat is 3 times the thickness of the component）.

The material selecting, processing and shape selecting of the bilge-plates: The bilge-plates on the left and right sides should be made of the same material, with same specific gravity and thickness. If the weight of the two sides of the completed bilge-plates is different,

扎底
Binding the bottom plate

the draught of two sides of ship are different. The bilge-plates of Jiangcheng traditional dragon boat are generally made of three whole timbers, and the positions of the bilge-plates on both sides should be staggered. The connection part of each bilge-plate cannot overlap with the connection part of bottom plate, and should avoid the connection parts with keel and thickened shell. The connection part of the bilge-plates should be made by the form of "Zhaokou" double buckle joint as far as possible. After the bilge-plates are jointed, it is necessary to take shape of the bilge-plates, which is to snap the datum line of spliced bilge-plates according to the datum position (data value) of expansion, mark the corresponding station line between each point and the bottom plate expansion, measure the radian and height of the expanded bilge-plates to each corresponding station line, and connect the points, which is the expansion shape of the bilge-plate. The shape of the bilge-plates is one of the key factors to determine the beauty of the whole boat, and determines the smoothness of the streamline of the bottom, the resistance of the water inlet point at the front of the full waterline, and the wave-making resistance. Therefore, the shape of the bilge-plates should be taken repeatedly without deviation. Double-layer wood shall be used in each connection part of the bilge-plates to strengthen the bilge-plates to keep the boat from deformation and water seepage. Nailing is particular when installing a bilge-plate. The bottom of bilge-plate is fixed with the bottom plate by connecting nails, and the hook nails cannot be used, because the hook nail is easy to crack the bilge-plate. The bilge-plates and baffle plate are fixed with hook nails with a distance of 7 cm.

Processing the thickened shell: The thickened shell of the dragon boat is the longitudinal stiffener of the dragon boat. The material selection of thickened shell should be based on the shape of dragon boat. The profile radian of the position of thickened shell is relatively large. Three whole timbers selected for the thickened shell should be

挡板用4mm×50mm的勾头方钉将底部与挡板钉紧，钉距一般为7厘米（江城龙舟一般用钉的长度是构件厚度的3倍）。

大艕的选料、拼接、取形、打钉：左右两边的大艕要用同一种材质，比重一样，加工厚薄规格一样，如做好的两边大艕的重量不一样，船两侧吃水就不平行。江城传统龙舟的大艕一般是用三整材接驳而成，两边大艕的驳口位置要错开。每个大艕的驳口不能与底板的驳口重合在一处，还要避开与龙骨、甲筋的驳口。大艕的驳口尽量用顺水“钊口”双扣挣形式。大艕拼接好后，就要进行大艕取形工作，即把拼接好的大艕按展开时的基准位置（数据值）弹基准线，标记各点与底板展开的对应站线，把展开的大艕弧度及高度分别量度到各对应站线，将各点连接，便是大艕的展开形状。大艕的形状是影响全船美观程度的关键因素之一，决定了底部流线的光顺程度，决定了满载水线前端的进水点的阻力大小、兴波阻力的大小，所以大艕加工取形时要多次反复取形加工，不能有丝毫偏差。大艕的每个驳口里位都要用双层木，以加强大艕的强度，使船不变形、不渗水。装大艕时打钉特别讲究。大艕末端与底板用连钉固定，不能使用勾头钉，因为勾头钉易使大艕末端爆裂。大艕与挡板固定用勾头钉，钉距均为7厘米。

加工甲筋：龙舟的甲筋是龙船纵向加强筋，甲筋的选料应根据船的形状来选择。龙舟甲筋位置的线形弧度比较大，甲筋选用的三整材要与龙舟的流线型吻合，不破坏船的线形结构，甲筋的驳口不能与龙骨及其他构件的驳口重合。大艕与甲筋用勾头钉固定，钉距为15厘米。

钉坐板：龙舟的檀子面（凳子面）一般宽度为11～12厘米，厚度与大艕一样。檀子面的作用是把两边的甲筋与挡板固定并加强龙舟的横向力，是划船者坐的凳面。檀子面两端用两支勾头钉与甲筋钉牢固，其余部位以钉距为15厘米的勾头钉与当子面紧固。

钉花艕：花艕是龙舟外壳结构的一种加强艕板，可以阻挡浪花上船。花艕用料的好坏、安装的垂直角度是决定整船美观程度的关键因素之一。花艕的角度中间应向里斜入1.5厘米，与枕位置垂直，头尾向外斜2厘米。花艕分里、外花艕，先做外花艕后做里花艕。外花艕的连钉在外面之下，不用打钉眼，与甲筋接口处用勾头钉钉紧固；里花艕的驳口不能与外花艕的驳口重合。里、外花艕之间用勾头钉或丝钉紧固。

做龙骨：每艘传统龙舟都有一组龙骨，由三段木组成，龙骨的驳口在龙舟的校部位置。用龙骨锲将三段龙骨连接起来，头尾两段龙骨通过龙骨锲可以调节弧度。龙骨必须随着船形，打龙骨锲不能过紧或过松。这样龙舟在水中划行速度才会比较快。

最后的工序为安装戽斗，安装龙头龙尾。龙舟全部完工后，就要择良辰吉日下水。下水前，由民间法师主持庄重的“旺龙”仪式：龙头前摆放一张八仙桌，摆上一些供品、香、烛、油灯，法师手抓大雄鸡，划破鸡冠，将鸡血滴在龙头上，口

consistent with the streamline of dragon boat without damaging the linear structure of the boat. The connection part of thickened shell should not coincide with the connection part of the keel and other components. The bilge-plates and thickened shell are fixed with hook nails with a distance of 15 cm.

Nailing the sitting board: The sandalwood surface (stool surface) of the dragon boat is generally 11–12 cm wide, and the thickness is the same as the bilge-plate. The role of the sandalwood surface is to fix the thickened shell and the baffle surface on both sides, and strengthen the transverse force of the dragon boat. It is the stool surface on which the boatman sits. The two ends of the sandalwood surface are nailed down with two hook nails and thickened shell, and the rest parts are nailed down with the clearance surface by using a hook nail with a distance of 15 cm.

Nailing the pallets: The pallets are strengthening plates of hull structure of dragon boat and can prevent the waves from getting on the boat. The quality of the material and the vertical angle of the installation of the pallet are one of the key factors to determine the beauty of the whole boat. The angle of the pallets should be 1.5 cm inward, and position should be vertical to the crosstie, and the head and tail should be a slope of 2 cm out. The pallets should be divided into inner and outer pallet, and the outer pallet should be made before the inner pallet. The connecting nail of the outer pallet is under the outside without nail hole and the interface with thickened shell shall be nailed down with hook nails. The connection part of the inner pallet cannot coincide with the connection part of the outer pallet. The inner and outer pallets are nailed down with hook nails or wire nails.

Making the keel: Each traditional dragon boat has a set of keels, which are composed of three sections of wood. The connection part of the keel is located at the correcting position of the dragon boat. The keel wedge shall be used to connect three keels, and the head and tail keels can adjust the radian through the keel wedge. The keel must follow the ship shape, and the keel wedge should not be fixed too tight or too loose. In this way, the dragon boat can row faster in the water.

The final processes are installing the bailing bucket and the dragon head and tail. After completion of dragon boat, it is necessary to choose an auspicious day to launch the boat. Before launching the boat, the folk wizard will host a solemn “Wanglong” ceremony: a square table is placed in front of the head of dragon boat with some offerings, incense, candles, oil lamps, and the wizard had a big cock in hands. The wizard would cut the comb of the cock, drop blood of the chicken on the head of dragon, chant incantations in the mouth, draw the eyes of the head of dragon boat, comb the bun and beard, paint color, etc.. Then the “Longzhong” (the leader of dragon boat team) sits in the front cabin of dragon boat. The drummers board the boat. Every two of strong men place a thick wooden pole under the dragon boat. With the command of drummers, the strong men send the dragon boat into the water together. Next, they row to the nearby river port, and carry out the ceremony of plucking the greens under the bamboo forest and willow shade. The "Longzhong" will pick a plant that symbolizes the "greens" and insert it on the head of dragon. The ceremony of dragon boat launching is completed.

Main Features

(1) The length of Jiangcheng Traditional Upstream Dragon Boat is 30.24 meters, with 53 boatmen generally.

(2) The bottom plate of Jiangcheng dragon boat is very unique, and it is horizontal and straight without bottom keel. Jiangcheng dragon boat chooses the flat bottom plate without bottom keel due to the river conditions and competition mode in Yangjiang. The flat bottom dragon boat has shallow draught, small immersion area on the boat's surface, and small friction resistance, which is conducive to the accelerate rowing of the dragon boat.

(3) The valuing method of the outer plate(bilge-plate) of Jiangcheng dragon boat is different from that of other dragon boats. The shape value of the bilge-plates of Jiangcheng Traditional Upstream Dragon Boat is obtained from the "raw" value and the width of the bottom plate, the angle of the side of the bilge-plates and relevant values after expansion. The bilge-plates of the whole boat are spliced with the bottom plate after being formed. In other places, the shape of the bilge-plates of dragon boat are drawn by putting the board of the bilge-plates on bottom edge according to the "raw" shape of the bottom plate, and splicing it in sections.

(4) Jiangcheng Traditional Upstream Dragon Boat is better than other dragon boats in terms of structure and other aspects. For example, each cabin of Jiangcheng Traditional Upsream Dragon Boat shall be provided with a bulkhead, while dragon boats in other places shall be provided with a bulkhead every two cabins. The thickened shell of Jiangcheng Traditional Upstream Dragon Boat is placed in square horizontal and vertical, while that of dragon boats in other places is placed in flat and oblique. The two sides of connection part of bilge-plates of Jiangcheng Traditional Upstream Dragon Boat should be staggered, the length should span two bulkhead panels, the "buckle" connection part should be used and the dragon boat should be strengthened by double wood. In other places, the "clap" connection part is often used for the bilge-plates of the dragon boats.

中不停地边念着咒语，边给龙头点睛、梳髻、梳须、涂彩等。然后“龙种”披红戴花坐到龙舟的前舱，锣鼓手先后上船，壮丁们两人持一条粗木杆分别穿过龙舟底部，在锣鼓手的指挥下，响起锣鼓一起发力将龙舟送下水。接着将船划到附近的河埠头，在竹林、柳荫下进行采青仪式，“龙种”把一棵象征“青”的植物采下插在龙头上，下水仪式就完成了。

主要特征

（1）江城传统逆水龙舟的船身统一长30.24米，全船一般载运动员53人。

（2）江城龙舟的底板非常独特，底板横向平直，没有底骨。江城龙舟选用无底骨的平底板是由阳江的河流及比赛模式决定的。平底龙舟吃水浅，船外表浸水面积小，摩擦阻力小，有利于龙舟加速划行。

（3）江城龙舟的外侧板（称大艕）的取值方法与其他地方龙舟的做法不同。江城传统逆水龙舟的大艕形状数值是由底板的“生度”值、宽度值、大艕的侧边的角度及各相关数值展开后取值而得来的。整只船的大艕成形后再与底板相拼接。而其他地方龙舟大艕的形状是分段把做大艕的木板拍在底边按底板“生度”形状画出来，再分段拼接而成。

（4）江城传统逆水龙舟在结构等方面比外地龙舟强。如：每个隔舱都有隔舱板，其他地方龙舟隔2个舱做1个隔舱板；江城传统逆水龙舟的甲筋是方形水平竖立式放置，其他地方龙舟是扁板形斜放置；江城传统逆水龙舟的大艕驳口两边要错开，长度要跨2个舱壁板，要用“扣挣”驳口并用双木板加强，其他地方的龙舟大艕驳口多用“拍”式驳口。

重要价值

· 历史价值

江城区位于广东省西南沿海，河网水道纵横密布，形成了江城区历史悠久、颇具特色的传统节庆大型民俗活动端午逆水赛龙舟。传统逆水龙舟的制作技艺最具代表性的制作者是造船世家周氏家族。周家祖祖辈辈制作木船、龙舟，绝技代代相传，流传至今已有十五代。该项目的发展对于研究阳江江城的制造业有一定的历史价值。

· 学术价值

传统逆水龙舟的制作技艺涵盖力学和物理学原理，在设计中要考虑船体所受的风力、水的浮力与阻力，船体装拼要考虑各个板材的形状结构，以及船体的重心、长度、宽度、高度等，对于造船业有一定的研究价值。

Great Value

· Historical value

Jiangcheng District is located in the southwest coast of Guangdong Province, and river network and waterways are densely distributed, forming a large traditional festival folk activity "Dragon Boat Festival (Dragon Boat Race Upstream) " with a long history and characteristics in Jiangcheng District. The most representative craftsmen of the Jiangcheng Traditional Upstream Dragon Boat Manufacturing Craftsmanship is the Zhou family of boat making. The Zhou family has made wooden boats and dragon boats for generations. The unique skills have been handed down from generation to generation for 15 generations. The development of this project has certain historical value for studying the manufacturing industry of Jiangcheng, Yangjiang.

· Academic value

The manufacturing craftsmanship of traditional upstream dragon boat covers principles of mechanics and physics. The power of wind and the buoyancy and resistance of water supported by the hull should be taken into account in design. The shape and structure of various plates, as well as the center of gravity, length, width and height of the hull, should be taken into account in hull assembly, which has certain research value for shipbuilding industry.

主要传承人

周世赏，男，1948年6月出生，阳江市江城区人，是造船世家周氏家族第十四代传人。周世赏六七岁开始跟祖父、父亲学做木船、龙舟，十来岁时已经从他们那里学到造木船和造龙舟的手艺。1977年进入江城船厂工作时，他已是能独当一面的造船师傅。1984年，江城恢复造逆水龙舟，此时他已经是"领军""把脉"人了。历年来，他除被江城绝大部分的龙舟队聘请造龙舟外，还被江城区政府，东平镇政府，阳东北惯镇林屋、那霍、丹载、金村、端陶，以及阳西县程村镇下店村等聘请建造龙舟，很大程度上支持和促进了阳江市民间传统文化的弘扬和发展，为阳江

Main Inheritors

Zhou Shishang, male, was born in Jiangcheng District, Yangjiang City in June 1948. He is the 14th-generation of the Zhou family of boat making. Zhou Shishang began to learn to make wooden boats and dragon boats from his grandfather and father at the age of six or seven. In his teens, he had learned the skills of making boats and dragon boats from them. When he started to work in Jiangcheng Shipyard in 1977, he was already an excellent craftsman of shipbuilding. He has become the leading people when Jiangcheng resumed the construction of upstream dragon boats in 1984. Over the years, in addition to being hired by most dragon boat teams in Jiangcheng to make dragon boats, he has also been hired to make dragon boats by Jiangcheng District Government, Dongping Town Government, Linwu, Nahuo, Danzai, Jincun, Duantao villages in Beiguan Town of Yangdong, and Xiadian village in Chengcun Town, Yangxi County etc.. He has supported and promoted the promotion and development of Yangjiang's traditional folk culture to a large extent, and

周世赏
Zhou Shishang

made a great contribution to make the Yangjiang traditional folk culture activity—Upstream Dragon Boat Race be known to the world. He is the representative inheritor of the fifth batch of intangible cultural heritage projects in Yangjiang City now.

Zhou Ju, male, was born in Jiangcheng District, Yangjiang City in November 1955. At the age of 14 or 15, he began to learn to make boats from his father and several elder brothers. From 1972 to 1975, he worked as a carpenter in various shipyards in Yangjiang. From 1975 to retirement, he worked as a carpenter in Yangjiang Second Light Shipyard. In 1984, he began to participate in dragon boat building work in the dragon boat team organized by his father and brother. In 1985, he began to lead the dragon boat building team to make various dragon boats. All along, on the basis of learning and inheriting the ingenious data and skills of the Zhou family's dragon boat making, he has been studying hard, bringing forth new ideas, summarizing actively, and designing and manufacturing various dragon boats in combination with the actual situation. The Jiangcheng upstream dragon boats made by him are exquisite in craftsmanship, smooth in shape, light in body, low in resistance and good in performance, which can be called the best in Yangjiang. Therefore, most of the dragon boat teams in Jiangcheng, Yangjiang City hired him to make dragon boats. The dragon boats "Red Beard", "Single White Flag", "Double White Flag", "Shanglai" made by him have won the championship for many times. Over the years, he has also been hired by Jiangcheng District Government, Dongping Town Government, Nahuo, Danzai, Linwu, Jincun, Duantao, Tanwu Villages in Beiguan Town of Yangdong; and Xiadian villages in Chengcun Town, Yangxi County etc. to make dragon boats. He is the representative inheritor of the fifth batch of intangible cultural heritage projects in Yangjiang City now.

传统民俗文化活动“端午逆水赛龙舟”走出阳江、走向全世界作出很大的贡献。周世赏现为阳江市第五批非物质文化遗产项目代表性传承人。

周聚，男，1955年11月生，阳江市江城区人，十四五岁开始跟父亲及几位大哥学造船，1972—1975年在阳江各间船厂做木工工作。1975年至退休在阳江二轻造船厂做木工工作。1984年开始加入父亲及大哥组织的造龙舟团队，从事造龙舟工作。1985年开始带领造龙舟团队“担干”制造各种龙舟。一直以来，周聚在学习继承周氏家族造龙舟的奇巧数度及技艺的基础上，不断刻苦学习钻研、推陈出新、积极总结，结合实际设计制造各种龙舟。经他制造的江城逆水龙舟工艺精细，船型光顺流畅，船身轻便，阻力小，性能好，堪称阳江一绝。所以，阳江江城绝大部分龙舟队都聘请他建造龙舟。经他制作的“红须”“单白旗”“双白旗”“上濑”等江城逆水龙舟曾多次获得冠军。多年来，他还被江城区政府，东平镇政府，阳东北惯镇那霍、丹载、林屋、金村、端陶、谭屋，以及阳西县程村镇下店等聘请建造龙舟。周聚现为阳江市第五批非物质文化遗产项目代表性传承人。

周 聚
Zhou Ju

东水造纸技艺

保护单位 阳西县新墟镇东水村民委员会

Dongshui Papermaking Craftsmanship

Protection Unit Dongshui Village Committee, Xinxu Town, Yangxi County

东水造纸技艺是阳西县新墟镇东水村村民的一种传统手工造纸技艺，这种技艺的传承方式有师徒传承和家族传承两种，以家族传承为主。

阳西县大体可分为沿海地带和山区地带两大部分。山区地带主要有新墟镇、塘口镇以及程村、织篢两镇的西北部。山区地带砾质土多，土质相对松散。最高点鹅凰嶂海拔1337米，位于县的西北部，与电白区接壤、阳春市相邻。东水村就在鹅凰嶂山腰，这里山高林密，水力资源丰富。一条南北走向的V形长峡谷将东水山分开两半，这里植被浓厚，溪流遍布，土壤肥

东水传统手工造纸技艺
Dongshui traditional manual papermaking technology

Dongshui Papermaking Craftsmanship is a traditional handmade papermaking skill of Dongshui villagers in Xinxu Town, Yangxi County. There are two ways of inheritance: apprenticeship inheritance and family inheritance, and it mainly based on family inheritance.

Yangxi County can be roughly divided into two parts, the coastal zone and the mountainous zone. The mountainous zone mainly includes Xinxu Town, Tangkou Town, and the northwest of Chengcun Town and Zhilong Town. There are many gravel soils in mountainous areas and the soil is relatively loose. In the northwest of the county, the peak, Ehuangzhang, is 1337 meters above sea level, bordering Dianbai District and Yangchun City. Dongshui Village is located on the mountainside of Ehuangzhang, where the mountains are high, the forests are dense, and the water resources are abundant. A v-shaped north-south long canyon divides Dongshui Mountain into two halves. The vegetation here is dense, the streams are everywhere, and the soil is fertile. In addition, it's so suitable for the growth of bamboo that the mountains on both sides become natural barriers and the climate is warm in winter and cool in summer. According to statistics, the bamboo forest in Dongshui Mountain covers an area of 20,000 *mu*, providing a large amount of raw materials for papermaking. Dongshui River (the birthplace of the Wangfu River) is at the bottom of the canyon. The riverbed of Dongshui River is high in the north and low in the south, with a gradient slope to the south. Villagers build houses along the river, and papermaking workshops are also distributed along the river.

Historical Origin

According to the *Yangxi County Annals* (published in 2013), there were human beings living in the Yangxi region in the Neolithic Age. During the Spring and Autumn Period and the Warring States Period, Yangxi was the land of Baiyue. Since there were large number of beliefs, folk sacrifices, witch doctors and traditional medical activities were frequent led to a large demand for sacrificial and medicinal uses, which provides a social basis for the emergence of ancient papermaking craft.

After Named as Yangjiang County in the second year of Daye period of Sui Dynasty（606 AD）, the county government was set up in Yangjiang County for a long time. During the Tang and Song Dynasties, Yangjiang County developed into a political, economic and cultural center. Since the Song Dynasty, there have been frequent economic and trade exchanges between Yangjiang and other places, and various products have been transported to and from Yangjiang and other places by waterways and post roads, which accelerated the development of Yangjiang's handicraft industry. Ancient papermaking craft was gradually introduced into the Yangjiang area. During the Ming and Qing Dynasties, handmade paper gradually played its commercial role as life, sacrifice, and medical supplies.

In the early Qing Dynasty, with the opening of the post road, residents of the central plains and Guangfu areas began to enter the Yangxi area in large numbers due to war, trade, politics, etc., and papermaking craft began to be introduced into the Yangxi area. Due to the advantages of bamboo forest resources and water resources, the paper industry has gradually developed. During the Qing Dynasty and Republic of China, the paper-making workshops in the Dongshui area have formed a considerable scale.

In the early Republic of China, due to the large sales of paper produced, the paper industry radiated to the neighboring Shahe Village of Xinxu Town, Tongyou Village of Tangkou Town, and Huangsha Village of Shalang Town in Dianbai District.

By the 1980s, ancient Dongshui papermaking craft was at its peak, with 206 workshops, an annual output of 200,000 packages of paper（10 kilograms each package）and an output value of about about 400,000 *yuan*（current price）.

In recent years, because of the impact of the machine-made paper market, the price of handmade paper has dropped, so the villagers have lacked the enthusiasm to produce straw paper. Most of them go away to work or do business, and some villagers use bamboo for other purposes. At present, there are only 6 ancient paper-making workshops and about 20 papermaking villagers in Dongshui Village.

沃，加上两边高山形成天然屏障，气候冬暖夏凉，非常适合竹子生长。据统计，整个东水山的竹林面积就达2万亩，为造纸提供了大量原料。峡谷的底部是东水河（望夫河的发源地），河床北高南低，向南梯度倾斜。村民沿河建房，造纸作坊也沿河分布。

历史渊源

据《阳西县志》（2013年出版）的记载，新石器时期代阳西地域就有人类居住，春秋战国时阳西为百越之地，因为信仰众多，民间祭祀、巫医和传统医疗活动频繁，导致了祭祀冥镪、药用纸煤需求量很大，为古法造纸工艺的出现提供了社会基础。

自隋大业二年（606）阳江县得名以后，郡治长期设置在阳江县城。唐宋时期，阳江县城发展成为政治经济文化中心。宋代以来，阳江与外地经济贸易往来频繁，各类产品经水路、驿道运输往返于阳江和外地，加速了阳江手工业的发展，古法造纸技术遂逐渐传入阳江地区。明清时期，手工制造的草纸作为生活、祭祀、医疗用品，逐步发挥出其商业作用。

清初，随着驿道开辟，中原和广府地区居民因战争、商贸、政治等影响，开始大量进入阳西地区，造纸技术开始传入阳西。阳西东水山地区因为竹林资源和水力资源丰富的优势，逐渐发展出了造纸产业。在清朝、民国时期，东水地区的造纸作坊已经形成一定的规模。

民国初期，由于造出来的纸销量大，造纸业辐射到邻近的新墟镇沙河村、塘口镇同由村、电白区沙琅镇黄沙村。

20世纪80年代是东水古法造纸的鼎盛

时期，有作坊206间，年产草纸20万件（每件10千克），产值约40万元（时价）。

近几年，受机制纸市场带来的影响，手工制纸价格下降，村民生产草纸的积极性减弱，大部分村民外出经商或务工，也有一些村民把竹子改作其他用途。目前东水古法造纸作坊仅存6间，造纸村民约20人。

基本内容

东水造纸技艺最早可以追溯到清康熙五十九年（1720）。东水人民充分利用东水山竹林资源和水力资源丰富的优势，以竹子为原料，利用峡谷两边汇入东水河的溪流流水作动力推动水车带动水碓粉碎竹子来造纸。这种古法手工艺制造出来的草纸质地纯黄带粗，吸水性强，易燃且燃烧后无积炭，广受顾客青睐。目前该种草纸多用于制造鞭炮，以及作药疗用品及祭祀用品。起初只有龙骨田村村民从事东水古法造纸这项手工产业，后来遍布整个东水地区，造纸业发展到邻近的新墟镇沙河村、塘口镇同由村、电白区沙琅镇黄沙村。

主要特征

· **产品特征**

纸质棉韧而不柔，纸面平整，边沿整齐，有隐约竹帘纹。虽然表面看似粗糙，但手感润滑；质地较好，纹理清晰，吸水性强，易燃且燃烧后无积炭。

· **原料特征**

东水山生长的竹子肉质厚、韧性好，经过石灰腌制后质地纯黄、绒多，是造草纸的上等材料。东水地区河溪密布，水源充足，水质清澈凉滑，经石灰腌制后的竹片放到水里清洗，石灰会很快被清洗干净，且没有杂质，使成品草纸纸面无折

Basic Content

Dongshui Papermaking Craftsmanship can be traced back to the 59th year of Kangxi period in Qing Dynasty (1720). People of Dongshui make full use of the advantages of abundant bamboo forest resources and hydraulic resources, by using bamboo as raw material and using water flowing from the stream into the Dongshui River on both sides of the canyon as power to drive the watermill to crush the bamboos for paper making. The paper made by this ancient handicraft is pure yellow with thick texture with the characteristics of strong water absorption, flammable without carbon deposits after combustion, which is widely favored by customers. At present, this kind of paper is mostly used in the manufacture of firecrackers, medicinal supplies and sacrificial supplies. The handicraft industry of ancient Dongshui papermaking craft was originally engaged only by the villagers of Longgutian Village, and later spread throughout Dongshui area. The papermaking industry radiated to the neighboring Shahe Village of Xinxu Town, Tongyou Village of Tangkou Town, and Huangsha Village of Shalang Town in Dianbai District.

Main Features

· Features of product

The paper is flexible but not soft. The surface is flat and the edges are neat. There are faint bamboo curtain patterns. Although the surface looks a little rough, it feels smooth. The texture is good and clear. The product has strong absorption. It is flammable without carbon ashes after combustion.

· Features of raw materials

The bamboo grown in Dongshui Mountain is thick and it has good toughness. After being pickled with lime, the texture is pure yellow and

浸泡造纸原料——竹子

Soaked raw material of paper making —bamboo

fluffy. The bamboo is the best material for making paper. Rivers and streams are densely covered in Dongshui area. The water source is sufficient and the water quality is clear and cool. The bamboo chips pickled with lime are washed in water, and the lime will be cleaned quickly, and there are no impurities, so that the finished paper surface is free of folds, cracks, holes, grits and other attachments.

· Features of skill

Dongshui Papermaking Craftsmanship is ancient and simple, with long production cycle, multiple processes and high proficiency requirements. This craft is smoke-free and dust-free in the production process, which is suitable for the natural environment with zero pollution, and rarely affects human health.

The core crafts of Dongshui Papermaking Craftsmanship are pestling bamboo fibre and fishing out the paper from water. If the paper is pestled too thin, the paper cotton will float away with the water and not much paper will be fished out. If the paper is pestled too thick, the paper quality will be poor and cannot meet the requirements. It's most suitable to make bamboo fibre powder, bamboo fibre silk, and bamboo fibre roots with 1 to 2 centimeters long. If the pulps poured into the paper tank are too many, the paper will be made too thick and uneven. If the pulps poured into the paper tank are too few, the paper will be too thin and cannot be torn apart. So it is most suitable to put two large plastic barrels of pulp in one paper tank.

Due to its good quality, Dongshui Paper is widely favored by people, and the products sell well in Yangjiang and even sold to Hong Kong and Macao. It is widely used as *Zhimei* (paper roll, shaped like drinking straw, used for lighting pipe) for medicinal treatment and as *Mingqiang* (paper money to be burned for the dead) for sacrifice.

舂竹麻的工具
The tool for pestling bamboo fibre

子、裂口、洞眼、沙粒和其他附着物。

· 技艺特征

东水造纸技艺古朴，制作周期较长，工序较多，对熟练度要求较高；该技艺制作过程中无烟无尘，与自然环境相协调，零污染，同时也几乎不对人体健康造成影响。

东水造纸技艺的核心工艺是舂竹麻、捞纸。若舂得太烂，纸棉会随水漂走，捞出来的纸成数不高；若舂得太粗，捞出来的纸纸质差，达不到要求，以竹麻粉、竹麻丝、竹麻根为1～2厘米长最合适。倒入纸槽的纸浆倒多了，捞出来的纸厚并且不均匀；倒少了，捞出来的纸薄且撕不开，按一纸槽放两大胶桶的纸浆最合适。

因质量佳，东水草纸广受人们青睐，产品畅销阳江乃至远销港澳地区。被广泛用作药用纸煤和祭祀冥镪。

制作好的草纸在竹竿上晾晒
The prepared paper is drying on the bamboo pole

工匠正在捞纸
The craftsman is fishing out the paper

重要价值

·工艺价值

东水造纸工艺流程复杂，手工要求严谨。这种纯手工生产技艺都是靠祖辈言传身教，需要仔细钻研和长期实践，在原材料加工过程中大都采用浸泡、晾晒等方式自然天成，需要十分熟练地掌握工序和火候。

·经济价值

长期以来，草纸一直是东水村村民的经济来源，在当地的经济发展中发挥了十分重要的作用。草纸产业的发展解决了当地部分村民的就业问题，在20世纪古法造纸兴盛时期，几乎一个村有好几个造纸作坊，形成了以东水造纸为主的手工业产业和一定规模的特色产业群。全盛时期，造纸业曾占当地经济总量的45%。

·历史和文化价值

从南宋时期开始，东水地区李氏、黎氏、叶氏等姓杂居，不同历史时期因战乱、贸易和政治因素而导致的种族大迁徙促进了阳西东水地区的社会经济发展与文化交流。中原地区带来先进的造纸技术，激发了人民的生产劳动热情，促进了草纸的发展，这既是一种粤西与中原、广府地区民族文化融合交流的体现，也是阳西自

Great Value

· Craft value

Dongshui Papermaking craft has complex processes, and the manual requirements are rigorous. This pure handicraft is taught by ancestors, and requires careful study and long-term practice. In the process of raw material processing, most of the methods such as soaking and drying are used naturally. It requires the craftsman to master the process and *Huohou* (the duration and degree of heating and smelting) very proficiently.

· Economic value

For a long time, paper has been the source of income for the villagers in Dongshui Village and has played a very important role in the local economic development. The development of the paper industry solved employment problem of some local villagers. During the prosperous period of ancient papermaking craft in the 20th century, there were almost several papermaking workshops in one village, dominating a handicraft industry by Dongshui papermaking and forming a characteristic industrial group of certain scale. During its heyday, the paper industry accounted for 45% of the local economy.

· Historical and cultural value

Since the Southern Song Dynasty, the Li Family, Li Family, Ye Family and other families in the Dongshui area have lived together. The ethnic migration caused by war, trade and political factors in different historical periods has formed the social economy and culture exchanges of the Dongshui area of Yangxi County. The central plains region has brought advanced papermaking craft to inspire the enthusiasm of the people for production and labor, and promoted the development of paper. It is not only a manifestation of the integration and exchange of ethnic cultures between western Guangdong, the Central Plains and Guangfu region, but also a physical witness to the emergence and development of local

传承人用舂好的竹麻制作纸浆
The inheritor is using the pestled bamboo fibre to make paper pulp

characteristic paper culture in Yangxi County. Dongshui Papermaking Craftsmanship originated from the production skills of Cai Hou paper, which is a part of the culture of the Han nationality. At the same time, it is different from Cai Hou paper in many production details. It is more suitable for the sacrificial activities in the western Guangdong, Lingnan, in terms of material selection, proportion, and water seepage. Dongshui Papermaking craft, with local characteristics in Yangxi, is the embodiment of the localization of Han culture in western Guangdong, Lingnan.

· Scientific value

Dongshui papermaking Craftsmanship is a complete reservation of traditional Chinese papermaking craft, and a historical microcosm of ancient working people's exploration of scientific production technique. It has corroborative significance for the study of the development of related industries in China, especially the paper industry and other scientific and technological history.

身本土特色纸文化产生和发展的实物见证。东水造纸技艺始于蔡侯纸制作技艺，是汉民族文化的一部分，同时又在许多制作细节方面有别于蔡侯纸，选材、比例、渗水性等方面更适用于岭南粤西地区的祭祀活动习惯，具有阳西本土特色，是汉文化在岭南粤西地区本土化的体现。

· 科学价值

东水造纸技艺是中国传统造纸工艺的完整保留，是古代劳动人民探索科学生产技术的历史缩影，其对于研究我国相关产业尤其是造纸业等科学技术史具有佐证意义。

Main Inheritor

There isn't representative inheritor of Dongshui Paper Making Craftsmanship in provincial and municipal intangible cultural heritage projects. At present, there are three inheritance genealogies that can be traced back relatively completely to the project.

Li Yingjun Family

1st generation: Li Yingjun, male, was born in the period of Xianfeng in Qing Dynasty. He engaged in papermaking for about 30 years.

2nd generation: Li Yanchang, born in the period of Tongzhi in Qing Dynasty, the son of Li Yingjun, studied from his father, and engaged in papermaking for about 25 years.

3rd generation: Li Zhenquan, was born in 1903, the 5th son of Li Yanchang, studied from his father. He has specializing in papermaking for about 50 years.

4th generation: Li Xiuyuan, was born in June, 1949. He is a villager in Longgutian Village of Dongshui. Li Xiuyuan was influenced by elder generation, and followed his father to make paper after graduating from junior high school. He has engaged in papermaking for more than 50 years.

主要传承人

东水造纸技艺项目暂无省市级非物质文化遗产项目代表性传承人，该项目目前可较为完整追溯的传承谱系有以下三支。

黎英骏系

一代：黎英骏，男，咸丰年间人，从业时间约30年。

二代：黎衍昌，黎英骏之子，同治年间人，师从其父，从业时间约为25年。

三代：黎振全，黎衍昌第五子，生于1903年，师从其父，专攻造纸时间约50年。

四代：黎秀源，男，生于1949年6月，东水龙骨田村村民。黎秀源受父辈影响，初中毕业就跟随父亲造纸，已从业50多年。

黎居贵系

一代：黎居贵，男，咸丰年间人，从业时间约为50年。

二代：黎光朝，黎居贵次子，咸丰同治时期人，师从其父，从业时间约为40年。

三代：黎振声，黎光朝第三子，光绪年间人，师从其父，从业时间约为40年。

四代：黎春源，黎振声长子，生于民国时期，东水龙骨田村村民，师从其父，从业时间约有65年。

五代：黎达儒，黎春源长子，生于1965年8月，东水龙骨田村村民。他本人精通水车、水碓的安装维护，时常帮邻居维修造纸装置。他教授造纸技艺，积极保护传承东水造纸技艺。

黎振庆系

一代：无法溯源。

二代：黎振庆，清末民国时期人，东水龙骨田村村民，从业时间约40年。

三代：黎瑞源，黎振庆次子，生于20世纪40年代，师从其父，从业时间约50年。

四代：黎伙明，黎瑞源之子，生于1983年6月，东水龙骨田村村民，年轻时便随其父学习造纸。黎伙明打工之余常回家参与造纸活动，从业时间近20年。该支黎氏目前仍有年轻人在专职从事造纸，传承较好，传承人也较年轻。

Li Jugui Family

1st generation: Li Jugui, male, was born in the period of Xianfeng in Qing Dynasty. He engaged in papermaking for about 50 years.

2nd generation: Li Guangchao, the 2nd son of Li Jugui, was born in the period of Xianfeng and Tongzhi in Qing Dynasty, studied from his father. He engaged in papermaking for about 40 years.

3rd generation: Li Zhensheng, the 3rd son of Li Guangchao, born in the period of Guangxu in Qing Dynasty, studied from his father. He engaged in papermaking for about 40 years.

4th generation: Li Chunyuan, the eldest son of Li Zhensheng, was born in the period of Republic of China. He is a villager in Longgutian Village, Dongshui. He studied from his father and engaged in papermaking for about 65 years.

5th generation: Li Daru, the eldest son of Li Chunyuan, was born in August, 1965. He is a villager in Longgutian Village, Dongshui. He is proficient in the installation and maintenance of waterwheels and watermill and often helps neighbors repair papermaking installations. He teaches papermaking skills to protect and inherit Dongshui Papermaking Craftsmanship.

Li Zhengqing Family

1st generation: Untraceable.

2nd generation: Li Zhenqing, male, was born in the period of the late Qing Dynasty and the Republic of China, a villager in Longgutian Village, Dongshui. He engaged in papermaking for about 40 years.

3rd generation: Li Ruiyuan, the 2nd son of Li Zhenqing, was born in the 1940s. He studied from his father, and engaged in papermaking for about 50 years.

4th generation: Li Huoming, the son of Li Ruiyuan, was born in June, 1983, a villager in Longgutian Village, Dongshui. He learned papermaking craft from his father when he was young. He always goes back home to attend papermaking activities in his spare time. He has engaged in papermaking for nearly 20 years. There are young people in this branch of Li who are still engaged in papermaking full-time. The inheritance is good. Li Huoming is relatively young.

Part 7

Folklore

第七部分

民俗

疍家婚俗（疍家渔民婚俗）

广东省第二批省级非物质文化遗产名录

保护单位 阳江市闸坡镇渔家博览馆

The Tanka Wedding Custom（Tanka Fisherman Wedding Custom）

The Second Batch of the Provincial Intangible Cultural Heritage List of Guangdong Province

Protection Unit Fisherman Expo Hall of Zhapo Town, Yangjiang City

疍家渔民婚俗，是疍家渔民流传的一种特殊婚嫁礼俗。广东阳江疍家婚俗主要流传于阳江市海陵岛闸坡镇、阳东区东平镇、阳西县沙扒镇、阳春市内河等地区。

2007年，疍家婚俗（疍家渔民婚俗）被列入广东省第二批省级非物质文化遗产名录。

疍家渔民婚俗的娶亲队伍

The Tanka Fisherman wedding team

The Tanka Fisherman Wedding Custom is a special wedding custom circulated by Tanka fishermen. The Tanka Fisherman Wedding Custom of Yangjiang, Guangdong, is mainly distributed in Zhapo Town of Hailing Island in Yangjiang City, Dongping Town of Yangdong District, Shapa Town of Yangxi County, the inland river of Yangchun City, etc..

In 2007, the Tanka Wedding Custom（the Tanka Fisherman Wedding Custom）was selected into second batch of the provincial intangible cultural heritage list of Guangdong Province.

Historical Origin

The fishermen used to be called the Tanka（i.e. the residents who engaged in fishing or water transportation in coastal harbors and inland rivers in Guangdong, Fujian, Hainan, and Guangxi, mostly lived in boats）. In history, Tanka people migrated from the area of Jiangsu and Zhejiang to the south, then settled in Guangdong, gradually growing into a large group of fishermen. "Some people took the boat as their home, and only the fishing and loading were their business. Some people lived on the water and did not do farming or weaving for no plough land. Both of them were called Tanka."（from *Pros & Cons of the Country*, written by Gu Yanwu）. According to *Yangjiang County Annals*（published in 2000）, Tanka fishermen of Yangjiang began in the Eastern Jin Dynasty .

Basic Content

According to the Wedding Custom circulated by the Tanka fishermen in Zhapo, after obtaining the consent of their parents, young lovers should invite a talkative matchmaker to arrange a marriage, and then choose an auspicious day to hold a grand wedding ceremony.

In the process of wedding, the matchmaker is a very important person. As the saying goes, "The matchmaker telling a white lie is like repairing the pot by mud." After the agreement from parents and the hard work of the matchmaker, the couple's parents light three sticks of incense in front of the memorial tablets of their each ancestors to tell the ancestors about the marriage. Then they have to wait for the incense to burn smoothly to the end. After the incense is successfully burned, in order to thank the matchmaker who tried her best to make the marriage success, they give the matchmaker money (the matchmaker's money) , a pig head and four pig feet (expressing their gratitude to the matchmaker). After knowing the two young people's lunar birthday, the matchmaker and the couple's parents ask an experienced fortune-teller to choose an auspicious date which is suitable for the wedding. After choosing the auspicious date, the man's family write a letter about the auspicious date on red cloth and then ask the matchmaker to take it to the woman's family, telling the exact date of giving presents and picking up the bride (called the Songbao Day) .

一场隆重的疍家渔民婚礼

A grand Tanka fisherman wedding ceremony

历史渊源

渔民旧称疍家（即在广东、福建、海南、广西沿海港湾和内河从事渔业或水上运输业的居民，多以船为家）。历史上疍家从江浙一带向南部沿途迁徙，后在广东定居，逐渐发展壮大成为广大渔民群体。“疍户者以舟楫为家，惟捕鱼装载为业，或编篷濒水而居，无土者，不事耕织，齐民曰为疍家”（顾炎武《天下郡国利病书》）。据《阳江县志》（2000年版）记载，阳江渔民疍家始见于东晋时期。

基本内容

根据闸坡疍家渔民流传的婚嫁礼俗，相恋的青年男女在得到父母的同意后，要请一个能说会道的媒人做媒，然后选择一个良辰吉日，举行一场隆重的婚礼仪式。

男女婚嫁之时，媒婆是一个很重要的人物，俗话说“媒婆呷（合）大话，补锅要泥擦（涂）”。经过媒婆的说合和父母的同意后，男女双方父母各自向自家的祖先神位奉上三炷香，告知祖先，然后等香顺利烧完。香顺利烧完后，为了答谢把这门婚事说成而尽心尽力奔走忙碌的媒婆，男女双方送给媒婆钱财（媒人钱）、猪头和四只猪脚（表示感激媒婆）。媒婆在取得男女双方出生年庚后陪同双方父母去请资深的算命先生选择一个适合他们生辰八字的吉日结婚。选定这个吉日后，男方家用红布制成吉日单由媒婆传递到女方家，告诉女方家准确的过礼接新娘日子（称送报日）。

临行仪式前几天，男女双方的渔船回港休息，亲戚的渔船成群结队停泊在港口的一方，筹备着婚礼的工作。男方用一只

礼船上载满丰盛的食品与财物
The gift boat is abundant in food and possessions

过礼中的疍家大姐
The Tanka elder sister is giving gifts

较大较新的船作为“过礼船”，这条礼船十分讲究，整条船油光水滑，船周围挂满了“红”（即红色的布条），装饰着许多鲜艳的花灯和彩带，充满喜庆氛围。“礼船”上有许多竹篮，装着食品和财物送到女方家船上。“礼船”上人们穿着色彩鲜艳的衣服，敲锣、打鼓对答咸水歌，喜气洋洋地把礼品送到女方的嫁船上。

到第二天凌晨3点的时候，男方挑选8位男女与新郎共9人随礼船前往女方船接新娘，女方船一般停泊在渡口西南边，男方船停泊在港口的东边，距离100米左右，按结婚仪式行事，女方船不能占男方船的大首位（指东边）。接新娘的人选很讲究，成年人要生育有子女，夫妻健在，不能重婚，表示祝福新娘、新郎将来幸福快乐。男性都穿着唐装，女性穿侧胸衫，上有布制纽扣。男性摇着礼船，燃烧着鞭炮，缓缓向女方船方向行驶。虽然是凌晨时分，但港里的渔船上已有许多人站在各自的船上看热闹。男方的礼船靠近女方船时，女方船人头攒动，新娘父母、姐妹、亲戚、朋友都招待男方来接新娘的人，伴娘则陪在新娘的身边。新娘身穿大红衫，头发盘

A few days before the ceremony, the fishing boats of the man's and woman's family return to the port to rest, and the relatives' fishing boats moor in groups on one side of the port, preparing for the wedding. A larger and newer boat is used as the gift boat. This “gift boat” is very particular. The oily and glossy boat is covered with “red” (red cloth strips) , decorated with many colorful lanterns and ribbons, and is full of festive mood. There are many bamboo baskets on the gift boat, containing food and possessions that will be taken to the woman's boat. The people on the gift boat wear brightly colored clothes, beating gongs as well as drums, singing salt-water songs, and give gifts to the woman's wedding boat happily.

At 3 a.m. of the next day, the bridegroom, with 8 men and women together, a total of 9 people, take the gift boat to pick up the bride from her family boat. The woman's boats moor on the southwest side of the port, and the man's boats moor on the east side, about 100 meters away. According to the wedding custom, the woman's family boats cannot take the first place of the man's family boats (the east side of the man's family boats) . It is very particular to choose the adults to pick up the bride, who cannot be bigamous as well as widowed, and must have children. It means those suitable people should benefit the bride and bridegroom, for blessing them live a long and happy life in the future. Men all wear Tang-style suits, while women wear side-chest shirts with cloth buttons. The men row the gift boat, burn firecrackers, and slowly move to the woman's boat. Although it is dark, a crowd of people in the port standing on their boats to watch the ceremony. When the gift boat approaches the woman's boat that is crowded and hilarious at that time, the bride's parents, sisters, relatives, and friends all greet those people that come to pick up the bride accompanied by the bridesmaids. The bride wears a red shirt, with hair in a silver bun, holding a bamboo fan in her right hand, and a small handkerchief in her left hand. The bride wears her hair in this silver bun and finish dress-up for a day. A prestigious married woman is hired especially, who not only has experience in grooming and makeup but also knows the process of the wedding. Firstly, boil a pot of hot water, pour the water into a new washbasin, and keep the water at a suitable temperature. Next, in the water, put some pomelo leaves or pomelo peel and add "Mafuzi" (the bran ash burned from wheat). Wash the bride's hair several times until clean, wipe it off with a dry towel while combing, divide the hair into three or five equal parts, weave it into a long braid, and roll it into a fist-shaped bun on top of the head. Fix the bun with a silver hairpin, and then fix the hair with a silver bun hoop. It is said that it can bring good fortune and ward off evils.

When the bride is at the ceremony, she needs to take 6 bridesmaids to the gift boat. The man should give red packets to the woman's parents, brothers and sisters, bridesmaids and the matchmaker. If the woman's family thinks it too little, some people will stand up for them naturally and prevent the bride from leaving. At that time, the matchmaker comes to mediate, and then the bridegroom must fill the red packets with more money to meet the requirements of the bride's family for taking the bride back smoothly. After the bride gets off the gift boat, people on the two "gift boats" need to sing the salt-water songs (called *Tan Gexiong*) to each other, which means to express the sense of their nostalgia for their parents and sisters. Many fishermen watch the ceremony, while the gift boat taking the bride and bridegroom to the men's boat. The scene is more crowded and lively than the scene in New Year and some festivals. After arriving at the bridegroom's boat, the bridegroom and bride should do the "Chong Huayuan", meaning that a mage is asked to hold up a sharp sword and chant incantations to ward off evils for the couple, and lets the bride cultivate herself and grow up more, and wish the couple to live a long life, love and respect each other until old. At that time, the bridegroom and bride should worship their ancestors first, heaven and earth next, and then the couple worship each other. Then worship by using chicken, pork, cakes, and sweets. They pour some wine, serve up some tea, offer incense, and burn paper money and ingots. Finally, they worship the bow of the boat.

The next morning after the wedding ceremony, the bride needs to cook in the kitchen, and bring water to her parents-in-law to wash face, showing her filial piety.

On the day of the wedding feast, the bridegroom and bride sing

着一个银髻，右手拿着竹扇，左手拿着小手绢。新娘梳这个银髻要一天的时间，专门聘请一位有威望的已婚妇女，既要具备一定的梳洗化妆经验，又要懂得新婚嫁娶的礼节程序。先烧开一锅热水，用一只新脸盆调好水温，水里放一些柚子叶或柚子皮，再加上“麻麸子”（用麦子烧出来的糠灰），为新娘洗头数次直至干净，边梳边用干毛巾擦干，将头发分成三或五等份，编成一条长辫子然后在头顶上卷成一个拳头形的髻，先用银钗固定，再用银髻箍罩固定头发，据说可以迎吉避邪，大吉大利。

新娘出嫁时带6个伴娘下礼船，男方要给女方父母、兄弟姐妹、伴娘、媒婆红包，如果女方家嫌少的话，自然有人为女方出头，不让新娘下礼船。这时候，媒婆要出面调解，男方就要增加红包的金额，以满足女方的要求，以顺利把新娘接回。新娘下礼船后，两条礼船上的人互唱咸水

一对新人喜笑颜开，媒婆陪同在旁

A Tanka couple smile happily and a matchmaker stand beside

歌（“叹哥兄”），用于表示对父母姐妹的留恋之情，围观的众多渔民目送礼船把新娘、新郎送到男方船，那情景和场面赛过逢年过节，热闹非常。到男方船后，新郎、新娘要“冲花园”——请一个法师擎起利剑作法，口念咒文，虔诚地为新郎、新娘辟邪除恶，让新娘修身养性，成人长进；祝夫妻长寿百岁，白发齐眉。这时新郎、新娘要一拜祖先，二拜天地，三拜夫妻（对拜）；然后使用鸡、猪肉、糕点、糖果进行拜祭，接着斟酒，敬茶，奉香，燃烧纸钱、元宝，最后拜船头。

仪式后的第二天早晨，新娘要进厨房煮饭，端水给家公、家婆洗脸，以表孝敬。

在喝喜酒这一天，新郎、新娘都由伴郎、伴娘陪同，在礼船最大的船舱里对唱咸水歌，气氛很热闹，吸引亲戚和小孩前来观看。礼船与亲戚的船停泊在一起，成行成列，头尾相连。酒席设在各尾大船的船舱甲板上。等到下午3点开席时，各人都找自己喜欢的位置坐下喝喜酒。首席要设新郎新娘席，包括父母、伴郎、伴娘和媒婆等人。首席要凑齐整整10人，表示十全十美，将来有财、有物、有后代。酒席后新娘要端甜茶（用红枣、瓜茶、桂圆、冰糖做的糖水）给家公、家婆和其他长辈饮用。长辈饮茶后，要给新娘一个红包。

待三朝后（即出嫁后第三天）新娘要回娘家洗髻（洗头）。

以上就是疍家渔民新娘出嫁的过程，此习俗一直流传至今。

过礼仪式

Giving-gifts ceremony

salt-water song accompanied by the best men and bridesmaids, in the largest cabin of the gift boat. The lively atmosphere attracts relatives and children to watch. The gift boat is moored together with other relatives' boats and those boats connected end to end are all in rows. The feast is set up on the cabin deck of each boat. When the feast starts at 3 p.m., everyone finds their position to enjoy their meal. The first table is prepared for the married couple, including their parents, best men, bridesmaids, matchmakers, etc.. The table needs to be seated ten people, which means perfect in every aspect and abundant in possessions and generations in the future. After the feast, the bride should serve sweet tea (made of red dates, melon tea, longan, and rock sugar) to her parents-in-law and the elders respectively. After that, they will all give the bride a red packet.

On the third day after the wedding ceremony, the bride has to go back to her parent's home to wash her bun (referring to washing her hair) .

The above is the processes of Tanka fishermen's wedding, which has been inherited till now.

队伍唱着渔歌迎亲

The wedding team is singing fishing songs to pick up the bride

Main Features

(1) Different from the ordinary wedding custom, the boat is used as the carrier to hold the wedding on the water at night, which is called "Yejia", the night wedding.

(2) The long-term water life of fishermen, which made the unique water culture phenomenon of Tanka fishermen, has extensive mass and folk inheritance.

(3) The complicated etiquette and grand wedding ceremony reflect the great importance of the crowd of Tanka to marriage and the pursuit of a happy life.

Great Value

· Historical value

Tanka Fishermen's Wedding in Zhapo can be traced back to the Eastern Jin Dynasty, and has passed down as a kind of folk culture for a long time, around more than a thousand years till now.

· Cultural value

Tanka Fishermen Wedding in Zhapo is a prominent form of the traditional culture of the Zhapo people in Hailing Island, representing the spiritual pursuit, life belief, as well as value orientation of Zhapo fishermen, and showing hope and yearning for a happy life.

· Aesthetic value

The unique costumes of the Tanka wedding reflect the artistic aesthetics, superb craftsmanship, and creative ability of the Tanka fishermen.

主要特征

（1）与普通的婚嫁习俗不同，疍家婚礼是以船为载体，在水上并在夜间举行，即“夜嫁”。

（2）渔民在长期的水上生活中，形成了疍家渔民独特的水文化现象，具有广泛的群众性和民间传承性。

（3）繁缛的礼仪、隆重的婚礼，体现了疍家人对婚姻的极度重视以及对幸福美好生活的追求和希冀。

重要价值

· 历史价值

闸坡渔民疍家婚礼最早可追溯到东晋时期，作为一种民间的生活习俗流传下来，延续至今已有一千多年的历史。

· 文化价值

闸坡渔民疍家婚礼是海陵岛闸坡人民传统文化的突出表现形式，代表了闸坡渔民的精神追求、人生信仰、价值取向，代表着他们对幸福美好生活的向往。

· 审美价值

疍家婚礼独特的服饰打扮体现了疍家渔民的艺术审美观，同时展现出疍家高超的手工艺水平和创作才能。

疍家婚嫁队伍正在巡游

The Tanka wedding team is parading

主要传承人

Main Inheritors

杨美福，男，1962年出生于阳江市闸坡镇，从艺起始于1979年，是疍家婚俗第五代传人。深受其母亲影响，从小开始学习传统婚嫁风格和技艺，擅长对疍家婚俗进行创作设计和研究。多年来，他不断提高自己的艺术修养，积极探索和实践，每年每届配合南海（阳江）开渔节组织100多人举行疍家渔民婚俗巡游活动，并收藏3000余件渔家古物，有银髻、银钗、梅花肚兜链、银裤链等藏品。杨美福于2005年8月1日建立阳江市闸坡镇渔家博览馆。杨美福现为广东省第二批省级非物质文化遗产项目代表性传承人。

Yang Meifu, male, was born in 1962 in Zhapo Town, Yangjiang City. He started his career in 1979, the 5th-generation inheritor of the Tanka Wedding Custom. Influenced by his mother, he has learnt traditional wedding styles and crafts since childhood. He is good at the research on creative design of Tanka wedding. Over the years, he has continuously improved his artistic accomplishment and literacy, exploring and practicing actively. In the Nanhai (Yangjiang) Fishing Festival every year, he organizes more than 100 people to hold a parade of Tanka fishermen wedding custom and collects more than 3,000 pieces of fishermen's antiquities, such as silver bun, silver hairpin, bellyband chain with plum blossom, silver trousers chain and other collections. The Fishermen Expo Hall in Zhapo Town, Yangjiang City was established by Yang Meifu on August 1, 2005. He is the representative inheritor of the second batch of the provincial intangible cultural heritage projects of Guangdong Province now.

杨美福（右二）
Yang Meifu (The second person from the right)

吴银伟（前）
Wu Yinwei (front)

吴银伟，女，1978年2月出生于阳江市闸坡镇。2005年从艺，跟随杨美福深入研究疍家渔民婚礼的每项程序并建立疍家渔民咸水渔歌团队研究基地，在继承的基础上求发展。吴银伟现为广东省第六批省级非物质文化遗产项目代表性传承人。

Wu Yinwei, female, was born in February 1978 in Zhapo Town, Yangjiang City. In 2005, she followed Yang Meifu to study every process of Tanka Fishermen's Wedding Custom and established the Tanka Fishermen Salt-water Fishing Song Team Research Base to seek development based on inheritance. She is the representative inheritor of the sixth batch of the provincial intangible cultural heritage project of Guangdong Province now.

高流河墟

广东省第三批省级非物质文化遗产名录

保护单位 阳春市非物质文化遗产保护中心

Gaoliu River Market

The Third Batch of the Provincial Intangible Cultural Heritage List of Guangdong Province

Protection Unit Yangchun Intangible Cultural Heritage Protection Center

Gaoliu River Market was originally a market formed on the banks of the Gaoliu River on the fourth day of the fifth lunar month and the fourteenth day of the seventh lunar month every year and only the market day on the fourth day of the fifth lunar month is preserved. Centering on the bridge across the Gaoliu River, the river market extends along both sides of Gaoliu River. This is a market day naturally formed by the villagers in the agricultural society in order to go shopping easily before the lunar festival. Because it is only once or twice a year, it is unique. Every market day, people from Yangchun, Yangjiang, Gaozhou, Xinyi, Dianbai, and other places gather on both sides of the Gaoliu River for the market, which is very lively. According to folk legends, bamboo and wooden wares bought on the market day will never be damaged by worms after being soaked in the Gaoliu River. In 2009, Gaoliu River Market was selected into the third batch of the provincial intangible cultural heritage list of Guangdong Province.

高流河墟原为每年农历五月初四、七月十四在高流河畔形成的墟集，现仅保留五月初四一个墟日。河墟以横跨高流河的大桥为中心，沿高流河两岸延伸。这是农耕社会周围村民在农历节日前为方便购物而自然形成的墟日。因其一年仅有一两次，故显独特。每年墟日，来自阳春、阳江、高州、信宜、电白等地的人们会聚于高流河两岸赶集，非常热闹。据民间传说，墟日买的竹器、木器浸泡过高流河水后会永不被虫蛀。2009 年，高流河墟被列入广东省第三批省级非物质文化遗产名录。

高流河上盛大的墟市
The crowded market by the Gaoliu River

历史渊源

阳春市城北10多公里处有一条漠阳江支流，名为高流河。该河发源于合水镇东南部五点梅峰西南山谷，河长17.7公里，自东向西流入漠阳江。高流河在明代之前称“高僚河”（读音为“高老”，含义为“高凉俚僚人”），官方又写作“高僚水”。明嘉靖十年（1531），随着俚、僚部族与汉族的逐渐同化，时任阳春县令的俞文英与当时在北京任儒学教授的阳春人钟杰共议，取“高山流水识知音”的古义，把该河改名为“高流河”。同时把“高僚墟”更名为“高流墟”，民间亦有人称“高留河”“高留墟”。据明万历年间《阳春县志》载，“高流墟，城西22里，在南在堡牛栏湾（合水镇高流河桥边，距离县城13公里），迴龙寺（已废）前，无铺户，每年以农历五月初四和七月十四日为墟期”。农历七月十四日墟期在新中国成立后被废，其原因主要是当日为“鬼节”，加上群众认为只有上午趁墟，日中散市，时间较短，来回很不方便，故只保留每年农历五月初四的墟期。该集市主要买卖铁、竹、木制的农具。明万历十六年（1588），“高流墟”被载入《阳春县志》。阳春全县当时有16个集市，高流河墟就是其中之一。

高流河墟历史悠久，从有历史记载以来距今有400多年历史。从县志记载古代高凉俚、僚人在高僚河畔烽火台下举行一年一度的原始商品交易会遗俗这一史料推算，高流墟的起源时间应该更早。据《三国志》记载，当时三国之一的吴国（229—280年）皇帝孙权曾派吕岱、薛综等部属将领率兵征剿高凉俚僚，说明三国时高凉地区（阳春、阳江地域）已聚居着大批

Historical Origin

More than ten kilometers north of Yangchun City, there is a tributary of the Moyang River called the Gaoliu River. The river originates from the valley southwest of Wudianmei Mountain in the southeast of Heshui Town. The river is 17.7 kilometers long and flows into the Moyang River from east to west. Before the Ming Dynasty, the Gaoliu River was called the “Gaoliao River” (pronounce as “Gao lao”, meaning “Gaoliang Liliao people”), and “Gaoliao Water” in official terms. In the ten years of the Jiajing period in the Ming Dynasty (1531), with the gradual assimilation of the Li, Liao, and Han people, Yu Wenying, the governor of Yangchun County at that time, negotiated with Zhong Jie, a Yangchun native who was a professor of Confucianism in Beijing at that time, determined to take the ancient meaning of “high mountain and running water know the sound of bosom friends” and then rename the river “Gaoliu River”. At the same time, “Gaoliao Market” was renamed as “Gaoliu Market”, and some people also called “Gaoliu River” and “Gaoliu Market”. According to *Yangchun County Annals* published in the Wanli period of the Ming Dynasty, “Gaoliu Market, is about 22 *li* west of the city, in the Nanzaibao Niulan Bay (near the Gaoliu River Bridge in Heshui Town, 13 kilometers away from the county), in front of Huilong Temple (was abandoned), where there are no shops. Every year, the fourth day of the fifth lunar month and the fourteenth day of the seventh lunar month are identified as the Market Day.” The Market Day on the fourteenth day of the seventh lunar month was abandoned after the founding of the People's Republic of China because the day was the “Ghost Festival”. People thought that they could only come to the market in the morning and end the market at noon. The time was short and it was very inconvenient to go back and forth. Therefore, They preserved only the fourth day of the fifth lunar month as the market day every year. People sold iron, bamboo, and wood farm implements in the market. In the 16th year of the Wanli period in the Ming Dynasty (1588), “Gaoliu Market” was recorded in the *Yangchun County Annals*. There were 16 markets in Yangchun County at that time, and Gaoliu Market was one of them.

Gaoliu River Market has a long history with more than 400 years according to historical records. However, according to the annals, ancient Gaoliang Li and Liao people held an annual primitive commodity market under the beacon tower on both sides of the Gaoliu River, so the origin of the Gaoliu Market should be traced back even earlier. According to the *Records of the Three Kingdoms*, the Emperor Sun Quan of Wu (229 AD-280 AD) that was one of the

Three Kingdoms at that time, dispatched Lü Dai, Xue Zong, and other subordinates to lead troops to conquer Gaoliang Li and Liao Tribes, indicating that during the period of the Three Kingdoms, the Gaoliang area (Yangchun and Yangjiang areas) had been inhabited by a large number of Li and Liao people. What was the specific reason for the formation of Gaoliu Market? The *Yangchun County Annals* published in 1996 records that "it originally was a kind of temple fair". A legend has been passed down to this day. That is, there was a severe drought one year, the grain harvest failed, and thieves were everywhere. Among them, a gang of thieves planned to rob homes at the Dragon Boat Festival. However, the secret was leaked, the villagers in Gaoliu packed up their belongings and took refuge in the woods. On the fourth day of the fifth lunar month, the villagers found that many strangers were in their ranks. Knowing that they were robbers, they reported to the official government and agreed on a code. On that night, soldiers surrounded the camp where refugees were stayed on the banks of the Gaoliu River, catching all the thieves. To commemorate this victory, the villagers gathered on the bank of the river on the fourth day of the fifth lunar month to celebrate, and gradually developed into an annual market period. Due to the abundance of bamboo and wood in the local area as well as bamboo and wood products, Gaoliu River Market has become a trading market for bamboo and wood products.

In the first year of Liang Datong (535 AD) , Feng Bao, the prefecture chief of Gaoliang, married Madam Xian. Later, his son Feng Pu served as the prefecture chief of Yangchun, his grandson Feng Ang served as the prefecture chief of Moyang, and his great-grandson Feng Zhidai served as the prefectural governor of

俚、僚部族。高流河墟具体是什么原因形成的？1996年出版的《阳春县志》记载"原属山会形式"，有一传说流传至今：有一年天大旱，粮食歉收，盗贼四起，其中有一匪帮计划在端午节打家劫舍，消息走漏，高流村民纷纷收拾家当，到林中躲避。五月初四那天，村民发现许多陌生人混在他们的队伍中，知晓是强盗，报告官府，约定暗号，当晚官兵包围了高流河畔难民集中的营地，把盗贼一网打尽。为了纪念这次胜利，村民们每逢五月初四都在河边沙滩上聚会庆祝，逐渐发展为一年一度的墟期。由于当地盛产竹木，竹木制品丰富，高流河墟便成为民间约定俗成的竹木制品交易市场。

梁大同元年（535），高凉太守冯宝与冼夫人结婚，后其子冯仆任阳春太守、其孙冯盎任漠阳太守、曾孙冯智戴任春州刺史，至武周万岁通天二年（697）冯智戴逝世，冼夫人及其儿孙统辖、治理阳春地域共163年。其间冼夫人力排阻力，不搞分裂，坚持国家统一，加强民族团结，使岭南各族人民安居乐业，受到阳春人民的拥

墟市开设在高流河的两岸

The market is opened on both sides of Gaoliu River

人们在高流河边清洗竹具
People wash bamboo products by Gaoliu River

戴和崇敬。建在高流河后面的迴龙寺，里面不仅供有三公、观音，还有冼夫人、冯宝等的灵位供群众祭拜，而农历五月初四和七月十四的祭拜活动使高流河墟墟期更加固定，墟场除竹木制品外，本村和邻村的生意人还会携带当地土特产前来交易。

高流河墟的繁荣长盛不衰，与高流河的水有密切的关系。这里流传着一个神奇的传说：明万历初年，合水高河村有一钟姓人家，三代以耕田为生。有一次洪水过后，钟氏的三个孙子孙女同时长痱子，全身长满红斑点，奇痒难忍，服了不少药都不见好转。端午节前一天，钟氏带三个孙子孙女到附近山坡采集粽叶，途经高流河，因河水不深，天气闷热，三个小孩忍不住跳下河里戏水。谁知第二天，小孩们身上的痱子全都没了，身上也不痒了。这一神奇之事一下子便在高河村传开了，不少患热痱的孩子纷纷到河里洗澡，但此时却没有任何效果。第二年端午节前一天，全村的小孩子都到高流河洗澡，神奇的事又发生了——凡长痱子的，痱子都不见了，没长痱子的，身体更健壮了。钟氏从小孩们的经历想到了竹木制品。这一年的

Chunzhou. Feng Zhidai died in the second year of the Tongtian period of Wu Zhou (697) . Madam Xian with her children and grandchildren ruled and governed the Yangchun area for a total of 163 years. During this period, Madam Xian fought against resistance, prohibited division, and insisted on and strengthened national unity, so that the people of all ethnic groups in Lingnan lived and worked in peace and contentment. She was supported and revered by the people of Yangchun. The Huilong Temple built behind the Gaoliu River not only enshrines Sangong and Guanyin but also memorial tablets of Madam Xian, Feng Bao, of the masses to worship. The worship activities on the fourth day of the fifth lunar month and the fourteenth day of the seventh lunar month make the dates of Gaoliu market day more specific. In addition to bamboo and wood products, business people from their own village and neighboring villages will also bring local specialities to trade.

The long-term prosperity of the Gaoliu Market is closely related to the water of the Gaoliu River. There is a magical legend circulating here: In the early years of the Wanli period in the Ming Dynasty, there was a Zhong family in Gaohe Village, Heshui. Three generations of them lived a life by farming. After a flood, three grandchildren of the Zhong family suffered from the prickly heat at the same time, with red spots all over their bodies, and the itching was unbearable. After taking a lot of medicine, they did not get better. The day before the Dragon Boat Festival, Zhong took his three grandchildren to collect reed leaves at a nearby hillside passing through the Gaoliu River. The river was not deep and the weather was muggy, so the three children couldn't help but jump into the water to play. The next day, the children's prickly heat was all healed, and their bodies were no longer itchy. This magical thing suddenly spread in Gaohe Village, and many children suffering from prickly heat went to the river to bathe, but it had no effect. On the day before the Dragon Boat Festival of the following year, all

热闹的竹具买卖场景
Bustling scene of selling bamboo products

the children in the village went to the Gaoliu River to bathe, and a magical thing happened again—all those suffering prickly heat were healed, and those who did not have prickly heat became stronger. Zhong thought of bamboo and wood products from the children's experience. On the day before the Dragon Boat Festival, he put and soaked his bamboo and wood products in the Gaoliu River, then sold them in Gaoliu Market. Since then, the magical thing has appeared again—the bamboo baskets that have not been soaked in the Gaoliu River have been damaged by worms, but the bamboo wares soaked in the Gaoliu River have been as bright as new. This thing has been passed down widely. Since then, on the fourth day of the fifth lunar month (the day before the Dragon Boat Festival) , every child who comes to Gaoliu Market bathe in the river. The bamboo and wood products bought by adults are soaked in the river for a while. This custom has been passed down to this day.

The annual Gaoliu Market, from ancient times to the present, naturally forming a market, has never been interrupted. People and merchants far and wide are attracted by magical legends. The day before the Dragon Boat Festival each time, they gather here to trade. In 2006, the Guangdong Photographers Association organized a photographer group to Gaoliu Market to collect folk customs. Since 2004, on the fourth day of the fifth lunar month, the main leaders of the Yangjiang, Yangchun Municipal Party Committee and Government have visited Gaoliu Market, having fun with the people. A bell-ringing ceremony and related cultural activities have been held, which have played a leading role in the inheritance and development of the Gaoliu River Market.

端午节前一天，他把自家的竹木制品放进高流河里浸泡后拿到高流河墟卖。神奇之事又出现了——没浸泡过高流河水的竹箩等被虫蛀坏了，但浸泡过高流河河水的竹器却鲜亮如新。此事一传十，十传百，此后每逢五月初四（端午节前一天），凡到高流河墟的小孩都会到河里沐浴一番，大人们都会把买到的竹木制品拿到河里浸泡一会。此习俗一直流传至今。

一年一度的高流河墟，从古到今，自然成集，从未断过，远近的百姓与商贾为神奇传说所吸引，每逢端午节前一天，云集于此进行交易。2006年，广东省摄影家协会组织摄影家采风团到高流河墟采风；2004年起，每年农历五月初四，阳江、阳春市委市政府主要领导都会莅临高流河墟与民同乐，并举行撞钟开墟仪式和相关的文化活动，对高流河墟的传承和发展起到了主导作用。

今日的高流河墟规模已经十分宏大
Nowadays, Gaoliu River Market is on a grand scale

基本内容

高流河墟在每年端午节前的一天成墟。墟址以横跨高流河的一座大桥为中心，沿高流河两岸东西延伸和沿省道113线南北延伸各数里。是日，当地的农民和周边县市的商贾便带着农具、工艺品、生活器具等竹木制品以及农副产品到这里交易。特别是当地的编织工匠，每当临近墟期，他们便夜以继日地编织、加工竹木器。墟期前三天，即农历五月初一，他们就开始到河滩选地盘、搭档口，抢占商机。高流河墟摆卖的竹器主要有箩筐、畚箕、竹筛、菜篮、竹椅、谷围、竹梯等，木器主要有台、凳、椅、水桶、秧盆、扁担、梯等，还有竹、木、藤、草工艺品等。相传，在这里购买的竹器和木器放进高流河水中浸泡，就会永不被虫蛀，而小孩在端午节前一天在高流河里洗澡，日后体魄也会格外健壮，不生痱子，此习俗一直延续至今。除此之外，高流河墟还有几个传说：高流河墟当日下午必下雨；趁高流河墟必须连去三年，才能带来好运；未婚男女相约趁墟，大多能喜结良缘；趁高流河墟要早去早回，下午最后离墟者必死；等。这些世代相传的神奇传说，极大

Basic Content

Gaoliu River Market is formed on the day before the Dragon Boat Festival annually. The market is centered on a bridge spanning the Gaoliu River, extending from east to west along both sides of the Gaoliu River, and from north to south along Provincial Highway 113 for several li. On that day, local farmers and merchants from surrounding counties and cities bring their bamboo and wood products such as agricultural tools, handicrafts, and living utensils, as well as agricultural and sideline products to trade here. Especially the local weaving craftsmen work around the clock to weave and process bamboo and wood wares when approaching the market day. Three days before the market day, the first day of the fifth lunar month, they begin to go to the river banks to choose a site to seize business opportunities. The bamboo wares sold in Gaoliu River Market mainly include baskets, dustpans, bamboo sieves, vegetable baskets, bamboo chairs, grain walls, bamboo ladders, etc.. Wooden wares mainly include tables, benches, chairs, buckets, seedling pots, poles, ladders, etc.. There are also bamboo, wood, rattan, and grass handicrafts, etc.. According to legends, if the bamboo and wooden wares purchased here are soaked in the Gaoliu River, they will never be damaged by worms. If the children bathe in the Gaoliu River on the day before the dragon boat Festival, they will be exceptionally strong in the future, and they will not have prickly heat. This custom has continued to this day. In addition, there are several legends in Gaoliu River Market: It will rain on the afternoon of the market day. People should go three times continuously to bring good luck. Unmarried men and women dating in the market mostly can tie the knot. People should go to the Gaoliu River Market and return as early as possible, and the last person leaving the market in the afternoon will die, etc.. These mythical legends passed down from generation to generation

高流河墟上售卖的竹制手工艺品
Bamboo handicrafts are sold on Gaoliu River Market

have greatly enriched the cultural connotation of Gaoliu River Market, and it has also added a lot of mystery and attraction to Gaoliu River Market, making Gaoliu River Market a famous "strange market" far and near. Bamboo and wooden wares were the most popular commodities in Gaoliu Market. However, with the development of the times, various modern home appliances, gold and silver jewelry, clothing, etc. have also appeared in the Gaoliu River Market, adding elements rich in the characteristics of the times into the ancient market, so that Gaoliu River Market have infinite vitality and will last forever.

On the early morning of the fourth day of the fifth lunar month, the local government holds a ceremony to open the Gaoliu River Market—ringing the big bell, setting off firecrackers, organizing theatrical performances, etc., to have fun with the people. From 10 a.m., tens of thousands of marketers from Xinxing, Luoding, Yangjiang, Enping, and other places from neighboring counties gather. Suddenly, the river beaches and highways are crowded with people, bustling and spectacular. In addition to merchants, most of people come for shopping and sightseeing. In addition, some literati come to collect the folk customs. They recite poems and make couplets under the shade of the trees, and talking while drinking. There are also young man and woman making a date to meet near the river. Relatives and friends who come from afar are invited to reunite and share their feelings. The local villagers around Gaoliu River Market are not in a hurry to go to the market. They know when Gaoliu River Market is the most bustling by listening to the sound at home. This is because whenever crowds of people gather in Gaoliu River Market, there will be bursts of laughter floating out from the river. Then the local villagers go to the Market to buy things. However, they don't stay for a long time. Shortly after noon, they will rush home. First, it will rain on the afternoon of market day. Second, they believe that the last person leaving the market will die.

地丰富了高流河墟的文化内涵，也为高流河墟平添了不少神秘感和吸引力，使高流河墟成为远近闻名的一大“怪墟”。竹器、木器原是高流河墟自古以来成交最火爆的商品，但随着时代的发展，各种现代家电用品、金银首饰、服装等也登场于高流河墟，为高流河墟注入富有时代特色的元素，使高流河墟有了无限的生命力，历久不衰。

五月初四一早，当地政府会在高流河墟举行开墟仪式——撞响大钟、燃放爆竹、组织文艺演出等，与民同乐。上午10时始，来自邻近的新兴、罗定、阳江、恩平等地的赶集者，数以万计云集而来。一时间，河滩上、公路上人山人海，水泄不通，熙熙攘攘，蔚为壮观。他们当中除商贾外，大多数是来购物观光的，此外，也有文人墨客趁风而来，于林荫之下，吟诗作对，把盏阔谈；也有青年男女相约而至，在花间溪旁细斟月老相托之事；更有远道而来的亲友相邀团聚，共叙亲友情。而高流河墟周边的本地村民，并不急着去赶集，他们在家里听声音就能知道高流河墟什么时候最热闹，这是因为每当高流河墟人头攒动的时候，就会从河滩传来阵阵笑声。这时，当地的村民才趁墟买东西。然而，他们逗留的时间也不会很长，中午过后不久，他们就会急着回家，一是高流河墟当天下午必会下一阵雨，二是因为他们更相信“最后离墟者必死”这一说法。

热情的卖家展示着亲手制作的竹笼和竹篮
Enthusiastic sellers introduce their handmade bamboo cages and baskets

高流河墟的交易产品以当地的竹木器具为主
Local bamboo and wood products have always been the main commodities in Gaoliu River Market

主要特征

据记载，高流河墟成俗已有400多年的历史。历经沧桑，久经嬗变，形成了如下特征：

（1）一年一度。高流河墟只在每年的五月初四成墟。地点也仅限于高流河与省道113线交汇的方圆数千米。

（2）竹木制品一直以来都是高流河墟的主要商品，也是成交量最大的商品，见证了数百年来当地农业生产生活的演变。

（3）高流河墟被赋予了许多传奇色彩，这些传说为高流河墟平添了不少神秘感和吸引力，也为了解高流河墟对当地文化、经济、生产、生活所赋予的存在意义和产生的影响提供了研究依据。

重要价值

·历史价值

高流河墟历史悠久，据明朝《阳春县志》记载，高流河墟是阳春唯一的野地集市。高流河墟一年一度，自然成集，交易产品以当地盛产的竹木器具为主。在数百年的历史发展过程中，它从一个侧面反映了当地人民的智慧和勤劳，它通过商贾交

Main Features

Gaoliu River Market is recorded to have a history of more than 400 years. After vicissitudes of life and evolution, the following characteristics have been formed.

(1) The Market is set up once a year. Gaoliu River Market is only established on the fourth day of the fifth lunar month. The location is also limited to a few miles around the intersection of Gaoliu River and Provincial Highway 113.

(2) Bamboo and wooden products have always been the main commodities in Gaoliu River Market, and they are also the commodities with the largest transaction volume, witnessing the evolution of local agricultural production and life for hundreds of years.

(3) Gaoliu River Market is endowed with many legends, which add a lot of mystery and attraction to Gaoliu River Market and also provide a research basis for understanding the meaning and impact of the Gaoliu River Market on local culture, economy, production, and life.

Great Value

· Historical value

Gaoliu River Market has a long history. According to the records in the *Yangchun County Annals* of the the Ming Dynasty, Gaoliu River Market is the only wild market in Yangchun. Gaoliu River Market is a natural market annually. The trading products are mainly bamboo and wooden wares that are abundant in the local area. Hundreds of years of historical development reflect the wisdom and diligence of the local people from one side. It meets the needs of production and life through merchant activities and shows the reality of the people's safety and well-being life in this area. It is a historical legacy, which has important historical value for the study of the history of Yangchun, the local customs, and the development of productive forces in various eras after the formation of the market.

· Commercial value

Gaoliu River Market creates a precedent for the wild market trade of Yangchun. In the earliest days, people in Gaoliu Market mainly exchanged agricultural production and living tools, such as plows and rakes for farming, bamboo and wooden wares for harvesting and grain storage, etc.. With the changes of the times, the commodities traded in Gaoliu River Market have become more and more rich and diverse. Bamboo and wooden products have gradually developed from crude and simple ones in the past to beautiful and practical products. Nowadays, there is a wide range of commodities on sale in Gaoliu River Market, and everything is available. The number of people coming to the market is increasing every year. In recent years, the average number of people has reached more than 100,000, boosting the local economy effectively.

· Cultural value

As an ancient market, Gaoliu River Market has gone through vicissitudes of life. Many mythical legends have been passed down till today, making it a famous "strange market". And it has always attracted people to approach it, understand it, and study it. The first legend is that the bamboo and wooden wares bought by Gaoliu River Market soaked in the Gaoliu River are never damaged by worms. The second is that if children bathe in the water that day, they will not have prickly heat and become stronger in the future. The third legend is that it is rainy in the afternoon at Gaoliu River Market. The fourth legend is that people should go three times continuously to bring good luck. The fifth legend is that unmarried men and women dating in the market mostly can tie the knot. The rich, unique, and mysterious

易活动满足当地人民生产生活的需求，也体现了这个地区人民生活安康。它是一个历史产物，对研究阳春的历史、成墟后各时代社会的风土人情及生产力发展状况等均有重要的历史价值。

· 商业价值

高流河墟开创了阳春野集贸易之先河。最早，人们在高流河墟主要是交换农业生产生活工具，如农耕用的犁耙、收割和盛粮用的竹木器等。随着时代的变迁，高流河墟交易的商品也越来越丰富多样。其竹木制品从以前的粗陋简单逐步发展为美观实用。到今天，高流河墟上摆卖的商品琳琅满目，应有尽有，每年趁墟的人数呈增加趋势，近几年来，达10万人次以上，有力地拉动了当地的经济。

· 文化价值

高流河墟作为古墟，历经沧桑，许多神话般的传说一直流传至今，使之成为闻名遐迩的一大“怪墟”，并一直吸引人们走近它、了解它、研究它。其传说一：高流河墟买的竹木器放进高流河水中浸泡永不被虫蛀；传说二：小孩在墟日下水沐浴，日后不会生痱子，体魄会格外健壮；传说三：高流河墟当天下午必下雨；传说四：趁高流河墟要连续趁三年，才能给人带来好运；传说五：未婚男女相约趁墟，大多能喜结良缘；等等。丰富、独特、神秘的文化内涵，赋予了高流河墟无限的生命力，使之历久不衰，延续至今。

高流河墟上的销售场景

Sales scene on Gaoliu River Market

· 科学价值

高流河水浸泡过的竹木器为什么不会被虫蛀？小孩在墟日用高流河河水沐浴为什么不会生痱子？其河水中有什么特殊的成分和元素？这些未解之谜，都具有广阔的科学研究空间和价值。

cultural connotation endow Gaoliu River Market with infinite vitality, making it enduring till today.

· Scientific value

Why are the bamboo and wooden wares soaked in the Gaoliu River not damaged by worms? Why won't the children have prickly heat when they bathe in the Gaoliu River on the market day? What special ingredients and elements are there in the river? These mysteries have broad scientific research space and value.

主要传承人

Main Inheritors

黎文来，男，1956年5月出生。青年时期以种水稻、蔬菜为主，兼营梯、椅制作，后来在阳江市专营竹椅、竹梯制作。1970年开始跟随本村黎开远学艺，至今一直从事竹椅、竹梯制作。师徒两人培养出的传承人有黎开传、黎开华、黎开满等人。黎文来读小学时开始跟师父黎开远学艺，一直虚心求教，努力创新，善于比较和总结经验，做到精益求精，力求完美，可以说深得师父真传。在实践中，黎文来以一年一度的高流河墟为依托，多出精品，提高经济效益。近十年来，黎文来

黎文来
Li Wenlai

Li Wenlai, male, was born in May, 1956. He mainly planted rice and vegetables when he was young, and also ran ladders and chair manufacturing industries. Later, he specialized in the production of bamboo chairs and bamboo ladders in Yangjiang City. He began to learn the craft with Li Kaiyuan in his village in 1970 and has been engaged in the production of bamboo chairs and bamboo ladders. The inheritors cultivated by them include Li Kaichuan, Li Kaihua, Li Kaiman, etc.. Since he learned crafts from Li Kaiyuan in primary school, Li Wenlai has been able to seek advice with an open mind, and strive for innovation. He is good at comparing and summarizing experience, striving for perfection and excellence as well as receiving genuine teaching from the master. In practice, relying on the annual Gaoliu River Market, Li Wenlai produced more high-quality products and improved economic benefits. In the past ten years, the popularity of bamboo ladders and bamboo chairs made by Li Wenlai has been increasing day by day, so more and more merchants from surrounding counties and cities have came and called to order chairs and ladders. He is a very popular craftsman on the Gaoliu River Market. He is the representative inheritor of the first batch of intangible cultural heritage projects in Yangjiang City now.

Li Kaiyuan, male, was born in December 1949, is a native of Gaohe Village, Heshui Town, Yangchun City. He has been engaged in the production of bamboo chairs and ladders at home since 1979. At the age of 18, master Zhou from Yangjiang County (now Yangjiang City) came to the village to buy bamboo for making chairs and ladders, and lived in Li Kaiyuan's home. The master was deeply moved by the warm hospitality of the family. In return for their kindness, he passed on the craft of producing bamboo chairs and bamboo ladders to Li Kaiyuan without reservation. Li Kaiyuan is in his old age now and has made countless bamboo chairs and bamboo ladders. The bamboo wares he made are not only beautiful but also strong and durable, which are favored by merchants from far and near. He is the representative inheritor of the first batch of the intangible cultural heritage projects in Yangjiang City now.

制作的竹梯、竹椅的知名度日渐升高，周边县市来人来电订购椅、梯的客商越来越多，是高流河墟上相当受欢迎的手艺人。黎文来现为阳江市第一批非物质文化遗产项目代表性传承人。

黎开远，男，1949年12月生，阳春市合水镇高河村人，1979年至今一直在家从事竹椅、竹梯的制作。18岁那年，阳江县（现阳江市）一位周师傅到本村收购石竹、毛竹，代人制作椅子、梯子，并住在他家中。家人热情招待师傅，对方深受感动。为感恩图报，对方便将竹椅、竹梯的制作技术毫无保留地传授给黎开远。黎开远现已是古稀老人，经其手制作的竹椅、竹梯不计其数，他所制作的竹器不但美观，而且结实耐用，深受远近客商的青睐。黎开远现为阳江市第一批非物质文化遗产项目代表性传承人。

黎开远
Li Kaiyuan

端午节（端午逆水赛龙舟）

广东省第五批省级非物质文化遗产名录

保护单位 江城区文化馆

Dragon Boat Festival (Upstream Dragon Boat Race)

The Fifth Batch of the Provincial Intangible Cultural Heritage List of Guangdong Province

Protection Unit Jiangcheng District Cultural Center

端午逆水赛龙舟这一习俗主要在漠阳江沿岸的城西、城南和中洲三个街道办事处区域内的东砵村、那西村、洲头社区、洲尾社区、太傅渔洲社区、马洲社区、马福社区、麻演社区、西岸社区等地流行。

2013年，端午节（端午逆水赛龙舟）被列为广东省第五批省级非物质文化遗产。

Upstream Dragon Boat Race at the Dragon Boat Festival is mainly distributed in Dongbo Village, Naxi Village, Zhoutou Community, Zhouwei Community, Taifuyuzhou Community, Mazhou Community, Mafu Community, Mayan Community, Xi'an Community, and other places in three subdistrict offices of Chengxi, Chengnan, and Zhongzhou along the Moyang River.

In 2013, the Dragon Boat Festival (Upstream Dragon Boat Race) was selected into the fifth batch of the provincial intangible cultural heritage list of Guangdong Province.

历史渊源

江城区的端午赛龙舟习俗，据清《阳江县志》记载，"自初一至初五，棹龙舟，箫鼓喧阗。亲友相邀，结彩船游玩。备采物，放锦标，视先后为胜负。两岸老幼聚观，至晚始散"。由此可推断，江城端午逆水赛龙舟活动至今已经有近200年历史。

江城端午赛龙舟最早是为了纪念屈原，慢慢形成了独具特色的端午逆水赛龙舟大型民俗活动。据接受采访的东砵"白须"龙舟老龙种张陆艺（享年103岁，2013年春节期间去世）生前回忆，清末民初时期至20世纪30年代，是江城赛龙舟的盛行时期。在端午节这个传统节日里，民间每年都要举行盛大的端午逆水赛龙舟活动，且龙舟

Historical Origin

The dragon boat race custom in Jiangcheng District is recorded in *Yangjiang County Annals* of the Qing Dynasty. "From the first day to the fifth day, with the loud sound of gongs and drums, dragon boat race attracts relatives and friends to make an appointment to play together, and the winner will be determined by who puts the trophy first on board. The elderly and children on both riversides gather to watch, and don't disperse until the evening." It can be concluded that the Upstream Dragon Boat Race has a history of nearly 200 years.

The dragon boat race of the Jiangcheng District originated from the commemoration of Qu Yuan, and gradually formed a unique large-scale folk activity of Upstream Dragon Boat Race on the Dragon Boat Festival. According to an interview with Zhang Luyi who died at the age of 103 during the Spring Festival in 2013 and was the old Longzhong of Dongbo White-beard Dragon Boat, from the late Qing Dynasty and the early Republic of China to the 1930s, in the traditional "Dragon Boat Festival", a grand dragon boat race was held every year. It was a popular period of the Dragon Boat Race in Jiangcheng. The number of dragon boats was the most, with a total of 18 boats. There were dragon boats named as the Triangular White Flag of Shell Land, the Bamboo leaves Seven-star Flag of the Naxi North Emperor Temple, the White-beard Old Man of Huahao Great King Temple, the Big-ear Cow of the Xialai Four Sages Palace, the Yellow and Red Flag of the Shanglai Four Sages Palace, the Single White Flag of the Xi'an Ancestral Hall, the Double White Flag of the Shawei Ancestral Hall, the Red Flag of the Longtao Great King Temple, the Bamboo Leaves Red Flag of the Shangbao Five-king Temple, the Bamboo Leaves Red Flag of the Xiabao Five-king Temple, the Black-beard Old Man of the Dongbo Lin Family Ancestral Hall, the White-beard Old Man of the Dongbo Zhang Family Ancestral Hall, the Red-Beard Old Man of the Dongbo Zhang Family Ancestral Hall, the Single Belt Seven-star Flag of the Haiku North Emperor Temple, the Double Belt Seven-star flag of the Dazhashe North Emperor Temple, the Black-clad of the Xinju Great King Temple, the Red and Black Sign of the Tangjitou Great King Temple, and the Red-Flower Roll of the Guanguang Great King Temple, etc.. The participating rowers were young, strong, and lively. The participating masses were high in the mood. The atmosphere was warm.

Because of the outbreak of wars, Dragon Boat Race could only be carried out intermittently, and even interrupted for a while. By 1949, only 11 dragon boat teams including the White-Beard Old Man of Huahao Great King Temple, the Triangular White Flag of Shell Land, the Big-ear Cow of the Xialai Four Sages Palace, the Yellow and Red Flag of the Shanglai Four Sages Palace, the Single White Flag of the Xi'an Ancestral Hall, the Double White Flag of the Shawei Ancestral Hall, the Bamboo Leaves Red Flag of the Shangbao Five-king Temple, the Bamboo Leaves Red Flag of the Xiabao Five-king Temple, the Red-Beard Old Man of the Dongbo Zhang Family Ancestral Hall, the White-Beard Old Man of the Dongbo Zhang Family Ancestral Hall, the Bamboo leaves Seven-star Flag of the Naxi North Emperor Temple, participated in the competition. From the early days of founding of the Republic of China to the early 1960s, the Dragon Boat Race in Jiangcheng gradually resumed and was held every year. In 1956, the Central News Film Studio made a special trip to Jiangcheng, Yangjiang to make documentaries for screening across the country. The grand occasion of the Upstream Dragon Boat Race in Jiangcheng spread through movies all over the country. However, during the "Cultural Revolution", the Dragon Boat Race was regarded as the "four olds". All dragon boats in Jiangcheng were

数量最多，共有18艘，它们是蚬壳地的三角白旗、那西北帝庙的竹叶七星旗、华濠大王庙的白须公、下濑四圣宫的大耳牛、上濑四圣宫的黄红旗、西岸宗祠的单白旗、沙尾宗祠的双白旗、龙涛大王庙的红旗、上堡五王庙的竹叶红旗、下堡五王庙的竹叶红旗、东砵林氏宗祠的黑须公、东砵张氏宗祠的白须公、东砵张氏宗祠的红须公、海库北帝庙的单带七星旗、大闸社北帝庙的双带七星旗、新居大王庙的黑褂仔、塘基头大王庙的红黑签、观光大王庙的红花卷等。参与的划手年轻力壮，生龙活虎，群众情绪高昂，气氛热烈。

由于战争影响，赛龙舟活动只能断断续续地进行，甚至一度中断。至1949年仅有华濠大王庙的白须公、蚬壳地的三角白旗、下濑四圣宫的大耳牛、上濑四圣宫的黄红旗、西岸宗祠的单白旗、沙尾宗祠的双白旗、上堡五王庙的竹叶红旗、下堡五王庙的竹叶红旗、东砵张氏宗祠的红须公、东砵张氏宗祠的白须公、那西北帝庙的竹叶七星旗共11支龙舟队参加比赛。中华人民共和国成立初期至20世纪60年代

农历五月初一清晨举行旺龙仪式
Wanglong ceremony is held on the morning of the first day of the fifth lunar month.

初，江城赛龙舟活动逐渐恢复，每年都举行一次。1956年，中央新闻纪录电影制片厂工作人员专程来到阳江江城拍摄制作纪录片并在全国放映，江城逆水赛龙舟的盛况才通过电影传遍全国各地。但在“文革”时期，赛龙舟活动被视为“四旧”，江城所有龙舟被挖起砸毁，龙头、龙尾被拖进县人民广场焚毁，遭到毁灭性破坏，赛龙舟活动因此被中断。直至20世纪80年代初，江城赛龙舟活动才逐渐被恢复。1984年，渔洲、太傅、漠阳街道的干部、群众集资重新建造蚬壳地、华濠、上濑、下濑的4艘龙舟，并在当年端午节恢复赛龙舟活动。次年，城西街道的东砵村、那西村和中洲街道麻演村的干部、群众集资新造白须公、红须公、单白旗、双白旗、上堡红旗、下堡红旗、七星旗7艘龙舟，1985年共有11艘龙舟参加了端午赛龙舟活动。1997年，城南街道的群众又集资重造双带七星旗，参加当年的赛龙舟活动。目前，江城区域内有12艘传统龙舟。

江城每年农历五月初一、初三、初五举行的逆水赛龙舟大型民俗活动，受众面广，热闹非凡，现场人山人海，活动当天万人空巷，江城以及阳春、阳东、阳西各县镇城乡的群众纷纷前来观看、助威，邻近的江门、茂名、湛江、云浮等市县的游客以及港澳同胞、海外侨胞和外国游客也会专门前来观赛，使这一具有江城特色的赛龙舟民俗活动再次进入了一个全新的鼎盛时期。

基本内容

端午逆水赛龙舟活动在江城有着悠久的历史和传统以及广泛、深厚的群众基础，每年的农历五月初一、初三、初五（端午节）期间都要举行这项重要的民俗

dug up and smashed, and the dragon heads and tails were dragged into the People's Square of the county and burned down, so the dragon boat race was interrupted. It was not until the early 1980s that the Dragon Boat Race in Jiangcheng gradually resumed. In 1984, the cadres and masses of Yuzhou, Taifu, and Moyang streets raised funds to rebuild four dragon boats including the boats of Shell Land, Huahao, Shanglai, and Xialai, resuming the dragon boat race on the Dragon Boat Festival that year. The following year, the cadres and masses raised funds to build 7 new dragon boats including White-beard Old Man, Red-beard Old Man, Single White Flag, Double White Flag, Shangbao Red Flag, Xiabao Red Flag, and Seven-Star Flag Dragon Boats. In 1985, a total of 11 dragon boats participated in the Dragon Boat Race. In 1997, the people in Chengnan street raised funds to rebuild the Double-belt Seven-star Flag Dragon Boat and joined the Dragon Boat Race that year. At present, there are 12 traditional dragon boats in Jiangcheng District.

Jiangcheng holds a large-scale folk activity of Upstream Dragon Boat Race on the first, third, and fifth day of the fifth lunar month every year. The audiences are wide and lively. At that time, there are thousands of people, attracting people from Jiangcheng and Yangchun, Yangdong, Yangxi to cheer up. It also attracts tourists from Jiangmen, Maoming, Zhanjiang, Yunfu, and other cities and counties, as well as Hong Kong and Macao compatriots, overseas Chinese, and foreign tourists. The folk custom activity of the dragon boat race with Jiangcheng characteristics has once again entered a new heyday.

Basic Content

Upstream Dragon Boat Race on the Dragon Boat Festival has a long history and tradition in Jiangcheng, as well as a broad and profound mass base. This important folk activity is held every year during the Dragon Boat Festival on the first, third, and fifth day of the fifth lunar month. Moyang River, the mother river of the Yangjiang people, is the platform of this folk activity, and the dragon boat is the carrier of the activity. From the starting point Dabutou (Shell Land) to the finishing point of Shanglai Zhoutou of Moyang River, the race is upstream from south to north on the river about 1,300 meters, so it is called the Upstream Dragon Boat Race. The population along the river is dense, row upon row of houses line the riverbank, and the river avenue and the roofs of private buildings by the river embankment are all viewing fields and viewing platforms, which can accommodate about 100,000 spectators.

The Upstream Dragon Boat Race in Jiangcheng has strong local characteristics. Each dragon boat belongs to the local temple or ancestral hall, and each has its banner and title. They are as follows.

活动。阳江人民的母亲河——漠阳江是该项民俗活动的平台，龙舟是活动的载体，从起点漠阳江大埠头（蚬壳地）至终点上濑洲头大约1300米的江（河）面上自南向北逆水而赛，故该活动被称为“逆水赛龙舟”。沿河人口密集，房屋鳞次栉比，河堤边的沿河大道、民房楼顶都是观看场和观看台，约可容纳10万名观众。

江城逆水赛龙舟活动具有浓厚的地方特色，每艘龙舟都归属当地神庙或姓氏宗祠，各有自己的旌旗和称谓，它们分别是：

十二支传统龙舟队赛前集合
Twelve traditional dragon boat teams are gathered before the race

- the Shanglai Four Sages Palace Dragon Boat in Zhoutou Community, Chengxi Street
- the Xialai Four Sages Palace Dragon Boat in Zhoutou Community, Chengxi Street
- the Bamboo Leaves Seven-star Flag of the Naxi North Emperor Temple Dragon Boat in Naxi Village, Chengxi Street
- the Red-beard Old Man Dragon Boat of the Zhang Family Ancestral Hall in Dongbo Village, Chengxi Street
- the White-beard Old Man Dragon Boat of the Zhang Family Ancestral Hall in Dongbo Village, Chengxi Street
- the Huahao Great King Temple Dragon Boat in Taifuyuzhou Community, Chengnan Street
- the Triangular White Flag of Shell Land in Mazhou Community, Chengnan Street
- the Double Belt Seven-star Flag of the Dazhashe North Emperor Temple in Sanpumafu Community, Chengnan Street
- the Shangbao Red Flag Five-king Temple in Mayan Community, Zhongzhou Street
- the Xiabao Red Flag Five-king Temple in Mayan Community, Zhongzhou Street
- the Single White Flag of the Xi'an Ancestral Hall in Xi'an Community, Zhongzhou Street
- the Double White Flag of the Shawei Ancestral Hall in Xi'an Community, Zhongzhou Street

- 城西街道洲头社区的四圣宫上濑龙舟
- 城西街道洲尾社区的四圣宫下濑龙舟
- 城西街道那西村的那西北帝庙竹叶七星旗龙舟
- 城西街道东砵村的张氏宗祠红须公龙舟
- 城西街道东砵村的张氏宗祠白须公龙舟
- 城南街道太傅渔洲社区的大王庙华濠龙舟
- 城南街道马洲社区的蚬壳地三角白旗龙舟
- 城南街道三铺马福社区的大闸社北帝庙双带七星旗龙舟
- 中洲街道麻演社区的五王庙上堡红旗龙舟
- 中洲街道麻演社区的五王庙下堡红旗龙舟
- 中洲街道西岸社区的西岸宗祠单白旗龙舟
- 中洲街道西岸社区的沙尾宗祠双白旗龙舟

这些传统龙舟还有“雌”“雄”性别之分，也有“兄弟”“姐妹”之别。三角白旗、单白旗、双白旗龙舟属雌性（俗称妹仔船），归属女菩萨庙堂，三角白旗归属当地妈祖庙，单、双白旗是“姐妹船”同归属当地的观音堂；而上堡、下堡则是“兄弟船”，同归属当地的五王庙等。各龙舟所属地都设有自己的龙舟协会，负责人称为“龙种”，负责组织安排每年的比赛活动。

江城传统龙舟主要由龙头、龙身、龙尾三部分构成。龙身用柚木或梢木建造，龙舟建好后用油漆髹饰，舟身光亮乌黑。龙舟长、宽都有传统的尺寸规定，并以传统的周公尺为标准，传统龙舟长度是8丈7尺6寸，折合30～31米，中部最宽处3尺5寸，折合约1.2米。龙头高大生猛，长须飘逸，极为威武，正面宽0.27米，长0.55米，龙颈及连接舟身部分高约1.5米，用樟木制作，雕刻精致，色彩鲜艳，神态各异；龙角则是采用真鹿角安装在龙头上。龙尾造型弯翘，用樟木制作，鳞甲色彩斑斓，活灵活现。

江城传统龙舟全舟共配置54人，不能多也不能少。龙舟分为前、中、后三舱，中舱放置锣鼓，配锣鼓手4名；前舱设壮丁舱位，配划手24位，称12对，其中2名为头梢；后舱是壮丁舱位，配划手26位，称13对，其中1名为尾梢。

各艘龙舟都极力彰显自己的风格和特征，龙头上所竖立的形状、颜色和数量不同的龙旗，龙腮上所配的黑、白、蓝、红、青、靛等不同颜色的龙须等，都代表所属龙庙的文化内涵和特色。如属雌性的单、双白旗龙舟同归属当地的观音堂，其龙头均以粉红为主色，配以蓝绿颜色，龙

These traditional dragon boats are also divided into female and male genders, as well as “brothers” and “sisters”. For example, the Triangular White Flag, the Single White Flag, and the Double White Flag dragon boats are female (commonly known as female boats), worshipping Female Bodhisattva Temple. The Triangular White Flag Dragon Boat belongs to to the local Mazu Temple, and the Single and Double White Flag Dragon Boats which are “sister boats” belongs to the local Guanyin Hall, while the Shangbao and Xiabao are “brother ships”, which belongs to the local Five-king Temple and so on. Each dragon boat has its dragon boat association, and the person in charge is called “Longzhong (dragon seed) ”, that is responsible for organizing and arranging the annual competition activities.

The traditional dragon boat in Jiangcheng is mainly composed of three parts: the dragon head, the dragon body, and the dragon tail. The dragon body is built of teak or wood. After it is made, the dragon boat is painted and decorated with paint. The boat's body is bright and black. The length and width of the dragon boat have traditional size regulations. With the traditional Zhou Gong ruler as the standard, the length of the traditional dragon boat is 87 *chi* 6 *cun* (30-31 meters) , and the widest part in the middle is 3 *chi* 5 *cun* (1.2 meters) . The dragon head is tall and powerful with an elegant long beard. The front is 0.27 meters wide, 0.55 meters long and 1.5 meters high (including the dragon neck and the connecting part to the boat body) . It is made of camphor wood, with exquisite carving, bright colors, and different expressions. The dragon horn is installed on the dragon head with real antlers. The dragon tail is curved and made of camphor wood, and the scales and shell are colorful and vivid.

The traditional dragon boat of Jiangcheng is equipped with a total of 54 people, neither more nor less. The dragon boat is divided into three cabins—front, middle and rear cabins. The middle cabin is equipped with gongs and drums, with four drummers. The front cabin is equipped with strong men seats, with 24 rowers, called 12 pairs, two of them are the head tip, and the rear cabin is also equipped with strong men seats, with 26 rowers, called 13 pairs, one of them is the tail tip.

Each dragon boat strives to show its style and characteristics. The dragon flags of different shapes, colors and numbers erected on the dragon's head, and the dragon beard of different colors such as black, white, blue, red, blue, and indigo, etc., on the dragon's cheeks represent the cultural connotation and characteristics of the dragon temple to which they belong. For example, the female Single White Flag and the Double White Flag Dragon Boats, worshipping the local Guanyin Hall, use pink as the main color on the dragon head, with blue and green colors, and the dragon horns are erected with a square-shaped white flag (the Single White Flag one with a dragon flag, and the Double White Flag one with two dragon flags) , which looks pretty and dignified. Another example is the female Triangular White Flag Dragon Boat, worshipping the local Tianhou Palace. The head and tail of the dragon are mainly pink and light green, with a blue beard. The striking dentate Triangular White Flag is erected in the middle of the dragon's head, which looks heroic. The heads and tails of other dragon boats are colored, and the dragon flags, dragon beards, shapes and colors are also different. For example, Shanglai Dragon Boat, belonging to the fire of the five elements, is a fire dragon and belongs to the local Taifu Temple. The temple is dedicated to the statue of Zhang Taifu from the state of Yue, the privy envoy of the Song Dynasty. The head and tail are red and golden as the main colors, decorated with sub-colors such as white, green, and blue. The two red and yellow dragon flags are erected on the dragon horns. The characters written on the flag are respectively "Song Privy Envoy of the State of Yue, Zhang Taifu Dragon Label" "confer titles of nobility on Qingjing Three Hades Palaces Royal Sealing Dragon King and Dragon Label", indicating that they belong to the Taifu Temple and the Qingjing Palace. Huahao Dragon Boat, which belongs to the local Great King Temple, has a green face and white beard, with the word "king" engraved on its forehead. The flag is written "confer title of nobility on Xianying Palace", indicating that it belongs to Xianying Palace. The Bamboo Leaves Seven-Star Flag Dragon Boat belongs to the local Xuandi Palace. Its head and tail are mainly black. A bamboo pole stands beside the dark green dragon horn. A black pennant with white toothed edge and seven silver stars in the shape of Big Dipper in the middle is strung on the bamboo pole. The beard is black under the lips, which is very powerful. The Double Belt Seven-star Flag Dragon boat belongs to the local North Emperor Temple. The dragon's head and tail are mainly dark green, and a black triangle flag of a black-white ribbon with seven silver stars like the Big Dipper

角边竖着四方形的白旗（单白旗是一支龙旗，双白旗是两支龙旗），显得俏丽、端庄。又如同属雌性的三角白旗龙舟，归属当地的天后宫，其龙头、龙尾以粉红、淡绿为主，配以蓝须，龙头顶中间竖起醒目的牙边三角白旗，显得英姿飒爽。其他龙舟的首、尾着色，龙旗、龙须、形状、色彩也各有不同，如上濑龙舟的五行属火，是火龙，归属当地太傅庙，庙内供奉宋枢密使越国张太傅神像；龙头、尾以红、金黄为主色，白、绿、蓝为副色点缀，龙角边竖的红、黄色的两面龙旗上写的字号分别是“宋枢密使越国张太傅公龙标”“敕封清境三位阎官感应龙王龙标”，说明它是属于太傅庙、清境宫的。华濠龙舟，归属当地大王庙，其龙头绿脸白须，额上刻一“王”字，角上举载尖红底黑边四方旗，旗上书“敕封显应宫”，说明它是属于显应宫的。竹叶七星旗龙舟，归属当地的玄帝宫，其龙头、龙尾以黑色为主，深绿的龙角边竖着一根带叶的竹竿串着黑底、白牙边、中间崁着如北斗星形的七颗银星的三角令旗，唇下黑须髯髯，十分威猛。双带七星旗龙舟归属当地的北帝庙，其龙头、龙尾以墨绿色为主，龙角上举樱尖黑白飘带嵌着如北斗星座的七颗银星的黑色三角令旗，唇下挂着黑色长须，在江

激烈的龙舟赛场面
Fierce scene of a dragon boat race

面游弋，犹如黑色蛟龙，生猛威武。

“四月八，龙舟挖。”每年四月初开始，各支龙舟队的“龙种”便开始筹备本年度的赛龙舟工作，组织人员发动当地群众集资。各家各户都会踊跃支持，捐款捐物，出钱出力，积极参与，大家都想贡献一分力量，使自己的龙舟能够“扒”第一。初六、初七两天，各龙舟队由“龙种”牵头，带领队员到去年“淹龙舟”所在地附近的河岸上搭建舟棚（即“龙舟坛”），大小为一二百平方米，内设供奉神祇神牌的神台，还要放置七八张桌子和若干把凳子，供参赛鼓手、锣手、划手及其他相关人员休息、吃饭。煮饭的地点则设在“龙舟坛”附近的空地上。他们在建好的“龙舟坛”四周插上彩旗，贴上各种内容的对联，如双白旗龙坛的对联是“龙德普双林端庆滘州沾德泽，神恩覃下坎回南安盛沐恩波”，白须龙坛的对联是“东岸共观红粉女，西河争看白须公”，而双带七星旗龙坛张贴的对联是“沐神恩我方我土家家兴旺，承祖荫龙子龙孙代代相传”等。到四月初八早上8点左右，要举行庄重的“挖龙舟”仪式，趁退潮，各龙舟队的“龙种”带领本龙舟队壮丁十来人来到去年“淹龙舟”的地方，首先在淹龙舟处的四周燃放鞭炮，以示驱邪，保佑挖龙舟顺顺利利，然后才能正式开始挖龙舟。挖出后，立刻把龙舟清洗干净，抬上备好的木桩或石桩上，为龙舟补漆上油，进行修整粉饰，重新扎牢龙骨，装上龙头龙尾，把龙舟擦亮，再把龙舟抬下河涌。之后各“龙种”率各龙舟部分队员把准备好的“三牲”祭品送到各自的神庙或宗祠进行供奉和参拜，以敬祭神灵或祖先，之后请出其神祇神牌，一路来到所属的“龙舟坛”，等候在“龙舟坛”的部分队员则敲

is held on dragon horns. There is a long black beard hanging under the lips. The boat cruising on the river, like a black dragon, is fierce and spectacular.

“On the eighth day of the fourth lunar month, the dragon boat is dug.” From the beginning of April every year, the “Longzhong” of each dragon boat begins to prepare for the annual dragon boat race, organizing people to mobilize local people to raise funds. Every family actively supports the race and makes donations and contributions. Everyone participates actively in the hope of helping their dragon boat win the first prize. On the sixth and seventh day, each dragon boat team is led by the “Longzhong” to the nearby river bank of the location of “Drowning the Dragon Boat” to build a boat shed, also the “Dragon Boat Altar”, which is one or two hundred square meters. Inside, there is a shrine dedicated to the tablets gods, and 7 or 8 tables and several stools are also placed for the participating drummers, gong players, rowers, and other related personnel to rest and eat. The cooking place is located in the open space near the “Dragon Boat Altar”. They plant colorful flags around the built “Dragon Boat Altar” and paste couplets with various contents. For example, the couplet of the Double White Flag Dragon Boat Altar is “The dragon, Depu, stained in grace in the Dragon Boat Festival in double forests of Jiaozhou, and people can be blessed from the god back to the south, Ansheng, to bath under the blessing”. The couplet of the White Beard Dragon Boat Altar is “We watch the female red and pink dragon boat on the east coast as well as White Beard Male Dragon Boat by West River”. The Double Belt Seven-star Flag Dragon Boat Altar is posted with “My family and my living space is bathed under the God’s grace and the son, as well as grandsons related with the Dragon Boat, are stayed in the ancestors’ protection, spreading generation to generation”, etc. At around 8 o’clock in the morning on the eighth day of the fourth lunar month, a solemn “Digging the Dragon Boat” ceremony is held after the ebb. Each “Longzhong” of the dragon boat leads about a dozen strong men of the dragon boat team to the place where the dragon boat was drown last year. First, firecrackers are set off around the place where the dragon boat was drown to show exorcism and bless for digging the dragon boat smoothly, and then it can officially start digging the dragon boat. After the dragon boat is dug out, they clean the dragon boat immediately, lift it on the prepared wooden stake or stone stake, oil the dragon boat for dressing and whitewashing, re-anchor the keel, install the dragon tail and head, polish the dragon boat, and then carry the dragon boat down the river. Afterward, each “Longzhong” leads some members of the dragon boat team to send the prepared "three sacrifices" to their respective temples or ancestral halls to worship gods or ancestors, and then invites their tablets to come to their own "Dragon Boat Altar". Some members of the team waiting at the "Dragon Boat Altar" greet them with gongs and drums, the tablets of the ancestral gods are solemnly placed on the altar in the "Dragon Boat Altar", and pass incense burners on the head of the dragon boat to show that the gods entered into the dragon boat. After that, the competition training begins. First of all, the gongs and drummers must be selected to be the conductor of the competition. "Longzhong" puts the dragon boat drum in the "Dragon Boat Altar", and allows the strong men who participate in the election to come and beat. It is recognized that the best postural and the most outstanding percussion skills are among them, selecting four for serving as drummers and gong players (two each). Fifty strong males are selected as rowers. Each dragon boat is generally trained at the Moyang River section close to the territory. The training time is about 20 days. During the training, the "Longzhong" especially emphasizes the unity and cooperation of the team, concerted efforts, consistent rhythm, neat movements, and cooperation, to achieve the best competition results. Winning the championship is the dream and expectation of every dragon boat team.

Around 7 a.m. on the first day of the fifth lunar month, "Longzhong" leads a solemn "Wanglong" ceremony at the "Dragon Boat Altar" built on the river bank. Before each participating dragon boat is launched, this ceremony must be held. Drummers, gong players, rowers, and other related personnel attend it, and all women in the village can not be present to watch. The ceremony is specially presided over by a "priest". The priest is dressed in blessing clothes, cranks a celebrating bell, recites auspicious words like praying for

锣打鼓迎接，肃穆庄重地将祖宗神祇的牌位安放在“龙舟坛”内的神台上，并传香炉于龙舟头，以示神祇进驻龙舟。之后便要开始比赛训练，首先要选出锣鼓手做比赛时的指挥，“龙种”把龙舟鼓放到龙坛内，让参选的壮丁前来敲击，选其中姿势最好、敲击技艺最出众的四人担任鼓手、锣手（各二人），同时推选50名健壮的男子当划手，每支龙舟队一般都在靠近属地的漠阳江河段训练，训练时间约20天，训练中“龙种”会特别强调全队的团结协作、齐心协力、节奏一致、动作整齐、相互配合等要素，以期取得最好的比赛成绩，夺冠是每支龙舟队的梦想和期望。

五月初一早上7点左右，由“龙种”牵头，在河岸搭建的“龙舟坛”内举行庄重的“旺龙”仪式，各参赛龙舟在下水前，都要先举行此仪式。鼓手、锣手、划手等相关人员到场参加，全村所有女性均不能在场观看。仪式专门邀请“祭师”主持，祭师身穿福衣，手摇庆铃，口中念着祈求保佑风调雨顺、六畜兴旺、平平安安等寓意吉祥的话语，捧着装有泡着柚子叶的“圣水”的钵盂，用柚子叶沾着“圣水”，从龙头至龙尾轻洒一遍，接着由“龙种”用鸡血或朱砂给龙头点睛，然后

龙舟赛中的丰盛奖品，有金猪、龙包等
Great rewards in the dragon boat race contain roast pigs, dragon buns, etc.

“祭师”双手拿着点燃的篱火把，沿着在龙舟底部绕龙舟熏一圈，意为给龙舟驱邪旺气，接着用胭脂、五色线、鸡蛋、毛巾、镜子、剃刀等给龙舟梳髻、剃须、梳须、洗脸、化妆。之后，各船壮丁穿着统一的服装上船，沿着河涌上游，划到就近河埠竹林进行“采青”，即在竹林采摘竹枝放在龙舟颈部斗仓上，表示驱邪、避灾、祈福，以祈求当年风调雨顺、岁岁平安；然后由锣鼓手带领划手把船划出河涌，即龙舟“出涌”，整个过程敲锣打鼓、燃放鞭炮，场面非常庄严壮观。随后各龙舟相继到漠阳江上游弋亮相，当经过其他龙舟的龙坛或附近庙堂时，都必定“徐鼓”（即轻击锣鼓）、“放钞”（即向江面撒纸钱）、燃放鞭炮，表示欢迎和崇敬。

“旺龙”仪式结束后，各龙舟进入漠阳江面，就可自发、自由地与任何其他龙舟进行对抗比赛。在江上，两龙舟相会时，如哪艘龙舟有意，便可由锣手对着对方龙舟“亮锣”（即高举锣快速连敲）表示邀请对方比赛，使比赛富有挑战性，如果对方龙舟也“亮锣”呼应，即表示同意接受挑战。双方把船划到起点漠阳江蚬壳地河段，两龙舟分别坐东、西河道，“集鼓”（即停锣鼓）比齐船头，再一齐“亮锣”数下，双方进入比赛准备状态。一锤鼓响，比赛开始，两艘龙舟百桨齐飞，跟着锣鼓节奏，喊着“呵唷”“呵唷”的号子，一起朝漠阳江上游方向的终点——上濑洲头河段逆水而上，奋力拼搏，谁先冲过那条绑了红布条的绳子，谁就为第一，如不服输，双方又回到起点，交换赛道，重新进行比赛，采用三局两胜制，决出最后胜负。如此这般，十二艘龙舟尽显其能，各领风骚，一直持续至傍晚才结束这

good weather, the prosperity of the six kinds of animals as well as safety, and holds a “holy water” bowl soaked in pomelo leaves. Then he dips the “holy water” with pomelo leaves, sprinkles it lightly from the dragon’s head to tail. Then “Longzhong” uses the chicken blood or cinnabar to paint the dragon’s eyes. Next, the “priest” holding the bonfire in both hands goes around the bottom of the dragon boat to exorcise evil spirits and vitality from the dragon boat, and then uses rouge, five-color thread, eggs, towels, mirrors, razors, etc. to comb and shave the dragon boat beard, wash face, and make up. Afterward, the strong men of each boat wear uniform clothes and board the boat, along the upper reaches of the river, and row to the nearby Bamboo Forest by the river port for “Plucking the Greens”, that is, people pick bamboo branches in the bamboo forest and placing them on the bucket of the neck of the dragon boat, expressing getting rid of the evils, avoiding disasters, and praying for blessings, to pray for good weather and safety this year. Then the gong players and drummers lead the rowers to row the boat out of the river, which is called the dragon boat is “out of the river”. The whole processes include beating gongs and drums and setting off firecrackers, with a very solemn and magnificent scene. Subsequently, each dragon boat comes to the Moyang River one after another to cruise and appear. When dragon boats pass by dragon boat altars of other dragon boats or nearby temples, they must “Xugu” (referring to lightly beating gongs and drums), “Fangchao” (referring to throwing paper money on the river), and setting off firecrackers to express welcome and respect.

After the “Wanglong” ceremony, each dragon boat enters the Moyang River and can spontaneously and freely compete against any other dragon boat. When the two dragon boats meet on the river, if any dragon boat intends to compete, the gong players can face the opponent’s dragon boat and “Liangluo” (referring to holding the gong high and beating it quickly) to invite the opponent to race, making the race more challenging. If the other dragon boat “Liangluo” back, meaning that it agrees to accept the challenge. So the two teams row the dragon boat to the starting point of Moyang River Shell Land, and start on the East and West River roads respectively. They “Jigu” (referring to stopping the gongs and drums) and compare to the bow, and then “Liangluo” several times together, entering the preparation for the race. With a drum, the race begins. The two dragon boats flow together with hundreds of oars, following the rhythm of the gongs and drums, and the rowers shout “He yo”, and make concerted efforts to head towards the finishing point of the upper reaches of the Moyang River—the

Shanglai Zhoutou river section, going up upstream and fighting hard. Whoever rushes through the rope tied with red cloth first is the winner. If any team doesn't admit defeat, the two teams will return to the starting point, exchange the track, restart the race, and play in the best of three sets to decide the final result. In this way, the twelve dragon boats show their abilities and the competition lasted until evening, The dragon boat race is a strong physical exercise, the second and fourth days are set as rest days, and the third and fifth days continue to compete. At the last moment, people decide on the dragon boat champion of the year finally. At that time, noise and shouts are in great commotion along the river banks. The crowd cheer and the sound of gongs and drums, firecrackers, and cheers are loud, which not only celebrate the final victory but also announce the successful conclusion of this year's dragon boat race.

Every year on the morning of the first day, the third day, and the fifth day of the fifth lunar month, dragon boat fans from all over the country come early to occupy the position to see the grand occasion, and cheer for the dragon boats. During the race, there are a sea of people on both sides of the river, and the restaurants, houses, balconies, and roofs along the coast become viewing platforms for the masses. Whenever the dragon boat passes by, the shouts and cheers are endless and the sound of gongs, drums, and firecrackers is deafening. Whenever the dragon boat reaches the finish line of the competition and wins the championship, the audiences on both sides of the bank are passionate, dancing happily. The sound of firecrackers rises one after another, people raise a great shout and cheer, pushing the atmosphere of the Dragon Boat Festival to a climax.

After the event on the last day, each dragon boat distributes "Dragon Buns" (referring to a dim sum specially made for the dragon boat race—steamed stuffed bun) to every family in the

一天的比赛。由于龙舟竞赛是一项强体力运动，初二、初四被定为休整日，初三、初五两天继续进行比赛，到最后一刻，方决出本年度最后的冠军龙舟，届时沿河两岸鼎沸如潮，万众欢腾，锣鼓声、鞭炮声、欢呼声大作，既是庆祝最后的胜利，也是宣告本年度龙舟比赛圆满结束。

每年的农历五月初一、初三、初五一早，各地龙舟迷早早来到比赛河段抢先占位，争睹盛况，为龙舟鼓劲助威。在比赛过程中，江边两岸人山人海，摩肩接踵，沿岸的酒楼、民房、阳台、楼顶都成了群众的观看台，龙舟过处，呐喊声、喝彩声不绝于耳，锣鼓声、鞭炮声震耳欲聋，每当比赛龙舟到达终点夺冠时，两岸观众更是心情激动，手舞足蹈，鞭炮声此起彼伏，欢呼声一浪高过一浪，将端午的节日气氛推至高潮。

最后一天活动结束后，各支龙舟队要给所在区域的每家每户发“龙包”（即为龙舟赛专门制作的点心——包子），男女老少在户外摆桌一起吃“龙舟饭”，大家大块吃肉，大碗喝酒，欢声笑语，其乐融融，一派热闹又祥和的场面，羡煞旁人。

聚餐后，各龙舟队还要举行“还神”仪式：先双手合十，虔诚参拜；然后燃放

龙舟赛后热闹的龙舟饭
People enjoy hearty dragon boat meal after the race

鞭炮，表示告知神灵大功告成；再庄重地将从神庙或宗祠请出的祖宗神祇牌位送归原位；之后“龙种”宣布“散坛”，表示本年度赛龙舟活动结束。

赛龙舟活动结束后，各支龙舟队还要对龙舟进行“淹龙舟”（淹：阳江话读yàn），即对龙舟采取淹埋措施进行护理和保存。在五月初八前后趁漠阳江退潮之际，“龙种”组织壮丁在合适的河涌选择能够被水长期淹浸的地方，挖好船坞，然后拉线定好枕位，放好用来支撑龙舟不变形的“龙枕”，将龙舟上枕后，两旁打上木桩定位，使龙舟不会左右摆动，之后用泥土覆盖龙舟全身，避免日晒雨淋，并长期以河水淹盖，使龙舟不被氧化，目的是保护好龙舟，使其不变形、不变质。龙舟“淹”得好，待次年四月初八再起挖参加比赛时可省去了许多修补龙舟的工夫，龙舟也更加“长寿”。至此，本年度赛龙舟活动才真正全部结束。

主要特征

端午逆水赛龙舟，是江城地区一个具有浓厚地方特色的大型民俗活动，其主要特征表现为：

（1）每艘龙舟都归属当地神庙或姓氏宗祠。

（2）每艘龙舟有自己独特的旌旗和称谓。

（3）各龙舟所属地都设有龙舟协会，并由“龙种”负责组织安排每年的活动。

（4）有固定的活动时间，即每年农历五月的初一、初三、初五。

（5）有固定的活动仪式，如“挖龙舟”仪式、“旺龙”仪式、“请神”仪式、“还神”仪式、“淹龙舟”仪式等。

area. Men and women, children and the elder set tables outdoors to eat “Dragon Boat Meal” together. Everyone enjoys the meal with laughters and cheers. The lively and peaceful scene makes others envious.

After the dinner, each dragon boat team also holds a ceremony of “rewarding the gods”. First, put your hands together, worship devoutly; and next, set off firecrackers to inform the gods that you have accomplished your work; and then solemnly return the tablets of ancestral gods invited from the temple or ancestral hall. After that, the “Longzhong” announces “dissolving the altar”, indicating the dragon boat race of this year ends.

After the dragon boat race, each dragon boat team also needs to “drown the dragon boat” (drown: Yangjiang dialect reads yàn), that is, the dragon boat will be submerged and buried for care and preservation. When the tide ebbs around the Moyang River around the eighth day of the fifth lunar month, the “Longzhong” organizes strong men to choose a place that can be flooded for a long time in a suitable river to dig the dock, then pull the line to set the position, and put “Dragon Pillow” in place to maintain its shape. Put the dragon boat on the pillow and set wooden stakes on both sides to position it so that the dragon boat will not swing from side to side. Then cover the whole body of the dragon boat with mud to avoid sun and rain, and drown it in the river for a long time, so that the dragon boat will not be oxidized. The purpose is to protect the dragon boat from deforming or deteriorating. If the dragon boat is “drown” well, it will save a lot of repair work when it will be dug again on the eighth day of the fourth lunar month the next year to participate in the race and the dragon boat is also more “long-lived”. At this point, this year's dragon boat race truly ends.

Main Features

Upstream Dragon Boat Race at the Dragon Boat Festival is a large-scale folk activity with strong local characteristics in the Jiangcheng area. Its main features are as follows.

(1) Each dragon boat belongs to a local temple or ancestral hall.

(2) Each dragon boat has its own unique banner and title.

(3) Each dragon boat has its own dragon boat association, and the “Longzhong” is responsible for organizing and arranging annual activities.

(4) There is a fixed activity time, that is, the first day, the third day and the fifth day of the fifth lunar month every year.

(5) There are fixed activities and ceremonies, such as the "Diging the Dragon Boat" Ceremony, "Wanglong" Ceremony, " Inviting God" Ceremony, "Rewarding God" Ceremony, "Drowning the Dragon Boat" Ceremony, etc..

(6) There are fixed traditional activities, such as "Plucking the Greens", "Chuyong", sending "Dragon Buns", and eating "Dragon Boat Meal".

(7) Dragon boats are built in traditional sizes, unique shapes, and special materials.

(8) The dragon boat race has a traditional route, that is, about 1,300 meters on the river starting from Moyang River Dabutou (Shell Land) to Shanglai Zhoutou as the end.

(9) There are traditional racing formats. One is racing the dragon boat upstream, and the other is that each race is limited to two dragon boats for confrontation.

(10) There are traditional rules like each boat is free to invite the other ones, and those who do not admit defeat can continue to race until the result come out under the best of three sets. There is no full-time referee.

(11) There is a traditional number of people configuration. The whole boat has a total of 54 people, including 4 gong players and drummers, and 50 rowers. The number of participator is constant.

Great Value

· Historical value

Upstream Dragon Boat Race has a long history and tradition, a wide range of dissemination and influence, a great number of participants in Jiangcheng District, Yangjiang. In the process of historical development, it expresses the rich ideology and feelings of the people in Jiangcheng, Yangjiang, and their warm pursuit of happiness, peace, and healthy life. It is the crystallization of the wisdom of the people and also a concrete manifestation of the history and culture of Jiangcheng District, Yangjiang. It provides valuable research materials for the study of the history of various eras, the social situation and the development of productive forces of each period, and the conditions of cultural and recreational life in Jiangcheng.

· Cultural value

The festival is the foundation of a nation. The Dragon Boat Festival is a traditional festival in China. The Upstream Dragon Boat Race at the Dragon Boat Festival has a profound background and cultural connotation. It originated from the commemoration of Qu Yuan and

（6）有固定的传统活动内容，如“采青”“出涌”以及发“龙包”、吃“龙舟饭”等。

（7）龙舟建造有传统的尺寸、独特的造型和特殊的材质。

（8）龙舟比赛有传统的路线，即漠阳江大埠头（蚬壳地）至终点上濑洲头大约1300米的江（河）面上。

（9）有传统的赛法，一是逆水赛龙舟，二是每场比赛都只限两艘龙舟进行对抗赛。

（10）有传统的比赛规则，如采用自发、自由的邀请形式，不服输者可继续进行比赛；采用三盘两胜制决胜负；没有专职裁判；等等。

（11）有传统的人数配置，全舟共配置54人，包括4名锣鼓手、50名划手，多则不允，少则不许。

重要价值

· 历史价值

端午逆水赛龙舟在阳江江城区有着悠久的历史和传统，传播影响范围广泛，参与群众甚多。在历史发展过程中，它表达了江城人民丰富的思想感情和对幸福、平安、健康生活的热烈追求，它是江城人民智慧的结晶，也是江城历史文化的具体表现，为研究江城各个时代的历史、各时期社会发展情况与生产力发展情况以及文化娱乐生活状况等提供了宝贵的研究资料。

· 文化价值

节日是一个民族的根基，端午节就是中国民间传统节日，端午逆水赛龙舟有着深刻的背景和文化内涵，最早源于纪念屈原，慢慢演变为一个具有本地特色的大型节日民俗活动。逆水赛龙舟之意在于“逆水行舟，不进则退”，体现了一种不畏艰难、奋勇争先的龙舟精神，也体现了一种爱国主义和集体主义精神，彰显了“划的是龙舟，赛的是精神”的文化内涵。如今已发展成为集文化、艺术、科学、娱乐、饮食、社交、商业、体育于一体，促进文化、艺术交流，促进经济发展，促进社会和谐的载体和平台，江城龙舟文化已渗透在阳江人的血液里，成为江城特有的文化符号。

·民俗价值

在漫长的历史发展过程中，端午逆水赛龙舟活动始终是江城人民的传统习俗，人们对端午节的期盼、对龙舟精神的追求、对冠军荣誉的向往，都寄托在端午逆水赛龙舟活动中。龙舟文化长期的熏陶和影响哺育、滋养了一代代江城人，形成了知难而进、团结协作、顽强拼搏、力争上游的江城人精神，而项目诸多的传统内容，如祭祖、每家每户派发“龙包”、男女老少一起吃“龙舟饭”等，凝聚了民众的文化认同感，加深了彼此的交流和理解，让邻里乡亲感情和睦，让人与自然的关系融洽，营造了一方和谐平安的氛围。

·运动价值

赛龙舟活动是一项强体力运动，也能锻炼身体的协调能力，具有强身健体的功能。同时，其强调相互间的高度合作，以达到动作整齐、节奏一致，形成合力，提高龙舟行进速度。这也是这项古老的传统民俗活动流传至今、影响广泛的魅力之一。

slowly evolved into a festival with local characteristics. The large-scale folk activity, Upstream Dragon Boat Race, meaning that a boat sailing against the current must go ahead or it will be driven back, reflects a dragon boat spirit that is not afraid of difficulties and strives for the first, and also embodies the spirit of patriotism and collectivism, demonstrating the cultural connotation of “row a dragon boat, but race for the spirit”. Today, it has developed into a collection of culture, art, science, entertainment, food, social communication, business, and sports, and has become a carrier and platform for promoting cultural and artistic exchanges, promoting economic development and social harmony. In the blood of the Jiangcheng people, dragon boat culture has become a unique cultural symbol of Jiangcheng.

· Folk value

In the long historical development process, Upstream Dragon Boat Race on the Dragon Boat Festival has always been the traditional custom of the people of Jiangcheng. People's expectations for the Dragon Boat Festival, the pursuit of the dragon boat spirit, and the yearning for the honor of the champion, are all pinned on the activity. The influence of the long-term dragon boat culture has nurtured and nourished generations of Jiangcheng people, forming the Jiangcheng people's spirit of advancing despite difficulties, uniting and cooperating, tenaciously working hard, and striving for the upper reaches. Many traditional contents of the custom, such as the ancestor worship, distribution of “Dragon Buns” to every family, men and women, old and young eating “Dragon Boat Meal” together, gather the people's sense of cultural identity, deepen mutual communication and understanding, harmonize the feelings of neighbors and villagers, and the relationship between human and nature, and creates a harmonious and peaceful atmosphere.

· Sports value

Dragon boat race is a strong physical exercise that can also exercise the coordination ability of the body and has the function of strengthening the body. At the same time, it emphasizes a high degree of cooperation with each other to achieve neat movements and consistent rhythms, and form a joint force to improve the speed of the dragon boat, which is also one of the charms of this ancient traditional folk activity passed down to this day with a wide range of influences.

Main Inheritors

Chen Ruyao, male, a native of Jiangcheng District, was born in July 1950. He is the fourth-generation inheritor of Jiangcheng Double Belt Seven-star Flag Dragon Boat. Since the early 1980s, he has studied the craft relating to the Dragon Boat under the previous master Mo Shirong and Liang Jin. Since 1997, he has served as the "Longzhong" (person in charge) of the Double Belt Seven-star Flag Dragon Boat Association. In February 2014, he was recognized as the municipal representative inheritor of the Upstream Dragon Boat Race. In April 2017, he was recognized as the representative inheritor of the fifth batch of provincial intangible cultural heritage projects in Guangdong Province.

Chen Ruyao was born, grew up, lived, and worked in Mafu Community, Chengnan Street, where the Double Belt Seven-star Flag Dragon Boat belongs. He has been immersed in the dragon boat culture since he was a child. After the formal apprenticeship, he studied the traditional rituals, competition procedures, and various customs and habits of the Upstream Dragon Boat Race, He has mastered the project skills and the whole set of standardized procedures,such as "Digging the Dragon Boat" "Inviting God" "Plucking the Greens" "Wanglong" "Chuyong" Ceremony, etc..

The Double Belt Seven-star Flag Dragon Boat originally belonged to Dazhashe North Emperor Temple. It was one of the twelve traditional dragon boats in Jiangcheng District. The dragon boat was seriously damaged due to various reasons after the middle period of the Republic of China. It was not until 1997 when Chen Ruyao actively organized fund-raising for repairing the dragon boat that the boat was restored and inherited, reappearing the majestic appearance again.

Chen Ruyao carefully organized dragon boats to participate in races over the years, selected good athletes, conducted pre-competition training, and also hired experienced coaches from other places to teach. He was also an excellent rower. Under the leadership of Chen Ruyao, the only dragon boat training base was established in Jiangcheng District by the Double Belt Seven-star Flag Dragon Boat Association. There is special training equipment on land for improving the comprehensive quality of the players and achieving better training results, which makes outstanding contributions to the inheritance and development of dragon boat culture.

To make the project a sustainable inheritance, repairing boats and rebuild new dragon boats are required at irregular intervals. Chen

主要传承人

陈汝榣，男，江城区人，1950年7月出生，是江城双带七星旗龙舟第四代传人。他从20世纪80年代初开始师从上代师父莫仕荣、梁近学习龙舟技艺，1997年开始担任双带七星旗龙舟协会"龙种"（负责人）至今。2014年2月被认定为"端午逆水赛龙舟"项目市级代表性传承人，2017年4月被认定为广东省第五批省级非物质文化遗产项目代表性传承人。

陈汝榣出生、成长及生活工作都是在双带七星旗龙舟所属的城南街道马福社区，从小受龙舟文化耳濡目染，正式拜师后对"端午逆水赛龙舟"的传统仪式、比赛程序、各种风俗习惯等有深入研究，并熟练掌握了项目技艺和整套规范程序，如挖龙舟、请神、采青、旺龙、出涌等。

双带七星旗龙舟原属大闸社北帝庙，是江城区十二艘传统龙舟之一，该龙舟民国中期后由于各种原因遭严重破坏，直至1997年陈汝榣积极组织集资重建，才使这条龙舟得以恢复和传承，再现当年的雄姿。

陈汝榣（左）
Chen Ruyao(left)

陈汝榣认真组织龙舟队参加比赛，挑选好运动员，进行赛前训练，而且还聘请外地有经验的教练进行指导，他本人也是一名优秀的划手。在陈汝榣的带领下，双带七星旗龙舟协会还建立了江城区唯一的龙舟训练基地，在陆地上也有专门的训练器械，提高了选手的综合素质，达到更好的训练效果，为传承和发展龙舟文化事业作出了突出的贡献。

为了使项目得到可持续发展，还要不定期修葺和重造龙舟，陈汝榣每次都带头出资，并号召大家集资，每当协会修造龙舟，他都要亲自参与设计，亲临制作现场进行技术指导，使双带七星旗每一处构造都极具特色，龙头生猛、颜色鲜艳、栩栩如生。

近年来，在各级政府的领导下，在社会各界的支持下，在广大群众的积极参与下，陈汝榣所属的协会制定了保护规划，落实保护措施，使该项目得到了传承和健康发展，赛龙舟活动举办的规模也不断扩大，影响面也越来越广。为了更好地传承和发扬赛龙舟精神，项目传承人陈汝榣目前正着力培养谭进华、梁仕伟等第五代传承人，将宝贵经验传承下去，使承载着人们理想追求和美好愿望的"逆水赛龙舟"民俗在人类历史发展的长河中逆水挺进、永远向前。

谭进华，男，出生、成长及生活工作都是在双带七星旗龙舟所属地的城南马福社区，对"端午逆水龙舟"项目的传统仪式、比赛程序、各种风俗习惯等都有深入研究，掌握江城端午逆水赛龙舟的规范程序。其所属双带七星旗龙舟队有传统龙舟

Ruyao takes the lead in investing every time and calls on everyone to raise funds. Whenever the association builds a new dragon boat, he will personally participate in the design and come to the production site for technical guidance, so that each new dragon boat with the Double Belt Seven-star flag is very distinctive, and the dragon head is fierce, brightly colored, and lifelike.

In recent years, with the efforts of governments at all levels, the support of all sectors of society, and the active participation of the general public, The association which Chen Ruyan belongs, has formulated protection plans and implemented protection measures, so that the project has been inherited and healthily developed. The scale of the event has continued to expand, and the impact has become wider and wider. To better inherit and carry forward the spirit of the dragon boat, Chen Ruyao, the inheritor of the project, is currently focusing on cultivating the fifth-generation of inheritors such as Tan Jinhua and Liang Shiwei, passing on the valuable experience, and making the Upstream Dragon Boat Race that carries people's ideals and good wishes advance against the current and move forward forever in the long river of human history.

Tan Jinhua, male, was born, grew up, lived, and worked in Mafu Community, Chengnan Street, where the Double Belt Seven-star Flag Dragon Boat belongs. He has in-depth research on the traditional rituals, competition procedures, various customs, and habits of the Dragon Boat Race Upstream project, mastering the standard procedures for it in Jiangcheng. The Double Belt Seven-star Flag Dragon Boat team which he belongs to has two traditional dragon boats and six dragon boats for training, and a dragon boat training base has been built, with a batch of water and land training equipment.

Tan Jinhua is the chief coach of the dragon boat training base established by the Double Belt Seven-star Flag Dragon Boat Association. Tan Jinhua has developed special dragon boat training equipment on land through daily training. Combining with a complete set of training methods, he has helped improve the comprehensive quality of athletes, and has made outstanding contributions to the inheritance and development of the Upstream Dragon Boat Race project.

At present, Tan Jinhua mainly trains the inheritors of the new generation of the project and is committed to imparting the traditional

谭进华（右四）
Tan Jinhua (the fourth from the right)

skills and traditional customs of Upstream Dragon Boat Race , so that the dragon boat culture in Jiangcheng can continue to be inherited and carried forward. He is the representative inheritor of the fourth batch of intangible cultural heritage projects in Yangjiang City now.

2艘、训练龙舟6艘，建成龙舟训练基地1个，有水、陆训练器械一批。

双带七星旗龙舟协会建立有龙舟训练基地，其总教练谭进华通过日常训练经营，研制专门在陆地上训练划龙舟的器械，并归纳出一整套训练方法，有效提高运动员的综合素质，为传承和发展端午逆水赛龙舟项目作出了突出贡献。

目前谭进华主要培养新一代项目接班人，致力于传授逆水赛龙舟这一传统技艺及传统习俗，使江城龙舟文化继续传承及发扬。谭进华现为阳江市第四批非物质文化遗产项目代表性传承人。

三月三

保护单位 阳东区非物质文化遗产保护中心

The Third Day of the Third Lunar Month

Protection Unit Yangdong District Intangible Cultural Heritage Protection Center

阳东三月三主要在阳东区东平、新洲、大沟等乡镇流行，尤以东平良垌最为集中、最为正统，是李姓群众之传统节日。这一节日在当地非常隆重，且有“三月三大过年”的说法。

历史渊源

中原地区自古以来有“三月三，生轩辕”的民谚。拜祭轩辕黄帝，是中华民族的传统大典。最先见诸春秋时期史料。唐代以后，渐成规制，绵延至今。

据史料记载，河南新郑市在黄帝时期称有熊国，现有黄帝文化遗迹20多处，是黄帝出生、创业、建都之地。轩辕黄帝在这一带修德振兵、抚万民、度四方、融炎帝一统天下。

后人为纪念黄帝的功德，每年三月初三这天都要在黄帝故里举行各种拜祖活动，尤其到了春秋时期，郑国名相子产更是让这一民间活动进一步发扬光大，兴起了三月三登具茨山（位于新郑市，系黄帝活动遗迹）朝拜轩辕黄帝活动，并形成民俗延续下来。

The Third Day of the Third Lunar Month of Yangdong is mainly spread in Dongping, Xinzhou, Dagou and other towns in Yangdong District, especially in Liangdong, Dongping, which is the most concentrated and orthodox. It is a traditional festival for the people surnamed Li. This festival is very grand in the local area and there is a saying that “the Third Day of The Third Lunar Month is more important than the Chinese New Year” .

Historical Origin

There has been a folk proverb in the central plains since ancient times, that is, “On the third day of the third lunar month, Xuanyuan was born” . Worshiping the Yellow Emperor Xuanyuan is a traditional ceremony in the Chinese nation. It was first seen in historical materials probably about in the Spring and Autumn Periods. After the Tang Dynasty, it gradually became regulated and continued to this day.

According to historical records, Xinzheng City, Henan Province was called Youxiong Country during the Yellow Emperor period. There are more than 20 cultural relics of the Yellow Emperor, which is the place where the Yellow Emperor was born, started a business, and built his capital. The Yellow Emperor cultivated spirits, developed troops, appeased thousands of people, measured and planned the lands, and unified the world by integrating Yan Emperor.

To commemorate the merits of the Yellow Emperor, future generations held various ancestor worship activities in the hometown of the Yellow Emperor on the third day of the third lunar month every year. Especially in the Spring and Autumn Period, Zichan, prime minister of the country of Zheng, further carried forward this folk activity, climbing the Juci Mountain (located in Xinzheng City, which is the relic of the activities of the Yellow Emperor) and worshipping the Yellow Emperor Xuanyuan , and the folk customs has continued.

The reason of worshipping the Yellow Emperor on a large scale, is regarding the Yellow Emperor as not only a cultural idol in the era of civilization, but also the common ancestor of the Chinese nation, which is another important factor.

The Third Day of the Third Lunar Month of Yangdong, coming from Guangxi and Nanxiong, has been spread in Dongping, Xinzhou, Dagou, and other towns in the form of ancestor worship for hundreds of years. The reason why commemorating the Yellow Emperor is different from other places is difficult to study. According to the elder, the Third Day of the Third Lunar Month of Yangdong, started from ancestors who migrated from Guangxi and Nanxiong to Yangdong and has been passed down from generation to generation.

People did not worship ancestors during the time of Tomb Sweeping Day but on the third day of the third lunar month. It is said that the ancestor surnamed Li fled from Zhuji Lane, Nanxiong to Yangjiang and lived in the Old Village, Sanshan in Yangdong County (the village is abandoned now) to have children later. When he died, it happened to be the third day of the third lunar month, so people followed it down and set the third day of the third lunar month as a festival to commemorate his ancestors.

The origin of the Third Day of the Third Lunar Month is divided across the country. There is a legend to commemorate the ancestors in various places. Judging from the fact that there is the Third Day of the Third Lunar Month in most of places of the whole country, this is a new continuation derived from the ancient custom of commemorating the Yellow Emperor.

Main Content

The Third Day of the Third Lunar Month of Yangdong is the time that a unique ancestor worship ceremony is held in the Liangdong area. Its unique feature is that tomb sweeping and ancestor worship are not on Tomb Sweeping Day but on the third day of the third lunar month. On this day, people have to go back to hometown wherever they live and whatever the weather is. They have to do tomb sweeping and ancestor worship regardless of the weather. There aren't unoccupied persons on this day, there is a division of labor regardless of men, women, children for they should jointly carry out the activity of tomb sweeping and ancestor worship.

Tomb sweeping and ancestor worship is a traditional ritual. On the morning of the Third day of the Third Lunar Month, every family kills

历代对黄帝进行大规模祭奠，除了因为把黄帝看作是文明时代的文化偶像外，还有一个重要因素，那就是黄帝是中华民族的共同祖先。

阳东三月三由广西、南雄传入，历经几百年，一直以祭祖形式流传于东平、新洲、大沟等镇。而其纪念黄帝的这一形式与别的地方不同的原因却难以考究。据老一辈人讲述，三月三这一节日是先人由广西、南雄迁移到阳东才有的，一代传一代延续至今。

上坟不选择清明时节，而选择三月三日，据说是因为李姓的祖先由南雄珠玑巷逃难而来阳江，住在阳东县三山的旧村（该村现已废）生儿育女。其去世的时候刚巧是三月三，于是便沿袭下来，以三月三日为节日纪念先人。

三月三的由来，在全国众说纷纭，各地方都有一个纪念先人的传说。从全国各地都有三月三这一事实来看，这实际就是纪念黄帝这一古老习俗而衍生的一种全新延续。

主要内容

阳东三月三的扫墓、祭祖是良垌一带独特的祭祖仪式。其独到之处是扫墓祭祖不在清明节而在农历三月初三，这天人们不论在什么地方生活都要赶回乡，且不管天气如何都要扫墓祭祖。这一天没有闲人，不管男女老幼都有分工，共同参与扫墓祭祖这一活动。

扫墓祭祖是一种传统仪式。三月三这天，每家每户一早杀鸡杀鹅，全家人带上祭品、工具来到祖坟上，首先除草、添土，对祖坟修整一番，再进行祭祀。祭祀时人们口中念念有词，说着祈求祖先保佑的话，多为祈平安、祈健康、祈丰收、祈发财等，最后燃放鞭炮。不管有多少个祖坟，都用同样的祭品，在同一天完成祭祀。

吃“蒸赏”是另外一个习俗，是三月三的另一种延续。

老太公（曾祖以上）坟山一般秋祭，就是所谓“吃蒸赏”，是同姓人祭祖的一种大聚会、大聚餐，源自过去专门划出“蒸赏地”作为祭祖专用。春祭叫“祀”，夏祭叫“瀹”，秋祭叫“蒸”，冬祭叫“赏”。

主要特征

（1）具有地方特色。三月三作为阳东的一个民俗节日，与全国其他地方的三月三不同，是将扫墓祭祖、缅怀先人作为一种过节形式，有地方特色。

（2）时间性、意识性较强。阳东三月三的扫墓祭祖仪式必须在三月三这一天全部完成，且人们不管在什么地方都必须赶回乡过三月三，否则意味背叛、数典忘祖。

（3）参与人数多，范围广。三月三这一天没有闲人，凡是李姓后代不论老少都参与祭祖活动，家庭中各有分工，妇女杀鹅、杀鸡，准备三牲祭品等，男人则除草、修坟等。

重要价值

· **社会价值**

阳东三月三以扫墓祭祖形式表现对祖先的深切怀念，弘扬社会伦理道德，倡导敬祖精神，对促进村民人与人之间的友好团结与和谐、增强民族团结意识有重要意义。

chickens and geese, bringing sacrifices and tools to the ancestral tomb. First, weed and add soil to repair the ancestral tomb, and then offer sacrifices. During the worship, people chant words for the blessing of their ancestors, mostly praying for peace, health, a good harvest, wealth, etc., and finally set off firecrackers. No matter how many ancestral tombs there are, they are given the same sacrifice and worshiped on the same day.

Eating “Zhengshang” is another folk custom and another continuation of the Third Day of the Third Lunar Month.

The old man (above the great ancestor) cemetery is generally worshiped in autumn, called “eating Zhengshang”, which is a large gathering and dinner for people with the same surname to worship the ancester. It originates from the past that a “Zhengshang plot” was set specially aside for ancestor worship. The spring worship is called “si”, the summer worship is called “yue”, the fall worship is called “zheng”, and the winter worship is called “shang”.

Main Features

(1) Unique local characteristics. As a folk festival in Yangdong, the Third Day of the Third Lunar Month is different from that of other parts in the country. It is a festival to sweep graves, worship ancestors and cherish ancestors, which has local characteristics.

(2) Strong timeliness and consciousness. The tomb sweeping and ancestor worship ceremony of Yangdong on the Third Day of the Third Lunar Month must be completed on the third day of the third lunar month, and people must go back to hometown wherever they are, otherwise, it means betraying and forgetting their ancestors.

(3) The large number of participants and the wide scope. On the Third Day of the Third Lunar Month, there aren't unoccupied persons. All descendants surnamed Li, young and old, participate in ancestor worship activities. The family has a division of labor. Women kill geese and chickens, and prepare the three livestock offerings, while men weed and repair graves.

Great Value

· Social value

The Third Day of the Third Lunar Month of Yangdong expresses a deep remembrance of ancestors in the form of sweeping graves and worshiping ancestors, helps promote social ethics and morality and advocates the spirit of respecting ancestors, which is of great significance to promoting the friendly and united relationship between villagers, living in harmony, and enhancing the awareness of national unity.

· Cultural value

Sweeping graves and worshipping ancestors on the Third Day of the Third Lunar Month is an ancient traditional cultural form in Yangdong, and its content and significance are very rich. It is of great significance to the study of the origin and historical changes of folk culture in this region.

· Historical and archaeological value

The Third Day of the Third Lunar Month has historical reference value for the study of the origin of the people surnamed Li in Yangdong, as well as historical migration, cultural evolution development, and folk customs.

· 文化价值

三月三的扫墓祭祖是阳东一种古老传统的文化形式，其内容意义非常丰富，对研究本地区民俗文化起源、历史变迁有重要意义。

· 历史考古价值

三月三对研究阳东李姓百姓起源，以及历史迁徙、文化演变发展、民俗风情等都有历史参考价值。

阳东三月三的宣传横幅
Promotional banner on the The Third Day of the Third Lunar Month of Yangdong

主要传承人

Main Inheritors

李孟均，男，出生于1956年8月，阳江市阳东区东平镇人，从小跟随父亲参与三月三扫墓祭祖活动，继承传统习俗。在家乡参加大族祭祖活动时，他在活动中参与舞狮、举旗。从十五岁开始，每隔三年参加外地联合祭祖活动，并参加新会、台山、南雄等外地宗亲联合祭祖活动。他非常熟练地掌握三月三祭祖仪式内容，能独立组织实施三月三祭祖活动。李孟均现为阳江市第三批非物质文化遗产项目代表性传承人。

Li Mengjun, male, was born in August 1956 in Dongping Town, Yangdong District, Yangjiang City. He has followed his father to participate in the Third Day of the Third Lunar Month ancestral worship activities and inherited traditional customs since he was a child. When participating in the ancestral worship activities of the big clan in the hometown, he joined in the lion dance and flag-raising activities. From the age of fifteen, he has participated in the joint ancestral worship activities in other places every three years and the joint ancestral worship activities of Xinhui, Taishan, Nanxiong, and other foreign clans. He proficiently masters the content of the Third Day of the Third Lunar Month ancestral worship ceremonies, and is able to organize the Third Day of the Third Lunar Month ancestral worship activities independently. He is the representative inheritor of the third batch of intangible cultural heritage project in Yangjiang City now.

李孟均
Li Mengjun

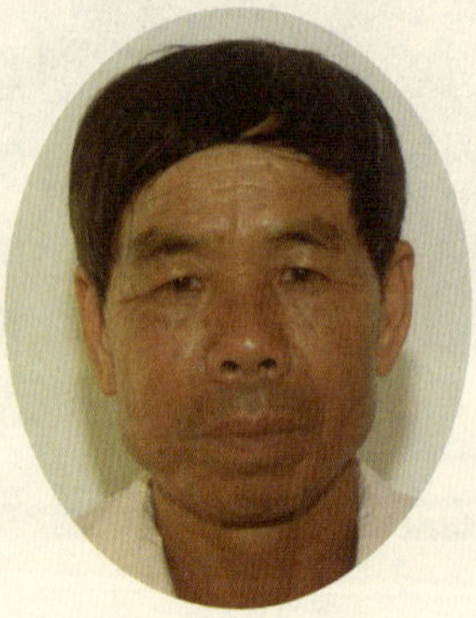

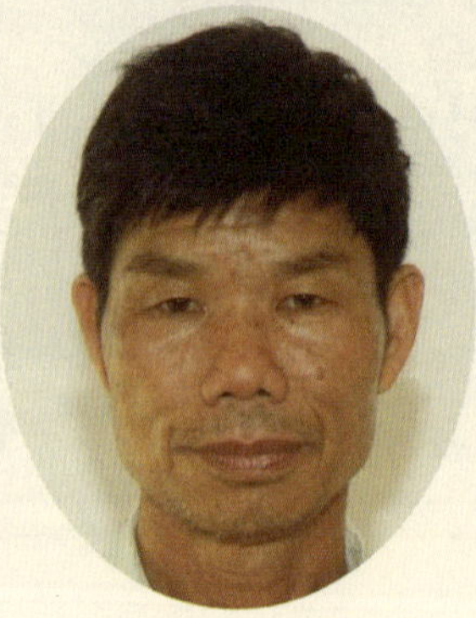

李俭
Li Jian

李俭，男，出生于1948年10月，阳江市阳东区东平镇人，从小跟随父亲参加每年的三月三祭祖活动，熟悉三月三祭祖仪式。成年后，每年坚持参加三月三祭祖活动，掌握三月三祭祖程序和方法，能独立组织实施三月三祭祖活动。李俭现为阳江市第三批非物质文化遗产项目代表性传承人。

Li Jian, male, was born in October 1948, in Dongping Town, Yangdong District, Yangjiang City. He has followed his father to participate in the Third Day of the Third Lunar Month ancestral worship activities every year since he was a child, and is familiar with the Third Day of the Third Lunar Month ancestral worship ceremonies. As an adult, he has insisted on participating in the Third Day of the Third Lunar Month to worship ancestors every year and masters the procedures and methods of worshiping ancestors of the Third Day of the Third Lunar Month. He is able to independently organize the Third Day of the Third Lunar Month ancestral worship activities. He is the representative inheritor of the third batch of intangible cultural heritage projects in Yangjiang City now.

陂面重阳古墟

保护单位 阳春市文化馆

Ancient Double Ninth Market in Beimian

Protection Unit Yangchun Cultural Center

The original site of Double Ninth Market in Beimian was located on the edge of Bidagang, Xinmin Village Committee, Beimian Town, Yangchun City. Later, due to the impassability of traveling by water, it was moved to Chongyanggang. After the reform and opening-up, due to a large number of participants, the two sides of County Road 601 in Chongyanggang, from Xinmin Village to Pozai Village, have gradually become a market. On August 13, 2009, the government of Yangchun city issued a document that the Ancient Double Ninth Market was listed as the intangible cultural heritage of Yangchun City, so that the ancient market culture was protected and would be inherited forever. On the ninth day of the ninth lunar month in 2016, the government of Beimian Town held the ancient Double Ninth Market Cultural Festival. The ancient market was officially named, and the activities of respecting the old and helping the students were carried out on that day.

陂面重阳古墟原址位于阳春市陂面镇新民村委会碧笪岗边，后因水路不通，迁至重阳岗。改革开放后，由于参与人数众多，重阳岗601县道新民村至坡仔村两侧逐步变成了墟集。2009年8月13日，市政府发文，将重阳古墟列为阳春市非物质文化遗产，古墟文化得以保护和传承。2016年农历九月初九，陂面镇政府举办了重阳古墟文化节，古墟正式命名，当天同时开展敬老助学活动。

陂面重阳古墟纪念石碑

The memorial stone of Ancient Double Ninth Market in Beimian

历史渊源

据新民村委会龙坡村老人伍尚来口述整理：春秋战国，吴国大将军伍子胥后代南迁于此，至隋朝伍壬公，医术高明，医德高尚，受人爱戴。惜哉一年重阳，草堂诊病，狂牛打架，壬公相劝，冲撞踩踏，致壬公惨死。民众痛惜，感念其人，拆除草堂，建慈云庵，祈福平安。每逢重阳，远近村民，庵前卖药，遂成墟期。

查阅广东省地方志，《阳春县志》（1996年出版）、《阳春市志》（2013年出版）均有记载陂面重阳古墟资料。

基本内容

陂面重阳古墟每年九月初九成墟，一年一度，摆卖草药，源远流长，历经一千四百载，名传四方。物换星移，重阳古墟规模不断扩大，商品种类逐年增多，已成为集商务、旅游、娱乐、饮食、社交、文化、艺术为一体的大型野地集市。古墟人气鼎盛，闻名遐迩，珠三角、粤西、广西的商贾纷纷慕名而来，络绎不绝，盛况空前。重阳古墟，是阳春民俗文

Historical Origin

According to the words of Wu Shanglai, an old man from Longpo Village, Xinmin Village Committee, in the Spring and Autumn Period and the Warring States Period, the descendants of Wu Zixu, the great general of the State of Wu, moved from north to this place. Wu Rengong, in the Sui Dynasty, who was well-known for his medical skills, was noble in medical ethics, and loved by others. It is a pity that on the ninth day of the ninth lunar month one year, he offered people medical service in a humble cottage when the wild bulls fought. He tried to stop the fight, but the bulls collided and stepped, resulting in his tragic death. The people mourned and missed him, demolishing the place and building Ciyun Nunnery to pray for safeness. Every Double Ninth Day, the villagers far and near sell medicine in front of the nunnery, gradually forming the market day.

Going through the local county chronicles of Guangdong Province, both the *Yangchun County Annals* (published in 1996) and the *Yangchun Annals* (published in 2013) record the data of the Ancient Double Ninth Market of Beimian.

Basic Content

The Ancient Double Ninth Market of Beimian forms on the ninth day of the ninth lunar month annually, selling Chinese herbal medicines, which have a long history and have been passed down for more than 1,400 years. With changing of the world, the scale of the market continues to expand, and the variety of commodities increases year by year. It has become a large-scale wild market integrating business, tourism, entertainment, food, social contact, culture,

陂面重阳古墟第三届文化节留影

Photo in the third Cultural Festival of Ancient Double Ninth Market in Beimian

and art. It is very popular and famous, attracting a large number of merchants from the Pearl River Delta, Western Guangdong, and Guangxi to come in an endless stream of unprecedented pomp. The Ancient Double Ninth Market is a characteristic brand of Yangchun folk culture.

Main Features

The Ancient Double Ninth Market of Beimian has been recorded to have a history of more than 1,400 years. Through vicissitudes of life and changes of the times, the following characteristics have been formed.

(1) The Ancient Double Ninth Market of Beimian is only on the ninth day of the ninth lunar month every year. The location is also limited to a radius of a few miles from the section of Xinmin Village Committee on County Road 601.

(2) The Ancient Double Ninth Market has been formed to commemorate the noble medical ethics and the behavior of curing patients and saving people of Wu Rengong in Sui Dynasty, and inherit the thousand-year Chinese herbal medicine culture. It can commemorate and inherit the medical ethos, medical ethics.

(3) Characteristic Chinese herbal medicine has always been the main commodity of the Ancient Double Ninth Market, which has not changed for more than thousand years. It has witnessed the development of local history, culture, and customs for more than 1,400 years, It also helped people understand and study the Double Ninth Market of Beimian in a broader imagination space for its significance and influence to local culture, economy, production and life.

Great Value

· Historical value

The Ancient Double Ninth Market of Beimian has a long history of more than 1,400 years. The Ancient Double Ninth Market is held once a year and is naturally assembled. The trading products are mainly local Chinese herbal medicines. The historical development process of more than 1,400 years, it has reflected the wisdom, diligence, and basic well-being of the local people from one aspect, and met their production and life needs through merchant activities. It is a historical product, which has important historical value for the study of the history of Yangchun, the customs of various eras after the formation of the market, and the development of productive forces.

· Commercial value

The Ancient Double Ninth Market of Beimian creates a precedent

重阳古墟
The Ancient Double Ninth Market in Beimian

化的一个特色品牌。

主要特征

据记载，陂面重阳古墟已有1400多年的历史。历经沧桑，时代变迁，形成了如下特征：

（1）陂面重阳古墟只在每年的农历九月初九成墟，地点也仅限于县道601线新民村委会段的方圆数里。

（2）重阳古墟因纪念隋朝伍壬公医德高尚、治病救人和传承千年中草药文化而形成。其具有纪念意义和传承医风、医德的作用。

（3）特色中草药一直以来都是重阳古墟的主要商品，千年不变，见证了1400多年来当地历史文化、风土人情的发展，也为了解、研究陂面重阳古墟对当地文化、经济、生产、生活所赋予的存在意义和产生的影响提供了更广阔的想象空间。

重要价值

· 历史价值

陂面重阳古墟，历史悠久，距今已有1400多年。重阳古墟一年一度，自然成集，交易产品以当地盛产的中草药为主。在1400多年的历史发展过程中，它从一个侧面反映了当地人民的智慧、勤劳和基本安康的生活状态，通过商贾活动满足了当地人们的生产生活需求。它是一个历史产物，对研究阳春的历史、成墟后各时代社会的风土人情及生产力发展状况等均有重要的历史价值。

·商业价值

陂面重阳古墟开创了阳春野集贸易之先河。最早，人们在重阳古墟主要是摆卖中草药等，随着时代的变迁，重阳古墟上的商品也越来越丰富多样。到今天，重阳古墟上摆卖的商品琳琅满目，应有尽有，每年趁墟的人数呈增加趋势，近几年来，平均每年有3万多人参加，为当地农民和商人创造了丰厚的经济效益。

·文化价值

陂面重阳古墟，历经沧桑，仍一直流传至今，成为闻名遐迩的阳春两大怪墟之一。这里有它独特的文化内涵，并一直吸引人们走近它、了解它、研究它。重阳古墟从一开始，就被人们赋予了许多神话般的传说，传说一：凡有病的人当天带着在重阳古墟买的中草药到慈云庵拜祭，回家后都能药到病除；传说二：小孩用了当天在重阳古墟买的中草药洗澡，体魄会格

游行队伍精美的轿子
Beautiful sedan chair in the parading team

for Yangchun wild market trade. In the earliest days, people mainly sold Chinese herbal medicines in Ancient Double Ninth Market. With the changes of the times, the commodities in Ancient Double Ninth Market have become more and more diverse. To this day, there is a wide range of commodities sold on the Ancient Double Ninth Market, and nearly everything is available. The number of people coming to the market is increasing every year. In recent years, the average number of people per year has reached more than 30,000, creating huge economic benefits for local farmers and merchants.

· Cultural value

The Ancient Double Ninth Market of Beimian has been passed down through vicissitudes of life to this day. It has its unique cultural connotation and always attracted people to approach it, understand it, and study it. From the very beginning, the Ancient Double Ninth Market has been endowed with many mythical legends. The first legend is that if the sick people bring the Chinese herbal medicines they bought in the Ancient Double Ninth Market to Ciyun Nunnery to worship on that day, they can be cured after returning home. The second legend is that if children bathe with the Chinese herbs they

穿着传统服饰的队伍奏乐游行
People wearing traditional clothes are parading in a team

bought in the Ancient Double Ninth Market that day, they will have extraordinarily strong physique. The third legend is that the old man will live longer when he goes to the Ancient Double Ninth Market three times continuously. Because of these legends, the connotation of the Ancient Double Ninth Market has been greatly enriched, and the Ancient Double Ninth Market has infinite vitality, enduring and moving from primitive to modern.

· Scientific value

In the more than 1,400 years of history from the very beginning to the present, Ancient Double Ninth Market is mainly based on selling Chinese herbal medicines in a great many varieties. It has a broad scientific research value for the study of traditional Chinese medicine culture.

外健壮；传说三：老人连续三年趁重阳古墟，会更加长寿。这些传说，极大地丰富了重阳古墟的内涵，使重阳古墟有了无限的生命力，历久不衰，从原始走向现代。

· 科学价值

重阳古墟从开墟至今的1400多年历史中，均是以摆卖中草药为主，品种繁多，对于研究我国的中医中药文化具有广阔的科学研究价值。

Main Inheritor

Zhou Zhihao, male, was born in January 1972, is a native of Zhougangwei Village of Xinmin Village Committee. He has been influenced by the ancient market culture since he was a child, and he was enthusiastic to participate. When he grew up, he traced roots back to the source of the ancient market and love the source and inheritance of Ancient Double Ninth Market. On the Double Ninth Festival every year, he gathers dozens of people to his home to promote the ancient market culture, and talk about the wonders of traditional Chinese medicine. After serving as a cadre in Xinmin Village since 2011, he is more committed to promoting the culture of the Ancient Double Ninth Market. Every year, he organizes the orderly sale of traditional Chinese medicine in Ancient Double Ninth Market, visits Chinese herbalists, and collects and collates ancient Chinese medicine books. He tries his best for the cultural inheritance of the Ancient Double Ninth Market and makes suggestions. He is the representative inheritor of the fifth batch of intangible cultural heritage projects in Yangjiang City now.

主要传承人

周志豪，男，1972年1月出生，新民村委会周岗尾村人，从小受古墟文化熏陶，热心参与，长大后追根溯源，对重阳古墟来源及传承更是热爱。每年重阳，周志豪均自行组织数十人到家中聚会，推介古墟文化，畅谈中医奇事。2011年任新民村干部后更致力于发扬重阳古墟文化，每年组织在重阳古墟有序摆卖中药，寻访中草药师，搜集、整理中医古本。为重阳古墟文化传承尽心尽力，出谋献策。周志豪现为阳江市第五批非物质文化遗产项目代表性传承人。

周志豪
Zhou Zhihao

书村“走公”

保护单位 阳西县沙扒镇乌石头村民委员会

Shu Village “Zougong”

Protection Unit Wushitou Village Committee, Shapa Town, Yangxi County

书村“走公”这一习俗主要在阳江市阳西县沙扒镇书村流行，参与村落有邻近的代仔村、巴斗村、潭仔村、高树下村、陇顶村、前步村、高山村、老马园村、前海村、流坑村、东坑村、南命村等十多条自然村，区域人口近两万人。

“Zougong” is mainly popular in Shu Village, Shapa Town, Yangxi County, Yangjiang City. The villages that participate in activities include the neighboring Daizai Village, Badou Village, Tanzai Village, Gaoshuxia Village, Longding Village, Qianbu Village, Gaoshan Village, Laomayuan Village, Qianhai Village, Liukeng Village, Dongkeng Village, Nanming Village, and so on, with a regional population of nearly 20,000 people.

历史渊源

早在清朝中期，从福建迁居书村的陈氏族人已繁衍至十几世代，本姓人口快速增长，再有他姓氏族的迁入，居住地域不断扩大，部分陈氏族人迁到邻近多个村落居住，可是，逢年过节以及其他的祭祀活动都会集中在三官堂（书村祖庙）举行，场面十分拥挤，于是，族中长者提议按地域范围建造西社官、旧社官（海仔官）、新社官、南社官等四座镜主大王庙，保境安民，方便祭祀，从此，书村人就有了社片的观念。那时候，书村人大多过着半渔半农的生活，半夜作罾（一种渔作方式）或早上出海打鱼，船回港便马不停蹄赶回村干农活。特别是到了农忙季节，从港口到村的路上更是你追我赶，自然而然地形

Historical Origin

In the middle period of the Qing Dynasty, the Chen family, whose ancestors moved from Fujian to Shu Village, multiplied to more than ten generations. The population of the family grew rapidly. With the influx of other families, the living area continued to expand. Some people of the Chen family moved to neighboring villages. However, during festivals and other sacrificial activities, they gathered together

书村“走公”的活动场景
The scene of Shu Village “Zougong”

in Sanguan Hall (Ancestral Temple in Shu Village) , which was very crowded. Therefore, the elders of the clan proposed to build four Jingzhu Great King Temples according to the geographical scope, including the Xishe Palace, the Jiushe Palace (Haizai Palace) , the Xinshe Palace, and the Nanshe Palace, to protect the territory and people, and facilitate sacrifices. Since then, the people of Shu Village have had a concept of community. At that time, most of the people in Shu Village lived a semi-fishing and semi-farming life. They fished by "Zeng" (a way of fishing) in the middle of the night or went fishing on the sea in the morning. When they returned, they rushed to the village to do the farm work continuously. Especially during the busy farming period, there was a chasing scene on the road from the port to the village. Naturally, they formed the habit of rushing and running, which reflected the hard-working and honest spirit of the ancestors of Shu Village. To inherit the traditional virtues of the ancestors, carry forward the spirit of unity and cooperation, and inspire future generations to forge ahead, the Sanguan Hall took the lead in organizing "Zougong" activities, dividing villagers into teams from four temples, including Xishe, Jiushe, Xinshe, Nanshe, on the fifth day of the fifth lunar month.

Basic Content

Shu Village "Zougong" ["Gong" (first tone) has the same pronunciation as "Gong" (falling tone) in the southern Fujian dialect, meaning "cuddle"] refers to the villagers holding statues of gods in a relay race. It is the most distinctive traditional temple fair folk custom activity in Shu Village. The customs and traditions were formed in the middle of the Qing Dynasty. The main contents of the activities are the "Four Great Kings Parade", "Piaose" parade, the men team's "Zougong", the women team's "Zougong", the dragon

活动中的女子队巡游
The women team is parading in the activity

成了赶路竞跑的习惯，同时也体现了书村先辈们勤劳、拼搏的精神与淳朴的性格。为传承先辈的传统美德，弘扬团结协作精神，激励后人奋发进取，三官堂牵头组织，以西社、旧社、新社、南社等四庙分片的村民各组队伍，每年农历五月初五举行“走公”活动。

基本内容

书村“走公”(“公”在闽南方言海话中与“共”同音，意思是“搂抱”)，是指村民抱着或举着神像接力赛跑，是书村最具特色的传统庙会民俗活动。该风俗传统形成于清朝中期，活动内容主要有“四大王巡游”、“飘色”游行、男子队“走公”、女子队

女子队举着旗帜巡游
The women team holding the flag is parading

巡游队伍中的“天女送花”花车
The float of "Fairy Giving Flowers" in the parading team

"走公"、舞龙醒狮表演、做社戏等。

每年端午节前，村中四社各挑选男女"走公"选手各18～20人，并组织仪仗队，精心制作"大王巡游"的道具，进行排练。

五月初五早上，各社精心组织的游行队伍聚于三官堂，各式旗帜招展，锣鼓雷鸣，唢呐清脆。各社的巡游队列依顺序游行，走在前面的是施炮手，旗手鸣锣开道，举牌手、端香炉者继之；大王座驾在中间，举绫罗伞者、鼓乐手紧随，其后是仪仗、飘色、舞龙醒狮队列。

"四大王巡游"完毕，各社庙主事人要恭请四位"大王"一起到潭仔村土地庙前的四社神坛"观水大"（观察海情），举行祭祀仪式，祈祷风调雨顺、国泰民安。

"观水大"仪式结束后，四位"大王"被恭迎到"走公"起跑点。确认各队选手就位、指定接力地点（俗称"排替"）后，主事人宣布"走公"正式开始。此时，2000多米的道路两旁早已挤满了村民和游客。"走公"是以各社的"大王"座驾（重3~4千克）传递接力，既增加了赛跑难度，同时也营造了"走公"的浓烈气氛。

"走公"结束，随后进行的是舞龙醒狮表演和连续数天的做社戏活动。

and lion dance performances, village theatrical performances, etc..

Every year before the Dragon Boat Festival, the village's four communities select 18-20 male and female contestants for "Zougong", organize an honor guard, and elaborately make props for the "Kings Parade" for rehearsal.

On the morning of the fifth day of the fifth lunar month, the parade queues carefully organized by each community gather in the Sanguan Hall, with all kinds of flags fluttering, gongs and drums thundering, and *suona* playing in a crisp sound. The queue of each community parades in sequence, with those who set off firecrackers walking in front, the flag bearers beating gongs to clear the way, followed by the holders of the placards and incense burners. The king's seat is set in the middle, followed by people taking silk umbrella and the drummers, and the ceremonial guard, the "Piaose", the dragon dance and lion dance team in the last.

After the "Four Kings Parade" is completed, the principal of each temple respectfully invites the four "Kings" to the Four Kings Altar in front of the Land God Temple in Tanzai Village, to "watch the grand water" (observing the sea conditions) , holding a sacrificial ceremony and praying for good weather, peace and security of the country.

After the ceremony of "watching the grand water", the four "Kings" are welcomed to the starting point of "Zougong". After confirming that the contestants of each team are in place at the designated relay location (commonly known as "row replacement"), the principal announces the official start of "Zougong". At that time, the two sides of the road of more than 2,000 meters are already crowded with villagers and tourists. Because the "King" ride (weighing 3-4 kg) should be passed on in "Zougong", the difficulty of the race and the strong atmosphere of "Zougong" are increased.

After "Zougong", dragon and lion dances will be performed, and several consecutive days of village theatrical performances will start.

选手们举着"大王"接力赛跑

Runners attend the rely race by holding the "King"

Great Value

"Zougong" activity is beneficial to inherit the traditional virtues of our ancestors, carry forward the spirit of unity and cooperation, and inspire future generations to forge ahead. The "Zougong" activity attracts around ten thousand people to watch and participate injecting profound humanistic elements into the construction of a strong tourism town of Shapa.

重要价值

"走公"活动传承先辈的传统美德，弘扬团结协作精神，激励后人奋发进取。"走公"活动参与及观看人数达数万人，为沙扒旅游强镇建设注入深厚的人文元素内涵。

Main Inheritors

Chen Jiadong, male, was born in July 1948, has retired after serving as the principal of the Primary School of Shu Village, Xinqiao Primary School, and No. 2 Primary School of Shu Village . To inherit the traditional culture of his hometown and the "Zougong" activity, the long-lasting and prosperous traditional folk activities of Shu Village on a large scale, he has been actively involved in planning, publicizing, organizing, and directing this traditional activity. Now he is the representative inheritor of the fourth batch of intangible cultural heritage projects in Yangjiang City.

Chen Meiyou, male, was born in 1957, is a local villager. He has been influenced by the local culture since he was a child. Since 1990, he has actively participated in, carefully planned, and organized the large-scale folk custom activity of "Zougong" in the Shu Village annually for more than 30 years. He is familiar with the various agendas of the activity. He plays an active role in cultivating the spirit of unity and progress, friendship and harmony, pioneering and hard-working among the villagers. He has certain representativeness, rallying point, and influence in the local area. He passes the custom to his children and grandchildren so that this folk custom activity can be passed on from generation to generation. Now he is the representative inheritor of the fourth batch of intangible cultural heritage projects in Yangjiang City.

主要传承人

陈家栋，男，1948年7月生，曾任书村小学、新桥小学、书村第二小学校长，现已退休。为秉承家乡传统文化、传承书村长盛不衰的大型传统民俗活动"走公"，陈家栋一直积极参与策划、宣传、组织并指挥这一传统活动。陈家栋现为阳江市第四批非物质文化遗产项目代表性传承人。

陈美油，男，1957年生，是一个地道的本土村民，自小受本土文化熏陶，从1990年开始，30多年来每年都积极参与、认真策划、精心组织书村"走公"这项大型民俗活动，熟悉活动的各项议程，在培养广大村民团结奋进、友好和谐、开拓拼搏精神等方面起到积极的推动作用，在当地具有一定的代表性、号召力和影响力，且身体力行传承给儿孙，使该项民俗活动得以薪火相传。陈美油现为阳江市第四批非物质文化遗产项目代表性传承人。

梁镇南将军府炮会

广东省第七批省级非物质文化遗产名录

保护单位 阳春市文化馆

General Liang Zhennan's Mansion Cannon Fair

The Seventh Batch of the Provincial Intangible Cultural Heritage List of Guangdong Province

Protection Unit Yangchun Cultural Center

梁镇南将军府炮会是流传于阳春市石望镇交岗村的一项传统民俗活动。石望镇交岗村位于粤西阳春市北部，古称铜陵垌。村庄四面环山、树竹苍翠，阳骄月朗、云缠雾绕，村中36口鱼塘三五成群、交相辉映，美景山水，如诗如画。在这样一个只有约190户人家、1100人的偏远小山村，每年的农历二月初二却万众云集，盛况空前。数以万计的宾客慕名来到这里，和当地村民欢聚一堂，共同参与梁镇南将军府炮会。

2018年，梁镇南将军府炮会被列入广东省第七批省级非物质文化遗产名录。

The General Liang Zhennan's Mansion Cannon Fair is a traditional folk custom activity spread in Jiaogang Village, Shiwang Town, Yangchun City. Jiaogang Village, Shiwang Town, is located in the north of Yangchun City, the west of Guangdong, known as Tonglingdong in ancient times. The village is surrounded by mountains and green trees, where the sun is gentle and the moon is bright surrounded by clouds and fog and there are 36 fish ponds in groups in the village, showing beautiful and picturesque scenery. In such a remote mountain village with only about 190 families and a population of 1,100, on the second day of the second lunar month every year, thousands of people gather, making the pomp unprecedented. Thousands of people gather and celebrate with the local villagers for the "General Liang Zhennan's Mansion Cannon Fair".

In 2018, the General Liang Zhennan's Mansion Cannon Fair was selected into the seventh batch of the provincial intangible cultural heritage list of Guangdong Province.

风景如画的阳春市石望镇交岗村

The picturesque scenery of Jiaogang Village, Shiwang Town, Yangchun City

Historical Origin

According to the records of *Annals Yangchun City (1979-2000)*, "The ancient Tongling archway and the archway of the general's mansion are located between the two mountains of Tonglingdong, Shiwang Town, 59 kilometers north of Yangchun. In the tenth year of the Kaihuang period in the Sui Dynasty (590), Tongling County was built in Tonglingdong, and destroyed in the eighteenth year of Kaiyuan period in the Tang Dynasty (730). In the sixth year of the Jiajing period in the Ming Dynasty (1527), Liang Zhennan, a native of Jiaogang Village in Tonglingdong, was the second-rank Huben general in front of the hall from the victory of Dateng Gorge in Guangxi. He contributed to the construction of the 'Ancient Tongling' archway to commemorate the historical site of Tongling County. In the seventh year of Jiajing period in the Ming Dynasty (1528), Liang Zhennan built the 'General's Mansion' in Jiaogang Village, an ancient building having three halls with three kaijian sections. Later generations held the General Liang Zhennan's Mansion Cannon Fair of Shiwang on the second day of the second lunar month every year to commemorate him."

General Liang Zhennan has made outstanding achievements in suppressing the bandits in Dateng Gorge. After returning to his hometown, he fought against the bully Rong Baiwan. He built an archway in ancient Tongling County for inheriting the culture. He respected teachers and teaching, built schools, and created the Yanyi School with lofty aspirations. He became a model for future generations, who was respected and loved by the villagers.

The General Liang Zhennan's Mansion Cannon Fair has been passed down for more than 500 years. It originated from the villagers firing five iron cannons in a row to welcome Liang Zhennan, the second-rank Huben general in front for the hall, who returned to his hometown. After the general's death, it evolved into a folk custom activity to commemorate and carry forward the general's spirit of loyalty and righteousness for defending the country; bravery and good fighting skills; might and integrity; and advocating literature and martial art, to remember the general's contribution to national unity and national reunification, praying that the general's spirit in heaven would bless the village with no disasters, abundant living materials and safe life.

历史渊源

据《阳春市志（1979—2000）》记载，“古铜陵牌坊和将军府牌坊在石望镇铜陵垌口两山夹峙处，距春城北59公里。隋开皇十年（590），在铜陵垌建铜陵县城，唐开元十八年（730）平毁。明嘉靖六年（1527），铜陵垌交岗村人梁镇南以从征广西大藤峡功著封殿前二品虎贲将军，他建筑‘古铜陵’牌坊记认铜陵县历史遗址。嘉靖七年（1528），梁镇南在交岗村建‘将军府’，三进三开间风格古建筑。后人为纪念梁镇南，于每年二月初二举办石望将军府炮会。”

梁镇南将军大藤峡剿匪战功显赫，回乡后为民除害，勇斗恶霸容百万，传承文化修建古铜陵县牌坊，尊师重教办学，心高志远创燕翼书室，成为后人的典范，受到村民的敬重和爱戴。

梁镇南将军府炮会延续传承至今已有500多年历史。最早起源于村民一连鸣放五枚铁铳大炮欢迎明代“殿前二品虎贲将军”梁镇南告老还乡荣归故里，将军逝世后，为了弘扬将军忠义卫国、骁勇善战、威武正直、崇文尚武的精神，缅怀将军为民族团结、国家统一作出的贡献，祈求将军在天之灵保佑此地灾难不起、物阜民安，该活动演变为一个纪念将军的民俗活动。

梁镇南将军练武石
The stone for General Liang Zhennan to practice martial art

基本内容

梁镇南将军府炮会历时三天，但正月已开始筹资集款、扎制土炮等，二月初一主要是做准备工作，如搭建炮会棚、八音棚，租借服装，集中收置鞭炮，垒灶搬台，采买备料，迎亲接友等，晚上还请戏班演粤剧折子戏；二月初三则主要是做善尾工作，如计数结账、拆棚撤灶、送还租借物品等。

二月初二为正式的炮会时间，一大早，八音班开棚奏乐庆贺，上一年抢到炮圈的人备好三牲酒礼到将军府拜祭，称之为“还福”； 八音班、舞狮队在将军府前吹奏、表演。八时左右，村长带领村民带上祭品前往将军府在将军灵牌前燃香祈福，参礼拜祭。上午，交岗村的村民杀猪、杀鸡、杀鹅、洗菜、煮饭、烧菜，或陪伴来宾到梁镇南将军府参观游览，青年男女充当服务员接待来宾。中午，在将军府内和将军府前的场地开流水席免费招待所有宾客。新朋老友欢聚一堂，谈笑风生，喜气洋洋。

下午三时左右，鸣响炮仗，由身穿古代服饰的队伍高擎着将军旗开路，大家抬着炮和爆竹，八音和醒狮簇拥，锣鼓喧天，炮声不断，一路人马浩浩荡荡前往位于将

Basic Content

The General Liang Zhennan's Mansion Cannon Fair lasts for three days, but in the first month of the first lunar month, people begin to raise funds and make cannons. On the first day of the second lunar month, they mainly make preparation, such as building cannon fair sheds and eight-instrument playing sheds, renting clothes and collecting firecrackers, building stove, buying materials, welcoming relatives and friends, etc.. In the evening, a troupe is also invited to perform Cantonese opera highlights. On the third day of the second lunar month, people mainly do the final work, such as settling accounts, dismantling sheds and stoves, and returning rental items.

The second day of the second lunar month is the official date of cannon fair. Early in the morning, the eight-instrument troupe starts to play music to celebrate. Those who grabbed the cannon ring in the last year prepare the three livestock with wine and present it to the general's mansion to worship, which is called “rewarding the blessing”. The eight-instrument troupe plays and the lion dance team performs in front of the general's mansion. Around 8 o'clock, the village chief leads the villagers to the general's mansion with offerings to burn incense in front of the general's tablets to pray for blessings, participating in the worship. In the morning, Jiaogang villagers are dispatched to kill pigs, chickens and geese, wash vegetables, cook dishes, or accompany guests to visit General Liang Zhennan's Mansion. Young people act as waiters to welcome the guests. At noon, a banquet is served inside and in front of the general's mansion to welcome all the guests for free. New and old friends gather together, talking and laughing happily.

Around 3 p.m., firecrackers are set off, and the team wearing ancient costumes holds the general's flag high to clear the path. People carry cannons and firecrackers, surrounded by the eight-instrument troupe and the lion dance team, with the loud gongs

村长带领村民在将军灵牌前燃香祈福，参礼拜祭

The village chief leads the villagers burn incense in front of the general's tablet to pray for blessings, participating in the worship and drums. They leave for the cannon fair place after the general's mansion, known as "cannon field".

After settling in, the cannon fair is announced by the president of the current cannon fair in the loud sound of firecrackers. The homemade cannon is the core of the cannon fair. Snatching the cannon ring is the highlight of the cannon fair. The whole cannon fair is also carried out with constant sound of firecrackers, while five homemade cannons are to be fired during the whole fair. In the ear-piercing sound of firecrackers, the lion dance team beats gongs and drums to congratulate the cannons. The beating drums and the dancing lions cheer and lead the first cannon out. The cannon is placed in the middle of the cannon field. The villagers or guests, who have made significant contributions to their hometown and the cannon fair, ignite the cannon. After a loud bang, the cannon goes up with the cannon ring and falls on the ground. At that time, people rush up to the place where the cannon ring lands, scrambling to grab it. Shouting, cheering and sound of firecrackers resound through the sky. Then, the lion dance team invites, the second, third, fourth, and fifth cannon one after another. Every time people try to grab the cannon hoop with much enthusiasm. The one who gets the cannon ring is so excited that he shouts as much as he can, and then people set off a boom.

After all the five cannons are fired, the president of the cannon fair puts on ribbons with the names for five cannon rings winners respectively and gives the bonuses stipulated in this year. Then the lion dance team and the eight-instrument troupe accompany the five cannon rings pickers back to their home. Those who get the cannon rings will hang the ribbon and the cannon rings in their atrium to show that the lucky star is lighting the family highly so that their family will be lucky, safe and full of prosperous grain, prosperous in population,

军府后面的炮会现场，也称“炮地”。

安顿完毕，在热闹的爆竹声中，本届炮会会长宣布炮会开始，自制土炮是炮会的核心，抢炮圈是炮会的重头戏，整个炮会也在不断的爆竹声中进行，其间要燃放五枚自制土炮。在震耳的爆竹声中，舞狮队敲锣打鼓，醒狮贺炮，鼓响狮腾，助威将第一炮请出，将其放在炮地中间，由为家乡和炮会作出重大贡献且德高望重的村民或嘉宾点燃炮引，土炮在发出一声巨响后，炮带着炮圈升空后落地，此时人们向着炮圈落地的地方哄拥而上，争相抢夺，叫喊声、欢呼声和爆竹声响彻云霄。接着四枚自制土炮按顺序由醒狮队一一请出，相继燃放第二炮、第三炮、第四炮、第五炮，每次抢炮圈时大家都群情激昂，争先恐后。抢得炮圈者兴奋无比，尽情呐喊，掀起一波又一波高潮，好不热闹。

五炮全部放完后，炮会会长分别给五位抢得炮圈者佩戴写有炮名的绶带，发放本届规定的奖金，然后由舞狮队、八音班将五位抢得炮圈者送回各自家中，他们将绶带和炮圈一起挂在自家的中堂上，以示福星高照，吉祥如意，五谷丰登，一年平安，人丁兴旺，万事亨通。整个炮会过程持续约两个半小时。

炮会会长点燃炮引
The president of the cannon fair ignites the cannon

抢炮圈场景
The scene of snatching the cannon ring

梁镇南将军府炮会使用的炮分为两种。一是爆竹，即一般燃放的鞭炮，有168万头、88万头、68万头、38万头、8.8万头、6.8万头等规格，通常是村民自觉自愿捐献给炮会燃放，捐赠数量按各家经济状况而定，经济好的人家会捐上3000多元的大爆竹，经济较差的也能捐上300~500元的爆竹，在炮会上由专人燃放。二是自制的土炮。在炮会前十天左右，制炮师傅就会开始扎制，五个炮约需用三天时间，提前扎好备用。

醒狮队燃炮祭神

The lion dance team set off the cannons to worship the gods

土炮由三个部分组成：一是炮座，二是炮胆，三是炮圈。炮座是外形，炮胆是核心，炮圈则是炮会上众人争夺的吉祥物。土炮的制作方法如下：

·炮座制作

（1）首先锯下一段竹子（长为一尺左右），然后用刀将竹破开，再用篾刀把竹削成小圆柱，晒干或鲜用均可。

（2）用小竹篾扎两个小圆圈（直径约8厘米）和一个大圆圈（直径约15厘米），再用砂纸连接接口处，用糨糊粘好，同时扎三个六边形，各用三条竹片交叉支撑六个角，中间点用包装绳扎好固定。

successful in everything in the whole year. The whole cannon fair lasts about two and a half hours.

There are two types of cannons used by the General Liang Zhennan's Mansion Cannon Fair. One is firecracker, that is, the kind of firecracker that is normally set off, including 1.68 million, 880 thousand, 680 thousand, 380 thousand, 88 thousand, 68 thousand firecrackers, etc.. Usually, the villagers voluntarily donate to the cannon fair to set off. The amount of donations are varies according to the economic conditions of each family. People with a good economic condition will donate more than three thousand *yuan* of large firecrackers, and those poor ones will donate 300 to 500 *yuan* of firecrackers, which are set off by specially-assigned person at the fair. The other one is homemade cannons. About ten days before the fair, the cannon makers start to tie cannons, and it takes about three days for five cannons to be tied up in advance.

A homemade cannon consists of three parts: the base, the core part, and the ring. The cannon base shows the shape, the cannon core part reflects the core, and the cannon ring is the mascot that everyone competes for at the cannon fair. The methods to make homemade cannons are as follows:

· Cannon base production

(1) Cut off a section of bamboo (about one *chi* long) . Then break it with a knife, and cut it into small cylinders with a knife. The bamboo strips can be used after drying out or directly.

(2) Use small bamboo strips to make two small circles (about 8 cm in diameter) and a large circle (about 15 cm in diameter). Then use sandpaper to connect the interface, stick it with paste, and make three hexagons at the same time. Use three bamboo pieces cross support the six corners, and the middle point is tied and fixed with a packaging rope.

(3) Use six bamboo strips with a length of 1.5 meters to string two small circles, a large circle, and three hexagons in a certain proportion, and tie each joint with sandpaper. Tie them with six bamboo strips of about 1.2 meters long at the midpoint. Use small bamboo strips to make a hexagon to reinforce the periphery, and the frame of the cannon base is considered complete.

(4) After the frame of the cannon base is completed, it is mounted on five-color paper or pattern paper, but the color of each layer cannot be the same. After mounting, write auspicious words with colored pens on each side of each layer, such as "Huakai Fugui" "Zhubao Ping'an" "Fengtiao Yushun" "Guotai Min'an", etc.. Then write the name of the cannon on the periphery of each cannon base. the General Liang Zhennan's Mansion Cannon Fair has

村民在制作土炮

The villagers are making homemade cannons.

a total of five cannons, and they have respectively named: The first cannon is "Wanzi Qianhong" (meaning a riot of color), the second cannon is "Huakai Fugui" (meaning rich and honored), the third cannon is "Tianding Facai" (meaning having a baby born into the family and getting rich), the fourth cannon is "Mantang Jiqing" (meaning all the place and people are safe and happy), and the fifth cannon is "Fushou Shuanghui" (meaning enjoying both felicity and longevity).

· Firecrackers core part production

(1) First, cut the kraft paper, and then roll the kraft paper into a cylinder. Usually roll the kraft paper three layers to make it thicker and stronger. After the cylinder is completed, put black powder (about 50 grams of gunpowder in a cylinder) in it. After placing the gunpowder, use a small wooden pestle to gently compact the gunpowder, and then use strips to tie the cannon powder cylinder three layers vertically, and then tie three layers horizontally and tightly. This will make the cannon sound loud and lift off higher.

(2) After tying the cannrn core part tightly with bamboo strips, use a small bamboo tube about 6 *cun* long to make a hole down from the top of the cannon core part (but can not through the bottom), and then put a fuse made of sandpaper rolled into gunpowder in the bamboo tube. It would be used when the cannon is fired.

· Cannon ring production

After using grass (grass implies "abundant grain") to form a small circle with a diameter of about 5 cm, use small bamboo strips to wrap around the small circle, and a small iron wire of 2 mm long to wrap the cannon ring again. After that, hang a red rope about 2 *chi* long on the cannon ring to hang the cannon core part.

After the cannon core part and cannon ring are completed, they are placed on the top floor of the cannon base together for setting off.

（3）用六条约1.5米长的竹条将两个小圆圈、一个大圆圈和三个六边形按一定比例串起来，用砂纸扎紧各个接点；用六条约1.2米长的竹条扎在中点处，再用小竹篾做一个六边形在外围加固，炮座框架才算完成。

（4）炮座框架做好后，再用五色纸或图案纸进行装裱，但每一层的色泽不能雷同。装裱后，在每一层的每一面用彩色笔写上吉祥语，如"花开富贵""竹报平安""风调雨顺""国泰民安"等，然后，在每一个炮座的外围写上该炮的名称。梁镇南将军府炮会共有五炮，第一炮为"万紫千红"、第二炮为"花开富贵"、第三炮为"添丁发财"、第四炮为"满堂吉庆"、第五炮为"福寿双辉"。

· 炮胆制作

（1）先裁好牛皮纸，然后把牛皮纸卷成圆筒，通常用牛皮纸卷三层，使其加厚加固。圆筒完成后，再放进黑火药（一个圆筒装入约50克火药），装入火药后，再用小木杵轻轻把火药压实，然后用篾青将火药筒按纵向扎三层再横向扎三层严密包扎。这样就能让炮声响亮，升空更高。

（2）用竹篾扎紧炮胆后，再用一根约6寸长的小竹筒从炮胆的顶端向下打一个洞（但不能打过底），然后将一根用砂纸卷进火药做的导火索，放进小竹筒，待点炮时用。

· 炮圈制作

用禾草（禾草寓意"五谷丰登"）绕成一个直径约5厘米的小圆圈后，先用小竹篾沿小圆圈缠绕一遍，再用2毫米长的小铁线将炮圈缠绕一遍。最后，在炮圈上挂上长约2尺的红绳，使其挂上炮胆。

炮胆、炮圈制作完成后一起放到炮座的顶层，以备燃放。

梁镇南将军府炮会的五炮
Five cannons on the General Liang Zhennan's Mansion Cannon Fair

主要特征

梁镇南将军府炮会从明弘治年间形成至今，已有500多年的历史，其主要特征如下。

（1）时间、地点固定。炮会只在每年的农历二月初二举行，地点也仅限在石望镇交岗村梁镇南将军府后面的稻田里，面积约为60亩。

（2）自扎自制土炮。炮会所燃放的炮为自制土炮，仅限五枚，并有固定的名称，按顺序燃放。抢炮圈是炮会的重头戏，抢得炮圈者为本年度幸运村民，可获本届炮会规定的奖金。

（3）带有浓厚的纪念色彩，有固定的祭拜场所。炮会主要是为纪念“殿前二品虎贲将军”梁镇南而举行的。炮会开始之前，在将军府有庄重的祭拜仪式，炮会全过程鞭炮声不断。

（4）炮会的影响力、号召力和凝聚力远超其他传统节日。只要是本村人，不论职位高低，不论贫贱富贵，不论路途远近，不用通知也不用催促，都会自动自觉从各自生活、工作的地方赶回家乡参加炮会。其中很多人即使春节不一定回家，但到了炮会也一定会回家，故有“炮会大过

Main Features

The General Liang Zhennan's Mansion Cannon Fair has a history of more than 500 years since it was formed during the Hongzhi period of the Ming Dynasty. Its main features are as follows.

(1) The time and place are fixed. The cannon fair is only held on the second day of the second lunar month every year, and the location is limited to the rice fields behind General Liang Zhennan's Mansion in Jiaogang Village, Shiwang Town, with an area of about 60 *mu*.

(2) Homemade cannons. The cannons fired on the cannon fair are homemade cannons, which are only five cannons with fixed names, and fired in sequence. Snatching the cannon ring is the highlight of the fair. The winners are the lucky villagers this year, and they can receive bonuses stipulated by the cannon fair this year.

(3) There are fixed places of worship with a strong commemorative color. The cannon fair is mainly held to commemorate the "the second-rank Huben general in front of the hall" Liang Zhennan. Before the cannon fair starts, there is a solemn worship ceremony in the general's mansion, and the firecrackers are set off uninterruptedly throughout the cannon fair.

(4) The influence, appeal, and cohesion of the cannon fair are higher than those of other traditional festivals. As long as one is a member of the village, regardless of position, poverty, wealth, or distance, without notice or urging, he will automatically and consciously rush back to hometown from where he lives and works to participate in the cannon fair. Many of them may not go home during the Spring Festival, but must go home during the cannon fair, so there is a saying that "The cannon fair is more important than the Chinese New Year".

(5) The dinner is free and everyone can enjoy it. On the second day of the second lunar month, Jiaogang villagers are dispatched to kill pigs, chickens and geese, wash vegetable and cook dishes. Young people act as waiters to welcome the guests. At noon, a banquet is served for all guests for free, with more than 500 tables at most.

Great Value

· Historical value

The General Liang Zhennan's Mansion Cannon Fair has a long history of more than 500 years. The commemorative character is real and clear, and Liang Zhennan's life and deeds also have a real historical basis. During the historical development of hundreds of years, the cannon fair had an extremely significant impact on the Jiaogang Village and the formation of the core values of the people in the Shiwang area. It has disseminated and passed on general's spirit through the form of fair, making him a model for future generations. The fair provides truth and precious historical data for the history, customs, humanistic spirit, social conditions, productivity development, culture, education, entertainment, and other aspects of Jiaogang Village, Shiwang area and even Yangchun.

· Cultural value

The cannon fair originates from the celebration of General Liang Zhennan's return to his hometown. The spirit of Liang Zhennan is the embodiment of the excellent traditional Chinese culture. Because of admiration and love for General Liang Zhennan, the villagers evolved celebrations into commemorations to carry forward the spirit of Liang Zhennan and inspire descendants. With the development of society, it has gradually been given new contents. It integrates culture, art, entertainment, food, social networking, tourism and commerce, making the cannon fair activities keep pace with the times and integrate the fashion culture and aesthetic requirements, and making the cannon fair attractive and cohesive. In addition to the core content of worship and setting off cannons, there are also eight-instrument troupe as well as lion dance performances, playing operas, singing and dancing, visiting and dining together, calligraphy, literary and artistic award ceremonies, off-road vehicle competitions and other cultural and recreational activities. In recent years, the cannon fair has attracted artists from all over the country to come here to collect folk customs and create works, which become a highlight of cultural construction in Guangdong. Various cultural elements greatly enhance the influence and popularity of the fair, enriching

年”之说法。

（5）免费聚餐，见者有份。农历二月初二，交岗村的村民杀猪、杀鸡、杀鹅、洗菜、煮饭、烧菜，青年男女则充当服务员接待招呼来宾，中午开流水席免费招待所有宾客，最多时摆席500多台。

重要价值

· 历史价值

梁镇南将军府炮会有着500多年的悠久历史，其纪念的人物真实清晰，梁镇南的生平事迹也有真实的历史依据。在数百年的历史发展过程中，炮会对交岗村以及石望地区人民群众价值观的形成产生了极其重大的影响，并通过炮会的形式传播和传承将军的精神，成为一代又一代后人的典范。这对研究交岗村以及石望地区乃至阳春的历史、风土人情、人文精神以及各时代社会状况、生产力发展情况和文化、教育、娱乐等方面都提供了真实而宝贵的史料。

· 文化价值

炮会起源于梁镇南将军告老还乡之时的庆祝活动，梁镇南精神是中华优秀传统文化的体现。村民出于对梁镇南将军的仰慕、敬爱，为了使梁镇南精神发扬光大和激励后人，将庆祝活动演变延续为纪念活动。随着社会的发展，炮会渐渐被赋予了新的内容，它集文化、艺术、娱乐、饮食、社交、旅游、商业于一体，使炮会活动与时俱进，融合时尚文化和审美要求，将炮会办得具有吸引力和凝聚力，除核心内容拜祭、放炮外，还有八音班吹奏、醒狮表演、唱戏、歌舞、参观、聚餐、书法家即席挥毫、文艺颁奖仪式、越野车比赛等文化娱乐活动。近年来，吸引了全国各地文艺家到此采风、创作，成为广东文化建设的一大亮点。各种丰富的文化元素极大地提高了炮会的影响力和知名度，也丰富了村民的文化生活，进一步促进了当地的精神文明建设，使炮会成为村民了解外界、外界了解当地文化的桥梁和平台，使子孙后代认同并牢记梁镇南将军精神的内涵，这对于弘扬优秀传统文化、弘扬梁镇南将军精神、弘扬社会主义核心价值观都起到十分重要的启迪示范作用。

·科学价值

梁镇南将军府炮会以炮贯穿整个活动过程，而土炮的制作有较严格的要求，其中的炮座、炮胆和炮圈原材料不同、功能不同、比例不同，各部位需合理配置，火药需精细利用，炮的声音、炮圈升空的高度等均要获得最佳效果。其制作过程涉及空气动力学、金属炼制技术等科技领域，因此炮会还具有科学研究的价值。

the cultural life of the villagers, further promoting the local mental civilization construction, and making the fair a bridge and platform for the villagers to understand the outside world and for the outside world to understand the local customs, so that future generations can recognize and remember the connotation of General Liang Zhennan's spirit, which plays a very important and model role in promoting the excellent traditional culture, the spirit of General Liang Zhennan, and the core values of Chinese socialism.

· Scientific value

The General Liang Zhennan's Mansion Cannon Fair runs through the entire activity process with cannons, while the production of homemade cannons has strict requirements. The cannon base, cannon core part, and cannon ring have different raw materials, different functions, and different proportions. The reasonable configuration of each part, the fine utilization of gunpowder, the sound of the cannon, and the height of the rising cannon ring should obtain the best effect. The production process involves aerodynamics, metal refining technology, and other scientific and technological fields, so the cannon fair also has scientific research value.

大王诞炮会

保护单位 阳春市石望镇石望村民委员会

The Great King's Birthday Cannon Fair

Protection Unit Shiwang Village Committee, Shiwang Town, Yangchun City

The Great King's Birthday Cannon Fair, commonly known as "burning cannons", is a typical traditional folk custom activity in Tanwei Natural Village, Shiwang Village Committee, Shiwang Town, Yangchun City. The Great King's Birthday Cannon Fair was formed to commemorate the favor of the "Great King" who killed the evil python to eliminate the plague more than 400 years ago, and to praise the great achievements of the "Great King", expressing the villagers' desire to eliminate the evil, praise the good, and hope a peaceful world.

Historical Origin

Tanwei Village is adjacent to Daxiang Mountain in the west and Gui Mountain in the east. Looking from the front, there are two smaller stone mountains connected to Daxiang Mountain. The shape is like an armchair. There are two natural stone caves in the small stone mountain. There is a deep pool in the center of the village. The east, south, and north sides of the village are surrounded by walls, so it is named Tanwei. During the Jiajing period of the Ming Dynasty, old man Yuanxiong (the adopted father of old man Qiubo), the great ancestor of the Liang family, brought his adopted son old man Qiubo to Tanwei Village from Furong Village.

According to the words of Liang Kunrong (male, was born on September 10th, 1935), the president of the 16th cannon fair association, based on the oral legend of the ancestors, after their ancestors settling down, the crops and fields were often destroyed for unknown reasons, and plagues often occurred. On the first and fifteenth day of the lunar month, people would go to the stone cave in the south, worshipping the "Great King" and praying for peace.

大王诞炮会俗称"烧炮"，是阳春市石望镇石望村委会潭围自然村典型的传统民俗活动。大王诞炮会是为纪念"大王"在400多年前斩恶蟒驱瘟疫的恩惠，以及歌颂"大王"的丰功伟绩而形成，也表达了村民期盼除恶扬善、天下太平的愿望。

历史渊源

潭围村西靠大象山，东朝龟山，正面看，有两座小一点的石山与大象山相连，形状如太师椅。小石山都有两个天然的石洞，寨中央有深潭一口，村庄东、南、北三面用围墙围起来，因此得名潭围。梁氏始祖远雄公（秋波公养父）于明嘉靖年间携养子秋波公从芙蓉寨迁居潭围寨。

据第十六世炮会会长梁坤荣（男，1935年9月10日出生）口述：据祖辈口口相传，祖辈定居后，庄稼田经常因不明原因被破坏，经常发生瘟疫，人们逢初一、十五都要到南边的石洞祭拜"大王"，祈求平安。有一个初一的早上，当人们去祭拜"大王"时，发现"大王"竟然不见了，只看见沿路滴落一地的香烛油，跟踪香烛油的

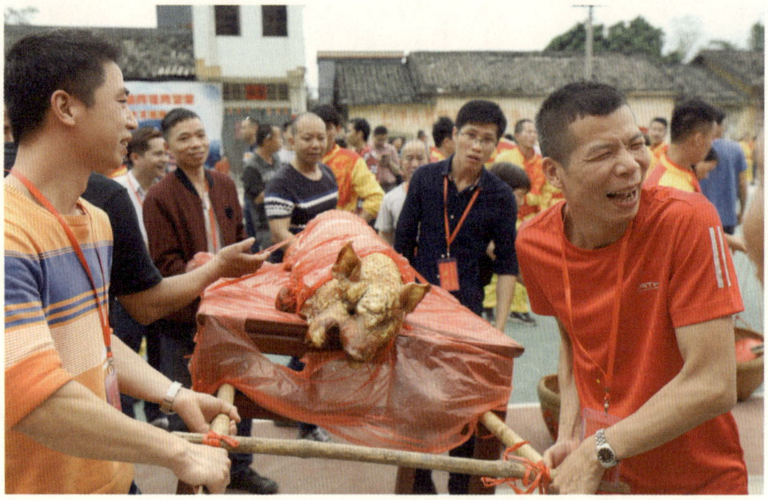

家家户户备三牲祭拜“大王”
Every family prepare the three livestock sacrifices to worship the “Great King”

痕迹，竟发现“大王”在北边的石洞中。人们百思不得其解。后一位高人云游到潭围寨，说“大王”其实是“石龙大王”，刚打败了深潭中的蟒蛇，是很有灵气的，人们要扎龙安龙，以农历二月十三为“石龙大王”的诞辰，举行怡神烧炮活动，这样“石龙大王”会一直在石洞中，保寨中平安。

秋波公决定立“石龙大王”神位，扎制金龙两条，并将石洞修葺一新，命名为“大王宫”。近年来，每到“大王诞”日，人们准备三牲祭拜“大王”，八音迭奏，恭请“大王”乘“金龙”巡游，举行搭戏棚、唱大戏、舞金龙、抬烧猪、烧花炮、抢炮圈等活动。自举行了炮会活动后，庄稼田再没有被破坏，瘟疫也没有了，于是炮会就一直举行下去。

后秋波公将炮会传给儿子宾辉公，并一代一代相传至孙大培公、昊培公，玄孙镇隆公、镇泰公、镇英公、镇时公、镇中公、镇宇公、镇盘公等，到现在已传至第十九代，400多年从未间断。潭围寨村民深信，只要有“大王”在，有“龙”在，才能保佑这方水土平安无事，因此必须举行大王诞炮会活动，“舞双龙”也因此成为炮会活动的必备程序，且有丰富完整的舞龙套式和独特造型。

On one morning of the first day of the lunar month, when people went to worship the “Great King”, they found that the “Great King” disappeared, and only saw the joss stick and candle oil dripping down the road. Tracking the traces of the joss stick and candle oil, people found that the “Great King” had gone to the stone cave in the north. people couldn’t understand. Later, a talented person wandered to Tanwei Village and said that the “Great King” was actually the “Shilong King”, who had just defeated the python in the deep pool, and was very spiritual. People had to appease dragons, set the thirteenth day of the second lunar month as the birthday of the “Shilong King”, hold a cannon-burning activity to delight the “Shilong King”, so that it would always be in the cave to keep the village safe.

Old man Qiubo decided to establish the tablet of “Shilong King”, made two golden dragons, repaired the cave, and named it the “Great King Palace”. In recent years, on the “Great King’s Birthday”, people prepare three livestock to worship the “Great King”, playing octave music, and respectfully inviting the “Great King” to ride “Golden Dragon” to parade, setting up a stage, singing traditional Chinese opera, dancing the golden dragon, carrying roast pigs, burning cannons, snatching cannon rings, and holding other activities. Since the cannon fair was held, the crops have not been destroyed, and the plague has disappeared. Therefore, the cannon fair has been held forever.

Later, old man Qiubo passed on the cannon fair to his son old man Binhui, grandson old man Dapei, Haopei, the great-great-grandson old man Zhenlong, Zhentai, Zhenying, Zhenshi, Zhenzhong, Zhenyu, Zhenpan, and so on, and it has had nineteen generations until now, without interruption for more than 400 years. The villagers in Tanwei Village are convinced that as long as there is the “Great

King" and "Dragon", they can bless the water and soil in peace, so the activities of the Great King's Birthday Cannon Fair must be held. Therefore, "dancing double dragons" has become an inevitable process for the activities of the cannon fair. There are rich and complete dragon dance sets and unique shapes.

According to the "Shiwang chapter" of *Looking for Rhyme in Chunzhou*, "On the thirteenth day of the second lunar month, the 'Great King's Birthday', people hold the worship ceremony with dragon dance in the village, setting up a stage to sing and celebrate, which attracts a crowd of people, and hold a ceremony of snatching the cannon rings with the drums and cannons sounds, for blessing good weather, peace and security of the country. The excitement is extraordinary."

Basic Content

The thirteenth day of the second lunar month is the birthday of the "Great King". The "Great King" fights the evil python to eliminate the plague which is deeply rooted among the villagers. On this day, the villagers hold a series of activities to thank and worship the "Great King", such as worshiping the "Great King", respectfully inviting the "Great King" to a parade, having double dragon performances, and burning cannons, calling it the "Great King's Birthday Cannon Fair". Over the past few hundred years, the activities of the Great King's Birthday Cannon Fair have gone through vicissitudes of life, but they have been constantly inherited, and the Great King's Birthday has gradually become a cultural and traditional festival in Tanwei Village.

On the morning of the thirteenth day of the second lunar month, the council of the cannon fair brings three livestock sacrifices to the "Great King Palace" in the back mountain of Tanwei Village

《春州寻韵》"石望篇"记载："每逢农历二月十三日'大王诞'日，人们都要在村里举行舞龙祭祀，并搭戏棚唱戏庆祝，人山人海，鼓炮齐鸣并举行抢花炮活动，祈求风调雨顺、国泰民安，热闹程度非凡。"

基本内容

农历二月十三是"大王"诞辰。"大王"斗恶蟒驱瘟疫，在村中深入人心。村民在这一天举行祭祀"大王"、恭请"大王"巡游、双龙表演、烧花炮等系列活动，感恩"大王"，敬奉"大王"，故称"大王诞炮会"。几百年来，大王诞炮会活动历经沧桑，但始终得以传承，大王诞也逐渐成为潭围村的文化传统节日。

农历二月十三早上，炮会理事会带三牲贡品到潭围村后山"大王宫"祭拜"大王"，禀告"大王"，敬请"大王"巡游，巡游由双龙相伴。巡游队伍所到之处，村民摆香案焚香拜"大王"，鸣鞭炮，接龙符（掌印人印制大量的"龙春符"作为"龙符"广发），以示迎吉消灾。

巡游队伍最后到达烧炮地，将"大王"神位伫立在烧炮地中间，再次接受村

大王诞活动

The activity of the Great King's birthday

民的集中祭拜。上一年抢到炮圈的人要还炮。请一枚炮，需备大金猪一只，油炸糍粑、粽子、水果若干作为贡品，另备长鞭炮几大串、檀香香烛。将金猪、贡品放置在一张八仙桌上，由四个壮汉抬着桌来到烧炮地，沿路锣鼓齐鸣，燃放鞭炮。七张八仙桌、七只大金猪、七枚炮整齐地摆放在“大王”神位前，众人焚香祭拜“大王”。

接着进行舞龙表演。舞龙队按不同造型进行表演，再现双龙勇缚恶蟒、斩除祸害的勇猛行为。舞龙完毕，开始烧炮。

烧炮开始，先由司仪宣读点炮人。七枚炮由不同人点燃。点炮人由大王诞炮会理事会推举，一般推举村中德高望重的人或者热心捐款人士担任。一枚炮推举一个或几个点炮人。点炮人按照“燃香—参拜大王—点炮”的程序进行点炮，非常隆重。七枚炮按次序点燃，烧完一炮，待炮圈被抢到，再接着烧下一炮。众人争先恐后去抢炮圈，抢到炮圈的幸运儿高举炮圈，其他人则立即停止争抢。抢到炮圈的人先是拜祭“大王”，然后领取“炮银”。整个烧炮活动持续一个半小时。

烧炮是大王诞炮会活动的核心内容。炮由三个部分组成：一是炮座，二是炮胆，三是炮圈。炮圈是炮会上众人争夺的吉祥物，抢到炮圈者可获花红奖励。各炮都有吉祥的寓意，并能带来好运气。原先是燃放五枚炮，后来增加两枚。原来在民国时期，本乡一位殷实的梁姓人士抢到一枚添丁炮，当年就添了一男丁，他为了谢恩，在第二年还炮时（按规定，抢到炮圈者第二年必须送还新炮座和花红），捐资设立了副三炮。

to worship the “Great King”, report to the “Great King”, and invite the “Great King” to parade accompanied by two dragons. Wherever the parade team goes, the villagers set up incense tables to burn incense to worship the “Great King”, set off firecrackers, and get dragon amulet (the people in charge print a large number of “Longchunfu” to widely distributed as “dragon amulet”) to welcome good luck and eliminate disasters.

The parade team finally arrives at the cannon-burning site, stands the tablet of “Great King” in the middle of the cannon-burning site, to accept the concentrated worship of the villagers again. Those who grabbed the cannon ring last year have to return the cannon. To invite a cannon, people need to prepare a big roast pig, fried *ciba*, *zongzi*, some fruits as sacrifices, as well as several large strings of long firecrackers, and sandalwood candles. The roast pig and the sacrifices are placed on a square table and four strong men carry the table to the cannon-burning site. Along the road the gongs and drums blare together and the firecrackers are set off. Seven square tables, seven big roast pigs, and seven cannons are neatly placed in front of the tablet of the “Great King”. Everyone burns incense to worship the “Great King”.

Then the dragon dance performance starts. The dragon dance is performed according to different shapes, reproducing the brave behavior of the double dragons binding the evil python and eliminating the scourge. After the dragon dance is completed, the cannon is fired.

The firing of the cannon begins with the master of ceremonies announcing the person ignites the cannon. The seven cannons are lit by different people who are recommended by the council of the Great King's Birthday Cannon Fair. Generally, the people who are of noble character and high prestige in the village, or enthusiastic donors will be elected as the person ignites the cannon. One or several people

抢到炮圈的年轻人

The youth who grabs the cannon ring

are recommended for one cannon. The person ignites the cannon according to the procedure of "burning incense-making a pilgrimage to the Great King-igniting the cannon", which is very saint. The seven cannons are ignited in order. One cannon is burned, and only after the cannon ring is grabbed can the next cannon be ignited. Everyone scrambles to grab the cannon ring. The lucky one who gets the cannon ring raises it high, and the others immediately stop snatching. Those who get the cannon ring first worship the "Great King", and then gain the "cannon bonus". The whole cannon-burning activity lasts for an hour and a half.

Burning cannons is the key activity of the King's Birthday Cannon Fair. The cannon consists of three parts: the cannon base, the cannon core part, and the cannon ring. The cannon ring is the mascot that everyone competes for at the Cannon Fair. Who grabs the cannon ring can be rewarded with bonus. Each cannon has auspicious meanings and can bring good luck. Originally, five cannons were fired, and later two are added. It turned out that during the period of Republic of China, a local well-off man surnamed Liang got a cannon that blesses the person with a new child, and Liang family had a new baby boy that year. To show gratitude, when he returned the cannon in the second year (according to regulations, those who obtained the cannon must return the new cannon base and bonus in the second year), he donated funds to set up the secondary of the third cannons.

There is a local saying that the cannon fair is more important than the Chinese New Year. No matter how far the villagers go out, they must back to hometown to worship the "Great King" and participate in the cannon fair. The Great King's Birthday Cannon Fair also attracts villagers in surrounding villages and their relatives and friends to watch, even the people from surrounding cities. The Great King's Birthday Cannon Fair is a typical representative of traditional folk activities in Yangchun City and an important part of traditional Chinese folk customs activities. The Great King's Birthday Cannon Fair reflects that the villagers in Tanwei and surrounding areas reverence nature, be grateful to nature, and their good wishes of praying for good weather, peace, and happiness, with Lingnan cultural characteristics.

Main Features

· Historic significance

The Great King's Birthday Cannon Fair originates in Wanli's period in the Ming Dynasty (1573-1620). It is a traditional custom that the villagers in Tanwei Village participate in every year and inherit

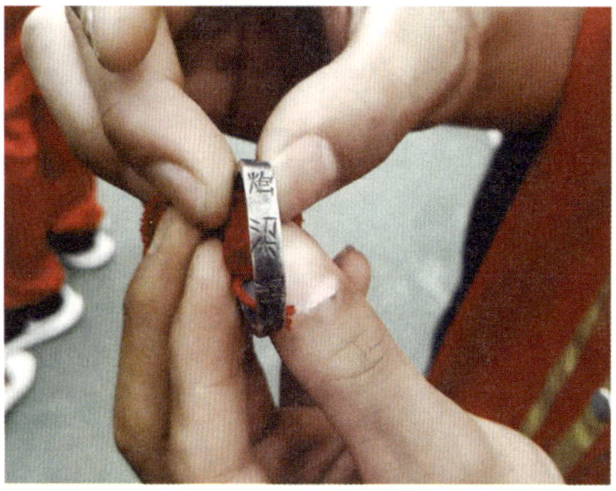

炮圈

The cannon ring

当地有“烧炮大过年”的说法。外出的村民无论离家多远，都必须回乡祭拜“大王”并参与炮会活动。大王诞炮会还吸引了周边村寨的村民以及亲朋好友，甚至是周边地市的人员前来观看。大王诞炮会活动是阳春市传统民俗活动的典型代表，也是中国传统民俗活动的重要组成部分。大王诞炮会活动体现了潭围及周边村民敬畏自然、感恩自然，并祈求风调雨顺、平安幸福的美好心愿，具有鲜明的岭南文化特色。

主要特征

· 历史性

大王诞炮会源于明万历年间（1573—1620），是潭围村一项村民年年参与、代代传承的传统习俗，具有较长的传承历史。

· 原生态

每年农历二月十三，村民自发备三牲、香祭拜大王，恭请“大王”巡游，并舞金龙、烧花炮、争抢炮圈、燃鞭炮、奏鼓乐等。大王诞炮会是民间性的祈福求愿、文化娱乐的一种形式。

· 地域性

大王诞炮会有着较强的地域文化特色，“大王”神位就立在谭围寨后山的

"大王宫"里，村民祭拜大王这一习俗，未曾中断。每年农历二月十三，恭请"大王"巡游。"大王"神位伫立于烧炮地，接受各方来客参拜；民间有"炮会大过年"的说法。

· **舞龙文化**

舞龙是大王诞炮会的一个特色。双龙按照"行龙—舔龙身—碌球—龙头滚龙尾—龙尾滚龙头—走龙柱、走五点梅—走金钱—走半边月—走榄形—龙门阵—长蛇阵—金虾鹤阵"的顺序进行表演。龙身用竹篾扎成，用多层砂纸粘在龙身周围，画上龙鳞，并用竹篾扎制鲤鱼、虾、鹤各一只。

· **唯一有七个炮的炮会**

七个炮分别是：一炮"万紫千红"、二炮"福禄双全"、三炮"添丁发财"、副三炮"满堂吉庆"、四炮"花开富贵"、五炮"丁财贵寿"、副五炮"福禄寿全"。炮全由扎炮传承人手工扎成。先扎好1.5米高炮身框架，四周贴上砂纸，下部为炮座，上部为装炮口，待砂纸自然干后，画上各种花图案，寓意花开富贵。接着制作炮胆。炮胆如同一个大炮仗，底部放黑火药，上部放炮圈。最后一步是装炮圈。炮圈是一个直径2厘米的铁圈。将炮圈放到炮的上部，装上引线。

村民备三牲、香祭拜大王

The villagers prepare three livestock and incense to worship the "Great King"

from generation to generation, with a long history of inheritance.

· Original ecology

Every year on the thirteenth day of the second lunar month, the villagers spontaneously prepare three livestock and incense to worship the "Great King", respectfully invite the "Great King" to the parade, dance golden dragons, burn cannons, grab cannon rings, set off firecrackers and play drums, etc.. The Great King's Birthday Cannon Fair is a form of praying, blessing, and cultural entertainment.

· Regionality

The King's Birthday Cannon Fair has strong regional cultural characteristics. The tablet of the "Great King" is located in the "Great King Palace" in the mountain behind the village. The villagers worship the "Great King" without interruption. Every year on the thirteenth day of the second lunar month, the "Great King" is respectfully invited to parade. The tablet of the "Great King" stands in the cannon-burning place, accepting visitors' worship from all over the world, and there is a saying that the cannon fair is more important than the Chinese New Year.

舞龙表演

Dragon dance performance

· Dragon dance culture

The dragon dance is a feature of the King's Birthday Cannon Fair. The double dragons follow the sequence of "walking dragon—licking the dragon body—roll ball—dragon head rolling dragon tail—dragon tail rolling dragon head—walking dragon pillar and walking a route of quincuncial piles—striking a pose of a copper coin—striking a pose of half the moon—walking elvis shape—dragon gate array—long snake array—golden shrimp and crane array". The dragon's body is made by tying the bamboo strips and using layers of sandpaper to stick around with painted drew dragon scales on. One carp, one shrimp, and one crane are made by tying bamboo strips.

· The only cannon fair with seven cannons

The seven cannons are as following: the first cannon is "Wanzi Qianhong" (meaning "a riot of color"), the second cannon is "Fulu Shuangquan" (meaning having both fame and wealth), the third cannon is "Tianding Facai" (meaning having a baby born into the family and getting rich), the secondary of the third cannon is "Mantang Jiqing" (meaning auspicious and festive mood in the house), the fourth cannon is "Huakai Fugui" (meaning getting rich when blossoming), the fifth cannon is "Dingcai Guishou" (meaning the blessing for a prosperous family, rich wealth, a prosperous career and long life), and the secondary of the fifth cannon is "Fulu Shouquan" (meaning the luck, rich and longevity). The cannons are all tied by hand by the cannon inheritors. First, tie the frame of the 1.5-meter-high cannon body and stick sandpaper around it. The lower part is the cannon base, and the upper part is the muzzle. After the sandpaper dries naturally, paint various flower patterns, which means getting rich when flower blossoming. Then make the cannon core part, which is like a big cannon, with black powder at the bottom and a cannon ring at the top. The last step is to install the cannon ring. The cannon ring is an iron ring with a diameter of 2 cm. The cannon ring is placed on the upper part of the cannon and fitted with a lead.

Great Value

· Historical value

The King's Birthday Cannon Fair in Tanwei Village originates in Wanli period in the Ming Dynasty (1573–1620) and has a history of more than 400 years. It is a traditional custom to worship the "Great King" and pray for good weather, abundant grains, happiness and peace. In the process of historical development, it carries the common memory of the villagers in Tanwei Village. The King's Birthday Cannon Fair is a microcosm of the villagers' spontaneous

装炮圈
Install the cannon ring

重要价值

· 历史价值

潭围村的大王诞炮会源于明万历年间（1573—1620），距今已经有400多年的历史，是为祭祀"大王"神灵，祈求风调雨顺、五谷丰登、幸福平安的一项传统习俗。在历史发展过程中，承载着潭围村村民共同的记忆。大王诞炮会是村民们自发传承和保护传统文化的一个缩影。舞双龙和抢炮圈是大王诞炮会的一大特色，寓意平安和丰收，它是一个历史产物，代表了一方水土的文化特色，对研究阳春的历史和此后各时代社会的风土人情及生产力发展状况均有重要的历史价值。

· 文化价值

大王诞炮会历经400多年，仍一直流传至今，这是因为它具有独特的文化内涵，吸引人们走近它、了解它、研究它。在潭围村大王宫石洞的对联"大德无私能载物，王灵有感祝千秋"，体现了潭围村深厚的文化底蕴。

· 学术价值

大王诞炮会作为民俗活动，具有历史学、社会学等方面的特殊价值，烙印着潭围村的历史变迁，凝结着潭围人的情感和思维，传承着岭南文化的内涵，因此具有一定的学术价值。

· 社会价值

随着时代的变迁，炮会内容不断丰富和完善。炮会期间，村民在家里大摆筵席，邀请乡里和亲朋好友到家中聚会，并举行炮会文艺晚会。炮会对凝聚向心力、营造和睦的邻里关系、培育文明乡风、推动农村产业兴旺、带动乡村旅游有重要意义。

inheritance and protection of traditional culture. Dancing double dragons and snatching cannon rings are major features of the Great King's Birthday Cannon Fair, implying peace and harvest. It is a historical product and represents the cultural characteristics of one place. It has important historical value for the study of the history of Yangchun and the social customs, productivity development, etc. of various eras since then.

· Cultural value

After more than 400 years of vicissitudes, the Great King's Birthday Cannon Fair has been passed down to this day. This is because it has its unique cultural connotation, attracting people to approach it, understand it, and study it. There is a couplet in the stone cave of the Great King's Palace in Tanwei Village, that is, "Selflessness and virtues can carry things. The immortal of the Great King has spirit and protects the place for thousand years." which reflects the profound cultural heritage of Tanwei Village.

· Academic value

As a folk activity, the Great King's Birthday Cannon has special value in history, sociology, etc.. It imprints the historical changes of Tanwei Village, condenses the emotions and thinking of Tanwei people, and inherits the connotation of Lingnan culture. Therefore, it has a certain academic value.

· Social value

With the changes of the times, the content of the cannon fair is also constantly enriched and improved. During the fair, the villagers hold a feast at home, inviting the other villagers, relatives, and friends to gather. A cannon fair entertainment evening party are also held. It is of great significance to keep cohesion, create harmonious neighborhood relations, cultivate civilized rural customs, promote the prosperity of rural industries, and drive rural tourism.

拾获炮圈者

The person who grabs the cannon ring

Main Inheritor

Liang Zhouji, male, was born in May 1964, is a native of Tanwei Natural Village, Shiwang Village Committee, Shiwang Town, Yangchun City, and the eighteenth-generation inheritor of the Great King's Birthday Cannon Fair (his master is Liang Kunrong) . He has learned the skill of making cannon and dragon from his father in his hometown since he was a child. He has strong comprehension, and once he saw the skill of making cannons, he couldn't forget it. He could make cannons according to his father's way, and has mastered the essentials. He has always been an expert in making cannons in the village. He preserves the frame of the old dragon head, two performing dragons, gongs and drums and other dragon dance instruments, seven cannon frameworks, and the cannon rings. His apprentice is Liang Yuesheng. He contributes to the smooth holding of the Great King's Birthday Cannon Fair. He is the representative inheritor of the fifth batch of intangible cultural heritage projects in Yangjiang City now.

Liang Jinkang, male, was born in October 1965, is a native of Chunwan Town, Yangchun City, and the eighteenth-generation inheritor of the Great King's Birthday Cannon Fair. He used to learn to make dragons and cannons. Since he started to work, he has participated in the planning and organization of the Great King's Birthday Cannon Fair with his uncle Liang Guangzhong every year. He keeps a dragon seal. In recent years, as the president of the Liang Clan Association in Tanwei, Shiwang Village, Liang Jinkang has made important contributions to holding the Tanwei Great King's Birthday Cannon Fair successfully every year. He is the representative inheritor of the fifth batch of intangible cultural heritage projects in Yangjiang City now.

主要传承人

梁周基，男，1964年5月生，阳春市石望镇石望村委会潭围自然村人，大王诞炮会第十八代传承人（师傅梁坤荣）。从小跟随父亲在家乡学扎炮、扎龙，领悟性强，对扎炮技术过目不忘，能按父亲的方式动手扎炮，并掌握要领，一直是村里负责扎炮的能手。他保存有老龙头框架、表演的舞龙两条、锣鼓等舞龙乐器、七枚炮框架及炮圈，并带有徒弟梁月生，为大王诞炮会活动的顺利举行作出了贡献。梁周基现为阳江市第五批非物质文化遗产项目代表性传承人。

梁锦康，男，1965年10月生，阳春市春湾镇人，大王诞炮会第十八代传承人。曾学过扎龙、扎炮，自参加工作起，每年与伯父梁光中一起参加大王诞炮会的策划和组织工作，保管有龙印一枚。近年来，梁锦康作为石望村潭围梁氏宗亲会会长，为每年潭围大王诞炮会的成功举办作出了重要贡献。梁锦康现为阳江市第五批非物质文化遗产项目代表性传承人。

梁锦康
Liang Jinkang

梁鉴治，男，出生于1968年10月。阳春市石望镇人，大王诞炮会第十八代传承人。自小随堂叔梁周基长大，并学习扎龙、扎炮，了解扎龙、扎炮的过程，对烧炮非常感兴趣。1987年参加工作后，每年都参与大王诞炮会的组织策划、主持，以及龙符制作与龙鳞制作等工作，记录炮会、宣传炮会，注重在潭围村年轻人中宣传炮会文化，为炮会传承与发展作出了重要的贡献。梁鉴治现为阳江市第五批非物质文化遗产项目代表性传承人。

Liang Jianzhi, male, was born in October 1968, is a native of Shiwang Town, Yangchun City, and the eighteenth-generation inheritor of the Great King's Birthday Cannon Fair. He grew up with his uncle Liang Zhouji since childhood and learned about the process of making dragons and cannons. He was very interested in burning cannons. Since working in 1987, he has participated works of the fair every year, such as organizing, planning and hosting the Great King's Birthday Cannon Fair, and making dragon amulet and dragon scale every year. He has recorded and publicized the cannon fair, and paid attention to the promotion of the cannon fair culture among young people in Tanwei Village, making important contributions to the inheritance and development of the cannon fair. He is the representative inheritor of the fifth batch of intangible cultural heritage projects in Yangjiang City now.

金堡盘皇庙炮会

保护单位 阳春市河口镇金堡村民委员会

Jinbao Pan Emperor Temple Cannon Fair

Protection Unit Jinbao Village Committee, Hekou Town, Yangchun City

The Jinbao Pan Emperor Temple Cannon Fair is a large-scale traditional folk activity that prevails in Jinbao Village, Hekou Town, Yangchun City. In history, the Jinbao Pan Emperor Temple Cannon Fair started from Nadan in the east to Yangjiang in the south, Lanshuping in the west, and Jianshui in the north, with Jinbao Market as the core. Jinbao Village is located in the south of Hekou Town, Yangchun City, adjacent to Shuangjie Town in the east, Chengcun Town in the south, Shihe Village, Hekou Town in the west, and Henan Village, Hekou Town in the north. The fair is distributed in 25 natural villages and spreads to Foshan, Shenzhen, Yunfu, Maoming, Jiangmen, Xinxing, Gaozhou, Enping, Yangjiang and other places.

Historical Origin

The *Yangchun County Annals* records that "Pan Emperor Temple was founded in the Jiachen Year of Qianlong period in the Qing Dynasty at the Jinbao Market of Nadanbao, Nanxiang". According to the words of the ancestors of Jinbao Village, heaven and earth were created by Pangu, and he turned his body into everything in heaven and earth, making the newly born universe rich and beautiful. To commemorate and thank Pan Emperor for his great virtues and gifts, the ancestors of Jinbao Village built Pan Emperor Temple in the Jiachen year of the Qianlong period in the Qing Dynasty (1784) . On the sixth day of the fourth lunar month in the same year, when the temple was built, the villagers of Jinbao held a grand cannon fair on the ground in front of the temple (later called "Cannon-burning Ground"), praying that Pan Emperor would protect the villagers forever, the weather would be good, the grain would be abundant,

金堡盘皇庙炮会，是盛行于阳春市河口镇金堡村的一项大型传统民俗活动。历史上的金堡盘皇庙炮会，以金堡墟为核心，东起那旦，南至阳江，西到榄树坪，北至涧水。金堡村地处阳春市河口镇南面，东与双捷镇相邻，南与程村镇相接，西与河口镇石河村相邻，北面是河口镇河南村。该项目分布于25条自然村并辐射至佛山、深圳、云浮、茂名、江门、新兴、高州、恩平、阳江等地。

历史渊源

《阳春县志》记载："盘皇庙在南乡都那旦堡金堡墟清乾隆甲辰年创建。"据金堡村祖辈口口相传，天地为盘古所造，他把自己的身体变成天地万物，使新诞生的宇宙丰富而美丽。为纪念和感恩盘皇的伟德和赐予，金堡村祖先在清乾隆甲辰年（1784年）修建了盘皇庙，该庙建好的当年农历四月初六，金堡乡民在盘皇庙前的坪地上（后称"烧炮坪"）举办盛大的炮会，祈求盘皇永远守护乡亲，风调雨顺、五谷丰登、六畜兴旺、国泰民安。此后金堡乡民每年农历四月初六都在烧炮坪举办盛大的炮会活动，一直延续至今。

金堡盘皇庙炮会有着200多年的历史。炮会传承人邹振煌叙述，当年金堡盘皇庙内，曾用石板铭刻当时捐资兴建盘皇庙的金堡乡民的芳名并镶嵌于墙壁上。但1982年8月，盘皇庙被拆除建校舍，捐资芳名无法追溯。在1785年以志纪念盘皇庙落成而专铸的、现仍供奉于盘皇庙内的大铁钟上，铭刻了诸位乡亲当时为铸造盘皇庙大铁钟捐资的信息，也佐证了该项目悠久的历史。

至2004年，邹振煌、赖方政、罗运明、赖明发动乡民踊跃筹资重建金堡盘皇庙于现址，成立炮会理事会，全面恢复炮会活动。赖明任炮会理事长，成员有邹振煌、赖方政、罗运明、邹家应、黎新福、罗圣崧、赖金许。

2019年2月，选举产生了新一届金堡盘皇庙炮会理事会成员，赖明任永久荣誉理事长，邹家应任理事长，成员有罗圣落、赖金许、黎新福、林进苏、盘仕诚、陈宗岳、罗圣桥、罗圣标、罗圣崧。

根据邹氏族谱和赖氏族谱共同记载，金堡盘皇庙炮会是以金堡村的两大姓氏邹姓和赖姓为传承脉络；而且邹氏祖先邹仕奇，赖氏祖先赖时宽、赖时衡由于捐资铸造大铁钟，名字被镌刻在大铁钟上，也可佐证。邹氏后代邹芳业、邹大杞、邹德熙、邹振煌（1937年3月出生）、邹家应（现任炮会理事长），以及其子邹李和（1985年7月出生），赖氏后代赖习常、赖有龙、赖朋庆、赖自生、赖水木、赖方政（1925—2004），以及其子赖明（上届炮会理事长）、赖金许（1963年2月出生）、赖美星（1968年12月出生）等辈辈相传，他们积极组织和参与炮会活动，熟悉炮会

the six livestock would be prosperous, and the country would be peaceful. After that, the Jinbao villagers, have held a grand cannon fair on the sixth day of the fourth lunar month on the Cannon-burning Ground every year, which has continued to this day.

Jinbao Pan Emperor Temple Cannon Fair has a history of more than 200 years. Zou Zhenhuang, the inheritor of the cannon fair, recounted that in the Jinbao Pan Emperor Temple, names of those villagers of Jinbao donating to the construction of the temple were inscribed on the wall with stone slabs. However, in August 1982, Pan Emperor Temple was demolished to build a school, the name of the donation could not be traced back. The big iron bell, which was specially cast in 1785 to commemorate the completion of the Pan Emperor Temple and is still enshrined in Pan Emperor Temple, is engraved with the information that the villagers donated money to cast it at that time, which also proves that the project has a long history.

Until 2004, Zou Zhenhuang, Lai Fangzheng, Luo Yunming, and Lai Ming mobilized the villagers to actively raise funds to rebuild the Jinbao Pan Emperor Temple at the current site, established the cannon fair council, and the activities of the cannon fair are fully resumed. Lai Ming was selected as the chairman of the council. The members of the cannon fair council included Zou Zhenhuang, Lai Fangzheng, Luo Yunming, Zou Jiaying, Li Xinfu, Luo Shengsong, and Lai Jinxu.

In February 2019, a new council of Jinbao Pan Emperor Temple Cannon Fair was elected. Lai Ming serves as the permanent honorary chairman, and Zou Jiaying as the chairman. The members include Luo Shengluo, Lai Jinxu, Li Xinfu, Lin Jinsu, Pan Shicheng, Chen Zongyue, Luo Shengqiao, Luo Shengbiao, and Luo Shengsong.

According to the records of Zou's and Lai's genealogies, Jinbao Pan Emperor Temple Cannon Fair is inherited by the Zou and Lai families of Jinbao Village. It can be identified that Zou's ancestor Zou Shiqi, Lai's ancestor Lai Shikuan and Lai Shiheng engraved their names on the big iron bell for the donations to the casting of the big iron bell. Zou's descendants Zou Fangye, Zou Daqi, Zou Dexi, Zou Zhenhuang (was born in March 1937) Zou Jiaying (current chairman of the council) , and his son Zou Lihe (was born in July 1985) , Lai's descendants Lai Xichang, Lai Youlong, Lai Pengqing, Lai Zisheng, Lai Shuimu, Lai Fangzheng (1925-2004) , and his son Lai Ming (chairman of the previous council) , Lai Jinxu (was born in February 1963) , Lai Meixing (was born in December 1968) and other generations have passed the cannon fair down. They actively organized and participated in the activities of the fair, and were familiar with the regulations of the fair, became the backbone of the cannon fair's inheritance, so that the Jinbao Pan Emperor Temple Cannon Fair has been passed down from generation to generation and has continued to this day.

Basic Content

The cannon fair takes Pan Emperor Temple as the carrier. On the sixth day of the fourth lunar month when the Pan Emperor Temple was built, in order to commemorate and thank the great virtues and gifts of the former emperor, pray for the protection of the former emperor and live a good-weather, peaceful and safe life, a grand cannon fair is held by the villagers of Jinbao on the ground in front of the Pan Emperor Temple and has been passed down to this day. It has become an enduring local folk custom activity, making the Pan Emperor Temple culture of "selfless dedication, solidarity and friendliness, mutual help, and harmonious coexistence" take root in the hearts of the people and become the spiritual home jointly guarded by the villagers.

From the fourth day of the fourth lunar month, the cannon fair holds a rewarding activity at Pan Emperor Temple. Those who got the cannon rings last year, together with their family members or relatives and friends, carry the slaughtered whole pig, followed by dancing lion, beating gongs and drums, and setting off firecrackers all the way, take the cannon plate enshrined at home back to Pan Emperor Temple to worship, and then entertaine relatives and friends in their respective homes to celebrate the good luck brought by the cannon.

On the fifth day of the fourth lunar month, people prepare the scene arrangement of the cannon fair. They construct the stove, set the stage, buy some relative objects, and then invite the troupe to perform Chinese Opera that night.

The sixth day of the fourth lunar month is the day of the cannon fair activities. In the early morning, the villagers take three livestock

各项规程，成为炮会传承的骨干力量，使金堡盘皇庙炮会得以薪火相传，延续至今。

基本内容

炮会以盘皇庙为载体。在盘皇庙建好当年的农历四月初六，金堡乡民为纪念和感恩先皇的伟德和赐予，祈求得到先皇的庇荫，过上风调雨顺、国泰民安的生活，在盘皇庙前的坪地上举办盛大的炮会活动并传承至今，成为当地一项长盛不衰的民俗活动，使“无私奉献、团结友善、互帮互助、和睦相处”的盘皇庙文化扎根民心，成为乡民共同守护的精神家园。

炮会从农历四月初四开始在盘皇庙举行酬炮活动，上年接到炮圈者，与家人或亲朋好友，抬着已宰好的全猪，醒狮跟随，敲锣打鼓，一路燃放鞭炮，把供奉在家的炮牌送回盘皇庙祭拜，然后在各自家里宴请亲朋好友，庆贺得炮带来的好运。

四月初五进行炮会场景布置、垒灶搬台、采购物料等，当晚请戏班唱大戏。

四月初六是炮会活动正日，一大早乡民备足三牲酒礼前往盘皇庙祭拜。然后，在醒狮的引领下，抬着盘皇神像，披红戴绿，敲锣打鼓，燃放鞭炮，巡游村寨。完毕后在盘皇庙前的坪地上开始热闹的重头戏——烧炮。烧炮一是指燃放鞭炮，二是按顺序逐个点燃精心制作的炮，炮名分别为“雄鸡报晓”“财源茂盛”“健康长寿”“龙马精神”“六畜兴旺”“马到成功”“喜气洋洋”“牛气冲天”的8个土

乡民抬着盘皇神像巡游村寨
The villagers are parading through the village with the statue of the Pan Emperor

乡民抢炮圈

The villagers are snatching the cannon ring

炮。土炮由炮座、炮胆和炮圈三部分组成，被点燃后随着一声炮响，炮圈腾空而起，这个被视为吉祥物的炮圈，被众人竞相抢接。抢到炮圈者由工作人员引领到主席台登记并领取相应的炮牌。其场面热闹而友好，高潮迭起又井然有序，彰显盘皇庙文化之底蕴和风采。

主要特征

（1）一年一度，时间、地点固定。炮会只在每年的农历四月初六举行，地点也仅限在河口镇金堡村金堡盘皇庙前面，设有1000多平方米的“烧炮坪”，并立有“烧炮坪”地名石一座。

and wine to Pan Emperor Temple to worship. Then, under the guidance of the dancing lions, they carry the statue of the Pan Emperor, dressing in red and green, beat gongs and drums, set off firecrackers, and parade in the village. After that, the highlight begins on the ground in front of the Pan Emperor Temple—burning cannons. Burning cannons means setting off firecrackers, and light 8 homemade cannons in order, called as “the rooster announcing the dawn” “the wealth coming from many ways” “people healthy and longevous” “energetic spirit as dragon and horse” “the prosperity of the six livestock” “success made instantly” “a scene full of joy” “an imposing aura like ox”. The homemade cannons consists of three parts: the cannon base, the cannon core part, and the cannon ring. After being ignited, the cannon ring rises into the air with the sound of cannon fired. The cannon ring, which is regarded as a mascot, is rushed by everyone. The person who grabs the cannon ring is led by the staff to the rostrum of register and receives the corresponding cannon plate. The scene is lively and friendly, with high tides and orderly sights, highlighting the cultural details and demeanour of Pan Emperor Temple.

Main Features

(1) The fair is held once a year, and the time and place are fixed. The cannon fair is only held on the sixth day of the fourth lunar month every year. Its venue is only in front of the Jinbao Pan Emperor Temple in Jinbao Village, Hekou Town. There is a “Cannon-burning Ground” with more than 1,000 square meters, and a place name stone of the “Cannon-burning Ground”.

(2) A strong commemorative mood. Worshipping Pan Emperor God has become one of the main contents of the cannon fair to commemorate and thank Pan Emperor for his virtues and gifts.

抢炮圈场景

The scene of snatching cannon ring

接炮后的喜悦

The excitement after receiving cannons

（2）带有浓厚的纪念色彩。为纪念和感恩盘皇的伟德和赐予，祭拜盘皇神成为炮会主要内容之一。

（3）炮会的影响力、号召力和凝聚力超过其他传统节日。每逢炮会，金堡乡民都在“烧炮坪”上举行盛大的炮会活动，当天，金堡乡民和外出乡贤，不论职位高低，不论贫贱富贵，不论路途远近，都汇聚金堡参加炮会。

（4）举行千人流水席，免费宴请参加炮会的乡亲和嘉宾，最多时摆席100多桌。

（5）自扎自制土炮。炮会所燃放的“炮”：一是燃放鞭炮，二为自扎自制的土炮。土炮仅限8枚，有固定的名称，并对应制作刻有鸡、财神、寿星公、龙、猪、马、羊、牛图案的炮牌。燃放自制土炮是炮会的核心，抢炮圈是炮会的重头戏。燃放鞭炮后，接着按顺序燃放8枚土炮。燃放土炮前，先请有关领导、嘉宾，或为村作出贡献的乡贤“净手”（用柚子叶水洗手，以示虔诚）后点燃土炮。一声巨响，炮圈腾空而起，乡民竞相接之。抢到炮圈者到主席台登记，领取相应炮牌。炮圈是众人争夺的吉祥物，据说，接到炮圈者，当年会有好运。

随着8枚土炮相继点燃，产生8名抢得

(3) The influence, appeal and cohesion of the fair are higher than those of other traditional festivals. Every time on the day of the fair, the villagers of Jinbao hold a grand cannon fair on the “Cannon-burning Ground”. On that day, the villagers of Jinbao and the sages of the outgoing villagers, regardless of their positions, wealth, poverty, or distance, all gather in Jinbao to participate in the cannon fair.

(4) A banquet of thousands of people will be held, and the villagers and guests who participate in the fair will be entertained for free, with more than 100 tables at most.

(5) Homemade cannons. The “cannons” set off by the fair include firecracker, and homemade cannons. The number of homemade cannons are limited to 8 cannons and have their respective fixed name, with corresponding cannon plate engraved with the pattern of chicken, the God of Wealth, the God of Longevity, dragon, pig, horse, sheep, and cow. The igniting of homemade cannons is the core of the cannon fair, and snatching the cannon ring is the highlight of the cannon fair. After the firecrackers are set off, 8 homemade cannons are ignited in sequence. Before the cannon is ignited, relevant leaders, guests, or local sages who have contributed to the village “clean their hands” (wash their hands with grapefruit leaf water to show their piety) and ignite the cannon. With a loud bang, the cannon ring takes off, and the villagers compete to get it. Those who grab the cannon ring go to the rostrum to register and receive the corresponding cannon plate. The cannon ring is the mascot that everyone competes for. It is said that those who receive the cannon ring will have good luck in the year.

As the 8 homemade cannons are ignited one after another, 8 lucky people who get the cannon rings appear. In the end, the chairman of the cannon association gives the 8 people ribbons with the name of the cannon written on them to wear , and issues honorary certificates

“烧炮坪”碑石
The “Cannon-burning Ground” stone

自制的八个各有寓意的土炮

8 homemade cannons with its own meaning

炮会理事长分别给8名抢获炮圈者颁发荣誉

The chairman of the cannon association gave rewards to the 8 people who won the cannon hoop

炮圈的幸运者。最后由炮会理事长分别为8名抢获炮圈者佩戴写有炮名的绶带，并发放荣誉证书和本届规定的奖金。

抢得炮圈者次年炮会前要酬炮。每位得炮圈者把炮牌送回盘皇庙祭拜，并奉上多于前一年得炮时所获奖金数的酬金。

重要价值

· 历史价值

金堡盘皇庙炮会历史悠久。金堡盘皇庙正门悬挂“恩光普照”四个金字，蕴含了丰富的文化底蕴，见证了几百年来当地历史、人文、风土、人情的嬗变历程，为了解、研究河口镇的历史、文化、民俗等社会状况提供了重要的依据。

金堡盘皇庙炮会有丰富的红色历史。1942年，在金堡盘皇庙旁的金堡小学建立的中共金堡支部，利用炮会募集经费，支援抗日救国运动和漠南武装斗争；改革开放时期，党和政府在中共金堡支部旧址设立思源堂，建立爱国主义教育基地。炮会期间，理事会组织人们到思源堂参观，厚植爱国主义情怀，对加强爱国主义教育有重要的意义。

and bonuses stipulated in this year.

Those who get the cannon ring will be rewarded with the cannon before the next fair. Each winner of the cannon should send the cannon plate back to Pan Emperor Temple to worship and offer a reward that is more than the bonus he received last year.

Great Value

· Historical value

Jinbao Pan Emperor Temple has a long history. The four golden characters of “Enguang Puzhao” (meaning “the golden light illuminates all things”) are hung on the main entrance of Jinbao Pan Emperor Temple, which contains a rich cultural heritage and witnesses the evolution of local history, humanities, customs, and human feelings over the past few hundred years. It provides an important basis for understanding and studying the history, culture, folk customs, and other social conditions of Hekou Town.

The Jinbao Pan Emperor Temple Cannon Fair has a rich red history. In 1942, the Jinbao Branch of the Communist Party of China, established at the Jinbao Primary School next to the Jinbao Pan Emperor Temple, raised funds through the cannon fair to support the Anti-Japanese National Salvation Movement and the Monan Armed Struggle. During the reform and opening-up period, the Party and the Government set up the Siyuan Hall on the former site of the Jinbao Branch of the Communist Party of China and established the Patriotism Education Base. During the cannon fair, people must be organized by the council to visit the Siyuan Hall to cultivate patriotism, which is of great significance to strengthening patriotism education.

· Social value

During the cannon fair, a banquet of thousands of people is held to entertain the guests, providing a platform for people to exchange information. The guests gather in Jinbao to exchange information and experience, impart technology, do good deeds, and help the needy, creating a neighborhood relationship of mutual help, solidarity and friendship, and harmonious neighborly relations. It promotes the development of local rural areas and agricultural industrialization and helps to promote poverty reduction and the enrichment of farmers.

· Cultural value

The Jinbao Pan Emperor Temple Cannon Fair has been passed down for more than 200 years. Pan Emperor Temple culture has taken root in the hearts of the people. It is not only the embodiment of the excellent traditional Chinese culture but also the embodiment of the value of the villagers. It has a certain role in promoting the formation of village customs and has great value for the study of folk culture in Yangchun.

Jinbao Pan Emperor Temple Cannon Fair takes Pan Emperor's belief as the core and takes praying for blessings and welcoming auspiciousness as its important content, attracting many artists to participate. The cannon fair not only organizes activities, such as singing and dancing performances, singing revolutionary songs and Hakka hill songs, calligraphy exhibitions, root carving exhibitions, etc., and also sells local specialties, Hakka snacks, and daily necessities, etc.. It reflects a wide range of mass nature and becomes a rich local cultural feast, not only activates rural cultural activities which have great significances in strengthening cultural self-confidence, promoting cultural revitalization, the constructing rural red tourism and implementing the rural revitalization strategy but also helping create a harmonious atmosphere in society, then resulting in gradually increasing social and economic benefits.

· 社会价值

炮会期间，大摆千人筵席款待宾客，为人们提供了一个信息交流平台。宾客云集金堡，互通信息，交流经验，传授技术，行善助善，营造互帮互助、团结友好、和睦相处的邻里关系，对带动当地农业产业化发展、农民脱贫致富有促进作用。

· 文化价值

金堡盘皇庙炮会，历时200多年传承，盘皇庙文化扎根民心，既是中华优秀传统文化的体现，更是村民价值观的体现。对村俗、村风的形成有一定的促进作用，对研究阳春的民俗文化有着重要的价值。

金堡盘皇庙炮会以盘皇信仰为核心，以祈福迎祥为重要内容，吸引众多艺术家参与。炮会不仅有歌舞表演、唱革命歌曲与客家山歌、书法展览、根雕展览等活动，而且还出售地方土特产、客家小食及日常生活用品等，体现出广泛的群众性，成为当地丰富的文化盛宴，不仅活跃了农村文化活动，对坚定文化自信、促进乡风文明建设、推动乡村红色旅游发展、实施乡村振兴战略有着重要的意义，而且有利于社会和谐气氛的营造，由此产生的社会效益和经济效益日渐增大。

千人流水席
a banquet of thousands of people

村民们观看演出
The villagers are watching the performances

主要传承人

邹家应，男，1961年7月出生，金堡村东坑自然村人。2004年，在其父辈的带领下，逐步熟悉炮会全流程，成为炮会传承的骨干力量。他积极参与炮会谋划，历经多年打造，2019年1月，金堡盘皇庙炮会被列入阳春市第四批县（市）级非物质文化遗产代表性项目名录。2019年2月，邹家应任金堡盘皇庙炮会理事会理事长，他带领理事会成员发动乡亲集资，成功举办了“文化兴，金堡旺”2019年金堡盘皇庙炮会活动，在群众中引起强烈反响。邹家应现为阳江市第五批非物质文化遗产项目代表性传承人。

Main Inheritor

Zou Jiaying, male, was born in July 1961, is a native of Dongkeng Natural Village, Jinbao Village. In 2004, under the leadership of his male relatives of senior generation, he gradually became familiar with the whole process of the cannon fair and became the backbone of the cannon fair's inheritance. He actively participated in the planning of the cannon fair. Developed after many years, in January 2019, the Jinbao Pan Emperor Temple Cannon Fair was listed in the fourth batch of representative projects of county (city) level intangible cultural heritage in Yangchun City. In February 2019, he served as the chairman of the council of the Jinbao Pan Emperor Temple Cannon Fair. He led the members of the council to mobilize the villagers to raise funds and successfully held the 2019 Jinbao Pan Emperor Temple Cannon Fair with the slogan "More prosperous culture, more advanced Jinbao", which aroused recognition of the masses. He is the representative inheritor of the fifth batch of intangible cultural heritage projects in Yangjiang City now.

邹家应（左五）
Zou Jiaying (The fifth person from the left)